Mastering Docker

from

Scratch to Scale

From Basics to CI/CD, Orchestration, and Production Deployment — Security, Scaling, Monitoring, and Hands-on Labs for DevSecOps, SRE, and Cloud Engineers

---

Unofficial Docker Certified Associate (DCA) Exam Preparation Self-Study Guide

---

First Edition

Author: Sudipta Biswas

Mastering Docker from Scratch to Scale

"From Basics to CI/CD, Orchestration, and Production Deployment — Security, Scaling, Monitoring, and Hands-on Labs for DevSecOps, SRE, and Cloud Engineers"

Unofficial Docker Certified Associate (DCA) Exam Preparation Self-Study Guide

Author: Sudipta Biswas

Disclaimer

This book is an independent work of nonfiction created for educational and professional development purposes. While every effort has been made to ensure accuracy, the author and publisher assume no responsibility for errors or omissions.

"**Docker**" and the **Docker logo** are trademarks or registered trademarks of **Docker, Inc**. in the United States and other countries. **Docker Certified Associate** is a certification managed by **Mirantis Inc**. This book is an independent publication and is not affiliated with, sponsored by, or endorsed by **Docker, Inc**. or **Mirantis Inc**.

"**Kubernetes**" is a registered trademark of **The Linux Foundation**. This publication is not endorsed by or affiliated with **The Linux Foundation**.
All product names, logos, and brands used in this book are the property of their respective owners. Their use is for identification and instructional purposes only and does not imply endorsement.

Publishing Details

Published by: Sudipta Biswas (via Amazon KDP)
First Edition – 2025
ISBN: 978-93-342-7874-3
Printed and distributed worldwide via Amazon Kindle Direct Publishing (KDP).

Design & Lab Resources

Cover Design: Sukanta Biswas
Interior Design: Sukanta Biswas
Lab Files & Resources: Scan QR Code / visit GitHub repository

Contact

For feedback, corrections, or inquiries:
✉ **Email:** mailsudiptabiswas@gmail.com

No Warranty

This book is provided "as-is," without warranty of any kind, express or implied. The author disclaims all warranties, including, but not limited to, implied warranties of merchantability and fitness for a particular purpose.

Preface

In today's fast-paced world of software delivery, automation, and cloud-native scale, **Docker** is more than a developer convenience—it's the foundation of modern application infrastructure. From microservices and serverless deployments to hybrid cloud orchestration and secure CI/CD pipelines, mastering Docker has become a **critical skill** for developers, DevOps engineers, SREs, platform architects, and security professionals alike.

Mastering Docker from Scratch to Scale is a comprehensive, hands-on journey crafted for both learners and leaders. Whether you're just running your first container or designing multi-region Swarm clusters and GitOps pipelines, this book is structured to grow with you. It blends **theory, practice, certification-readiness, and enterprise-grade scenarios** into a unified experience.

What makes this book truly stand out is its **real-world applicability**. It goes beyond the basics of `docker run` or `docker build`. You'll explore:

- Advanced container lifecycle management
- Secure and compliant image creation
- Multi-node orchestration with Swarm and Compose
- CI/CD integration using GitHub Actions
- Monitoring, logging, and alerting with Prometheus and Grafana
- Kubernetes transition insights via Docker workloads
- Infrastructure-as-Code with YAMLs, backup strategies, and volume planning
- Troubleshooting real errors with real fixes

Each chapter is paired with **live lab exercises** using **Play With Docker** and downloadable local environments, enabling you to apply what you learn—immediately and confidently.

This book is also **fully aligned with the Docker Certified Associate (DCA)** exam blueprint, covering all six domains:

- **Orchestration**
- **Image Creation & Management**
- **Installation & Configuration**
- **Networking**
- **Security**
- **Storage & Volumes**

But this isn't just a self-study certification guide (unofficial). It's a **career-growth toolkit** for professionals who want to lead container adoption, secure cloud-native infrastructure, and master automation from end to end.

Why This Book?

Despite Docker's widespread usage, many only explore its surface. True Docker proficiency means understanding:

- Image layers and optimization techniques
- Container hardening, rootless execution, and trusted content
- Advanced networking, secrets, and service discovery
- Swarm clustering and failover strategies
- Scalable CI/CD workflows with DockerHub integration
- Logging, monitoring, and observability
- Backup, recovery, and production readiness

This book was written to:

- Demystify Docker and its ecosystem
- Teach via labs, not just pages
- Build confidence for real deployments and the DCA exam
- Help professionals deliver secure, scalable, production-grade apps
- Serve as both a **learning resource** and a **practical reference**

How This Book Is Structured

We begin with the fundamentals—containers, images, volumes—and progress all the way to production orchestration, monitoring, security, and automation. You'll learn to:

- Build efficient, optimized Dockerfiles and multi-stage builds
- Manage services with Docker Compose and Swarm
- Secure containers using best practices (DCT, rootless, AppArmor)
- Monitor containers with Grafana, Prometheus, and Loki
- Automate CI/CD pipelines using GitHub Actions and DockerHub
- Backup and restore volumes and images safely
- Troubleshoot and debug like a production engineer
- Leverage real case studies (Netflix, Amazon, Flipkart, Blockchain)

This book is designed to mirror the real-world journey of mastering Docker — beginning with core fundamentals, advancing through production hardening and security, and culminating in resilience, troubleshooting, automation, and Kubernetes scaling. Each chapter builds logically upon the last, ensuring a seamless, practical transition from beginner skills to enterprise-ready deployment strategies.

Every section includes **step-by-step labs**, diagrams, output snapshots, cheat sheets, and ready-to-run configurations.

Who This Book Is For

Whether you're aiming for certification, deploying at scale, or transitioning into a DevOps or SRE role, this book is for:

- Developers who want to ship containers securely
- DevOps engineers managing modern CI/CD pipelines
- SREs building observable, resilient platforms
- Sysadmins containerizing legacy systems
- Cloud engineers deploying Docker in ECS, AKS, or GKE
- Students, self-learners, or job switchers mastering Docker and DevSecOps

If you've ever struggled with inconsistent environments, manual deployments, or hard-to-debug container behavior—this book will help you to fix all of that.

What You'll Need

To follow the labs and projects, you'll need:

- A working knowledge of the Linux command line
- Docker Engine and Docker Compose (on Linux/macOS/Windows)
- Git and GitHub account (for CI/CD labs)
- Optional: VS Code, Prometheus, Grafana, or Play With Docker

All code, YAMLs, dashboards, and lab assets are included in a downloadable ZIP with live tracking sheets and JSON dashboards.

Scan the QR Code for Practice Labs

Let's Get Started

This isn't just a technical book—it's a **learning path, a toolkit, a portfolio**, and a **launchpad** for your career in modern cloud-native engineering.

Whether you're reading it end-to-end or diving straight into a CI/CD lab or container security, you'll walk away with confidence, clarity, and skills that matter in the real world.

Welcome to a journey where you don't just learn Docker—you master it.

Let's begin—From Scratch to Scale.

Sudipta Biswas
Author • Engineer • Educator – Building the Next-Gen Cloud Talent

Foreword by Rakesh Shaw

Senior DevOps Engineer | Kubernetes & Cloud-Native Consultant

"Having worked with Docker since its early days, I've seen firsthand how transformative containers have been in reshaping application delivery. But despite its popularity, many professionals still struggle to move beyond basic usage.

Mastering Docker from Scratch to Scale is one of the most complete, practical, and forward-thinking Docker books I've reviewed. What makes it different is not just the technical depth—but the **real-world perspective** it brings. From Docker fundamentals to advanced orchestration, CI/CD, DevSecOps practices, and production monitoring, it's all covered in a structured, lab-driven approach.

Whether you're a developer shipping your first container or a DevOps engineer preparing for the DCA exam, this book provides you with **the skills and confidence to build, deploy, secure, and scale containerized applications** in enterprise environments.

Sudipta has done a remarkable job distilling complex concepts into hands-on, actionable knowledge. This book doesn't just teach you Docker—it prepares you to lead with it."

Foreword by Shankar Pandit

Cloud Architect | SRE & Platform Security Lead

"***Mastering Docker from Scratch to Scale***" is more than a book—it's a blueprint for building secure, scalable, and production-ready containerized systems. As someone deeply involved in platform security and SRE architecture, I was especially impressed by how well the book integrates **Docker best practices, DevSecOps principles, real-world failure scenarios, and recovery strategies**.

The structured labs, practical CI/CD pipelines with GitHub Actions, monitoring dashboards, and resource planning tools make this not just a study guide, but a real operational playbook for modern engineering teams.

What stands out is the author's ability to cover **both breadth and depth**—ranging from Dockerfiles and Swarm to security scanning, rootless containers, content trust, and cloud-native deployments on AWS, Azure, and GCP.

If you're serious about mastering Docker and applying it in real operational settings, **this book is the gold standard**. Highly recommended for engineers, architects, and learners aiming for long-term mastery."

These insights from respected practitioners set the tone for your journey ahead. You're not just reading—you're preparing to lead in the containerized world.

Acknowledgements

Authoring a book like ***Mastering Docker from Scratch to Scale*** is not a solo journey, it's the product of encouragement, collaboration, feedback, and support from many people who've contributed directly or indirectly along the way.

Primarily, I would like to express my sincere gratitude to my family for their patience, unwavering support, and constant encouragement during the long hours and weekends I spent immersed in research, writing, and building labs. Your belief in me is the foundation of this work.

To the **DevOps, Cloud, and Security communities** I've been fortunate to work with—thank you. The real-world challenges we've solved together inspired many of the patterns, labs, and hardening techniques you'll find in these pages. This book reflects the practical knowledge we've applied in the trenches of high-scale deployments and CI/CD pipelines.

Special thanks to **Rakesh Shaw** and **Shankar Pandit** for reviewing this book and contributing insightful forewords that capture the spirit of modern containerization and engineering excellence. Your experience and leadership in the industry bring tremendous value to the readers of this book.

I'd also like to acknowledge the open-source communities behind Docker, Kubernetes, Prometheus, Grafana, GitHub Actions, and countless others. These projects not only power the future of software delivery—they've made this book and its hands-on approach possible.

To my students, mentees, colleagues, and everyone who's ever asked, "Can you show me how to do this in Docker?"—this book is for you. Thank you for motivating me to explain better, document deeper, and teach in a way that scales.

Finally, to the readers: thank you for trusting me to guide your learning. Whether you're starting your journey or deepening your expertise, I hope this book helps you not only master Docker but grow as an engineer.

Let's continue building scalable, secure, and resilient systems—together.

Sudipta Biswas
Author • Engineer • Educator – Building the Next-Gen Cloud Talent

About the Author

Sudipta Biswas is a multifaceted technology leader, author, and architect with over 20 years of experience spanning **cloud-native platforms, cybersecurity, Information Security, Enterprise DevOps, and Automation Engineering**. With a rare blend of hands-on implementation expertise and deep architectural vision, he has played a critical role in modernizing technology infrastructures for global enterprises and mission-driven organizations alike.

Currently serving in senior technical leadership roles across security operations and transformation programs, Sudipta specializes in building **high-performance, scalable, and secure DevSecOps ecosystems** that integrate containerization, microservices, CI/CD, infrastructure as code, and compliance automation.

His technical portfolio includes:

- **Enterprise-grade Docker and Kubernetes deployments**
- **Penetration testing platforms aligned with OWASP, PTES, and MITRE ATT&CK**
- **FAIR-based cyber risk engines with Kafka, Superset, and ML modelling**
- **SSL monitoring platforms, AI-driven threat detection, and automated reporting systems**

As an author and engineer, Sudipta is known for his ability to **simplify complex systems into actionable blueprints**, which is exactly what he delivers in ***Mastering Docker from Scratch to Scale***. The book reflects not just his mastery of containerization, but also his passion for knowledge-sharing, platform reliability, and engineering excellence.

He has also contributed to real-world projects in:

- **Cloud Security Posture Management (CSPM/CNAPP)**
- **IoT/OT security frameworks**
- **Blockchain trust models**
- **Post-quantum cryptography readiness**

This book is a culmination of years of hands-on experience, research, knowledge sharing and teaching — designed to bring clarity, practicality, and depth to the world of containerization and infrastructure automation. Outside of his professional pursuits, Sudipta is committed to shaping the next generation of engineers through open-source contributions, practical training environments, and building full-stack lab platforms for hands-on learning.

Contents

Chapter 1: Introduction – Understanding Docker and Containerization

Docker History – From Innovation to Ubiquity

To fully understand the impact of Docker, we need to appreciate the journey it took — from a niche internal project to a global technology standard that reshaped software development and deployment.

Origins of Docker: dotCloud and the Early Days

Docker was born as an internal project at a Platform-as-a-Service (PaaS) company called **dotCloud**, founded by **Solomon Hykes**. Initially, dotCloud used **Linux Containers (LXC)** to provide isolated environments for hosting applications. This sparked the idea of packaging these containers into a portable and user-friendly format.

In **March 2013**, Docker was open-sourced and presented at **PyCon** — and within days, it went viral in the developer community. Developers finally had a way to reliably "build once, run anywhere," and infrastructure engineers saw a massive simplification of deployment and scaling.

"We're trying to do for the other 80% of developers what AWS did for the top 20%."
— Solomon Hykes, Docker Creator

Name Origin

The name **"Docker"** reflects its foundational metaphor:

A dock worker (or "docker") loads, ships, and unloads standardized cargo containers.

Just like how port docks load and unload standardized shipping containers onto vessels, Docker "containers" allow developers to **build once and run anywhere**, standardizing software delivery across environments. The container icon and ship wheel motif became iconic symbols of modern DevOps and microservices.

Fun fact: before being named Docker, the internal tool was known as "**dotCloud Container Engine**". Once it spun out into its own project, it needed a simpler and catchier name—hence, **Docker**.

Evolution of Docker Architecture

Docker initially relied on LXC as its default container runtime. But by **late 2013**, it had replaced LXC with its own execution environment called `libcontainer`, giving the Docker team full control over container behavior, performance, and security.

This enabled significant improvements:

- Native Go implementation
- Better isolation
- Improved resource control (via cgroups)
- Enhanced portability

The Rise of the Docker Ecosystem

As Docker gained traction, its ecosystem rapidly evolved:

Year	Milestone
2013	Docker 0.1 released; based on LXC
2014	DockerHub launched; Docker 1.0; Docker Compose introduced
2015	Docker Swarm introduced (native orchestration)
2016	Docker Engine split into CE (Community Edition) and EE (Enterprise Edition)
2017	Moby Project launched; OCI standardization with runc
2019	Docker Enterprise sold to Mirantis; Docker refocuses on developers
2020+	Docker Desktop growth; Docker Compose v2 rewrite; WSL2 integration

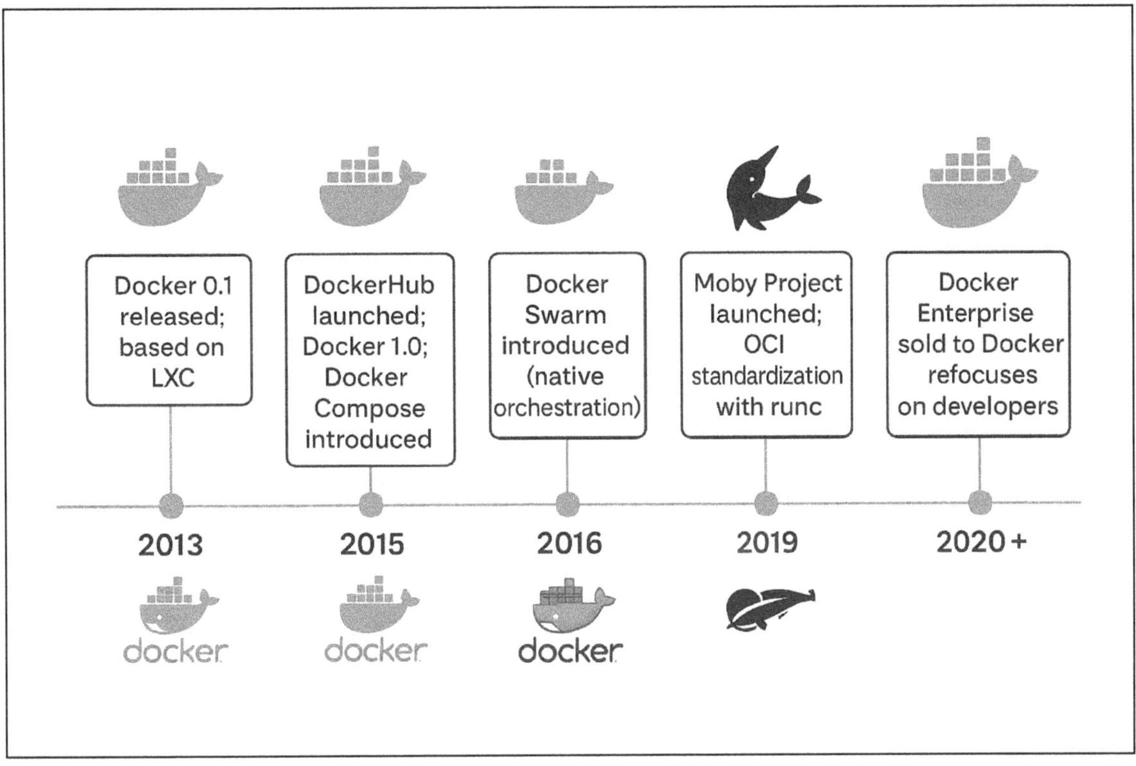

Figure 1.1: The Rise of the Docker Ecosystem

The OCI Revolution: Standardizing Containers

One of Docker's greatest contributions was the formation of the **Open Container Initiative (OCI)** in June 2015 under the Linux Foundation. OCI defined standardized formats for container images and runtimes, leading to industry-wide compatibility and interoperability.

Thanks to Docker, containers could now run on:

- Docker Engine
- Podman
- containerd
- Kubernetes
- CRI-O

This opened the door for **Kubernetes** to become the dominant orchestrator — and Docker images remained the universal package format.

From Containers to Cloud-Native: The New Paradigm

Docker's philosophy of immutable, portable containers fueled the rise of the **Cloud-Native movement**:

- CI/CD pipelines became faster and safer

- Dev, Test, and Prod environments became identical
- Infrastructure-as-Code became standard
- Scaling microservices became manageable

This led to the rise of:

- **Kubernetes** for orchestration
- **Helm** for application packaging
- **Istio** for service mesh
- **OpenShift** and **Rancher** for enterprise container platforms

Docker's Modern Role (Post-2020)

While **Docker Inc.** exited the enterprise space by selling Docker Enterprise to Mirantis, it refocused on developer tools and productivity. Today, Docker maintains a dominant presence via:

- Docker Desktop (Windows/macOS)
- Docker Compose v2
- DockerHub and Docker Extensions
- Docker BuildKit and image signing
- GitHub Actions integrations

Docker is now developer-first — helping individuals and teams build, test, and share containerized apps with speed and security.

What is Docker?

Docker is an open-source platform designed to simplify application development, shipment, and execution using containerization. At its core, Docker allows developers to package applications and their dependencies into isolated environments known as **containers**. These containers ensure that the application will run reliably in any computing environment — whether on a developer's laptop, a testing server, or a production cloud system.

Imagine you've developed a Python web application on your laptop. It works fine locally, but when you try to deploy it to a server, the application crashes due to differences in the runtime environment — maybe a different Python version, missing libraries, or conflicting system settings. Docker solves this problem by encapsulating your application with everything it needs to run, right down to system libraries and configurations.

Why Containerization Matters

The Traditional Way: Virtual Machines (VMs)

Before containers, many organizations used virtual machines for isolation. VMs run an entire operating system (OS), which makes them bulky and resource intensive. If you needed 10 applications running in parallel, you might end up with 10 different OS instances — a maintenance and performance nightmare.

The Container Way

Containers, unlike VMs, share the host machine's kernel and run as isolated processes in user space. This makes containers incredibly lightweight and fast to start.

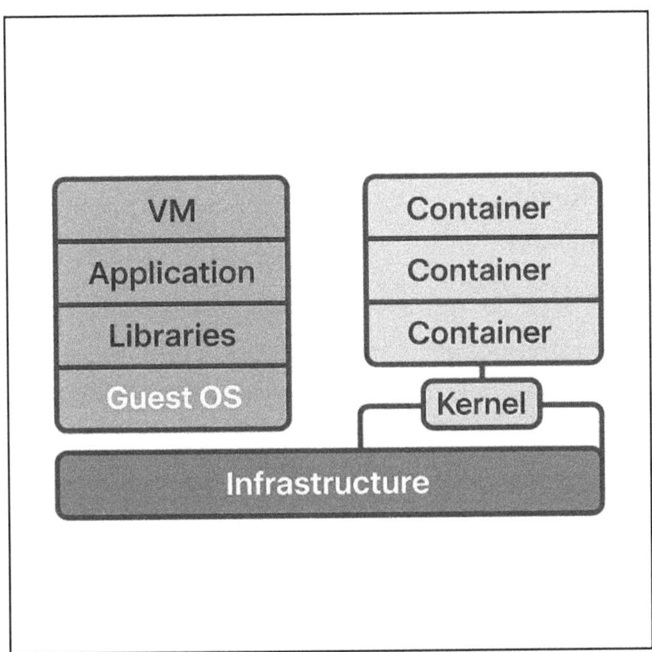

Figure 1.2: Traditional VM vs. Docker Containers

Key Benefits of Docker Containers

- **Portability:** "It works on my machine" is no longer an excuse. A Docker container runs the same everywhere.
- **Consistency:** Staging and production environments can be exact replicas.
- **Isolation:** Apps are sandboxed, which prevents interference from other containers.
- **Efficiency:** Containers use less memory and CPU compared to VMs.

Let's take an example. Suppose you're running a `Node.js` app with `MongoDB` and `Nginx`. With Docker, each component runs in its own container:

- `node-app`
- `mongo`
- `nginx`

You can build, test, and deploy them consistently without worrying about the underlying OS or hardware.

Docker vs. Docker Compose

- **Docker (Engine):** Used for building, running, and managing single containers.
- **Docker Compose:** Used for defining and running multi-container applications. It helps manage complex deployments by defining all services in a single YAML configuration file.

For instance, if an application stack includes:

- A backend written in Django
- A frontend using React
- A PostgreSQL database
- A Redis cache

Managing these individually with `docker run` commands can become tedious. Docker Compose simplifies this with one `docker-compose.yml` file and a single command.

```
$ docker compose up
```

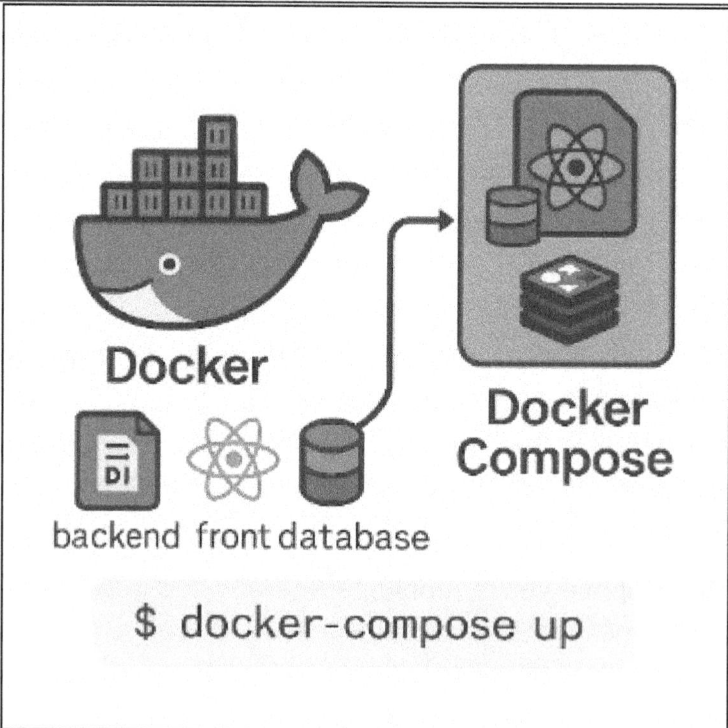

Figure 1.3: Docker vs. Docker Compose

How Docker Changed the DevOps Landscape

Before Docker, developers and operations teams often worked in silos. Developers would write code and throw it over the wall to operations teams, who were responsible for deploying it. This often led to friction and bugs in production.

Docker bridged that gap:

- Developers ship containers.
- Operations deploy the same containers without worrying about how the app is built.

This shift in how software is developed and deployed is one of the foundational changes that paved the way for modern DevOps practices, Continuous Integration/Continuous Deployment (CI/CD), and microservices architectures.

Real-World Example

Let's say you're building a Flask web application. Traditionally, you'd need to:

- Install Python and Flask on the server
- Set up Gunicorn and Nginx
- Configure environment variables
- Make sure it runs reliably at startup

With Docker, you can containerize this entire app. Here's a simple `Dockerfile`

```
FROM python:3.10
WORKDIR /app
COPY . .
RUN pip install -r requirements.txt
EXPOSE 5000
CMD ["python", "app.py"]
```

With this, your application can be spun up anywhere using

```
$ docker build -t flask-app .
$ docker run -p 5000:5000 flask-app
```

Done. No manual setup, no dependency nightmares.

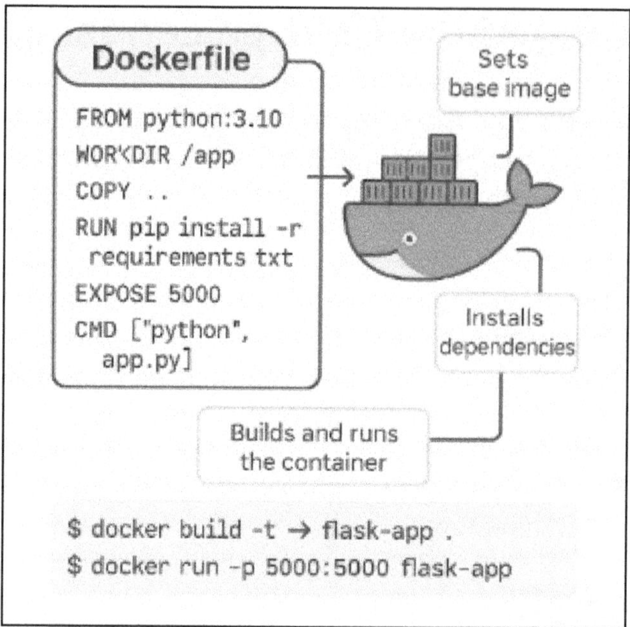

Figure 1.4: Docker and Dockerfile relationship

Docker Ecosystem at a Glance

- **Docker Engine:** The core runtime that builds and runs containers.
- **Docker CLI:** Command-line interface to interact with the engine.
- **Docker Hub:** A public registry of prebuilt images (e.g., nginx, postgres).
- **Docker Compose:** A tool to define and run complex applications using multiple services.

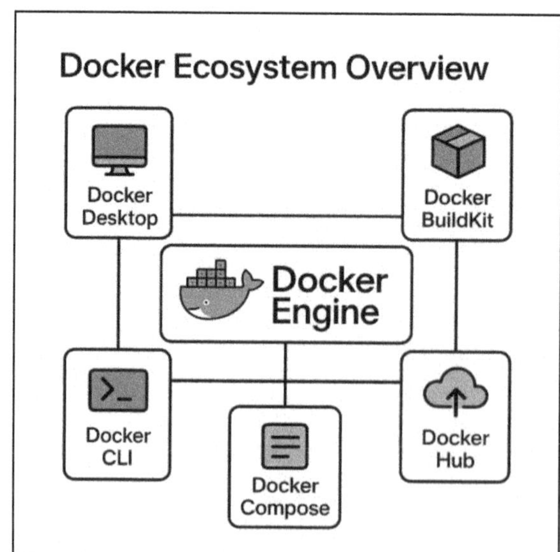

Figure 1.5: Docker Ecosystem

As we proceed, you'll learn how to use each of these components — not just in theory, but with step-by-step real-world use cases.

Summary

- Learned how Docker originated from dotCloud and evolved into a game-changing open-source technology.
- Understood Docker's client-server architecture: Docker CLI, Docker Daemon, Docker REST API, and Docker Registry.
- Clarified the difference between Docker images (blueprints) and containers (running instances).
- Explored the benefits of containerization: portability, consistency, efficiency, and isolation.
- Examined how Docker integrates with CI/CD pipelines, DevOps workflows, and cloud-native infrastructure.
- Comparing containers with virtual machines to highlight performance and resource advantages.
- Introduced Docker Compose for managing multi-container applications.
- Reviewed a real-world use case by containerizing a Flask web application.

Key Takeaways

- In this chapter, we explored Docker's journey from an internal project at dotCloud to a global standard that redefined software development and deployment. We learned how Docker introduced lightweight, portable containers that contrasted sharply with traditional virtual machines, offering unmatched speed, consistency, and efficiency. The emergence of the Docker ecosystem, the establishment of industry standards through the Open Container Initiative (OCI), and Docker's pivotal role in fueling the cloud-native revolution were highlighted. By understanding Docker's history, architecture, and core advantages, we lay the foundation for mastering containerization — a skill now essential for modern development, DevOps practices, and scalable cloud infrastructure.

Knowledge Check

1. **What is a container in the context of Docker?**
   A) A virtual machine
   B) A lightweight, standalone, executable package of software
   C) A Linux kernel replacement
   D) A network protocol
2. **Which of the following best describes Docker?**
   A) A programming language
   B) A hypervisor
   C) A containerization platform
   D) A database engine
3. **What is the main advantage of Docker over traditional VMs?**
   A) Better GUI
   B) Requires more resources
   C) Faster startup and lightweight
   D) Requires a dedicated OS
4. **What command is used to check installed Docker version?**
   A) `docker check`
   B) `docker -v`
   C) `docker install version`
   D) `docker show`
5. **Which component of Docker builds images from a Dockerfile?**
   A) Docker Engine
   B) Docker Daemon
   C) Docker Builder
   D) Docker CLI
6. **True or False: Containers include an entire guest operating system.**
   A) True
   B) False
7. **What is the default base image for most minimal containers?**
   A) Ubuntu
   B) CentOS
   C) Alpine
   D) BusyBox
8. **Which command is used to list all Docker containers (running and stopped)?**
   A) `docker ls -a`
   B) `docker container show`
   C) `docker ps -a`

D) `docker run list`

9. **What is the name of the Docker component that runs in the background and manages containers?**

   A) Docker CLI

   B) Docker Client

   C) Docker Daemon

   D) Docker Machine

10. **Which of the following commands pulls a Docker image from DockerHub?**

    A) `docker push`

    B) `docker get`

    C) `docker pull`

    D) `docker fetch`

11. **What does** `docker run hello-world` **do?**

    A) Starts a new Docker container with a test image

    B) Runs the Docker daemon

    C) Launches a web server

    D) Displays Docker networking info

12. **Which of the following is NOT true about Docker containers?**

    A) They are lightweight

    B) They can run isolated services

    C) They always run on Windows

    D) They are based on images

13. **What flag is used with** `docker run` **to remove a container after it stops?**

    A) `–kill`

    B) `–rm`

    C) `–clean`

    D) `--prune`

14. **What is DockerHub?**

    A) A text editor

    B) A monitoring dashboard

    C) A public container image registry

    D) A GUI for Docker Desktop

15. **Which command shows Docker system-wide information?**

    A) `docker status`

    B) `docker show`

    C) `docker stats`

    D) `docker info`

Answers

Q#	Correct Answer	Explanation
1	B	Containers are lightweight environments that bundle an app and its dependencies.
2	C	Docker is a containerization platform.
3	C	Containers are faster and lightweight than traditional VMs.
4	B	`docker -v` or `docker --version` shows the installed version.
5	A	Docker Engine builds and runs containers based on Dockerfile instructions.
6	B	Containers share the host OS kernel — no full OS included.
7	C	Alpine is the most lightweight base image.
8	C	`docker ps -a` lists all containers.
9	C	The Docker Daemon (`dockerd`) manages containers.
10	C	`docker pull` fetches images from DockerHub.
11	A	Runs a test image to verify Docker installation.
12	C	Containers can run on Windows or Linux, not just Windows.
13	B	`--rm` auto-removes the container after exit.
14	C	DockerHub is the default public registry for images.
15	D	`docker info` shows system-wide configuration and resource info.

Chapter 2: Installing Docker and Docker Compose

Setting up Docker and Docker Compose is the first hands-on step toward building containerized applications. This chapter will guide you through installing Docker on various platforms—Linux (Ubuntu/Debian), macOS, and Windows—along with Docker Compose, ensuring you're ready to build and run containers confidently.

System Requirements

Hardware Requirements:

- 64-bit processor
- At least 4 GB of RAM (8+ GB recommended for larger projects)
- Stable internet connection for downloading Docker packages

OS Compatibility:

OS	Supported	Notes
Ubuntu 18.04+	☑	Recommended for Linux users
Debian 10+	☑	Stable support
Windows 10+	☑	Requires WSL2 (for Home)
macOS 11+	☑	Uses Apple's Hypervisor

Installing Docker on Ubuntu/Debian (Linux)

Step-by-step Installation on Ubuntu 22.04

We'll install Docker Engine, CLI, containerd, and Docker Compose plugin.

Step 1: Update Your System

```
$ sudo apt update
$ sudo apt upgrade -y
```

Step 2: Install Required Dependencies

```
$ sudo apt install \
    ca-certificates \
    curl \
    gnupg \
    lsb-release -y
```

Step 3: Add Docker's Official GPG Key

```
$ sudo mkdir -p /etc/apt/keyrings
curl -fsSL https://download.docker.com/linux/ubuntu/gpg | \
    sudo gpg --dearmor -o /etc/apt/keyrings/docker.gpg
```

Step 4: Set Up the Docker Repository

```
$ echo \
"deb [arch=$(dpkg --print-architecture) signed-
by=/etc/apt/keyrings/docker.gpg] \
https://download.docker.com/linux/ubuntu \
$(lsb_release -cs) stable" | \
sudo tee /etc/apt/sources.list.d/docker.list > /dev/null
```

Step 5: Install Docker Engine

```
$ sudo apt update
$ sudo apt install docker-ce docker-ce-cli containerd.io docker-buildx-
plugin docker-compose-plugin -y
```

Step 6: Enable and Start Docker

```
$ sudo systemctl enable docker
$ sudo systemctl start docker
```

Step 7: Run Docker as Non-Root User

```
$ sudo usermod -aG docker $USER
$ newgrp docker
```

Test Docker Installation

Run the classic "Hello World" test:

```
$ docker run hello-world
```

Expected Output:

`Hello from Docker!`
This message shows that your installation appears to be working correctly.

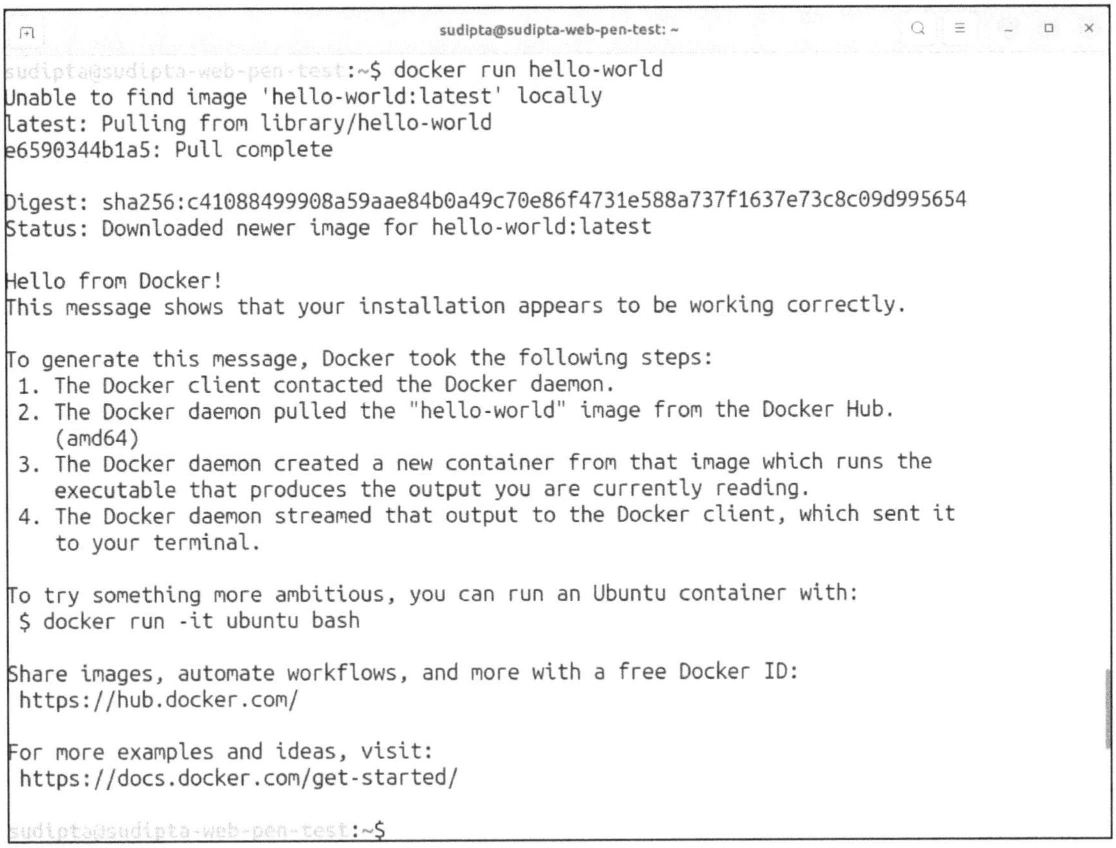

```
sudipta@sudipta-web-pen-test: ~
sudipta@sudipta-web-pen-test:~$ docker run hello-world
Unable to find image 'hello-world:latest' locally
latest: Pulling from library/hello-world
e6590344b1a5: Pull complete
Digest: sha256:c41088499908a59aae84b0a49c70e86f4731e588a737f1637e73c8c09d995654
Status: Downloaded newer image for hello-world:latest

Hello from Docker!
This message shows that your installation appears to be working correctly.

To generate this message, Docker took the following steps:
 1. The Docker client contacted the Docker daemon.
 2. The Docker daemon pulled the "hello-world" image from the Docker Hub.
    (amd64)
 3. The Docker daemon created a new container from that image which runs the
    executable that produces the output you are currently reading.
 4. The Docker daemon streamed that output to the Docker client, which sent it
    to your terminal.

To try something more ambitious, you can run an Ubuntu container with:
 $ docker run -it ubuntu bash

Share images, automate workflows, and more with a free Docker ID:
 https://hub.docker.com/

For more examples and ideas, visit:
 https://docs.docker.com/get-started/

sudipta@sudipta-web-pen-test:~$
```

Figure 2.1: Hello from Docker

Installing Docker on macOS

Step 1: Download Docker Desktop

- Visit: `https://www.docker.com/products/docker-desktop/`
- Choose the **macOS (Intel/Apple Chip)** version as per your hardware.

Step 2: Install Docker Desktop

- Open the downloaded `.dmg` file and drag Docker to Applications.
- Launch Docker from Applications.
- Give necessary permissions (network, filesystem).

Step 3: Verify Docker Installation

Open Terminal

```
$ docker version
```

You should see both `Client` and `Server` information.

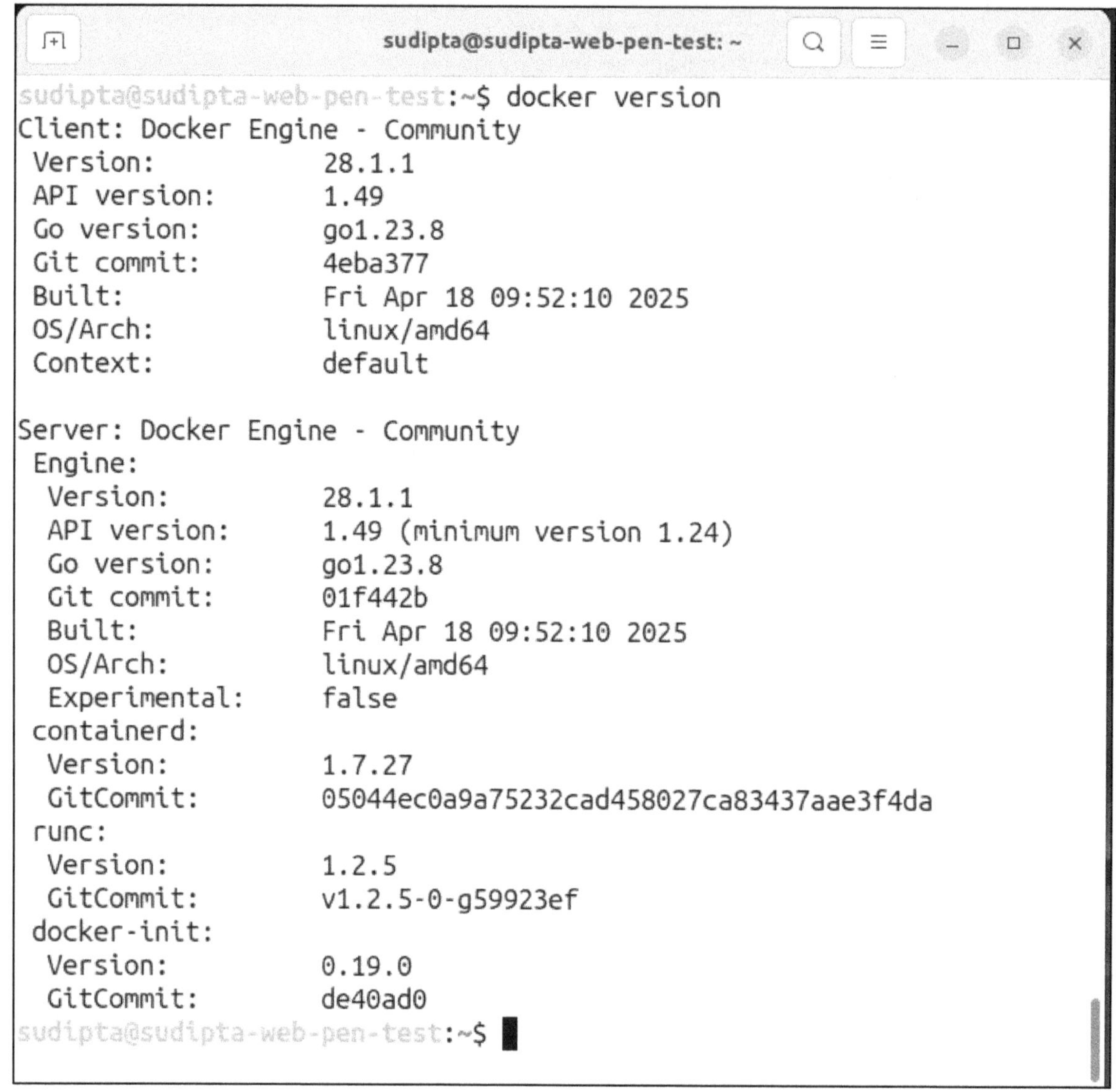

Figure 2.2: Docker Client and Server information

Installing Docker on Windows 10/11

Docker Desktop (Recommended)

For Windows Home edition, WSL2 is required.

Step 1: Install WSL2

Open PowerShell as Admin:

```
PS C:\> wsl –install
```

Reboot your system if prompted.

Step 2: Download Docker Desktop for Windows

- Visit: https://www.docker.com/products/docker-desktop/
- Run the installer and follow the GUI prompts.
- Enable WSL2 integration and choose your default distro (usually Ubuntu).

Step 3: Test in PowerShell or WSL Terminal

```
$ docker run hello-world
```

Installing Docker Compose Manually (Linux Only)

If `docker compose` plugin wasn't installed via `apt`, you can install it manually:

Step 1: Download the Binary

```
$ sudo curl -L \
"https://github.com/docker/compose/releases/download/v2.20.2/docker-compose-
$(uname -s)-$(uname -m)" \
-o /usr/local/bin/docker-compose
```

Step 2: Apply Executable Permission

```
$ sudo chmod +x /usr/local/bin/docker-compose
```

Step 3: Verify Installation

```
$ docker compose version
```

Common Issues & Fixes

Problem	Solution
`docker: command not found`	Check if Docker is in your `$PATH`. Reinstall or log out/in.
`permission denied` when running Docker	Add your user to the `docker` group: `sudo usermod -aG docker $USER`
WSL2 backend not working on Windows	Make sure virtualization is enabled in BIOS and WSL2 is correctly set up
Docker won't start on macOS	Check security settings in System Preferences > Security & Privacy

Real-World Setup: Dev Environment with Docker

Let's say you're a Python developer using Django + PostgreSQL. Without Docker, you'd install dependencies manually. With Docker, just run:

```
$ docker run -d \
  --name my-postgres \
```

```
  -e POSTGRES_USER=admin \
  -e POSTGRES_PASSWORD=admin123 \
  -e POSTGRES_DB=mydb \
  -p 5432:5432 \
  postgres:15
```

PostgreSQL server is now running in a container — clean, isolated, and portable. Connect to it using pgAdmin or a Django app.

Figure 3.3: Postgres SQL Setup in Docker

Docker Desktop vs Docker Engine (Linux): Platform Differences at a Glance

Feature / Command	Linux (Docker Engine)	Windows (Docker Desktop)	macOS (Docker Desktop)
Base Engine	Native Docker Engine on Linux	Docker runs inside WSL2 / Hyper-V VM	Docker runs inside lightweight VM (hyperkit)
Default Volume Mount Path	/var/lib/docker/volumes	C:\Users\<user>\.docker\volumes (mounted to /host_mnt)	/Users/<user>/.docker/volumes (via /host_mnt)
File System Behavior	Native Linux FS	NTFS to ext4 (WSL) translation layer	APFS to ext4 translation layer
Path Mapping in Volumes	/data:/data	C:\data:/data maps to /host_mnt/c/data:/data	/Users/data:/data maps to /host_mnt/Users/data:/data
Performance of Volume Mounts	Fast	Moderate (WSL2 overlay)	Slower for large mounts

Feature / Command	Linux (Docker Engine)	Windows (Docker Desktop)	macOS (Docker Desktop)
Networking Mode (host)	Supported	Not natively supported, requires workarounds	Not supported
Rootless Docker	[✓] Native support	[X] Not supported	[X] Not supported
Access to host services	Native loopback (`localhost`)	Use `host.docker.internal`	Use `host.docker.internal`
CLI Location	Native `/usr/bin/docker`	`docker.exe` accessible in PowerShell, WSL	`/usr/local/bin/docker`

Explanation: ***Note:*** *Most real-world production deployments run Docker on Linux servers. While Docker Desktop is ideal for development on Windows/macOS, always test critical behaviors (e.g., file permissions, symlinks, volume mounts) in a Linux environment before deploying to production.*

Summary

In this chapter, you've learned:

1. How to install Docker on Ubuntu, Windows, and macOS
2. How to install Docker Compose and verify it
3. Best practices like enabling non-root access
4. Common errors and how to fix them
5. A sample containerized database setup (PostgreSQL)

Key Takeaways

In this chapter, you successfully learned how to install Docker and Docker Compose across Linux, macOS, and Windows environments, setting up a complete container runtime. You understood critical steps like enabling non-root access, verifying installations, and troubleshooting common issues such as WSL2 configuration and permissions errors. With the real-world example of running PostgreSQL inside a Docker container, you are now equipped to build, run, and manage containerized applications confidently, laying the foundation for future hands-on work with Docker.

Knowledge Check

1. **What is the minimum supported OS for Docker Engine on Linux?**
   A) Ubuntu 16.04+
   B) Windows XP
   C) Fedora CoreOS
   D) Alpine only
2. **Which command is used to install Docker on Ubuntu from the official repo?**
   A) `sudo apt install docker.io`
   B) `docker install ubuntu`
   C) `apt docker`
   D) `docker start`
3. **What is the purpose of the docker group on Linux?**
   A) Add GUI support
   B) Manage Docker networking
   C) Run Docker as non-root
   D) Enable Docker Enterprise
4. **Which command checks if the Docker service is running?**
   A) `docker status`
   B) `docker run`
   C) `systemctl status docker`
   D) `docker-service`
5. **What is the official method to install Docker Compose v2+?**
   A) Python pip
   B) Built-in with Docker CLI
   C) `docker-compose install`
   D) Snap store
6. **Which command verifies Docker Compose is installed?**
   A) `docker-compose -version`
   B) `docker compose version`
   C) `docker compose -v`
   D) All of the above
7. **What file needs to be present to run `docker compose up`?**
   A) `Dockerfile`
   B) `.env`
   C) `docker-compose.yml`
   D) `compose.json`
8. **What port does Docker typically expose for its internal registry?**
   A) 8080

B) 5000
C) 3000
D) 443

9. **What is required before installing Docker Compose on CentOS manually?**
   A) `Yum` update
   B) `Go` compiler
   C) `pip3`
   D) `curl` & `Git`

10. **Which command installs Docker on Amazon Linux 2?**
    A) `yum install docker`
    B) `apt install docker`
    C) `dnf docker-install`
    D) `amazon-linux-docker`

11. **Docker Compose v1 was written in which language?**
    A) Python
    B) Go
    C) JavaScript
    D) Rust

12. **What command pulls Docker images defined in the Compose file without starting containers?**
    A) `docker compose pull`
    B) `docker compose images`
    C) `docker pull`
    D) `compose fetch`

13. **What's the easiest way to install Docker on macOS?**
    A) Brew install
    B) .pkg installer
    C) Docker Desktop
    D) Build from source

14. **After installing Docker, which group must a Linux user join?**
    A) `root`
    B) `docker`
    C) `wheel`
    D) `daemon`

15. **Which Docker Compose command brings down the services and removes volumes?**
    A) `docker compose kill`
    B) `docker compose down -v`
    C) `docker compose stop`
    D) `docker remove`

Answers

Q#	Correct Answer	Explanation
1	A	Docker officially supports Ubuntu 16.04+ and other modern Linux distros.
2	A	`sudo apt install docker.io` installs Docker on Ubuntu.
3	C	Adding a user to the docker group lets them run Docker without `sudo`.
4	C	`systemctl status docker` checks the Docker daemon status.
5	B	Compose v2 is built into the Docker CLI (as docker compose).
6	D	All three commands verify Docker Compose installation depending on the version.
7	C	The `docker-compose.yml` file is required to define services.
8	B	Docker registries commonly use port 5000.
9	A	Yum must be updated before installing dependencies like curl.
10	A	Amazon Linux uses `yum install docker` for Docker setup.
11	A	Docker Compose v1 was originally written in Python.
12	A	`docker compose pull` pulls images without starting containers.
13	C	Docker Desktop is the easiest method for macOS and Windows.
14	B	Add users to the docker group to avoid using `sudo`.
15	B	`docker compose down -v` stops and removes services and volumes.

Chapter 3: Docker Architecture and Basic Commands

In this chapter, we'll take a closer look at the internals of Docker, understand its layered architecture, and work hands-on with essential Docker CLI commands. You'll also learn how containers are created, started, stopped, inspected, and removed—all foundational for building more complex systems later.

How Docker Works: High-Level Architecture

Docker follows a client-server architecture and consists of the following key components:

Docker Engine

The Docker Engine is the core software that enables containers to run. It consists of:

- **Docker Daemon (dockerd):** The background service that handles image building, container management, and other core functions. Internally, Docker uses a lightweight container runtime called containerd to manage container lifecycle operations such as create, start, stop, pause, and remove. It listens for Docker API requests, then **builds, runs, and manages containers** and manages Docker objects (images, containers, networks, volumes).
- **Docker CLI (docker):** The command-line tool that sends commands to the Docker daemon via REST API. Commands such as `docker build`, `docker run`, or `docker pull`.
- **Docker REST API:** Acts as the communication layer between the CLI and daemon. It allows Docker clients to **interact with Docker Daemon remotely or locally**, enabling automation and scripting. External tools like Portainer and Kubernetes also interact with Docker via this API.
- **Docker Host:** The **physical or virtual machine** where Docker Daemon runs. It hosts containers and handles resource management, networking, and volume mounting.
- **Docker Registry: It is a repository of Docker images**. Docker Daemon uses `docker pull` to retrieve images and `docker push` to upload images to docker registry. **Docker Hub** is the default public registry, though private registries can be configured.

Docker Objects

Object	Description
Image	Read-only blueprint to create containers
Container	A running (or stopped) instance of an image
Volume	Persistent data storage managed by Docker
Network	Allows containers to communicate with each other and with the host

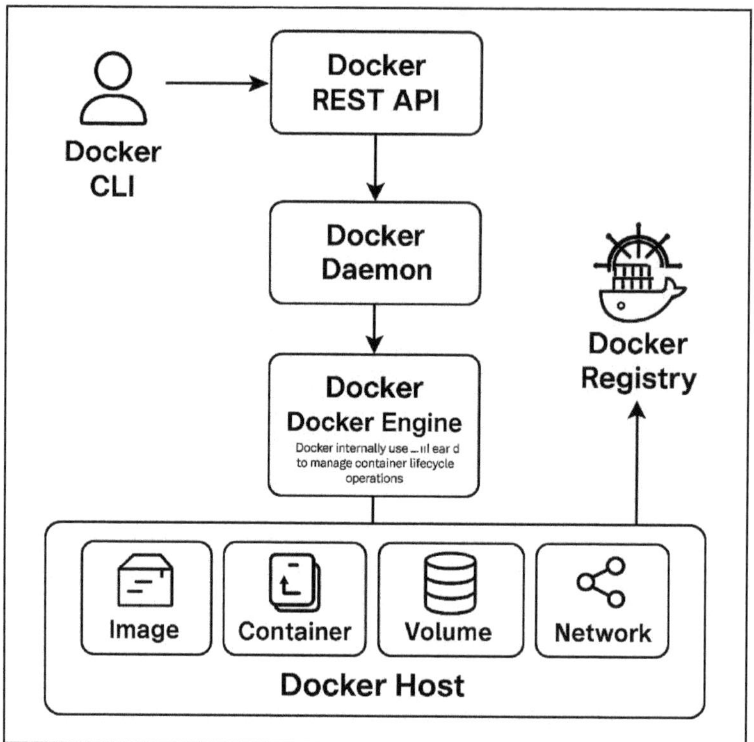

Figure 3.1: High Level Docker Architecture

Docker Architecture operates on a client-server model that facilitates efficient containerized application development and deployment.

At the user-facing layer lies the Docker Command-Line Interface (CLI), which enables developers and administrators to interact with the Docker environment using intuitive commands such as `docker build`, `docker run`, and `docker pull`.

These commands are internally converted into REST API calls and transmitted to the Docker Daemon—a background service that orchestrates the lifecycle of containers. Acting as the core engine, the Docker Daemon is responsible for building, managing, and running containerized applications.

It operates within the Docker Host, which may be a physical or virtual machine, and oversees the execution of key Docker objects such as images, containers, volumes, and networks.

Communication between CLI and Daemon is handled through the Docker REST API, which supports both local and remote interactions. In addition to local operations, the Docker Daemon interfaces with the Docker Registry—a centralized repository, such as Docker Hub—allowing it to pull application images or push newly built images for storage and distribution.

This modular yet integrated architecture promotes isolation, portability, and scalability across the application lifecycle, from development to production, making Docker a cornerstone technology in modern DevOps and cloud-native infrastructure.

First Docker Commands (Hands-On)

Let's begin using Docker with real examples. Open the terminal and follow along.

Example: Running the hello-world Container

```
$ docker run hello-world
```

What Happens:

1. Docker checks if the `hello-world` image is present locally.
2. If not, it pulls it from Docker Hub.
3. Then it runs the container, which prints a friendly message.

Output:

```
Hello from Docker!
```

This message shows that the installation appears to be working correctly.

Images and Containers: What's the Difference?

- **Image:** A snapshot or template with everything needed to run an application (code, dependencies, system tools).
- **Container:** A running (or stopped) instance of an image. Think of it as a live session of an image.

Analogy:

- **Image = Class**
- **Container = Object**

Basic Docker Commands (With Real Output)

Let's explore the most commonly used Docker commands.

`$ docker images`

Lists all locally available images.

```
$ docker images
```

Output:

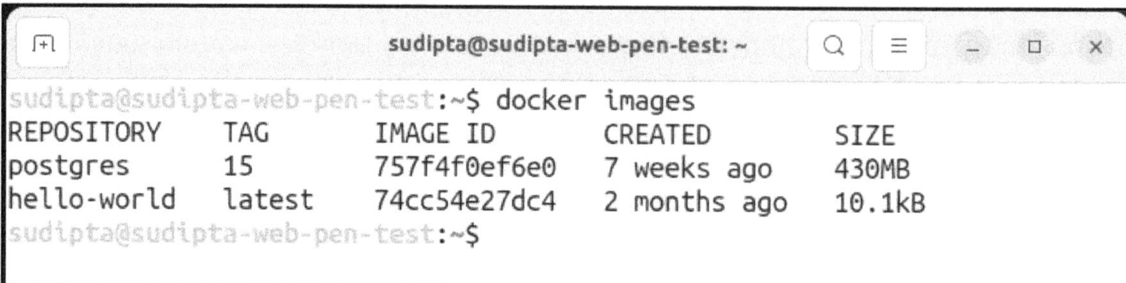

Figure 3.2: Docker image command output

`$ docker run`

Runs a container based on an image.

```
$ docker run -it ubuntu bash
```

- `-it`: Interactive + TTY (opens a terminal session)
- `ubuntu`: Image name
- `bash`: Command to run inside the container

Once inside, you'll be in the container's shell:

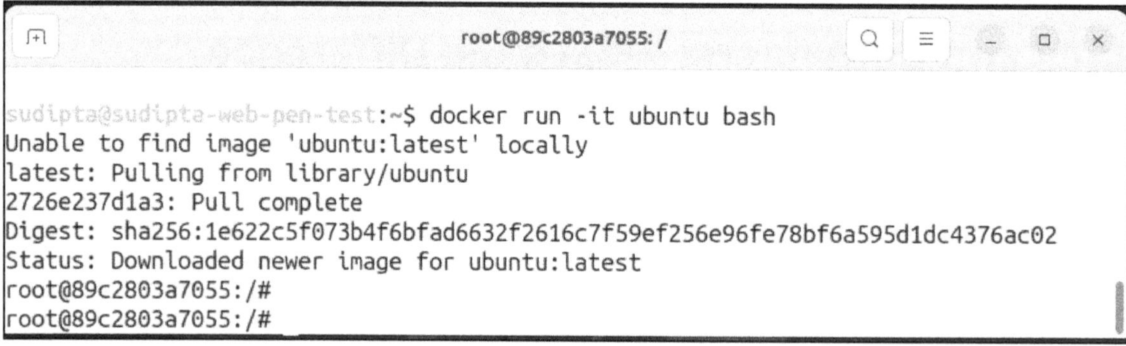

Figure 3.3: Docker run command output

`$ docker ps`

Lists running containers.

```
$ docker ps
```

Output:

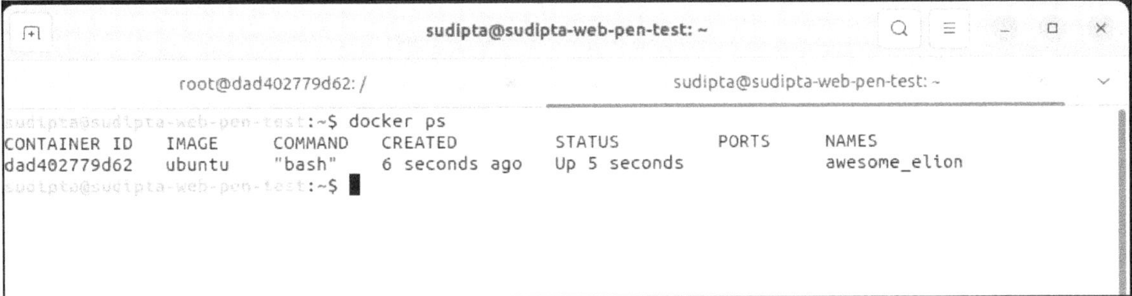

Figure 3.4: Docker ps command output

`$ docker ps -a`

Lists **all** containers (running + stopped).

```
$ docker ps -a
```

Output:

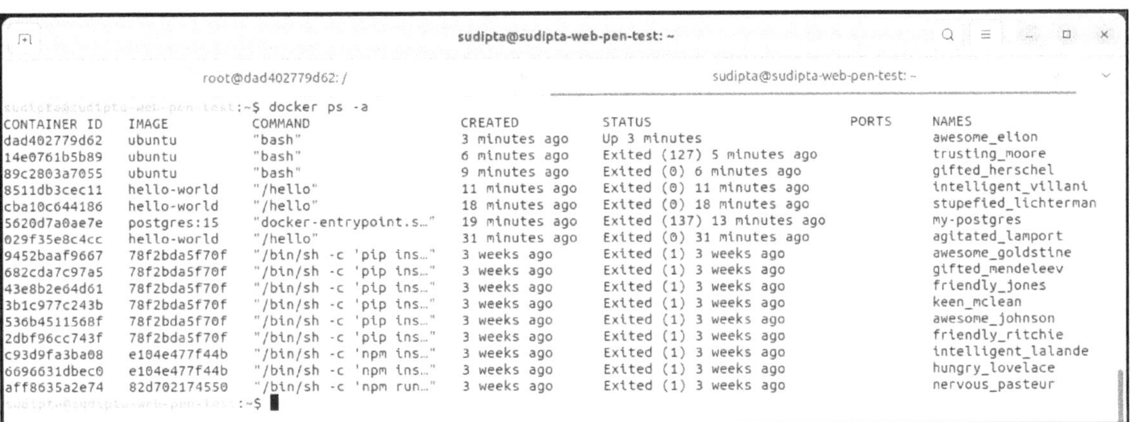

Figure 3.5: Docker ps -a command output

`$ docker stop`

Stop a running container.

```
$ docker stop <container_id_or_name>
```

Output:

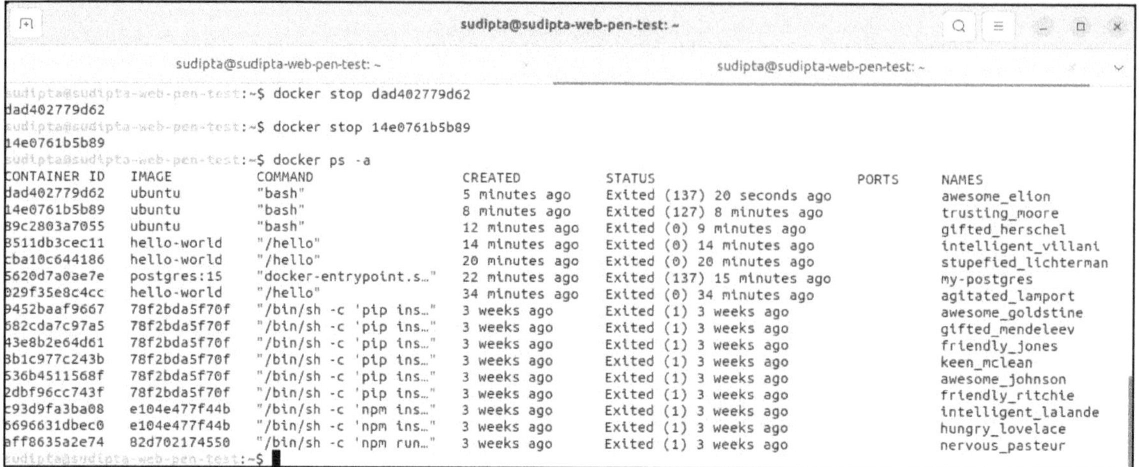

Figure 3.6: Docker stop command output

`$ docker rm`

Removes a **stopped** container.

```
$ docker rm <container_id_or_name>
```

Output:

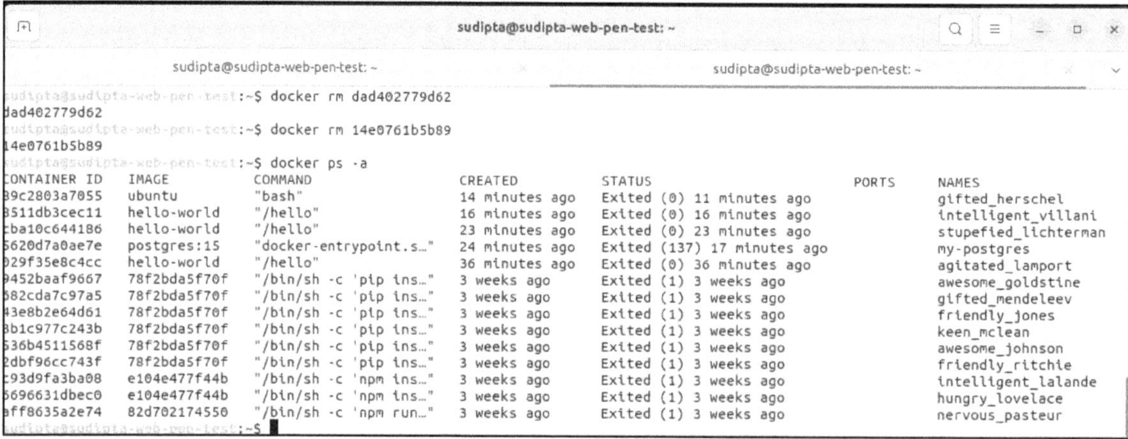

Figure 3.7: Docker rm command output

`$ docker rmi`

Removes an image from system.

```
$ docker rmi <container_id_or_name>
$ docker rmi ubuntu
```

Note: You must stop and remove the container image before deleting the image.

Output:

```
sudipta@sudipta-web-pen-test: ~
sudipta@sudipta-web-pen-test: ~                                   sudipta@sudipta-web-pen-t
sudipta@sudipta-web-pen-test:~$ docker ps -a
CONTAINER ID   IMAGE    COMMAND   CREATED         STATUS         PORTS     NAMES
a499914e8b8d   ubuntu   "bash"    8 seconds ago   Up 8 seconds             amazing_wu
sudipta@sudipta-web-pen-test:~$
sudipta@sudipta-web-pen-test:~$ docker stop a499914e8b8d # Step 1 "Stop the Container"
a499914e8b8d
sudipta@sudipta-web-pen-test:~$
sudipta@sudipta-web-pen-test:~$ docker rm a499914e8b8d # Setp 2 "Remove the container"
a499914e8b8d
sudipta@sudipta-web-pen-test:~$
sudipta@sudipta-web-pen-test:~$
sudipta@sudipta-web-pen-test:~$ docker rmi a499914e8b8d # Setp 3 "Remove the image"
```

Figure 3.8: Docker rmi command output

Container Lifecycle Explained

A Docker container moves through the following lifecycle stages:

1. **Create** → `docker create`
2. **Start** → `docker start`
3. **Running** → Container executes commands
4. **Stop** → `docker stop`
5. **Paused (optional)** → `docker pause`
6. **Exited** → Process ends, or container stopped
7. **Remove** → `docker rm`

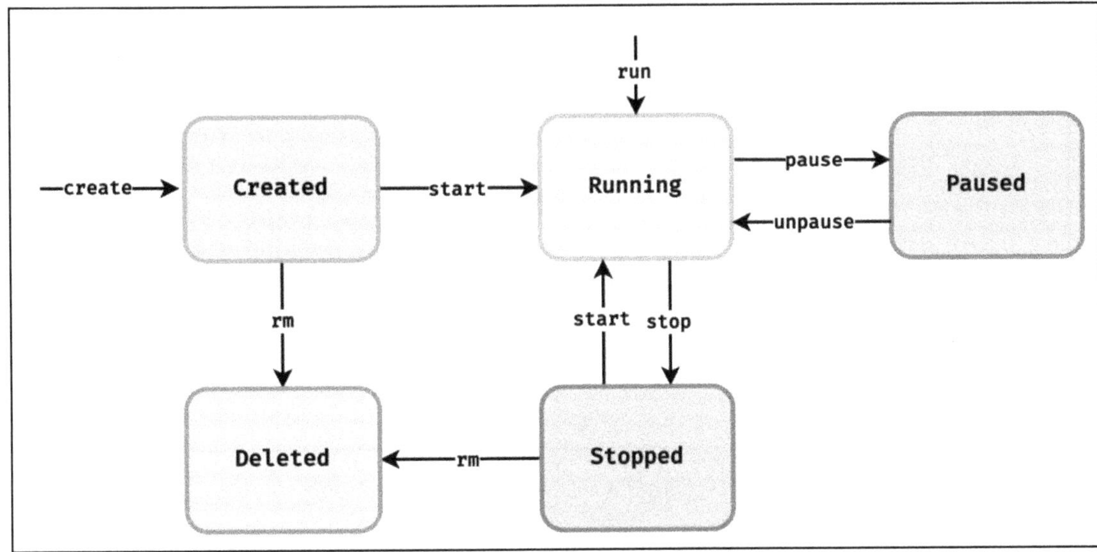

Figure 3.9: Docker Container Lifecycle

🏴 In most cases, `docker run` combines `create + start`.

Interactive vs Detached Mode

Interactive Mode

Run a container in the foreground with your terminal attached.

```
$ docker run -it ubuntu bash
```

Output:

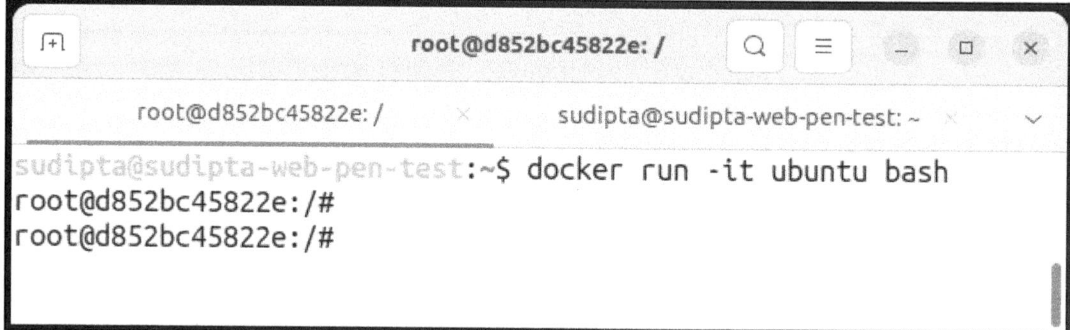

Figure 3.10: Docker interactive mode

Detached Mode

Runs a container in the background.

```
$ docker run -d nginx
```

Output:

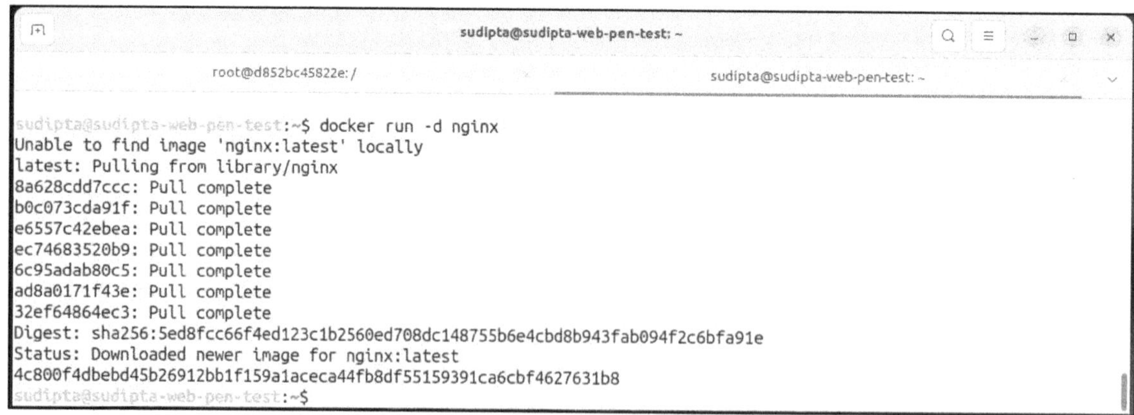

Figure 3.11: Docker detached mode

Check the logs

```
$ docker logs <container_id>
```

Output:

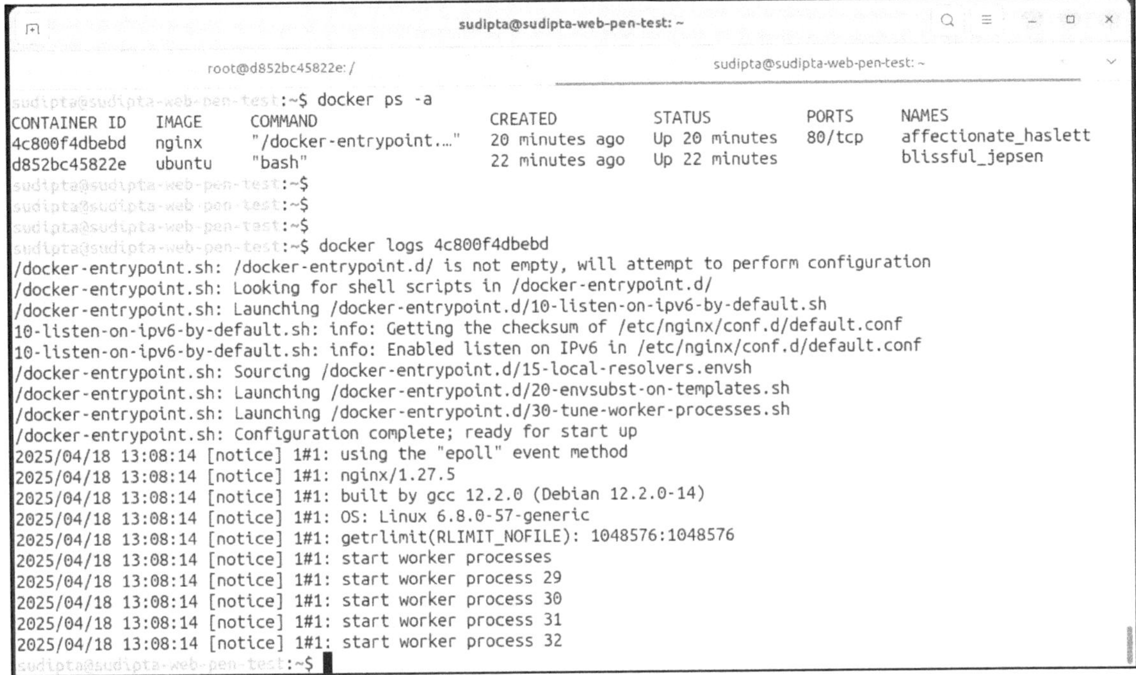

Figure 3.12: Docker logs command output

Exposing Ports

To make a container accessible via the host:

```
$ docker run -d -p 8080:80 nginx
```

- `-p`: Maps `host_port:container_port`
- `8080` (host) → `80` (nginx)

Visit `http://localhost:8080` and you'll see the Nginx welcome page.

Output:

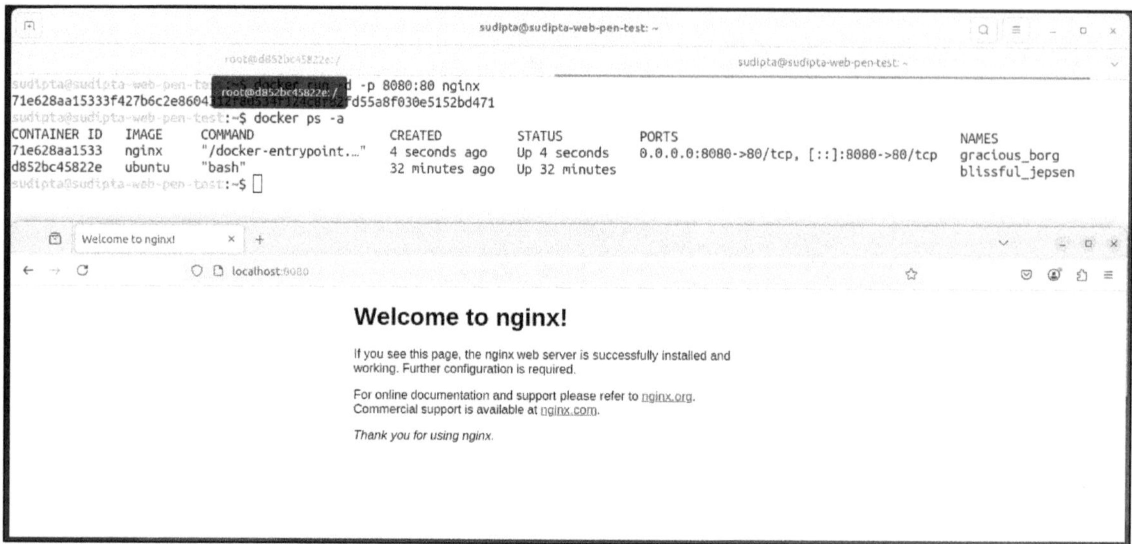

Figure 3.13: Exposing docker ports mapping - internal & external port

Working with Named Containers

Instead of using auto-generated names (hopeful_morse), assign a name

```
$ docker run -d --name webserver nginx
```

Output:

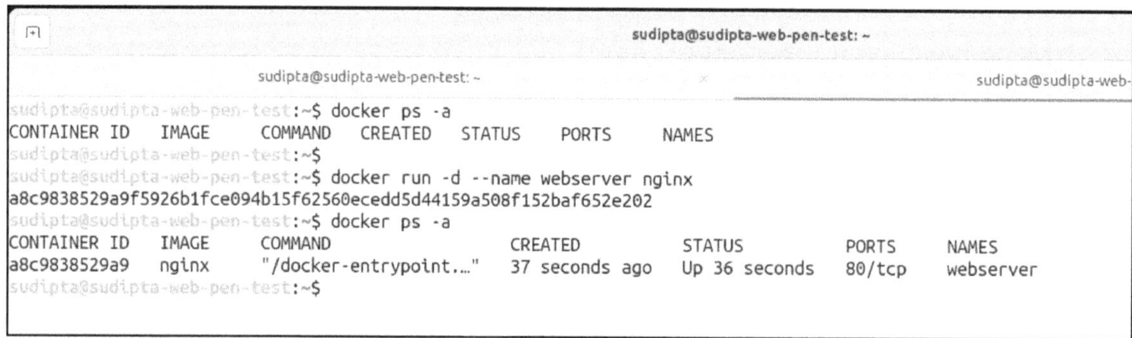

Figure 3.14: Naming Docker container

Start/stop by name:

```
$ docker stop webserver
$ docker start webserver
```

Output:

Figure 3.15: Starting and stopping container by names

Inspecting Docker Objects

Inspect a Container:

```
$ docker inspect webserver
```

Output:

```
sudipta@sudipta-web-pen-test: ~                    sudipta@sudipta-web-pen-test: ~
sudipta@sudipta-web-pen-test:~$ docker inspect webserver
[
    {
        "Id": "a8c9838529a9f5926b1fce094b15f62560ecedd5d44159a508f152baf652e202",
        "Created": "2025-04-18T13:41:16.789167838Z",
        "Path": "/docker-entrypoint.sh",
        "Args": [
            "nginx",
            "-g",
            "daemon off;"
        ],
        "State": {
            "Status": "running",
            "Running": true,
            "Paused": false,
            "Restarting": false,
            "OOMKilled": false,
            "Dead": false,
            "Pid": 16231,
            "ExitCode": 0,
            "Error": "",
            "StartedAt": "2025-04-18T13:50:03.637419571Z",
            "FinishedAt": "2025-04-18T13:49:19.134842911Z"
        },
        "Image": "sha256:4e1b6bae1e48cdbde8e6ec3e6ee42d86ad4780156e75790465bf6fb16c551c27",
        "ResolvConfPath": "/var/lib/docker/containers/a8c9838529a9f5926b1fce094b15f62560ecedd5d44159a508f152baf652e202/resolv.conf",
        "HostnamePath": "/var/lib/docker/containers/a8c9838529a9f5926b1fce094b15f62560ecedd5d44159a508f152baf652e202/hostname",
        "HostsPath": "/var/lib/docker/containers/a8c9838529a9f5926b1fce094b15f62560ecedd5d44159a508f152baf652e202/hosts",
        "LogPath": "/var/lib/docker/containers/a8c9838529a9f5926b1fce094b15f62560ecedd5d44159a508f152baf652e202/a8c9838529a9f5926b1fce094b15f62560ecedd5d44159a508f152baf652e202
-json.log",
```

Figure 3.16: Inspecting docker container by names

Returns low-level details as JSON: networking, mount points, IP address, etc.

Inspect a Network:

```
$ docker network inspect bridge
```

Output:

```
sudipta@sudipta-web-pen-test: ~
sudipta@sudipta-web-pen-test: ~        sudipta@sudipta-web-pen-test: ~

sudipta@sudipta-web-pen-test:~$ docker network inspect bridge
[
    {
        "Name": "bridge",
        "Id": "8f2a11cbf9b9948d922a698a19fb145b2f4024b19595176e1ca98678e28d5646",
        "Created": "2025-04-18T17:42:00.321508418+05:30",
        "Scope": "local",
        "Driver": "bridge",
        "EnableIPv4": true,
        "EnableIPv6": false,
        "IPAM": {
            "Driver": "default",
            "Options": null,
            "Config": [
                {
                    "Subnet": "172.17.0.0/16",
                    "Gateway": "172.17.0.1"
                }
            ]
        },
        "Internal": false,
        "Attachable": false,
        "Ingress": false,
        "ConfigFrom": {
            "Network": ""
        },
        "ConfigOnly": false,
        "Containers": {
            "a8c9838529a9f5926b1fce094b15f62560ecedd5d44159a508f152baf652e202": {
                "Name": "webserver",
                "EndpointID": "a480a3bca76e22dc25491c1ed549d84153cb9dc2c0511336e12fc16bf522f282",
                "MacAddress": "fa:9c:a1:d9:0e:5a",
                "IPv4Address": "172.17.0.2/16",
                "IPv6Address": ""
            }
        },
        "Options": {
            "com.docker.network.bridge.default_bridge": "true",
            "com.docker.network.bridge.enable_icc": "true",
            "com.docker.network.bridge.enable_ip_masquerade": "true",
            "com.docker.network.bridge.host_binding_ipv4": "0.0.0.0",
            "com.docker.network.bridge.name": "docker0",
            "com.docker.network.driver.mtu": "1500"
        },
        "Labels": {}
    }
]
sudipta@sudipta-web-pen-test:~$
```

Figure 3.17: Inspecting default docker bridge network

Copying Files Into/Out of a Container

Copy from Host → Container

```
$ docker cp myfile.txt webserver:/usr/share/nginx/html
```

Output:

```
sudipta@sudipta-web-pen-test: ~

sudipta@sudipta-web-pen-test: ~                                   sudipta
sudipta@sudipta-web-pen-test:~$ touch myfile.txt # Create a File
sudipta@sudipta-web-pen-test:~$
sudipta@sudipta-web-pen-test:~$ ls -l myfile.txt
-rw-rw-r-- 1 sudipta sudipta 0 Apr 18 19:57 myfile.txt
sudipta@sudipta-web-pen-test:~$
sudipta@sudipta-web-pen-test:~$ docker cp myfile.txt webserver:/usr/share/nginx/html
Successfully copied 1.54kB to webserver:/usr/share/nginx/html
sudipta@sudipta-web-pen-test:~$
```

Figure 3.18: Copying file from system to container

Copy from Container → Host

```
$ docker cp webserver:/etc/nginx/nginx.conf ./nginx.conf
```

Output:

```
sudipta@sudipta-web-pen-test: ~

sudipta@sudipta-web-pen-test: ~                                   sudipta@sud
sudipta@sudipta-web-pen-test:~$ ls -l nginx.conf
ls: cannot access 'nginx.conf': No such file or directory
sudipta@sudipta-web-pen-test:~$
sudipta@sudipta-web-pen-test:~$ docker cp webserver:/etc/nginx/nginx.conf ./nginx.conf
Successfully copied 2.56kB to /home/sudipta/nginx.conf
sudipta@sudipta-web-pen-test:~$
sudipta@sudipta-web-pen-test:~$ ls -l nginx.conf
-rw-r--r-- 1 sudipta sudipta 644 Apr 16 17:44 nginx.conf
sudipta@sudipta-web-pen-test:~$ cat nginx.conf

user  nginx;
worker_processes  auto;

error_log  /var/log/nginx/error.log notice;
pid        /run/nginx.pid;


events {
    worker_connections  1024;
}


http {
    include       /etc/nginx/mime.types;
    default_type  application/octet-stream;

    log_format  main  '$remote_addr - $remote_user [$time_local] "$request" '
                      '$status $body_bytes_sent "$http_referer" '
                      '"$http_user_agent" "$http_x_forwarded_for"';
```

Figure 3.19: Copying file from container to local system

Docker Command Recap Table

Command	Description
`docker run`	Run a new container
`docker ps`	List running containers
`docker ps -a`	List all containers
`docker stop <id>`	Stop a container
`docker rm <id>`	Remove a container
`docker images`	List images
`docker rmi <image>`	Remove an image
`docker exec -it <id> bash`	Run bash inside a running container
`docker logs <id>`	View logs of a container
`docker inspect <id>`	View detailed container info

Hands-On Lab: Build and Run a Static Website

Let's build a simple container running a static HTML site using Nginx.

Difficulty Level: Basic

Step 1: Create a Directory and HTML File

```
$ mkdir mysite && cd mysite
$ echo '<h1>Welcome to MySite!</h1>' > index.html
```

Step 2: Create a Dockerfile

```
FROM nginx:alpine
COPY index.html /usr/share/nginx/html/index.html
```

Step 3: Build the Image

```
$ docker build -t mysite:latest .
```

Output:

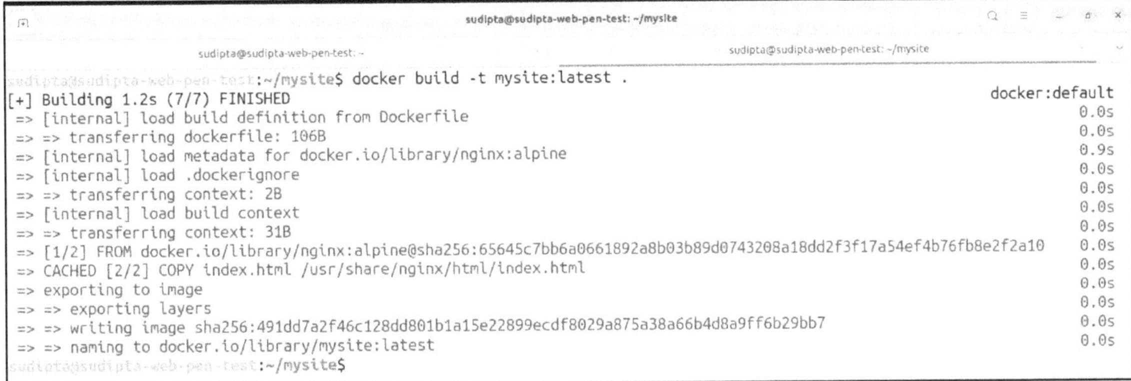

Figure 3.20: Building and hosting website in container

Step 4: Run the Container

```
$ docker run -d -p 8080:80 mysite:latest
```

Open `http://localhost:8080` in your browser.

Output:

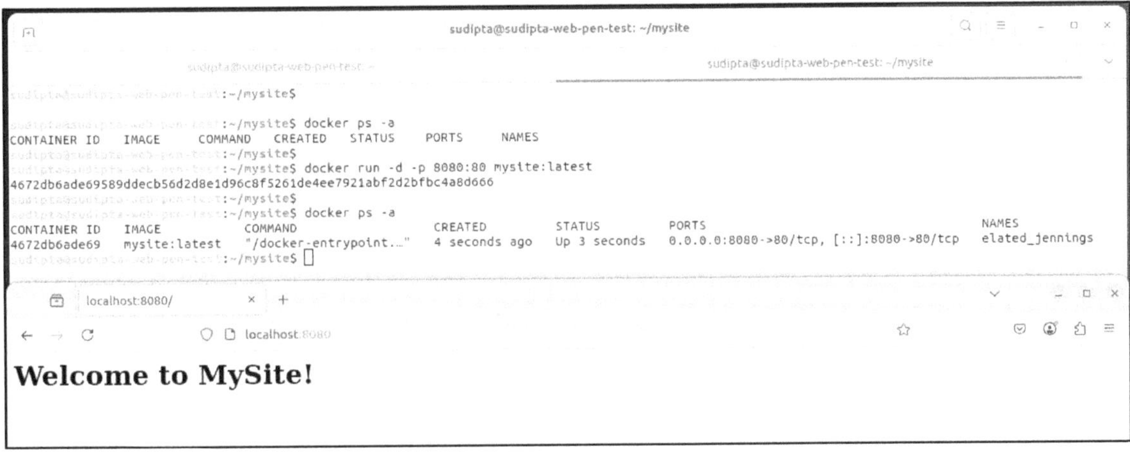

Figure 3.21: Running the container and accessing it from browser

Summary

In this chapter, you've learned:

- How Docker works under the hood
- What images, containers, and volumes are
- How to run, stop, inspect, and remove containers
- The difference between interactive and detached modes
- How to map ports, name containers, and copy files
- A full hands-on project to build and run a containerized static site

Key Takeaways

In this chapter, you mastered Docker's layered client-server architecture, learned the difference between images and containers, and practiced fundamental container lifecycle operations. You gained hands-on experience with commands like docker run, docker ps, docker exec, and docker inspect, setting the foundation for building and managing complex containerized applications.

Knowledge Check

1. **What are the three core components of Docker architecture?**
   A) Docker Engine, Docker Hub, Docker Swarm
   B) Docker Client, Docker Daemon, Docker Objects
   C) Docker Compose, Docker API, Dockerfile
   D) Docker VM, Docker OS, Docker Agent
2. **What role does the Docker Daemon (dockerd) play?**
   A) Hosts the Docker GUI
   B) Builds Docker images only
   C) Listens to requests from Docker client and manages Docker objects
   D) Only deploys Swarm services
3. **What is a Docker object?**
   A) An image only
   B) Any unit of configuration like image, container, volume, or network
   C) A file on the host
   D) A log file
4. **What does the command docker images do?**
   A) Lists active containers
   B) Lists all Docker images stored locally
   C) Downloads new images
   D) Runs image stats
5. **What is the difference between `docker stop` and `docker kill`?**
   A) stop kills instantly; kill exits gracefully
   B) No difference
   C) stop sends SIGTERM, kill sends SIGKILL
   D) kill pauses the container
6. **What does docker exec allow you to do?**
   A) Create a volume
   B) Launch a new container
   C) Run a command inside a running container
   D) List Docker services
7. **What flag is used to run a container interactively with a terminal session?**
   A) `-d`
   B) `–volume`
   C) `-it`
   D) `-rm`
8. **Which of the following commands lists all Docker networks?**
   A) `docker networks`

B) `docker list network`

C) `docker network ls`

D) `docker show net`

9. What is the purpose of docker inspect?

A) Start container

B) See low-level JSON details of containers, networks, volumes, etc.

C) Clean image cache

D) View log summary

10. What command is used to attach your terminal to a running container's output?

A) `docker connect`

B) `docker attach`

C) `docker logs`

D) `docker shell`

11. Which command permanently deletes a Docker image?

A) `docker delete`

B) `docker clean`

C) `docker rmi`

D) `docker shutdown`

12. Which Docker command lets you rename an existing container?

A) `docker rename`

B) `docker tag`

C) `docker alias`

D) `docker label`

13. What does the `docker ps` command show by default?

A) Running containers

B) All containers

C) Only stopped containers

D) All active volumes

14. What command is used to tag an image before pushing to a registry?

A) `docker mark`

B) `docker tag`

C) `docker push`

D) `docker version`

15. Which component handles building and running containers in Docker's architecture?

A) Docker Registry

B) Docker Client

C) Docker Daemon

D) Docker Container Engine

Answers

Q#	Correct Answer	Explanation
1	B	Docker architecture includes Client (CLI), Daemon (Server), and Docker Objects like containers/images.
2	C	The Docker Daemon manages images, containers, and listens to client commands.
3	B	Docker objects include images, containers, networks, volumes, and plugins.
4	B	`docker images` lists all local images.
5	C	`docker stop` sends a SIGTERM (graceful), `docker kill` sends a SIGKILL (force).
6	C	`docker exec` runs commands in running containers.
7	C	`-it` allows interactive shell with a container.
8	C	`docker network ls` lists all networks on the Docker host.
9	B	`docker inspect` returns detailed JSON output of Docker objects.
10	B	`docker attach` connects your terminal to the container's STDOUT.
11	C	`docker rmi` permanently deletes an image.
12	A	`docker rename` renames an existing container.
13	A	`docker ps` shows running containers by default.
14	B	`docker tag` assigns a new name or registry path to an image.
15	C	Docker Daemon is the engine responsible for managing all containers and images.

Chapter 4: Building Docker Images — Writing Efficient Dockerfiles and Optimizing Layers

Docker images are the foundation of every container. If you think of a container as a running application, the image is its blueprint. In this chapter, you'll learn how to write `Dockerfiles` to build your own custom images, optimize builds using caching and layering, and follow the industry's best practices.

What Is a Docker Image?

A **Docker image** is a read-only template that contains:

- The base operating system
- Application code
- Dependencies
- Configuration files
- Runtime instructions

You can think of it like a snapshot. When you **run** an image, Docker creates a new **container**, which is a live, writable instance of the image.

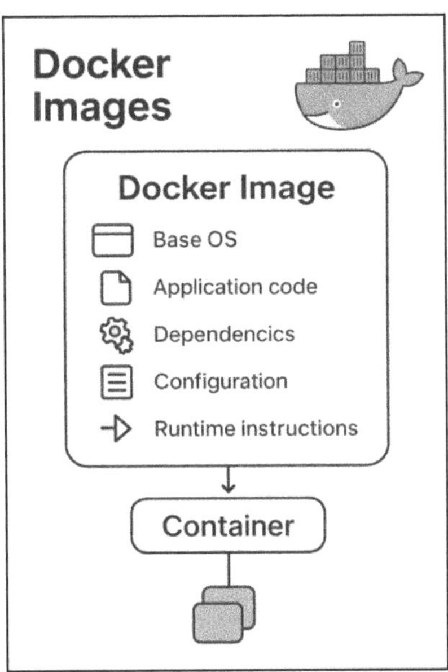

Figure 4.1: Container consists of Docker Images

What Is a Dockerfile?

A **`Dockerfile`** is a simple text file that contains instructions to build a Docker image. Each line in the Dockerfile represents a layer in the final image.

Let's take a simple Node.js app as an example:

`Example Node.js App:`

```
🗁 my-node-app/
├── Dockerfile
├── package.json
└── index.js
```

🗎 index.js ($ nano index.js)

```
const http = require('http');
const port = 3000;
const server = http.createServer((req, res) => {
  res.end("Hello from Docker!");
});
server.listen(port, () => {
  console.log(`Server running at http://localhost:${port}`);
});
```

🗎 package.json ($ nano package.json)

```
{
  "name": "dockerapp",
  "version": "1.0.0",
  "main": "index.js",
  "dependencies": {}
}
```

Writing a Basic Dockerfile

🗎 Dockerfile ($ nano Dockerfile)

```
# Step 1: Use base image
FROM node:18

# Step 2: Set working directory
WORKDIR /usr/src/app

```

```
# Step 3: Copy package files first (for caching)
COPY package*.json ./

# Step 4: Install dependencies
RUN npm install

# Step 5: Copy the rest of the code
COPY . .

# Step 6: Expose port
EXPOSE 3000

# Step 7: Define default command
CMD ["node", "index.js"]
```

Building and Running the Image

Step 1: Build the Image

```
$ docker build -t my-node-app .
```

Output:

```
Sending build context to Docker daemon  4.096kB
Step 1/7 : FROM node:18
 ---> d7d8ff2cbfdf
Step 2/7 : WORKDIR /usr/src/app
 ---> Running in 0a6f6fd7db50
...
Successfully built 87fbac72cb50
Successfully tagged my-node-app:latest
```

Output:

```
sudipta@sudipta-web-pen-test: ~                    sudipta@sudipta-web-pen-test: ~/my-node-app
sudipta@sudipta-web-pen-test:~/my-node-app$
sudipta@sudipta-web-pen-test:~/my-node-app$ nano index.js
sudipta@sudipta-web-pen-test:~/my-node-app$ nano package.json
sudipta@sudipta-web-pen-test:~/my-node-app$ nano Dockerfile
sudipta@sudipta-web-pen-test:~/my-node-app$ docker build -t my-node-app .
[+] Building 177.2s (10/10) FINISHED                                                   docker:default
 => [internal] load build definition from Dockerfile                                            0.1s
 => => transferring dockerfile: 391B                                                            0.0s
 => [internal] load metadata for docker.io/library/node:18                                      3.3s
 => [internal] load .dockerignore                                                               0.1s
 => => transferring context: 2B                                                                 0.0s
 => [1/5] FROM docker.io/library/node:18@sha256:df9fa4e0e39c9b97e30240b5bb1d99bdb861573a82002b2c52ac7d6b8d6d773e  161.9s
 => => resolve docker.io/library/node:18@sha256:df9fa4e0e39c9b97e30240b5bb1d99bdb861573a82002b2c52ac7d6b8d6d773e    0.2s
 => => sha256:df9fa4e0e39c9b97e30240b5bb1d99bdb861573a82002b2c52ac7d6b8d6d773e 6.41kB / 6.41kB    0.0s
 => => sha256:de20d623379fc7c7ccf845a22c3153b920d57446ba7c8e64ba25d21a60b48ad6 6.39kB / 6.39kB    0.0s
 => => sha256:23b7d26ef1d294256da0d70ce374277b9aab5ca683015073316005cb63d33849 48.49MB / 48.49MB  11.2s
 => => sha256:aa6c239d30ee04dede270729f9502389b1a9546687ce656872536340ee0a9e03 2.49kB / 2.49kB    0.0s
 => => sha256:07d1b5af933d2dfc3d0dd509d6e20534825e4a537f7b006a6cb5b8e5a1f20905 24.01MB / 24.01MB  14.5s
 => => sha256:1eb98adba0eb44a2e4facf9ca3626a4a66feedd0dd56d159cca90a35205744e7 64.40MB / 64.40MB  31.7s
 => => sha256:b617a119f8a27982374d94ec6eb3738ae3d38d6fc2c34c865813926cf596a621 211.33MB / 211.33MB 53.7s
 => => extracting sha256:23b7d26ef1d294256da0d70ce374277b9aab5ca683015073316005cb63d33849        46.8s
 => => sha256:ee496386c5de1ce84096ca486e1aabcdf7cb8f0afd5a9b4863dbf870b340744f 3.32kB / 3.32kB    15.0s
 => => sha256:058db40e534297246fb14bc4e107d2f6ddc140494a26793e1e90696cd6b2507a 45.68MB / 45.68MB  43.8s
 => => sha256:04deb1529fda049f44f9be8d16ca833a53961813ce07eda3cefd50cd3fd74880 1.25MB / 1.25MB    33.7s
 => => sha256:3b3ca5178f3ece5f7e96b38b9c4b9c3a101a9d6777cf0f5c320f869512c80024 448B / 448B        34.6s
 => => extracting sha256:07d1b5af933d2dfc3d0dd509d6e20534825e4a537f7b006a6cb5b8e5a1f20905         5.7s
 => => extracting sha256:1eb98adba0eb44a2e4facf9ca3626a4a66feedd0dd56d159cca90a35205744e7        20.0s
 => => extracting sha256:b617a119f8a27982374d94ec6eb3738ae3d38d6fc2c34c865813926cf596a621        49.5s
 => => extracting sha256:ee496386c5de1ce84096ca486e1aabcdf7cb8f0afd5a9b4863dbf870b340744f         0.0s
 => => extracting sha256:058db40e534297246fb14bc4e107d2f6ddc140494a26793e1e90696cd6b2507a        19.1s
 => => extracting sha256:04deb1529fda049f44f9be8d16ca833a53961813ce07eda3cefd50cd3fd74880         1.0s
 => => extracting sha256:3b3ca5178f3ece5f7e96b38b9c4b9c3a101a9d6777cf0f5c320f869512c80024         0.0s
 => [internal] load build context                                                               0.2s
 => => transferring context: 791B                                                               0.0s
 => [2/5] WORKDIR /usr/src/app                                                                  2.9s
 => [3/5] COPY package*.json ./                                                                 1.0s
 => [4/5] RUN npm install                                                                       5.9s
 => [5/5] COPY . .                                                                              0.6s
 => exporting to image                                                                          0.7s
 => => exporting layers                                                                         0.6s
 => => writing image sha256:a595c8ac8ead52b6a26695184d3799942eac258ddbdce09ec09a05296debef35      0.0s
 => => naming to docker.io/library/my-node-app                                                  0.1s
sudipta@sudipta-web-pen-test:~/my-node-app$
```

Figure 4.2: Building Image

Step 2: Run the Container

```
$ docker run -d -p 3000:3000 my-node-app
```

Step 3: Access the App

Visit `http://localhost:3000` → Output should be:

```
Hello from Docker!
```

Output:

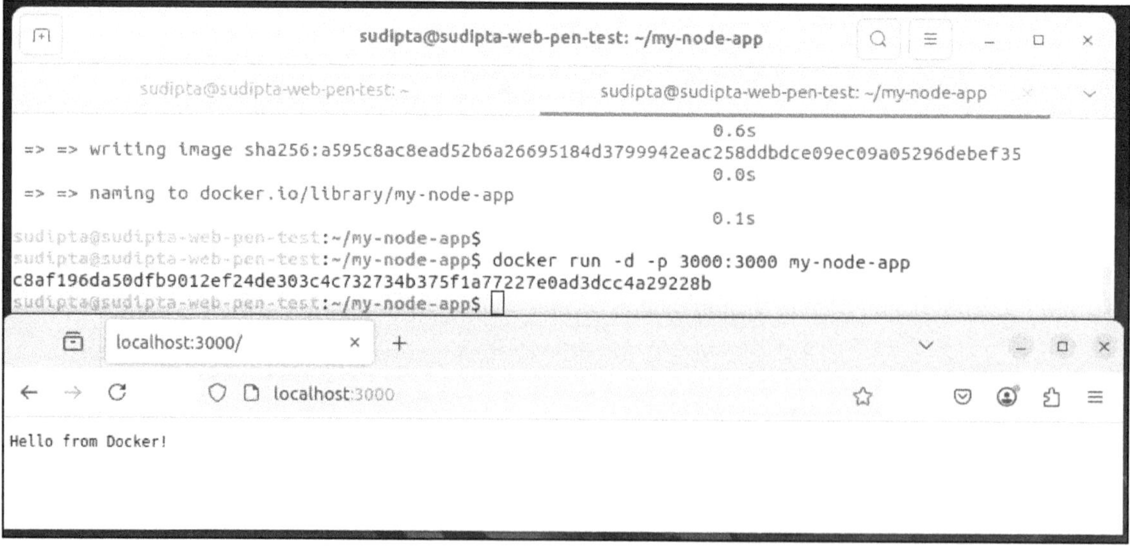

Figure 4.3: Access the app from browser

Understanding Dockerfile Instructions

Instruction	Purpose
`FROM`	Specifies the base image
`WORKDIR`	Sets the working directory inside the image
`COPY`	Copies files from host to container
`RUN`	Executes commands while building the image
`EXPOSE`	Inform Docker which port will be used
`CMD`	Sets the default command to run when the container starts
`ENV`	Sets environment variables
`ADD`	Similar to COPY but supports remote URLs and tar auto-extract
`ENTRYPOINT`	Sets a command that always runs (usually used with CMD)

ⓘ ***Note***: `ENTRYPOINT` and `CMD` can be combined — `ENTRYPOINT` defines the fixed executable, while `CMD` provides default arguments that can be overridden at runtime.

Layering and Caching in Docker

Each line in a `Dockerfile` creates a **layer** in the image. Docker caches these layers for efficiency. This is why ordering matters.

Efficient Dockerfile Example

```
FROM python:3.10-slim

WORKDIR /app

# Cache dependencies
COPY requirements.txt .

RUN pip install --no-cache-dir -r requirements.txt

# Copy application code
COPY . .

CMD ["python", "app.py"]
```

By placing `COPY requirements.txt` and `RUN pip install` before copying the rest of the code, Docker can cache the dependencies layer and avoid reinstalling them on every change to your code.

Multi-Stage Builds (Advanced)

Multi-stage builds are a powerful feature for creating small, production-ready images. You can use one stage to build the app and another to deploy it.

Example: Node.js + Nginx Static App

```
# Stage 1: Build
FROM node:18 AS builder
WORKDIR /app
COPY . .
RUN npm install
RUN npm run build

# Stage 2: Deploy
FROM nginx:alpine
COPY --from=builder /app/build /usr/share/nginx/html
```

Benefits:

- Keeps the final image lean (no source code or build tools)
- Improves security and startup time

ⓘ **Note:** Multi-stage builds require Docker version **17.05 or later** to work properly.

Best Practices for Writing Dockerfiles

☑ Use Official Images

Stick to Docker Hub's official images unless you need custom ones.

☑ Keep Layers Minimal

Combine commands where possible

```
RUN apt update && apt install -y curl git
```

☑ Use `.dockerignore`

Create a `.dockerignore` file to exclude files from build context (similar to `.gitignore`)

```
node_modules
```

```
.git
Dockerfile.old
```

ⓘ ***Note:*** Files listed in `.dockerignore` are excluded from the build context sent to the Docker daemon, which significantly speeds up builds and helps secure sensitive or unnecessary files from being included in images.

☑ Set Environment Variables

```
ENV NODE_ENV production
```

☑ Pin Version Tags

Avoid using `latest`. Use versioned images for stability

```
FROM python:3.11-slim
```

Real-World Use Case: Containerizing a Flask App

Let's containerize a simple Python Flask app.

🗎 `app.py ($ nano app.py)`

```
from flask import Flask
app = Flask(__name__)

@app.route('/')
def hello():
    return "Hello, Docker!"

if __name__ == "__main__":
    app.run(host="0.0.0.0", port=5000)
```

🗎 `requirements.txt ($ nano requirements.txt)`

```
Flask==2.3.2
```

🗎 `Dockerfile ($ nano Dockerfile)`

```
FROM python:3.11-slim
WORKDIR /app
COPY requirements.txt .
RUN pip install -r requirements.txt
```

```
COPY . .
EXPOSE 5000
CMD ["python", "app.py"]
```

Build & Run

```
$ docker build -t flask-docker-app .
$ docker run -d -p 5000:5000 flask-docker-app
```

Visit `http://localhost:5000` in your browser.

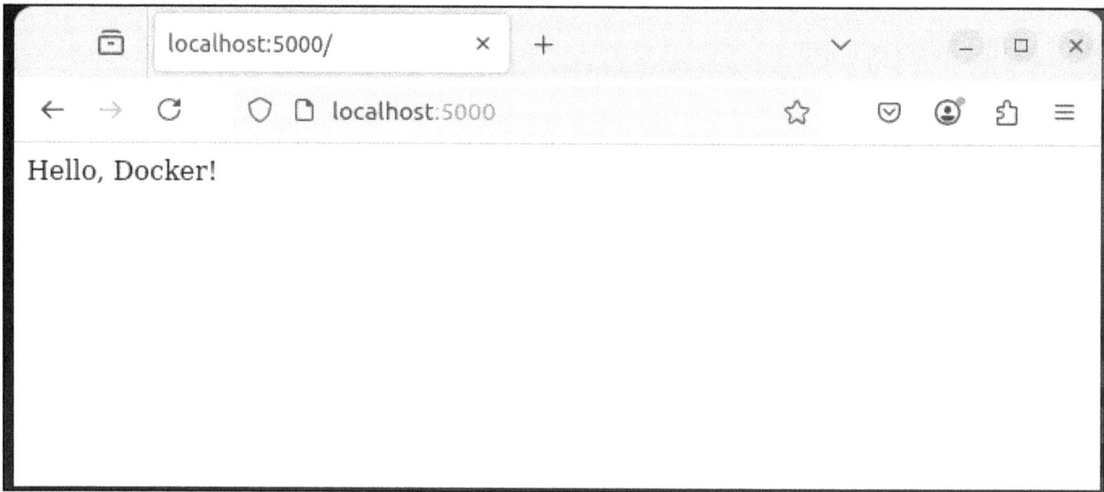

Figure 4.4: Access the app from browser

Exercise: Create a Custom Image

Goal: Create your own custom Docker image that:

- Runs a small Go, Python, or Node.js app
- Uses a `.dockerignore` file
- Exposes a port
- Has environment variables

Explanation: Tip: Try deploying it using Docker Compose.

Summary

In this chapter, you learned:

- What Docker images are and how they're built
- How to write, build, and run `Dockerfile`
- The difference between CMD and ENTRYPOINT
- Layer caching and image optimization tips
- How to write multi-stage builds for lean production images
- Real-world examples for Node.js and Flask apps

Key Takeaways

In this chapter, you mastered the basics of creating Docker images using Dockerfiles, understood how layering and caching optimize builds, explored multi-stage build techniques for production, and applied best practices to write secure, efficient, and maintainable container images.

Knowledge Check

1. **What is a Dockerfile?**
   A) A binary blob to store containers
   B) A configuration file used to build Docker images
   C) A tool to run Kubernetes clusters
   D) A backup file for container logs
2. **Which instruction in a Dockerfile sets the base image?**
   A) START
   B) COPY
   C) FROM
   D) BASE
3. **What is the correct syntax to copy files into an image?**
   A) COPY . to /path
   B) INTO ./app
   C) COPY src/ /app/
   D) ADD src app
4. **What is the difference between ADD and COPY in a Dockerfile?**
   A) COPY supports remote URLs
   B) ADD unpacks tar files and supports URLs
   C) ADD is deprecated
   D) COPY is for Windows only
5. **Which command in a Dockerfile sets environment variables?**
   A) EXPOSE
   B) ENV
   C) RUN
   D) ARG
6. **Which command runs only at build time?**
   A) CMD
   B) ENTRYPOINT
   C) RUN
   D) ENV
7. **What's the default command that executes when a container starts?**
   A) RUN
   B) CMD
   C) ENTRYPOINT
   D) ENV
8. **True or False: You can use multiple CMD instructions in a Dockerfile.**
   A) True
   B) False

9. **How can you reduce Docker image size?**
   A) Use multiple RUN instructions
   B) Use Alpine as base image
   C) Install everything in separate layers
   D) Always include GUI tools
10. **Where is the Docker image stored after build?**
   A) On DockerHub
   B) In the container
   C) In the local Docker image cache
   D) In the .dockerfile folder
11. **Which of the following are valid Dockerfile instructions?**
   ▢ FROM
   ▢ CMD
   ▢ RUN
   ▢ INIT
12. **In multi-stage builds, which benefits apply?**
   ▢ Smaller final image
   ▢ Better build-time separation
   ▢ More RAM usage at runtime
   ▢ Compile-time dependency exclusion
13. **Which files are commonly ignored by `.dockerignore`?**
   ▢ `.git`
   ▢ `node_modules/`
   ▢ `*.log`
   ▢ `Dockerfile`
14. **When using CMD, which form allows overriding at runtime?**
   ▢ `CMD ["python", "app.py"]`
   ▢ `CMD app.py`
   ▢ `CMD {"run": "bash"}`
15. **Which instructions support variable substitution via ARG?**
   ▢ ENV
   ▢ RUN
   ▢ COPY (as destination)
   ▢ FROM (before Docker v17.05)

Answers

Q#	Correct Answer	Explanation
1	B	A Dockerfile is a text script to define the steps for building an image.
2	C	Every Dockerfile starts with a FROM base image.
3	C	COPY src/ /app/ follows correct syntax: COPY <src> <dest>.
4	B	ADD has features like unpacking .tar and supporting remote URLs.
5	B	ENV sets key=value environment variables.
6	C	RUN executes during image build, not container runtime.
7	B	CMD is the default command when starting a container.
8	B	Only the last CMD in a Dockerfile is respected.
9	B	Alpine is a minimal base image, making images lightweight.
10	C	Docker caches images locally after build.

Q11. Which of the following are valid Dockerfile instructions?

- [✓] `FROM`
- [✓] `CMD`
- [✓] `RUN`
- [X] `INIT`
  Explanation: Only FROM, CMD, and RUN are valid instructions.

Q12. In multi-stage builds, which benefits apply?

- [✓] Smaller final image
- [✓] Better build-time separation
- [X] More RAM usage at runtime
- [✓] Compile-time dependency exclusion
  Explanation: Multi-stage builds allow optimized final images by excluding unnecessary tools.

Q13. Which files are commonly ignored by .dockerignore?

- [✓] `.git`
- [✓] `node_modules/`
- [✓] `*.log`
- [X] `Dockerfile`

Explanation: You usually want to exclude large or sensitive files, but **not** the `Dockerfile`.

Q14. When using CMD, which form allows overriding at runtime?

- **[✓]** `CMD ["python", "app.py"]`
- **[✓]** `CMD app.py`
- **[X]** `CMD {"run": "bash"}`
  Explanation: Shell and exec form of CMD support override; invalid JSON formats are not allowed.

Q15. Which instructions support variable substitution via ARG?

- **[✓]** `ENV`
- **[✓]** `RUN`
- **[✓]** `COPY` (as destination)
- **[X]** `FROM` (before Docker v17.05)
  Explanation: Variable substitution works in most layers but `FROM` support was added in v17.05+.

Chapter 5: Docker Containers in Action — Execution, Lifecycle, and Real-World Management

Once you've built a Docker image, the next step is to run containers based on that image. In this chapter, you'll learn how to manage containers, run applications interactively or in the background, and execute commands inside running containers.

What Is a Container?

A **Docker container** is a lightweight, standalone, and executable software package that includes everything needed to run a piece of software: code, runtime, libraries, environment variables, and configuration files.

A container creates from a Docker **image**, and it runs as a process on a system with its own isolated filesystem, network, and process tree.

Running Your First Container

Let's run a container using the official Ubuntu image:

```
$ docker run -it ubuntu
```

- `-i`: Interactive mode (keeps STDIN open)
- `-t`: Allocates a pseudo-TTY (terminal)
- `ubuntu`: The image to run

Now, you'll be dropped into an Ubuntu shell inside the container:

```
root@d83deaaf0863:/#
```

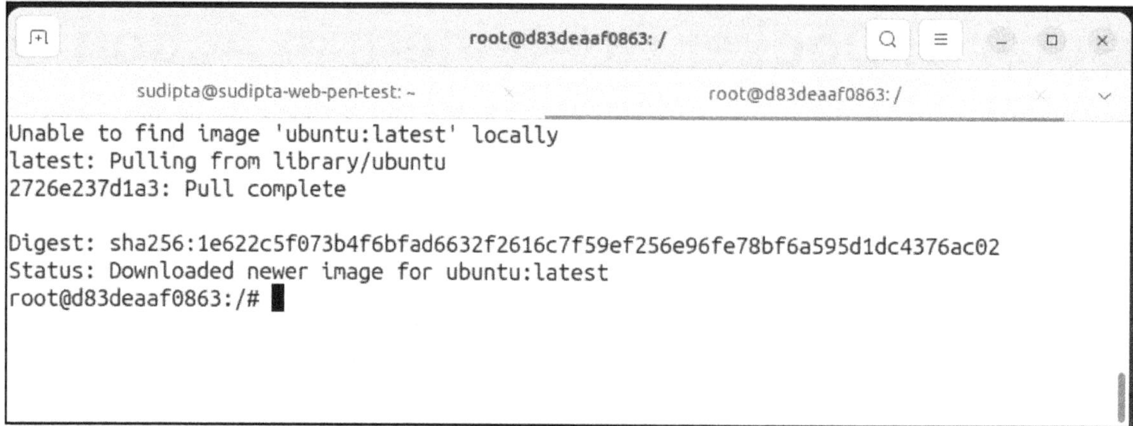

Figure 5.1: Running container in an Interactive mode

You're inside the container! Try running

```
# apt update
```

Exit the container

```
# exit
```

The container will stop as soon as you exit the shell unless it's running a background process.

```
root@d83deaaf0863:/# apt update
Get:1 http://security.ubuntu.com/ubuntu noble-security InRelease [126 kB]
Get:2 http://archive.ubuntu.com/ubuntu noble InRelease [256 kB]
Get:3 http://security.ubuntu.com/ubuntu noble-security/multiverse amd64 Packages [21.9 kB]
Get:4 http://archive.ubuntu.com/ubuntu noble-updates InRelease [126 kB]
Get:5 http://security.ubuntu.com/ubuntu noble-security/main amd64 Packages [941 kB]
Get:6 http://archive.ubuntu.com/ubuntu noble-backports InRelease [126 kB]
Get:7 http://archive.ubuntu.com/ubuntu noble/universe amd64 Packages [19.3 MB]
Get:8 http://security.ubuntu.com/ubuntu noble-security/universe amd64 Packages [1073 kB]
Get:9 http://security.ubuntu.com/ubuntu noble-security/restricted amd64 Packages [1088 kB]
Get:10 http://archive.ubuntu.com/ubuntu noble/multiverse amd64 Packages [331 kB]
Get:11 http://archive.ubuntu.com/ubuntu noble/restricted amd64 Packages [117 kB]
Get:12 http://archive.ubuntu.com/ubuntu noble/main amd64 Packages [1808 kB]
Get:13 http://archive.ubuntu.com/ubuntu noble-updates/main amd64 Packages [1294 kB]
Get:14 http://archive.ubuntu.com/ubuntu noble-updates/universe amd64 Packages [1371 kB]
Get:15 http://archive.ubuntu.com/ubuntu noble-updates/restricted amd64 Packages [1206 kB]
Get:16 http://archive.ubuntu.com/ubuntu noble-updates/multiverse amd64 Packages [26.4 kB]
Get:17 http://archive.ubuntu.com/ubuntu noble-backports/main amd64 Packages [48.0 kB]
Get:18 http://archive.ubuntu.com/ubuntu noble-backports/universe amd64 Packages [31.8 kB]
Fetched 29.3 MB in 8s (3637 kB/s)
Reading package lists... Done
Building dependency tree... Done
Reading state information... Done
1 package can be upgraded. Run 'apt list --upgradable' to see it.
root@d83deaaf0863:/# exit
exit
sudipta@sudipta-web-pen-test:~$ docker ps -a
CONTAINER ID   IMAGE    COMMAND       CREATED         STATUS                    PORTS   NAMES
d83deaaf0863   ubuntu   "/bin/bash"   4 minutes ago   Exited (0) 4 seconds ago          dreamy_colden
sudipta@sudipta-web-pen-test:~$
```

Figure 5.2: Update packages via apt update in container and exit from container

Once you type "`exit`", container stop, and you can see via command "`docker ps -a`" and `STATUS` would be "`Exited (0) 4 seconds ago`" in the output command as shown in the Figure 5.2

Interactive Mode vs Detached Mode

Interactive Mode

```
$ docker run -it ubuntu bash
```

- You stay inside the container until you exit.
- Great for debugging or experimentation.

Detached Mode (Background)

```
$ docker run -d nginx
```

- The container runs in the background.
- Ideal for servers or daemons.

ⓘ **Note:** When running in detached mode, you should monitor container health using `docker logs`, `docker ps`, and `docker inspect`. These tools help you ensure the container is running as expected without direct terminal interaction.

Output:

```
sudipta@sudipta-web-pen-test:~$ docker run -d nginx
Unable to find image 'nginx:latest' locally
latest: Pulling from library/nginx
8a628cdd7ccc: Already exists
b0c073cda91f: Pull complete
e6557c42ebea: Pull complete
ec74683520b9: Pull complete
6c95adab80c5: Pull complete
ad8a0171f43e: Pull complete
32ef64864ec3: Pull complete
Digest: sha256:5ed8fcc66f4ed123c1b2560ed708dc148755b6e4cbd8b943fab094f2c6bfa91e
Status: Downloaded newer image for nginx:latest
eca9602f323d8228a7bcb634800fd129a8cff5d68ac87e5bfe0dd2f11c330db4
sudipta@sudipta-web-pen-test:~$
sudipta@sudipta-web-pen-test:~$ docker ps -a
CONTAINER ID   IMAGE     COMMAND                  CREATED          STATUS                      PORTS     NAMES
eca9602f323d   nginx     "/docker-entrypoint.…"   15 seconds ago   Up 14 seconds               80/tcp    boring_lichterman
ae2a8fe08030   ubuntu    "bash"                   2 minutes ago    Exited (0) 41 seconds ago             adoring_borg
d83deaaf0863   ubuntu    "/bin/bash"              8 minutes ago    Exited (0) 4 minutes ago              dreamy_colden
sudipta@sudipta-web-pen-test:~$ docker ps -a
CONTAINER ID   IMAGE     COMMAND                  CREATED          STATUS                          PORTS     NAMES
eca9602f323d   nginx     "/docker-entrypoint.…"   53 seconds ago   Up 52 seconds                   80/tcp    boring_lichterman
ae2a8fe08030   ubuntu    "bash"                   2 minutes ago    Exited (0) About a minute ago             adoring_borg
d83deaaf0863   ubuntu    "/bin/bash"              9 minutes ago    Exited (0) 5 minutes ago                  dreamy_colden
sudipta@sudipta-web-pen-test:~$
```

Figure 5.3: Running container in detached mode

Get logs using

```
$ docker logs <container_id>
```

Output:

```
sudipta@sudipta-web-pen-test:~$ docker ps -a
CONTAINER ID   IMAGE     COMMAND                  CREATED          STATUS                     PORTS     NAMES
eca9602f323d   nginx     "/docker-entrypoint.…"   2 minutes ago    Up 2 minutes               80/tcp    boring_lichterman
ae2a8fe08030   ubuntu    "bash"                   4 minutes ago    Exited (0) 3 minutes ago             adoring_borg
d83deaaf0863   ubuntu    "/bin/bash"              11 minutes ago   Exited (0) 7 minutes ago             dreamy_colden
sudipta@sudipta-web-pen-test:~$
sudipta@sudipta-web-pen-test:~$ docker logs eca9602f323d
/docker-entrypoint.sh: /docker-entrypoint.d/ is not empty, will attempt to perform configuration
/docker-entrypoint.sh: Looking for shell scripts in /docker-entrypoint.d/
/docker-entrypoint.sh: Launching /docker-entrypoint.d/10-listen-on-ipv6-by-default.sh
10-listen-on-ipv6-by-default.sh: info: Getting the checksum of /etc/nginx/conf.d/default.conf
10-listen-on-ipv6-by-default.sh: info: Enabled listen on IPv6 in /etc/nginx/conf.d/default.conf
/docker-entrypoint.sh: Sourcing /docker-entrypoint.d/15-local-resolvers.envsh
/docker-entrypoint.sh: Launching /docker-entrypoint.d/20-envsubst-on-templates.sh
/docker-entrypoint.sh: Launching /docker-entrypoint.d/30-tune-worker-processes.sh
/docker-entrypoint.sh: Configuration complete; ready for start up
2025/04/18 16:08:20 [notice] 1#1: using the "epoll" event method
2025/04/18 16:08:20 [notice] 1#1: nginx/1.27.5
2025/04/18 16:08:20 [notice] 1#1: built by gcc 12.2.0 (Debian 12.2.0-14)
2025/04/18 16:08:20 [notice] 1#1: OS: Linux 6.8.0-57-generic
2025/04/18 16:08:20 [notice] 1#1: getrlimit(RLIMIT_NOFILE): 1048576:1048576
2025/04/18 16:08:20 [notice] 1#1: start worker processes
2025/04/18 16:08:20 [notice] 1#1: start worker process 29
2025/04/18 16:08:20 [notice] 1#1: start worker process 30
2025/04/18 16:08:20 [notice] 1#1: start worker process 31
2025/04/18 16:08:20 [notice] 1#1: start worker process 32
sudipta@sudipta-web-pen-test:~$
```

Figure 5.4: viewing logs of a container

Naming Containers

By default, Docker assigns random names like `adoring_bhabha`. You can assign meaningful names

```
$ docker run -d --name mynginx nginx
```

Output:

```
sudipta@sudipta-web-pen-test:~$ docker run -d --name mynginx nginx
Unable to find image 'nginx:latest' locally
latest: Pulling from library/nginx
8a628cdd7ccc: Pull complete
b0c073cda91f: Pull complete
e6557c42ebea: Pull complete
ec74683520b9: Pull complete
6c95adab80c5: Pull complete
ad8a0171f43e: Pull complete
32ef64864ec3: Pull complete
Digest: sha256:5ed8fcc66f4ed123c1b2560ed708dc148755b6e4cbd8b943fab094f2c6bfa91e
Status: Downloaded newer image for nginx:latest
0a62f34b32bd176cc0454024a982256b212d8591d2015ffc1d26ed4a2ba6ad2c
sudipta@sudipta-web-pen-test:~$
sudipta@sudipta-web-pen-test:~$ docker ps -a
CONTAINER ID   IMAGE     COMMAND                  CREATED          STATUS          PORTS     NAMES
0a62f34b32bd   nginx     "/docker-entrypoint.…"   25 seconds ago   Up 24 seconds   80/tcp    mynginx
sudipta@sudipta-web-pen-test:~$
```

Figure 5.5: naming a container - mynginx

Now, you can refer to the container by name

```
$ docker stop mynginx
```

```
$ docker start mynginx
$ docker logs mynginx
```

Output:

```
sudipta@sudipta-web-pen-test:~$ docker ps -a
CONTAINER ID   IMAGE     COMMAND                  CREATED              STATUS              PORTS     NAMES
0a62f34b32bd   nginx     "/docker-entrypoint.…"   About a minute ago   Up About a minute   80/tcp    mynginx
sudipta@sudipta-web-pen-test:~$
sudipta@sudipta-web-pen-test:~$ docker stop mynginx
mynginx
sudipta@sudipta-web-pen-test:~$
sudipta@sudipta-web-pen-test:~$ docker ps -a
CONTAINER ID   IMAGE     COMMAND                  CREATED              STATUS                     PORTS     NAMES
0a62f34b32bd   nginx     "/docker-entrypoint.…"   About a minute ago   Exited (0) 3 seconds ago             mynginx
sudipta@sudipta-web-pen-test:~$
sudipta@sudipta-web-pen-test:~$
sudipta@sudipta-web-pen-test:~$
```

```
sudipta@sudipta-web-pen-test:~$ docker ps -a
CONTAINER ID   IMAGE     COMMAND                  CREATED         STATUS                      PORTS     NAMES
0a62f34b32bd   nginx     "/docker-entrypoint.…"   2 minutes ago   Exited (0) 51 seconds ago             mynginx
sudipta@sudipta-web-pen-test:~$
sudipta@sudipta-web-pen-test:~$ docker start mynginx
mynginx
sudipta@sudipta-web-pen-test:~$
sudipta@sudipta-web-pen-test:~$ docker ps -a
CONTAINER ID   IMAGE     COMMAND                  CREATED         STATUS         PORTS     NAMES
0a62f34b32bd   nginx     "/docker-entrypoint.…"   2 minutes ago   Up 2 seconds   80/tcp    mynginx
sudipta@sudipta-web-pen-test:~$
```

```
sudipta@sudipta-web-pen-test:~$ docker ps -a
CONTAINER ID   IMAGE     COMMAND                  CREATED         STATUS          PORTS     NAMES
0a62f34b32bd   nginx     "/docker-entrypoint.…"   3 minutes ago   Up 56 seconds   80/tcp    mynginx
sudipta@sudipta-web-pen-test:~$
sudipta@sudipta-web-pen-test:~$ docker logs mynginx
/docker-entrypoint.sh: /docker-entrypoint.d/ is not empty, will attempt to perform configuration
/docker-entrypoint.sh: Looking for shell scripts in /docker-entrypoint.d/
/docker-entrypoint.sh: Launching /docker-entrypoint.d/10-listen-on-ipv6-by-default.sh
10-listen-on-ipv6-by-default.sh: info: Getting the checksum of /etc/nginx/conf.d/default.conf
10-listen-on-ipv6-by-default.sh: info: Enabled listen on IPv6 in /etc/nginx/conf.d/default.conf
/docker-entrypoint.sh: Sourcing /docker-entrypoint.d/15-local-resolvers.envsh
/docker-entrypoint.sh: Launching /docker-entrypoint.d/20-envsubst-on-templates.sh
/docker-entrypoint.sh: Launching /docker-entrypoint.d/30-tune-worker-processes.sh
/docker-entrypoint.sh: Configuration complete; ready for start up
2025/04/18 16:19:49 [notice] 1#1: using the "epoll" event method
2025/04/18 16:19:49 [notice] 1#1: nginx/1.27.5
2025/04/18 16:19:49 [notice] 1#1: built by gcc 12.2.0 (Debian 12.2.0-14)
2025/04/18 16:19:49 [notice] 1#1: OS: Linux 6.8.0-57-generic
2025/04/18 16:19:49 [notice] 1#1: getrlimit(RLIMIT_NOFILE): 1048576:1048576
2025/04/18 16:19:49 [notice] 1#1: start worker processes
2025/04/18 16:19:49 [notice] 1#1: start worker process 29
2025/04/18 16:19:49 [notice] 1#1: start worker process 30
2025/04/18 16:19:49 [notice] 1#1: start worker process 31
2025/04/18 16:19:49 [notice] 1#1: start worker process 32
2025/04/18 16:21:28 [notice] 1#1: signal 3 (SIGQUIT) received, shutting down
2025/04/18 16:21:28 [notice] 29#29: gracefully shutting down
2025/04/18 16:21:28 [notice] 29#29: exiting
2025/04/18 16:21:28 [notice] 29#29: exit
```

Figure 5.6: start, stop, view logs of container, by container name – mynginx

Container Lifecycle Management

Create Container (without running it)

```
$ docker create ubuntu
```

Output:

```
sudipta@sudipta-web-pen-test:~$ docker ps -a
CONTAINER ID   IMAGE     COMMAND   CREATED   STATUS    PORTS     NAMES
sudipta@sudipta-web-pen-test:~$ docker create ubuntu
Unable to find image 'ubuntu:latest' locally
latest: Pulling from library/ubuntu
2726e237d1a3: Pull complete
Digest: sha256:1e622c5f073b4f6bfad6632f2616c7f59ef256e96fe78bf6a595d1dc4376ac02
Status: Downloaded newer image for ubuntu:latest
b62a07a23a520e3da487f054a5a2d20f7e04c5b4cd40259c125bee334571c7ae
sudipta@sudipta-web-pen-test:~$
sudipta@sudipta-web-pen-test:~$ docker ps -a
CONTAINER ID   IMAGE     COMMAND       CREATED          STATUS    PORTS     NAMES
b62a07a23a52   ubuntu    "/bin/bash"   19 seconds ago   Created             recursing_clarke
sudipta@sudipta-web-pen-test:~$
```

Figure 5.7: Create container without running it

Start Container

```
$ docker start <container_id>
```

Stop Container

```
$ docker stop <container_id>
```

Restart Container

```
$ docker restart <container_id>
```

Remove Container

```
$ docker rm <container_id>
```

List Containers

```
$ docker ps            # Running only
$ docker ps -a         # All containers
```

Executing Commands Inside a Running Container

Let's run NGINX in the background

```
$ docker run -d --name web nginx
```

Now, let's open a shell inside it

```
$ docker exec -it web /bin/bash
```

Inside the container, you can run

```
$ ls /usr/share/nginx/html
```

Exit

```
$ exit
```

Copying Files To/From a Container

Copy a file from your host into a container

```
$ docker cp index.html web:/usr/share/nginx/html/index.html
```

Copy a file from a container to your host

```
$ docker cp web:/etc/nginx/nginx.conf ./nginx.conf
```

Environment Variables

Pass environment variables into a container using **-e**:

```
$ docker run -e "APP_MODE=production" ubuntu env
```

This is useful for configuring apps dynamically without changing the image.

Exposing and Mapping Ports

Containers can expose internal ports, but you must **map them to host ports** for access

```
$ docker run -d -p 8080:80 nginx
```

- 8080: Host port (what your browser connects to)
- 80: Container port (used by Nginx)

Now, open `http://localhost:8080` to see the default Nginx page.

Output:

Figure 5.8: Access nginx web server from browser

Inspecting Containers

To view detailed container info

```
$ docker inspect nginx
```

This returns JSON output containing:

- IP addresses
- Mounts
- Configurations
- Networks
- Command and entrypoint

You can extract specific info

```
$ docker inspect -f '{{.NetworkSettings.IPAddress}}' nginx
```

Output:

```
sudipta@sudipta-web-pen-test:~$ docker ps -a
CONTAINER ID   IMAGE     COMMAND                  CREATED         STATUS         PORTS                                   NAMES
9d269aee0b68   nginx     "/docker-entrypoint.…"   9 minutes ago   Up 9 minutes   0.0.0.0:8080->80/tcp, [::]:8080->80/tcp   nginx
sudipta@sudipta-web-pen-test:~$
sudipta@sudipta-web-pen-test:~$
sudipta@sudipta-web-pen-test:~$ docker inspect -f '{{.NetworkSettings.IPAddress}}' nginx
172.17.0.2
sudipta@sudipta-web-pen-test:~$
```

Figure 5.9: Filtering by IP Address from docker inspect

Networking Between Containers

Let's run two containers on the same custom bridge network so they can communicate.

Step 1: Create a network

```
$ docker network create mynet
```

Step 2: Run containers on the same network

```
$ docker run -d --name web1 --network mynet nginx
$ docker run -it --rm --network mynet busybox
```

Inside busybox

```
$ ping web1
```

Output:

```
/ # ping web1
PING web1 (172.18.0.2): 56 data bytes
64 bytes from 172.18.0.2: seq=0 ttl=64 time=2.439 ms
64 bytes from 172.18.0.2: seq=1 ttl=64 time=0.095 ms
64 bytes from 172.18.0.2: seq=2 ttl=64 time=0.122 ms
64 bytes from 172.18.0.2: seq=3 ttl=64 time=0.085 ms
64 bytes from 172.18.0.2: seq=4 ttl=64 time=0.129 ms
64 bytes from 172.18.0.2: seq=5 ttl=64 time=0.141 ms
^C
--- web1 ping statistics ---
6 packets transmitted, 6 packets received, 0% packet loss
round-trip min/avg/max = 0.085/0.501/2.439 ms
/ # █
```

Figure 5.10: Ping response from web1

This confirms that both containers are connected.

Monitoring Container Performance

View CPU and memory usage

```
$ docker stats
```

Output:

```
CONTAINER ID   NAME   CPU %   MEM USAGE / LIMIT     MEM %   NET I/O        BLOCK I/O     PIDS
5e2e148950a8   web1   0.00%   4.477MiB / 3.824GiB   0.11%   8.9kB / 798B   0B / 20.5kB   5
```

Figure 5.11: Container status

View container logs

```
$ docker logs mynginx
```

Tail logs in real-time

```
$ docker logs -f mynginx
```

Tips for Managing Containers

☑ Use meaningful container names for better maintainability.

Clean up unused containers

```
$ docker container prune
```

Output:

```
sudipta@sudipta-web-pen-test:~$ docker container prune
WARNING! This will remove all stopped containers.
Are you sure you want to continue? [y/N]
```

Figure 5.12: Pruning container

Press "y" to continue

Automatically remove containers on exit

```
$ docker run --rm ubuntu echo "Temporary container"
```

Set restart policies

```
$ docker run --restart always nginx
```

Hands-On Lab: PHP + Apache

Let's deploy a simple PHP application using Docker.

Difficulty Level : Basic

Step 1: Create Files

🗎 `phpapp/index.php`

```
<?php echo "Hello from PHP on Docker!"; ?>
```

🗎 Dockerfile

```
FROM php:8.2-apache
COPY . /var/www/html/
EXPOSE 80
```

Step 2: Build and Run

```
$ docker build -t phpapp .
$ docker run -d -p 8081:80 phpapp
```

Step 3: Test

Visit `http://localhost:8081` → you'll see the PHP output.

Output:

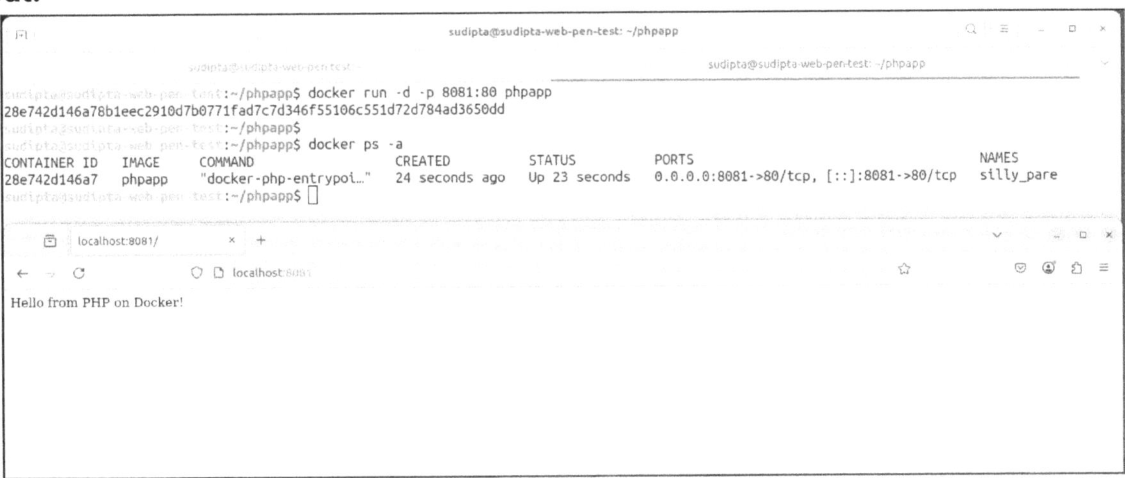

Figure 5.13: Accessing app from browser

Optional Extension: Try scaling the PHP app by running multiple containers and exposing them on different ports (e.g., 8082, 8083). This simulates running multiple service instances — a fundamental step toward container orchestration and load balancing.

Summary

In this chapter, you learned how to:

- Run containers in interactive and detached mode
- Name, start, stop, and remove containers
- Use `exec` to run commands inside containers
- Copy files between host and container
- Use environment variables and expose ports

- Monitor container health and performance
- Build a complete PHP+Apache app in Docker

Key Takeaways

In this chapter, you mastered running Docker containers in interactive and detached modes, managing container lifecycles, monitoring performance, networking multiple containers, and deploying real-world applications – building strong foundational skills for production container management.

Knowledge Check

1. **What does the `docker run` command do?**
   A) Starts Docker Engine
   B) Pulls an image and starts a container
   C) Installs Docker
   D) Builds Docker images
2. **Which command starts a stopped container?**
   A) `docker init`
   B) `docker restart`
   C) `docker start`
   D) `docker create`
3. **How do you name a container when launching it?**
   A) `docker run --title mycontainer`
   B) `docker run --container-name mycontainer`
   C) `docker run --name mycontainer`
   D) `docker create --setname mycontainer`
4. **Which flag removes a container once it stops?**
   A) `–destroy`
   B) `--auto-remove`
   C) `–rm`
   D) `--exit`
5. **What does `docker ps -a` show?**
   A) Only running containers
   B) Only stopped containers
   C) All containers (running and stopped)
   D) Only system containers
6. **What command allows executing a command inside a running container?**
   A) `docker bash`
   B) `docker exec`
   C) `docker attach`
   D) `docker load`
7. **How do you stop a running container gracefully?**
   A) `docker kill`
   B) `docker stop`
   C) `docker pause`
   D) `docker delete`
8. **What happens when you run `docker container prune`?**
   A) Restarts containers

B) Shows logs
C) Removes all stopped containers
D) Deletes volumes

9. **What does `docker logs <container>` display?**
A) Docker CLI history
B) Container event stream
C) STDOUT and STDERR of the container
D) System logs

10. **How do you list all volumes on your system?**
A) `docker show volumes`
B) `docker volumes`
C) `docker volume ls`
D) `docker logs --volumes`

11. **What flags can be used with docker run?**
- [ ] `–rm`
- [ ] `–name`
- [ ] `-d`
- [ ] `--compose`

12. **Which of the following are valid container lifecycle commands?**
- [ ] `docker start`
- [ ] `docker stop`
- [ ] `docker restart`
- [ ] `docker repeat`

13. **Which of these helps debug a running container?**
- [ ] `docker logs`
- [ ] `docker exec`
- [ ] `docker top`
- [ ] `docker rename`

14. **Which commands remove a container permanently?**
- [ ] `docker rm`
- [ ] `docker container rm`
- [ ] `docker delete`
- [ ] `docker stop`

15. **What can you do with `docker attach`?**
- [ ] Reconnect to a container's STDOUT/STDERR
- [ ] View interactive processes
- [ ] Execute new commands

☐ Attach to a stopped container

Answers

Q#	Correct Answer	Explanation
1	B	`docker run` creates and starts a new container, pulling the image if not already available.
2	C	`docker start` restart a stopped container.
3	C	The `--name` flag is used to assign a custom container name.
4	C	`--rm` deletes the container after it stops.
5	C	`docker ps -a` shows all containers (running and exited).
6	B	`docker exec` allows executing commands in a running container.
7	B	`docker stop` uses SIGTERM to shut down gracefully.
8	C	`docker container prune` removes all stopped containers.
9	C	`docker logs` shows STDOUT and STDERR logs of the container.
10	C	`docker volume ls` lists all Docker-managed volumes.

Q11. What flags can be used with `docker run`?

- [✓] `--rm`
- [✓] `--name`
- [✓] `-d`
- [X] `--compose`

  Explanation: These are valid container options; `--compose` is not a valid run flag.

Q12. Which of the following are valid container lifecycle commands?

- [✓] `docker start`
- [✓] `docker stop`
- [✓] `docker restart`
- [X] `docker repeat`

  Explanation: `docker repeat` is not a real command.

Q13. Which of these helps debug a running container?

- [✓] `docker logs`
- [✓] `docker exec`
- [✓] `docker top`
- [X] `docker rename`

  Explanation: `logs, exec`, and `top` help inspect containers; rename does not.

Q14. Which commands remove a container permanently?

- [✓] `docker rm`
- [✓] `docker container rm`
- [X] `docker delete`
- [X] `docker stop`

  Explanation: `docker rm` variants remove containers; `stop` only halts them.

Q15. What can you do with docker attach?

- [✓] Reconnect to a container's STDOUT/STDERR
- [✓] View interactive processes
- [X] Execute new commands
- [X] Attach to a stopped container

  Explanation: `attach` connects you to the container's live output.

Chapter 6: Data Management in Docker — Volumes, Mounts, and Networks Made Simple

One of the key challenges in containerized applications is handling **persistent data** and **service communication**. Containers are ephemeral by nature — when they stop or are removed, everything inside them is lost unless stored externally. That's where **volumes** and **networks** come into play.

This chapter teaches you how to use volumes to persist application data and Docker networks to enable container-to-container communication — all through clear, practical examples.

Why Persistence Matters

When you stop and remove a container, all data written inside it (unless part of an external volume or mount) is **erased**.

Example:

```
$ docker run -it ubuntu
```

Inside the container

```
$ echo "Hello" > /data/hello.txt
$ exit
```

Now restart the container

```
$ docker ps -a
$ docker start -ai <container_id>
```

Check `/data` — your file is gone.

ⓘ **Note:** Because containers are ephemeral, external storage is critical for any stateful applications like databases, websites, and enterprise apps.

This is why we need **volumes** — a method to store persistent data outside of the container's writable layer.

Docker Volumes

Volumes are the preferred mechanism for persisting data in Docker. They are:

- Created and managed by Docker

- Stored in `/var/lib/docker/volumes/`
- Isolated from the host filesystem
- Used by multiple containers

Create and Use a Volume

```
$ docker volume create mydata
$ docker run -d --name datacontainer -v mydata:/data busybox sleep 3600
```

Now let's write something into it

```
$ docker exec -it datacontainer sh
$ echo "Volume working!" > /data/test.txt
$ exit
```

Stop and remove the container

```
$ docker rm -f datacontainer
```

Reattach the same volume in a new container

```
$ docker run -it -v mydata:/data busybox sh
$ cat /data/test.txt
```

Output:

```
Volume working!
```

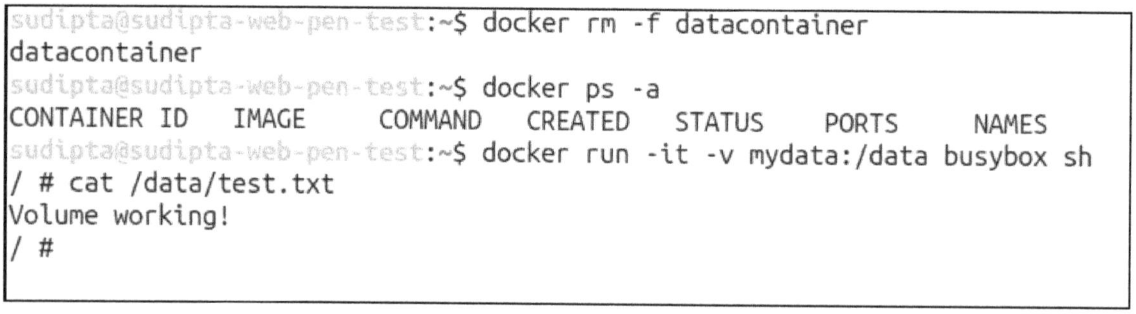

```
sudipta@sudipta-web-pen-test:~$ docker rm -f datacontainer
datacontainer
sudipta@sudipta-web-pen-test:~$ docker ps -a
CONTAINER ID   IMAGE     COMMAND   CREATED   STATUS    PORTS     NAMES
sudipta@sudipta-web-pen-test:~$ docker run -it -v mydata:/data busybox sh
/ # cat /data/test.txt
Volume working!
/ #
```

Figure 6.1: Create volume and file inside volume

Bind Mounts vs Named Volumes

Feature	Bind Mount	Named Volume
Host path	Specified manually	Managed by Docker
Portability	Less portable	Portable and Docker-native
Use cases	Dev environments	Databases, shared app data
Example path	`/home/user/app/data`	`/var/lib/docker/volumes/...`

Bind Mount Example

```
$ mkdir -p $PWD/data
$ echo "Dev Data" > $PWD/data/dev.txt

$ docker run -it -v $PWD/data:/app busybox sh
$ cat /app/dev.txt
```

Any changes made in `/app` will directly reflect in your local $PWD/data.

Explanation: Use bind mounts during development and named volumes in production.

Quick Comparison for `--mount` vs `-v`

Feature	`-v / --volume`	`--mount`
Syntax	Short, flexible	Verbose, clear
Readability	Harder in complex setups	Easier to read for complex configs
Features	Older, compatible with Compose v2	Full support for driver options, labels, and more
Best Use Case	Quick commands and dev work	Production setups, advanced features

Inspecting Volumes

List volumes

```
$ docker volume ls
```

Inspect a volume

```
$ docker volume inspect mydata
```

Output:

```
sudipta@sudipta-web-pen-test:~$ docker volume create mydata
mydata
sudipta@sudipta-web-pen-test:~$ docker volume ls
DRIVER    VOLUME NAME
local     mydata
sudipta@sudipta-web-pen-test:~$ docker volume inspect mydata
[
    {
        "CreatedAt": "2025-04-19T01:53:04+05:30",
        "Driver": "local",
        "Labels": null,
        "Mountpoint": "/var/lib/docker/volumes/mydata/_data",
        "Name": "mydata",
        "Options": null,
        "Scope": "local"
    }
]
sudipta@sudipta-web-pen-test:~$
```

Figure 6.2: Volume Inspect

Remove a volume

```
$ docker volume rm mydata
```

Output:

```
sudipta@sudipta-web-pen-test:~$ docker volume rm mydata
Error response from daemon: remove mydata: volume is in use - [4c1ebbf77e917cbde139de28d9ad65f928ed6849b7
7a0da68840ff786651760e, 414f203ea1b5bee8cad360c38a7b41b22e8e1718975a960eaa444391c5f382d7]
sudipta@sudipta-web-pen-test:~$
```

Figure 6.3: Error removing Volume

NOTE: *You can't remove a volume if it is in use, stop & remove the container then remove the volume*

Output:

```
sudipta@sudipta-web-pen-test:~$ docker volume ls
DRIVER    VOLUME NAME
local     mydata
sudipta@sudipta-web-pen-test:~$ docker ps -a
CONTAINER ID   IMAGE     COMMAND   CREATED          STATUS          PORTS     NAMES
23dbf148b988   busybox   "sh"      32 seconds ago   Up 32 seconds             funny_yonath
sudipta@sudipta-web-pen-test:~$ docker stop 23dbf148b988
23dbf148b988
sudipta@sudipta-web-pen-test:~$ docker volume rm mydata
Error response from daemon: remove mydata: volume is in use - [23dbf148b9881521e217531872f2041c6e6dd16513
0b33b805415c17a28c47e3]
sudipta@sudipta-web-pen-test:~$ docker rm 23dbf148b988
23dbf148b988
sudipta@sudipta-web-pen-test:~$ docker volume rm mydata
mydata
sudipta@sudipta-web-pen-test:~$ docker volume ls
DRIVER    VOLUME NAME
sudipta@sudipta-web-pen-test:~$
```

Figure 6.4: Volume remove successfully

Remove all unused volumes

```
$ docker volume prune
```

Output:

```
sudipta@sudipta-web-pen-test:~$ docker volume prune
WARNING! This will remove anonymous local volumes not used by at least one container.
Are you sure you want to continue? [y/N] y
Total reclaimed space: 0B
sudipta@sudipta-web-pen-test:~$
```

Figure 6.5: Remove all unused volumes

Real-World Example: PostgreSQL with Persistent Storage

```
$ docker volume create pgdata

$ docker run -d \
  --name mypostgres \
  -e POSTGRES_PASSWORD=mysecret \
  -v pgdata:/var/lib/postgresql/data \
  -p 5432:5432 \
  postgres:16
```

Output:

```
sudipta@sudipta-web-pen-test:~$ docker volume ls
DRIVER    VOLUME NAME
sudipta@sudipta-web-pen-test:~$
sudipta@sudipta-web-pen-test:~$ docker volume create pgdata
pgdata
sudipta@sudipta-web-pen-test:~$ docker volume ls
DRIVER    VOLUME NAME
local     pgdata
sudipta@sudipta-web-pen-test:~$
sudipta@sudipta-web-pen-test:~$ docker run -d \
  --name mypostgres \
  -e POSTGRES_PASSWORD=mysecret \
  -v pgdata:/var/lib/postgresql/data \
  -p 5432:5432 \
  postgres:16
Unable to find image 'postgres:16' locally
16: Pulling from library/postgres
8a628cdd7ccc: Pull complete
061d38a4b4b6: Pull complete
0ee947678059: Pull complete
b83b3351f389: Pull complete
77835859ece0: Pull complete
002bfa82406b: Pull complete
632d3e125710: Pull complete
35942c92517e: Pull complete
e5baf548ac99: Pull complete
f486b50b9884: Pull complete
62963168ef8d: Pull complete
2139f5af38ec: Pull complete
acee9f076f01: Pull complete
915ee56c56b2: Pull complete
Digest: sha256:cef2d22004db69e3d601442ca4cac142adda0987ad7ca4f28c4e998bef690951
Status: Downloaded newer image for postgres:16
437c170d1f69dc748966ae211c2da0c2f3e7ce80ffa3244e926bc4a4881faed6
sudipta@sudipta-web-pen-test:~$
```

Figure 6.6: Creating persistent storage volume for PostgreSQL

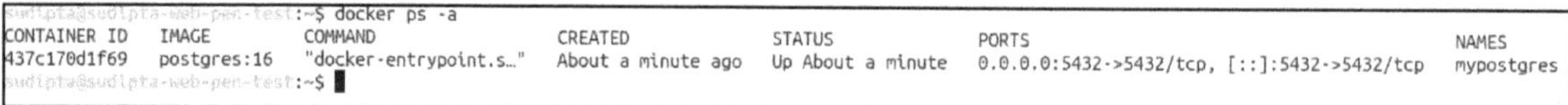

Figure 6.7: Checking newly create PostgreSQL

This ensures your PostgreSQL database persisted even if the container is deleted.

Docker Networks

Docker uses networks to allow containers to talk to each other and to external services. By default, Docker creates

Network Name	Type	Description
`bridge`	Bridge	Default for standalone containers
`host`	Host	Uses host's network stack (Linux only)
`none`	None	No network access

Creating a Custom Bridge Network

```
$ docker network create mynet
```

Output:

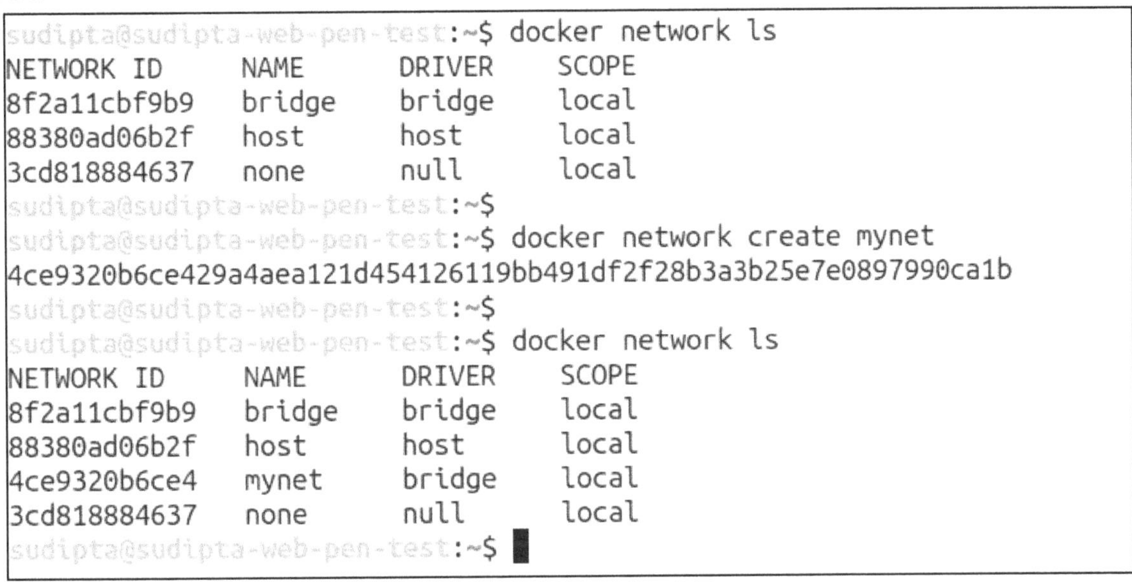

Figure 6.8: Creates custom bridge network

ⓘ **Tip:** Custom bridge networks provide automatic DNS-based container discovery and better isolation compared to the default bridge network.

Run Containers on Same Network

```
$ docker run -d --name redis --network mynet redis
$ docker run -it --network mynet busybox
```

Output:

```
sudipta@sudipta-web-pen-test:~$ docker run -d --name redis --network mynet redis
Unable to find image 'redis:latest' locally
latest: Pulling from library/redis
8a628cdd7ccc: Pull complete
3ff860482ac5: Pull complete
811af041d785: Pull complete
a7e27cf18de4: Pull complete
8ae1ad8ce35e: Pull complete
759939a29cb5: Pull complete
4f4fb700ef54: Pull complete
cbb99c664e48: Pull complete
Digest: sha256:fbdbaea47b9ae4ecc2082ecdb4e1cea81e32176ffb1dcf643d422ad07427e5d9
Status: Downloaded newer image for redis:latest
715ff729b9b942cd44d23c8ff303b104a99f32a65be28fbe3f0ff09ca10bddd6
sudipta@sudipta-web-pen-test:~$ docker ps -a
CONTAINER ID   IMAGE     COMMAND                  CREATED         STATUS         PORTS      NAMES
715ff729b9b9   redis     "docker-entrypoint.s…"   9 seconds ago   Up 8 seconds   6379/tcp   redis
sudipta@sudipta-web-pen-test:~$
```

Figure 6.9: Running container with custom bridge network - mynet

```
sudipta@sudipta-web-pen-test:~$ docker run -it --network mynet busybox
Unable to find image 'busybox:latest' locally
latest: Pulling from library/busybox
97e70d161e81: Pull complete
Digest: sha256:37f7b378a29ceb4c551b1b5582e27747b855bbfaa73fa11914fe0df028dc581f
Status: Downloaded newer image for busybox:latest
/ #
```

Figure 6.10: Running container with custom bridge network - mynet

Inside busybox

```
$ ping redis
```

Output:

```
/ # ping redis
PING redis (172.18.0.2): 56 data bytes
64 bytes from 172.18.0.2: seq=0 ttl=64 time=2.497 ms
64 bytes from 172.18.0.2: seq=1 ttl=64 time=0.072 ms
64 bytes from 172.18.0.2: seq=2 ttl=64 time=0.085 ms
64 bytes from 172.18.0.2: seq=3 ttl=64 time=0.074 ms
^C
--- redis ping statistics ---
4 packets transmitted, 4 packets received, 0% packet loss
round-trip min/avg/max = 0.072/0.682/2.497 ms
/ #
```

Figure 6.11: Pinging inside from container by name

This shows container-to-container DNS works out of the box.

Lab: Docker Compose + Volumes + Networks (All-in-One)

Difficulty Level: Basic

Let's build a web + DB app with Docker Compose and volumes.

🗁 Folder Structure:

```
docker-demo/
├── docker-compose.yml
├── web/
│   └── index.html
```

🗎 index.html ($ nano web/index.html)

```
<!-- docker-demo/web/index.html -->
<!DOCTYPE html>
<html>
<head>
  <title>Welcome to Docker Demo</title>
</head>
<body>
  <h1>Hello from Nginx + Docker!</h1>
  <p>This is served from the local /web/index.html</p>
</body>
</html>
```

🗎 docker-compose.yml ($ nano docker-compose.yml)

```
services:
  web:
    image: nginx:alpine
    ports:
      - "8080:80"
    volumes:
      - ./web:/usr/share/nginx/html
    networks:
      - appnet

  redis:
    image: redis
    networks:
```

```
      - appnet

networks:
  appnet:
```

Run:

```
$ docker compose up -d
```

Output:

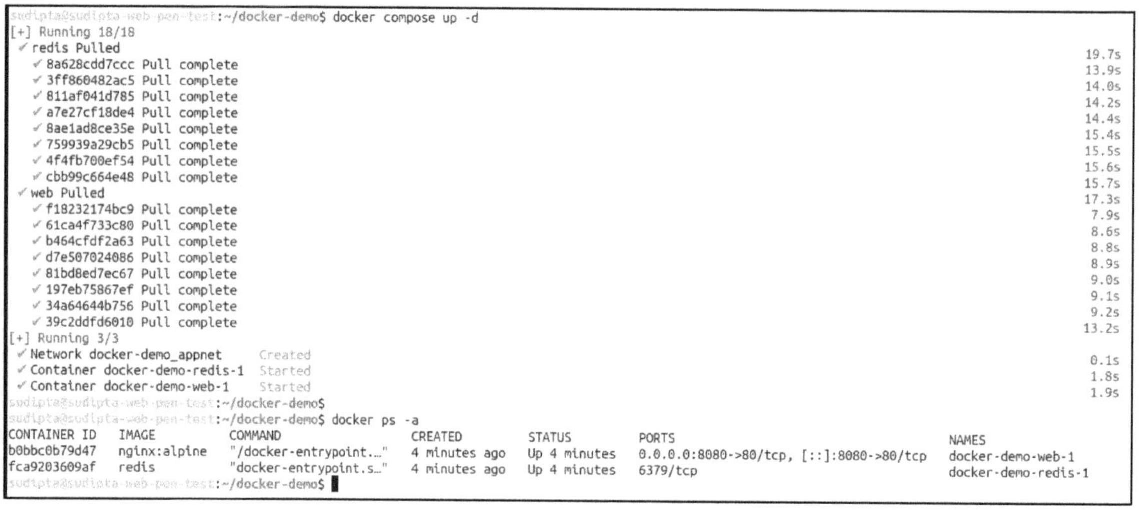

```
sudipta@sudipta-web-pen-test:~/docker-demo$ docker compose up -d
[+] Running 18/18
 ✓ redis Pulled                                                        19.7s
   ✓ 8a628cdd7ccc Pull complete                                        13.9s
   ✓ 3ff860482ac5 Pull complete                                        14.0s
   ✓ 811af041d785 Pull complete                                        14.2s
   ✓ a7e27cf18de4 Pull complete                                        14.4s
   ✓ 8ae1ad8ce35e Pull complete                                        15.4s
   ✓ 759939a29cb5 Pull complete                                        15.5s
   ✓ 4f4fb700ef54 Pull complete                                        15.6s
   ✓ cbb99c664e48 Pull complete                                        15.7s
 ✓ web Pulled                                                          17.3s
   ✓ f18232174bc9 Pull complete                                         7.9s
   ✓ 61ca4f733c80 Pull complete                                         8.6s
   ✓ b464cfdf2a63 Pull complete                                         8.8s
   ✓ d7e507024086 Pull complete                                         8.9s
   ✓ 81bd8ed7ec67 Pull complete                                         9.0s
   ✓ 197eb75867ef Pull complete                                         9.1s
   ✓ 34a64644b756 Pull complete                                         9.2s
   ✓ 39c2ddfd6010 Pull complete                                        13.2s
[+] Running 3/3
 ✓ Network docker-demo_appnet       Created                             0.1s
 ✓ Container docker-demo-redis-1    Started                             1.8s
 ✓ Container docker-demo-web-1      Started                             1.9s
sudipta@sudipta-web-pen-test:~/docker-demo$
sudipta@sudipta-web-pen-test:~/docker-demo$ docker ps -a
CONTAINER ID   IMAGE          COMMAND                  CREATED         STATUS         PORTS                                   NAMES
b0bbc0b79d47   nginx:alpine   "/docker-entrypoint.…"   4 minutes ago   Up 4 minutes   0.0.0.0:8080->80/tcp, [::]:8080->80/tcp   docker-demo-web-1
fca9203609af   redis          "docker-entrypoint.s…"   4 minutes ago   Up 4 minutes   6379/tcp                                docker-demo-redis-1
sudipta@sudipta-web-pen-test:~/docker-demo$
```

Figure 6.11: Running container with docker compose

- Visit: `http://localhost:8080`
- Redis is running and accessible to other services on the `appnet` network

Output:

Figure 6.12: Access the app from web browser

Inspecting Docker Networks

List networks

```
$ docker network ls
```

Output:

Figure 6.13: Listing docker network

Inspect network:

```
$ docker network inspect appnet
```

Output:

```
sudipta@sudipta-web-pen-test:~/docker-demo$
sudipta@sudipta-web-pen-test:~/docker-demo$ docker network inspect docker-demo_appnet
[
    {
        "Name": "docker-demo_appnet",
        "Id": "901266f6a81183e61f461fddf9e10e22a503bbda43813435271e81c5b17525bc",
        "Created": "2025-04-19T03:12:20.151474174+05:30",
        "Scope": "local",
        "Driver": "bridge",
        "EnableIPv4": true,
        "EnableIPv6": false,
        "IPAM": {
            "Driver": "default",
            "Options": null,
            "Config": [
                {
                    "Subnet": "172.18.0.0/16",
                    "Gateway": "172.18.0.1"
                }
            ]
```

Figure 6.14: inspect docker network configuration

You'll see connected containers and their internal IP addresses.

Tips for Volumes and Networks

- **Never store secrets** in bind mounts or inside images
- Use **named volumes** for databases
- Use **custom networks** to isolate microservices
- Clean up unused volumes and networks regularly
- Avoid using host mode unless absolutely necessary (security risk)

Lab: MySQL + Adminer with Persistent Storage

Difficulty Level: Intermediate

🗎 docker-compose.yml ($ nano docker-compose.yml)

```
services:
  mysql:
    image: mysql:8.0
    environment:
      MYSQL_ROOT_PASSWORD: root
    volumes:
      - db_data:/var/lib/mysql
```

```
    networks:
      - backend

  adminer:
    image: adminer
    ports:
      - 8080:8080
    networks:
      - backend

volumes:
  db_data:

networks:
  backend:
```

Run:

```
$ docker compose up -d
```

Visit: `http://localhost:8080`

Use:

- Server: `mysql`
- User: `root`
- Password: `root`

Output:

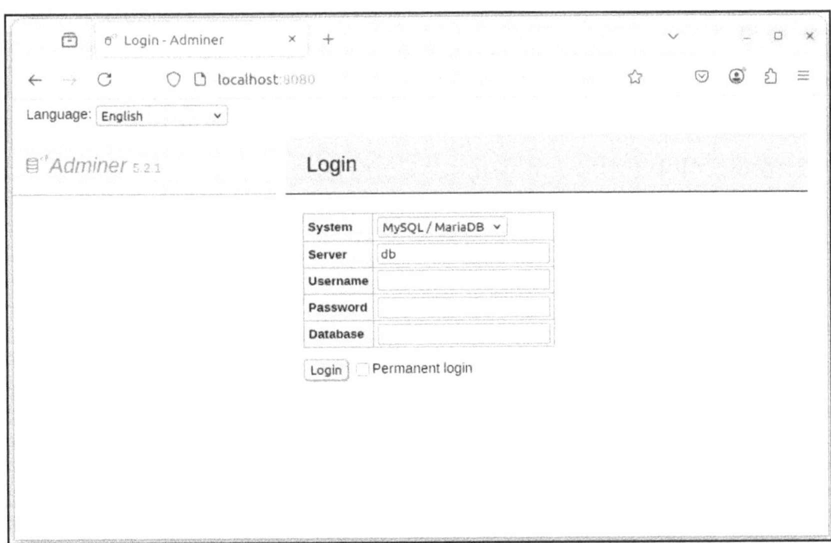

Figure 6.15: Adminer Login Page

Post Login

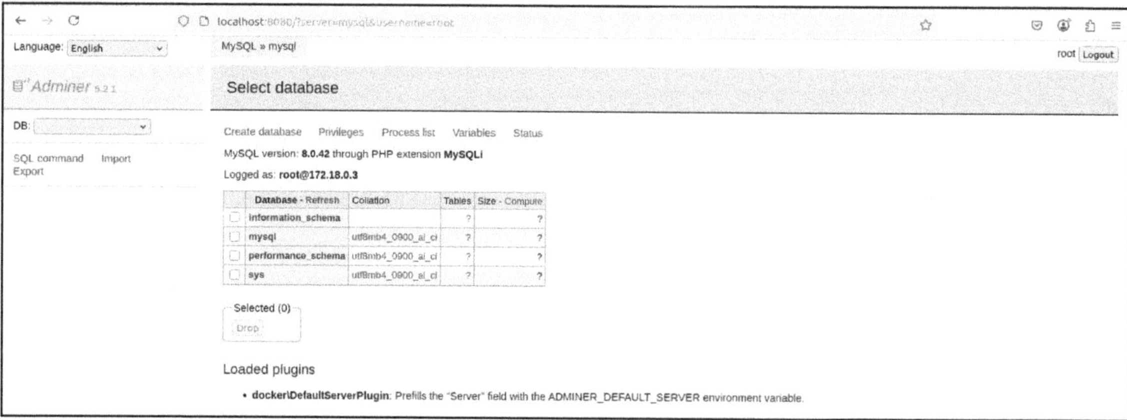

Figure 6.15: Adminer successful Login

Summary

In this chapter, you learned:

- The difference between bind mounts and Docker volumes
- How to persist data across container restarts
- How to manage and inspect volumes
- How to create and use custom Docker networks
- How services communicate internally via Docker DNS
- Real-world labs using PostgreSQL, MySQL, Redis, and Nginx

Key Takeaways

In this chapter, you learned how to manage persistent data with Docker volumes and bind mounts, network containers using custom bridge networks, and integrate both data and networking in real-world multi-service applications through Docker Compose.

Knowledge Check

1. **Which command creates a named volume in Docker?**
   A) `docker create volume myvol`
   B) `docker volume create myvol`
   C) `docker volume --new myvol`
   D) `docker new volume myvol`
2. **What is the default mount path for Docker volumes inside** containers?
   A) `/docker`
   B) `/mnt`
   C) `/var/lib/docker/volumes`
   D) `/data`
3. **Which of the following are types of Docker volumes?**
   A) Bind Mounts, Named Volumes, tmpfs
   B) USB Mounts, Logs, RAMFS
   C) S3 Buckets, Git Mounts, Swap
   D) Hard Links, Symlinks, ISO
4. **Which flag is used to mount a volume when running a container?**
   A) `–bind`
   B) `–mount`
   C) `--volume` or `-v`
   D) Both B and C
5. **How would you inspect a volume named `mydata`?**
   A) `docker volume ls mydata`
   B) `docker inspect volume mydata`
   C) `docker volume inspect mydata`
   D) `docker info volume mydata`
6. **What happens when you delete a volume in use by a container?**
   A) The container crashes
   B) The volume is marked deleted but not removed
   C) Docker throws an error
   D) The container deletes itself
7. **Which of these is a use case for bind mounts?**
   A) Sharing configuration files from the host
   B) Logging metrics into Elasticsearch
   C) Isolating container memory
   D) Running GPU workloads
8. **Which command lists all Docker networks?**
   A) `docker networks`

B) `docker net show`
C) `docker network ls`
D) `docker list networks`

9. **Which network driver is used by default in Docker?**
A) `overlay`
B) `host`
C) `bridge`
D) `none`

10. **What does docker** `network inspect <network>` **show?**
A) Only running containers
B) Low-level details like connected containers and configs
C) Docker registry logs
D) Kubernetes node list

11. **What are valid volume types in Docker?**
- ☐ Named Volumes
- ☐ Bind Mounts
- ☐ tmpfs
- ☐ Cloud Block Volumes

12. **What can you do with docker volume subcommands?**
- ☐ Create a volume
- ☐ Inspect a volume
- ☐ Remove a volume
- ☐ List container ports

13. **Which actions will not persist data after container restart?**
- ☐ Use bind mount
- ☐ Use named volume
- ☐ Use anonymous volume without reference
- ☐ Store data inside container FS

14. **Which of the following are valid `--mount` usage keys?**
- ☐ `type=`
- ☐ `source=`
- ☐ `target=`
- ☐ `input=`

15. **Which drivers support multi-host networking (Swarm)?**
- ☐ overlay
- ☐ bridge
- ☐ host

- ▢ macvlan

16. **What are effects of `--network=host`?**
    - ▢ Bypasses container NAT
    - ▢ Shares host's network stack
    - ▢ Isolates all ports
    - ▢ Used in performance-sensitive setups
17. **Docker volumes are useful for:**
    - ▢ Persisting databases
    - ▢ Sharing files between containers
    - ▢ Setting CPU limits
    - ▢ Backing up data
18. **What can be defined in a custom Docker network?**
    - ▢ Subnet and IP range
    - ▢ Network driver
    - ▢ Gateway address
    - ▢ Container filesystem layout
19. **What happens when you remove a network in use?**
    - ▢ Docker throws an error
    - ▢ It removes the network silently
    - ▢ It stops all containers
    - ▢ It switches to bridge network
20. **Which of the following will you typically find in a docker-compose.yml volume config?**
    - ▢ volumes: section
    - ▢ External volume flag
    - ▢ Named volume references
    - ▢ IP address bindings

Answers

Q#	Correct Answer	Explanation
1	B	`docker volume create myvol` is the correct syntax.
2	C	Docker stores persistent volumes in `/var/lib/docker/volumes`.
3	A	The three supported volume types are: bind mounts, named volumes, tmpfs.
4	D	Both `--mount` and `-v` can mount volumes into containers.
5	C	`docker volume inspect <name>` provides detailed volume info.
6	C	Docker throws an error if the volume is in use.
7	A	Bind mounts is used for sharing host paths like configs/logs.
8	C	`docker network ls` lists available Docker networks.
9	C	Docker uses `bridge` driver by default.
10	B	`docker network inspect` gives JSON output including connected containers.

Q11: What are valid volume types in Docker?

- **[√]** Named Volumes
- **[√]** Bind Mounts
- **[√]** tmpfs
- **[X]** Cloud Block Volumes

  Explanation: are the native supported volume types in Docker.

Q12: What can you do with docker volume subcommands?

- **[√]** Create a volume
- **[√]** Inspect a volume
- **[√]** Remove a volume
- **[X]** List container ports

  Explanation: `docker volume` is unrelated to networking or port management.

Q13: Which actions will not persist data after container restart?

- **[X]** Use bind mount
- **[X]** Use named volume
- **[√]** Use anonymous volume without reference
- **[√]** Store data inside container FS

  Explanation: Anonymous volumes and in-container files are ephemeral.

Q14: Which of the following are valid --mount usage keys?

- [✓] type=
- [✓] source=
- [✓] target=
- [X] input=
  Explanation: The `--mount` flag uses keys like type, source, and target.

Q15: Which drivers support multi-host networking (Swarm)?

- [✓] `overlay`
- [X] `bridge`
- [X] `host`
- [✓] `macvlan`
  Explanation: overlay enables cross-host networking in Swarm.

Q16: What are effects of `--network=host`?

- [✓] Bypasses container NAT
- [✓] Shares host's network stack
- [X] Isolates all ports
- [✓] Used in performance-sensitive setups
  Explanation: `--network=host` removes container-level NAT overhead.

Q17: Docker volumes are useful for:

- [✓] Persisting databases
- [✓] Sharing files between containers
- [X] Setting CPU limits
- [✓] Backing up data
  Explanation: Volumes persist and enable backup/restore across restarts.

Q18: What can be defined in a custom Docker network?

- [✓] Subnet and IP range
- [✓] Network driver
- [✓] Gateway address
- [X] Container filesystem layout
  Explanation: Network configuration includes these optional flags.

Q19: What happens when you remove a network in use?

- [✓] Docker throws an error
- [X] It removes the network silently
- [X] It stops all containers

- **[X]** It switches to bridge network
  Explanation: Docker blocks deletion of in-use networks.

Q20: Which of the following will you typically find in a docker-compose.yml volume config?

- **[√]** volumes: section
- **[√]** External volume flag
- **[√]** Named volume references
- **[X]** IP address bindings
  Explanation: Compose manages volume mappings, not IP configs.

Chapter 7: Docker Compose Essentials — Define, Run, and Scale Multi-Container Apps

Docker Compose is a tool that simplifies running multi-container Docker applications. Instead of manually running multiple `docker run` commands and linking containers together, you define everything in a single `docker-compose.yml` file and launch your stack with a single command.

What Does Docker Compose?

Docker Compose lets you:

- Define multiple containers (services) in a YAML file
- Set up volumes, networks, and environment variables
- Build images from Dockerfiles
- Scale services
- Manage everything with a single command

Why Use Compose?

Without Compose:

```
$ docker run -d --name db -e MYSQL_ROOT_PASSWORD=123 mysql:8
$ docker run -d --name web -p 80:80 --link db nginx
```

With Compose

```
$ docker compose up -d
```

All services, networks, and volumes are declared in one YAML file. That's **Infrastructure as Code (IaC)** made simple.

Basic Structure of `docker-compose.yml`

Here's a minimal example:

```
services:
  web:
    image: nginx
    ports:
      - "8080:80"
```

```
  redis:
    image: redis
```

Breakdown:

- `version:` The Compose file version (3.9 is commonly used)
- `services:` List of containers you want to run
- `web, redis:` The names of individual containers (services)

Real-World Example: Flask + Redis

Let's create a Flask web app that uses Redis for counting page visits.

🗁 `Folder Structure:`

```
flask-redis-app/
├── app.py
├── requirements.txt
├── Dockerfile
└── docker-compose.yml
```

🗎 `app.py ($ nano app.py)`

```
from flask import Flask
import redis

app = Flask(__name__)
r = redis.Redis(host='redis', port=6379)

@app.route('/')
def index():
    count = r.incr('hits')
    return f'Page viewed {count} times.'

if __name__ == "__main__":
    app.run(host='0.0.0.0', port=5000)
```

🗎 `requirements.txt ($ nano requirements.txt)`

```
flask
Redis
```

🗎 `Dockerfile ($ nano Dockerfile)`

```
FROM python:3.11-slim
WORKDIR /app
```

```
COPY requirements.txt .
RUN pip install -r requirements.txt
COPY . .
EXPOSE 5000
CMD ["python", "app.py"]
```

🖹 docker-compose.yml ($ nano docker-compose.yml)

```
services:
  web:
    build: .
    ports:
      - "5000:5000"
    depends_on:
      - redis

  redis:
    image: redis:alpine
```

Run the Stack

```
$ docker compose up -build
```

Visit `http://localhost:5000` and refresh to see the counter increase.

Output:

Refresh the page and count will be shown (for my case I have refreshed it 4 times)

Figure 7.1: Browse the website and page refresh count

Common Compose Options

Key	Description
`Build`	Build from Dockerfile instead of pulling an image
`Image`	Specify an image to use

Key	Description
`Ports`	Map container port to host
`Volumes`	Mount host or named volumes
`depends_on`	Start order dependency
`environment`	Set environment variables
`Networks`	Define network isolation

Adding Volumes and Networks

Let's persist Redis data using a volume.

Update `docker-compose.yml`:

```
services:
  web:
    build: .
    ports:
      - "5000:5000"
    depends_on:
      - redis
    networks:
      - appnet

  redis:
    image: redis:alpine
    volumes:
      - redisdata:/data
    networks:
      - appnet

volumes:
  redisdata:

networks:
  appnet:
```

Redis data now persists across container restarts.

Environment Variables in Compose

You can pass environment variables directly:

```
services:
  db:
    image: mysql:8
    environment:
      - MYSQL_ROOT_PASSWORD=secret
```

Or load them from a `.env` file:

`.env`

```
MYSQL_ROOT_PASSWORD=topsecret
```

Then reference it:

```
environment:
  - MYSQL_ROOT_PASSWORD=${MYSQL_ROOT_PASSWORD}
```

Viewing and Managing Compose Services

Command	Description
`docker compose up`	Start all services
`docker compose up -d`	Start in detached mode
`docker compose down`	Stop and remove all services
`docker compose logs`	View logs
`docker compose ps`	View running services
`docker compose exec web bash`	Open shell in web container
`docker compose build`	Rebuild services
`docker compose restart`	Restart services

Hands-On Lab: Static HTML Site with Nginx

Difficulty Level: Basic

🗁 `Folder Structure:`

```
nginx-site/
├── docker-compose.yml
└── site/
```

```
    └── index.html
```

🗎 site/index.html

```
<h1>Hello from Compose-powered Nginx!</h1>
```

🗎 docker-compose.yml

```
services:
  nginx:
    image: nginx:alpine
    ports:
      - "8080:80"
    volumes:
      - ./site:/usr/share/nginx/html
```

Run:

```
$ docker compose up -d
```

Visit: `http://localhost:8080`

Output:

Figure 7.2: Browse Static HTML Site with Nginx

Scaling with Compose

Use the `--scale` flag to horizontally scale a service.

```
$ docker compose up --scale nginx=3
```

⚠ **Troubleshooting Tip:** If you see the error bind: address already in use, it usually means multiple containers are trying to bind to the same host port. Avoid this by fronting services with a reverse proxy like NGINX and only exposing the proxy port to the host.

Output:

```
:~/nginx-site$ docker ps -a
CONTAINER ID   IMAGE          COMMAND                  CREATED          STATUS          PORTS                                     NAMES
0582767a4cc1   nginx:alpine   "/docker-entrypoint.…"   12 minutes ago   Up 12 minutes   0.0.0.0:8080->80/tcp, [::]:8080->80/tcp   site-nginx-1
:~/nginx-site$
:~/nginx-site$ docker compose up --scale nginx=3
[+] Running 4/4
 ✓ Network nginx-site_default     Created                                                                0.1s
 ✓ Container nginx-site-nginx-3   Created                                                                0.5s
 ✓ Container nginx-site-nginx-1   Created                                                                0.5s
 ✓ Container nginx-site-nginx-2   Created                                                                0.5s
Attaching to nginx-1, nginx-2, nginx-3
Gracefully stopping... (press Ctrl+C again to force)
Error response from daemon: failed to set up container networking: driver failed programming external connectivity on endpoint nginx-site-nginx-1 (9e1b19a3775
42a0a0ea06bdf2ceb9545243f4a2cb1e7f7a8d8c24f5ade7214d4): Bind for 0.0.0.0:8080 failed: port is already allocated
:~/nginx-site$ docker ps -a
CONTAINER ID   IMAGE          COMMAND                  CREATED          STATUS          PORTS                                     NAMES
e647e947553f   nginx:alpine   "/docker-entrypoint.…"   9 seconds ago    Created                                                   nginx-site-nginx-1
ead3c736c146   nginx:alpine   "/docker-entrypoint.…"   9 seconds ago    Created                                                   nginx-site-nginx-2
ad41915d7466   nginx:alpine   "/docker-entrypoint.…"   9 seconds ago    Created                                                   nginx-site-nginx-3
0582767a4cc1   nginx:alpine   "/docker-entrypoint.…"   12 minutes ago   Up 12 minutes   0.0.0.0:8080->80/tcp, [::]:8080->80/tcp   site-nginx-1
:~/nginx-site$
```

Figure 7.3: Scale 3 Nginx websites

This starts with 3 instances of the `nginx` service, but you can see it is unable to assign port 8080 as it is already assigned to other containers. Now we will configure it behind reverse proxy to access the web page to load balancer and distribute traffic.

🗁 `Folder Structure:`

```
nginx-site/
├── docker-compose.yml
├── nginx
│   ├── Dockerfile
│   ├── index.template.html
│   └── startup.sh
├── reverse-proxy
│   └── default.conf
```

🗎 `docker-compose.yml`

```
services:
  nginx-replica-1:
    build:
      context: ./nginx
    container_name: nginx-replica-1

  nginx-replica-2:
    build:
      context: ./nginx
    container_name: nginx-replica-2

  nginx-replica-3:
    build:
      context: ./nginx
    container_name: nginx-replica-3
```

```
  reverse-proxy:
    image: nginx:alpine
    container_name: reverse-proxy
    ports:
      - "8080:80"
    volumes:
      - ./reverse-proxy/default.conf:/etc/nginx/conf.d/default.conf:ro
    depends_on:
      - nginx-replica-1
      - nginx-replica-2
      - nginx-replica-3
```

🗎 nginx/index.template.html

```
<!DOCTYPE html>
<html>
<head><title>Docker Replica</title></head>
<body>
  <h1>Hello from docker replica: $CONTAINER_ID</h1>
</body>
</html>
```

🗎 nginx/startup.sh

```
#!/bin/sh

# Get the container ID (12 chars)
export CONTAINER_ID=$(hostname | cut -c1-12)

# Inject it into the HTML file
envsubst '$CONTAINER_ID' < /usr/share/nginx/html/index.template.html >
/usr/share/nginx/html/index.html

# Start nginx in foreground
nginx -g "daemon off;"
```

🗎 nginx/Dockerfile

```
FROM nginx:alpine

COPY startup.sh /startup.sh
COPY index.template.html /usr/share/nginx/html/index.template.html

RUN chmod +x /startup.sh
```

```
CMD ["/startup.sh"]
```

🗎 reverse-proxy/default.conf

```
upstream backend {
    server nginx-replica-1:80;
    server nginx-replica-2:80;
    server nginx-replica-3:80;
}

server {
    listen 80;

    location / {
        proxy_pass http://backend;
        proxy_http_version 1.1;
        proxy_set_header Connection "";

        proxy_set_header Host $host;
        proxy_set_header X-Real-IP $remote_addr;
        proxy_set_header X-Forwarded-For $proxy_add_x_forwarded_for;
        proxy_set_header X-Forwarded-Proto $scheme;

        add_header Cache-Control "no-store, no-cache, must-revalidate,
proxy-revalidate, max-age=0";
        proxy_no_cache 1;
        proxy_cache_bypass 1;
    }
}
```

Run:

```
$ docker compose up --scale nginx-replicas=3 --build
```

Test the Setup vis CLI

Run this command to simulate 10 sequential HTTP requests:

```
$ for i in {1..10}; do curl -s http://localhost:8080 | grep Hello; sleep 1;
done
```

Output:

```
sudipto@sudipto-web-pen-test:~/nginx-site$ for i in {1..10}; do curl -s http://localhost:8080 | grep Hello; sleep 1; done
  <h1>Hello from docker replica: 896cf19874c4</h1>
  <h1>Hello from docker replica: 896cf19874c4</h1>
  <h1>Hello from docker replica: 896cf19874c4</h1>
  <h1>Hello from docker replica: 0bd8a6051b9f</h1>
  <h1>Hello from docker replica: 896cf19874c4</h1>
  <h1>Hello from docker replica: cf0e487d0d56</h1>
  <h1>Hello from docker replica: 0bd8a6051b9f</h1>
  <h1>Hello from docker replica: 896cf19874c4</h1>
  <h1>Hello from docker replica: cf0e487d0d56</h1>
  <h1>Hello from docker replica: 0bd8a6051b9f</h1>
sudipto@sudipto-web-pen-test:~/nginx-site$ docker ps -a
CONTAINER ID   IMAGE                           COMMAND                  CREATED          STATUS          PORTS                                     NAMES
7b2162205c52   nginx:alpine                    "/docker-entrypoint.…"   10 minutes ago   Up 10 minutes   0.0.0.0:8080->80/tcp, [::]:8080->80/tcp   reverse-proxy
0bd8a6051b9f   nginx-site-nginx-replica-3      "/docker-entrypoint.…"   10 minutes ago   Up 10 minutes   80/tcp                                    nginx-replica-3
cf0e487d0d56   nginx-site-nginx-replica-2      "/docker-entrypoint.…"   10 minutes ago   Up 10 minutes   80/tcp                                    nginx-replica-2
896cf19874c4   nginx-site-nginx-replica-1      "/docker-entrypoint.…"   10 minutes ago   Up 10 minutes   80/tcp                                    nginx-replica-1
sudipto@sudipto-web-pen-test:~/nginx-site$
```

Figure 7.4: accessing website via curl behind reverse proxy

Open in browser:

`http://localhost:8080`

Hit refresh — you should see different containers like:

```
Hello from docker replica: 896cf19874c4
```

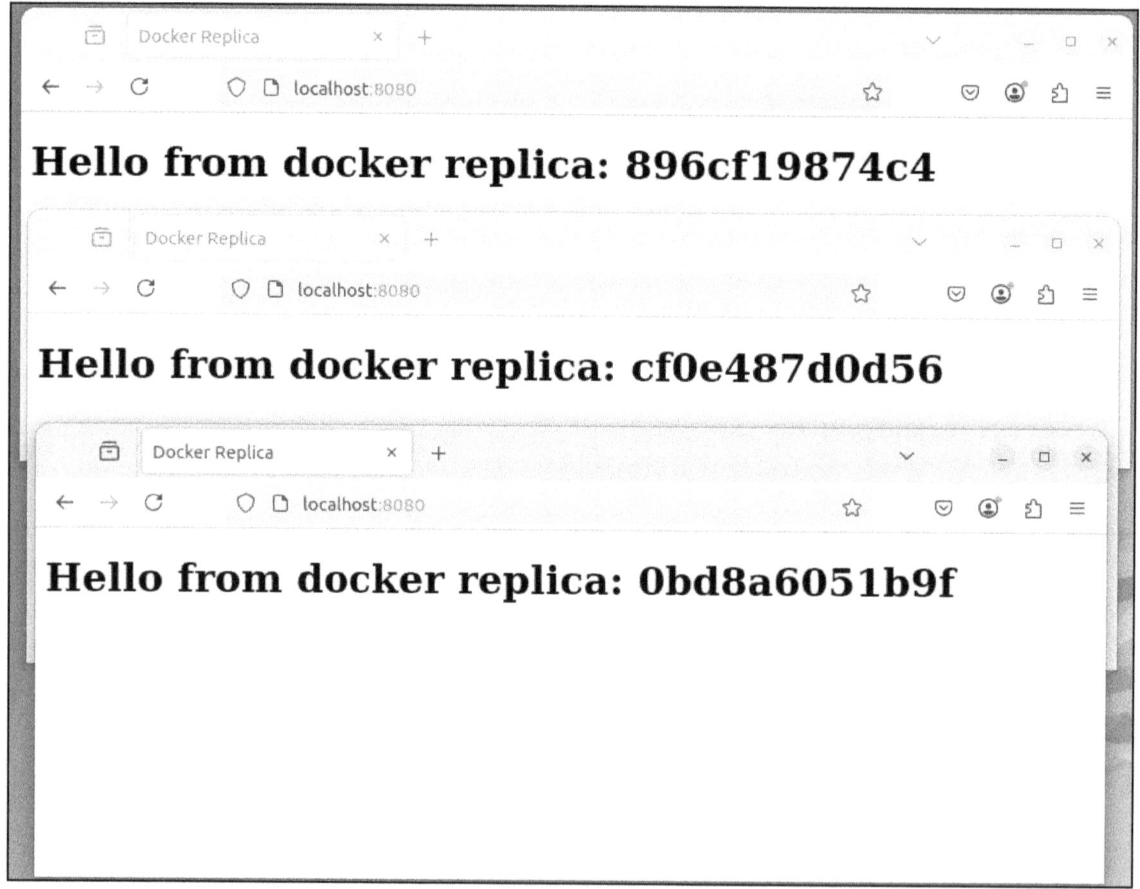

Figure 7.4: accessing website from browser behind reverse proxy

ⓘ **Tip:** Using a reverse proxy enables load balancing and SSL termination for scalable container-based applications.

Best Practices for Docker Compose

- Split configuration into multiple files:
    - `docker-compose.yml` (base)
    - `docker-compose.override.yml` (dev)
- Use `.env` for secrets/config
- Use named volumes for databases
- Use `depends_on` for startup order (but not for health checks)
- Don't hardcode passwords or API keys in Compose files

Summary

In this chapter, you learned:

- What Docker Compose is and why it's essential
- How to define multi-container applications
- How to build and run stacks using Compose
- How to pass environment variables, mount volumes, and define networks
- How to scale services using `--scale`
- Hands-on examples using Flask, Redis, MySQL, and Nginx

Key Takeaways

In this chapter, you mastered Docker Compose for defining and managing multi-container applications, scaling services, handling persistent storage and dynamic environments, and deploying applications behind a reverse proxy for better scalability and load balancing.

Knowledge Check

1. **What is the primary purpose of Docker Compose?**
   A) Managing Docker Swarm nodes
   B) Configuring container networking
   C) Defining and running multi-container Docker applications
   D) Building Docker images
2. **What is the default filename Docker Compose looks for?**
   A) `compose.yml`
   B) `docker-compose.json`
   C) `composefile.yaml`
   D) `docker-compose.yml`
3. **Which command starts all services in a Compose file?**
   A) `docker compose up`
   B) `docker compose start`
   C) `docker compose run`
   D) `docker start-compose`
4. **How do you run Docker Compose in detached mode?**
   A) `docker compose start`
   B) `docker compose run -d`
   C) `docker compose up -d`
   D) `docker compose deploy`
5. **What does `docker-compose` down do?**
   A) Stops services only
   B) Stops and removes containers, networks, and volumes
   C) Deletes all images
   D) Updates running containers
6. **In a `docker-compose.yml`, what section defines services?**
   A) `containers:`
   B) `docker:`
   C) `services:`
   D) `apps:`
7. **Which file is used to define environment-specific overrides?**
   A) `docker-compose.override.yml`
   B) `.env`
   C) `env_config.yml`
   D) `config.json`
8. **What does the depends_on keyword do?**
   A) Runs containers in sequence

B) Links to another image
C) Sets resource limits
D) Creates named volumes

9. **How can you scale a service using Docker Compose?**
   A) `docker compose scale service=3`
   B) `docker compose --replicas 3`
   C) `docker compose replicate`
   D) `docker compose deploy`
10. **What format is used for writing Compose files?**
   A) `JSON`
   B) `INI`
   C) `YAML`
   D) `XML`
11. **Which commands are valid for Docker Compose?**
   - [ ] `docker compose up`
   - [ ] `docker compose down`
   - [ ] `docker compose ps`
   - [ ] `docker compose mount`
12. **What can be defined inside a `docker-compose.yml` service?**
   - [ ] `image:`
   - [ ] `build:`
   - [ ] `volumes:`
   - [ ] `firewall:`
13. **What are the effects of using `docker compose stop`?**
   - [ ] Stops all running containers
   - [ ] Deletes networks and volumes
   - [ ] Removes images
   - [ ] Keeps containers on disk
14. **Which options can be passed to `docker compose up`?**
   - [ ] `–build`
   - [ ] `--remove-orphans`
   - [ ] `–save`
   - [ ] `--force-recreate`
15. **What behaviors are defined in `docker-compose.override.yml`?**
   - [ ] Environment overrides
   - [ ] Dev-time volume mounts
   - [ ] Registry replication

- ▢ Logging adjustments

16. Which sections can define volumes in Compose?

- ▢ `volumes:` root section
- ▢ `services.volumes:`
- ▢ `services.env:`
- ▢ `volumes.datafiles:`

17. What are reasons to use Docker Compose?

- ▢ Simplified orchestration
- ▢ Infrastructure-as-code
- ▢ Easy dev/test workflows
- ▢ Fine-grained RBAC

18. Compose files can include...

- ▢ Custom networks
- ▢ Logging configs
- ▢ Environment variables
- ▢ Host BIOS settings

19. What happens if a volume is not declared in Compose?

- ▢ It create as an anonymous volume
- ▢ The service fails
- ▢ It points to /tmp
- ▢ A warning is printed

20. Compose environments can be made dynamic by:

- ▢ Using `.env` files
- ▢ Variable substitution `${}`
- ▢ Multiple Compose files
- ▢ Editing Docker source code

Answers

Q#	Correct Answer	Explanation
1	C	Compose is designed for multi-container Docker apps.
2	D	The default Compose config is `docker-compose.yml`.
3	A	`docker compose up` starts and builds services.
4	C	`-d` runs services in the background.
5	B	down removes containers, networks, and volumes.
6	C	The `services`: section defines each container group.
7	A	Overrides are applied from `docker-compose.override.yml`.
8	A	`depends_on` sets service start order.
9	A	`scale` is used to increase replicas in Compose.
10	C	Compose is written in YAML for clarity and hierarchy.

Q11. Which commands are valid for Docker Compose?

- [√] `docker compose up`
- [√] `docker compose down`
- [√] `docker compose ps`
- [X] `docker compose mount`

  Explanation: Mounting is handled in YAML; no direct CLI command exists.

Q12. What can be defined inside a `docker-compose.yml` service?

- [√] `image:`
- [√] `build:`
- [√] `volumes:`
- [X] `firewall:`

  Explanation: Services can define build context, image, ports, networks, and volumes.

Q13. What are the effects of using `docker compose stop`?

- [√] Stops all running containers
- [X] Deletes networks and volumes
- [X] Removes images
- [√] Keeps containers on disk

  Explanation: `stop` only halts containers without removing resources.

Q14. Which options can be passed to `docker compose up`?

- [√] `--build`

- [√] `--remove-orphans`
- [X] `--save`
- [√] `--force-recreate`

  Explanation: Compose supports many options for rebuilding, cleaning, or recreating services.

Q15. What behaviors are defined in `docker-compose.override.yml`?

- [√] Environment overrides
- [√] Dev-time volume mounts
- [X] Registry replication
- [√] Logging adjustments

  Explanation: It allows fine-tuning config per environment.

Q16. Which sections can define volumes in Compose?

- [√] `volumes: root section`
- [√] `services.volumes:`
- [X] `services.env:`
- [X] `volumes.datafiles:`

  Explanation: Volumes can be declared globally and assigned per service.

Q17. What are the reasons to use Docker Compose?

- [√] Simplified orchestration
- [√] Infrastructure-as-code
- [√] Easy dev/test workflows
- [X] Fine-grained RBAC

  Explanation: RBAC is handled by Kubernetes, not Compose.

Q18. Compose files can include...

- [√] Custom networks
- [√] Logging configs
- [√] Environment variables
- [X] Host BIOS settings

  Explanation: Compose supports network, logging, envs — not hardware-level configs.

Q19. What happens if a volume is not declared in Compose?

- [√] It create as an anonymous volume
- [X] The service fails
- [X] It points to `/tmp`
- [√] A warning is printed

  Explanation: Docker will auto-create an unnamed volume if one isn't declared.

Q20. Compose environments can be made dynamic by:

- [√] Using `.env` files

- **[✓]** Variable substitution `${}`
- **[✓]** Multiple Compose files
- **[X]** Editing Docker source code
  Explanation: Compose supports `.env`, dynamic configs, and layering YAMLs.

Chapter 8: Advanced Docker Compose — Profiles, Pipelines & Production Patterns

Docker Compose isn't just for local development — it's a powerful tool that can scale to production-like environments and integrate with automation pipelines. This chapter covers Compose features that enable maintainability, reusability, health monitoring, scaling, and multi-environment management.

Multi-File Configuration with Compose

Large projects often need different settings for **development**, **testing**, and **production**.

Default Behavior

Docker Compose looks for:

- `docker-compose.yml`
- `docker-compose.override.yml`

You can override or layer Compose files like this

```
$ docker compose -f docker-compose.yml -f docker-compose.prod.yml up -d
```

Example: Development vs Production

🗎 `docker-compose.yml (base):`

```
services:
  app:
    build: .
    ports:
      - "5000:5000"
    environment:
      - APP_ENV=development
```

🗎 `docker-compose.prod.yml (override):`

```
services:
  app:
    environment:
      - APP_ENV=production
    restart: always
```

Use Case:

Build a dev container with

```
$ docker compose up
```

Deploy the prod version with

```
$ docker compose -f docker-compose.yml -f docker-compose.prod.yml up -d
```

Parallel Builds and Caching

If you have many services with their own `Dockerfiles`, Compose can **build them in parallel**:

```
services:
  frontend:
    build:
      context: ./frontend
  backend:
    build:
      context: ./backend
```

Run:

```
$ docker compose build -parallel
```

This speeds up image creation and improves CI/CD pipeline performance.

Restart Policies for Resiliency

Use `restart:` to auto-recover crashed containers.

Options:

- `no` (default)
- `always` – restart no matter what
- `on-failure` – only restart if container exits with non-zero
- `unless-stopped` – always restart unless stopped manually

Example:

```
services:
  app:
    image: myapp
    restart: always
```

Adding Health Checks

You can define custom **health checks** for services.

Example:

```
services:
  web:
    image: nginx
    healthcheck:
      test: ["CMD", "curl", "-f", "http://localhost"]
      interval: 30s
      timeout: 10s
      retries: 5
```

Then inspect

```
$ docker inspect --format='{{json .State.Health}}' <container_id>
```

Use it in scripts or monitoring.

Secrets and Configuration Management

While Compose doesn't encrypt secrets, you can manage them securely in production via Docker Swarm or mount secrets using volumes.

Using `.env`:

```
DB_USER=admin
DB_PASS=supersecret
```

Security Tip: Always add `.env` to your `.gitignore` to avoid accidentally pushing secrets or credentials to source control.

`docker-compose.yml:`

```
environment:
  - MYSQL_USER=${DB_USER}
  - MYSQL_PASSWORD=${DB_PASS}
```

Never commit `.env` to Git! Add it to `.gitignore`.

Build-Time vs Runtime Variables

Docker builds can accept **build args** and **runtime env vars**.

🗎 `Dockerfile`

```
ARG APP_VERSION
ENV VERSION=$APP_VERSION
```

🗎 `docker-compose.yml`

```
build:
  context: .
  args:
    APP_VERSION: "1.2.3"
```

At runtime

```
environment:
  - NODE_ENV=production
```

Compose + CI/CD Pipelines (GitHub Actions Example)

Here's how to run a Compose stack inside GitHub Actions

🗎 `.github/workflows/ci.yml`

```
name: CI Pipeline

on: [push]

jobs:
  build:
    runs-on: ubuntu-latest
    services:
      docker:
        image: docker:20
    steps:
      - uses: actions/checkout@v3
      - name: Set up Docker
        uses: docker/setup-buildx-action@v2

      - name: Build and test with Compose
        run: |
          docker compose up -d
          docker compose exec -T app pytest
```

Use `exec -T` to disable TTY for automated testing.

Compose with Profiles (v3.9+)

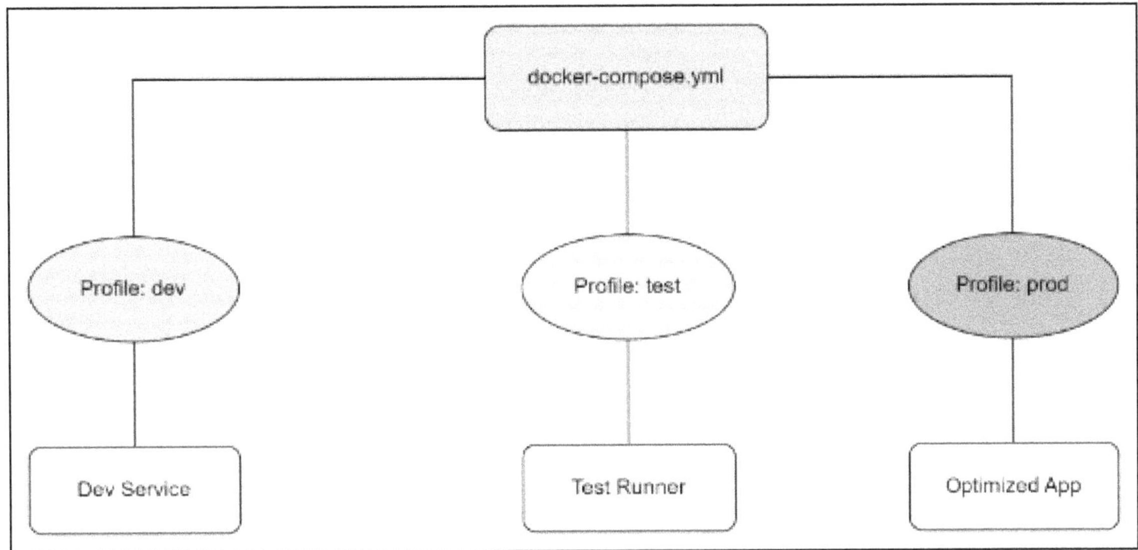

Figure 8.1: Profile-Based Deployment Flow

This diagram illustrates how Docker Compose uses profiles conditionally include or exclude services for different environments such as development, testing, and production.

Use `profiles` to include or exclude services conditionally.

Example:

```
services:
  web:
    image: myweb
  debug:
    image: busybox
    command: sleep 3600
    profiles:
      - debug
```

Run without debug

```
$ docker compose up
```

Run with debug profile

```
$ docker compose --profile debug up
```

Deploying Docker Compose to Production

While Compose isn't a full orchestrator like Kubernetes or Swarm, it can still be used in staging or production setups with:

- **NGINX / Traefik** for load balancing
- **Docker Secrets** (in Swarm)
- **Bind mount certs** (TLS)
- **Watchtower** for auto-updating containers
- **Volume drivers** for persistent cloud storage

Deploying Compose stacks in production

```
$ docker compose -f docker-compose.yml -f docker-compose.prod.yml up -d
```

Lab: Compose + GitHub Actions CI/CD project with Docker Compose Profiles

This setup allows you to **build, test, and deploy conditionally** based on profiles (`dev, test, prod`).

Difficulty Level: Advanced

🗁 `Folder Structure:`

```
ci-cd-compose-profile-app/
├── app/
│   ├── Dockerfile
│   ├── app.py
│   ├── requirements.txt
│   └── tests/
│       └── test_app.py
├── docker-compose.yml
├── docker-compose.prod.yml
└── .github/
    └── workflows/
        └── ci.yml
```

🗎 `app/Dockerfile`

```
FROM python:3.11-slim
WORKDIR /app
```

```
COPY requirements.txt .
RUN pip install --no-cache-dir -r requirements.txt

COPY . .
CMD ["python", "app.py"]
```

🗎 app/requirements.txt

```
flask
pytest
```

🗎 app/app.py

```
from flask import Flask

app = Flask(__name__)

@app.route('/')
def home():
    return "Hello from Docker Compose Profile App!"

if __name__ == '__main__':
    app.run(host='0.0.0.0', port=5000)
```

🗎 app/tests/test_app.py

```
def test_addition():
    assert 2 + 2 == 4
```

🗎 docker-compose.yml (**Dev + Test Profiles**)

```
services:
  web:
    build: ./app
    ports:
      - "5000:5000"
    volumes:
      - ./app:/app
    command: python app.py
    profiles:
      - dev

  test:
    build: ./app
    command: ["pytest", "-q", "--disable-warnings"]
    profiles:
      - test
```

🗎 `docker-compose.prod.yml` (**Prod Profile**)

```
services:
  web:
    image: yourusername/compose-profile-app:latest
    ports:
      - "80:5000"
    environment:
      - FLASK_ENV=production
    restart: always
    profiles:
      - prod
```

🗎`.github/workflows/ci.yml` (**GitHub Actions**)

```
name: CI Pipeline with Compose Profiles

on:
  push:
    branches: [main]
  pull_request:
    branches: [main]

jobs:
  build-test:
    runs-on: ubuntu-latest

    steps:
      - name: Checkout code
        uses: actions/checkout@v3

      - name: Set up Docker
        uses: docker/setup-buildx-action@v2

      - name: Run tests using 'test' profile
        run: |
          docker compose --profile test up --build --abort-on-container-exit
          docker compose down -v
```

Test Locally

```
# Start dev environment
$ docker compose --profile dev up
```

```
# Run tests only
$ docker compose --profile test up --build --abort-on-container-exit
```

Output Dev

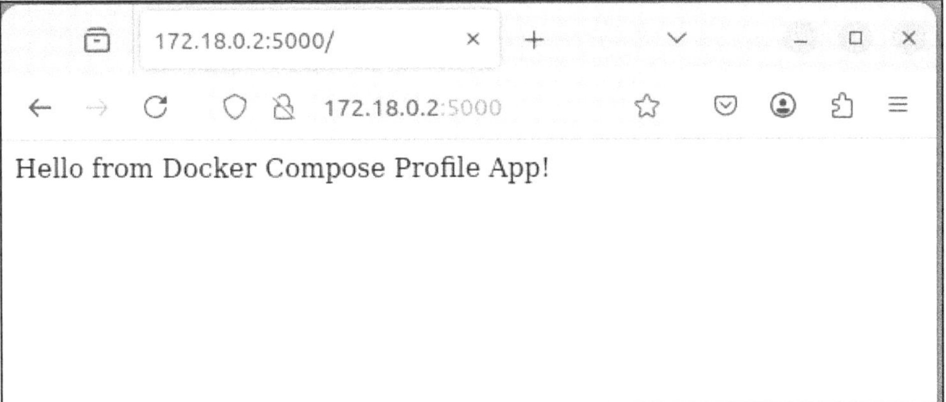

Figure 8.2: accessing website deployed via profile in development

Production Deployment

```
$ docker compose -f docker-compose.yml -f docker-compose.prod.yml -
-profile prod up -d
```

Output Prod:

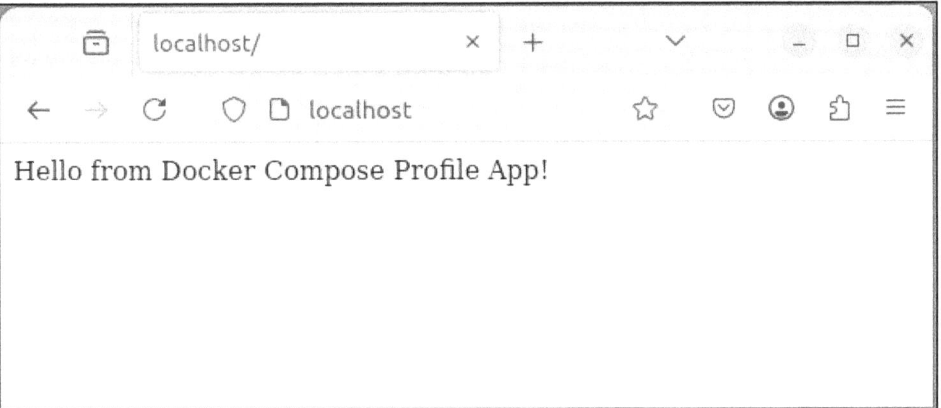

Figure 8.3: accessing website deployed via profile in production

Now you have successfully deployed the app in Production

Best Practices to be Followed

- Use specific versions of images (`node:18.17.1`) not `latest`
- Avoid hardcoding secrets into Compose files
- Don't rely on `depends_on` for timing; use health checks
- Split dev and prod Compose files

- Use `.dockerignore` to reduce build context size
- Don't bind mount your entire project in production
- Use named volumes for databases

✏ ***Note:*** `depends_on` does not wait for a service to be "ready" — it only manages container start order. Use `healthcheck` to ensure service readiness in pipelines.

Lab: Build a Scalable Node.js App with Profiles

Goal: Run a minimal Node.js app, optionally including a debugging container.

Difficulty Level: Advanced

🗁 `Folder Structure:`

```
nodejs-app/
├── app.js
├── package.json
├── Dockerfile
├── docker-compose.yml
```

🗎 `app.js` **(Simple Node.js HTTP Server)**

```
const http = require('http');
const PORT = process.env.PORT || 3000;
const HOSTNAME = require('os').hostname();

const server = http.createServer((req, res) => {
  res.writeHead(200, { 'Content-Type': 'text/plain' });
  res.end(`Hello from Node.js app!\nHostname: ${HOSTNAME}\n`);
});

server.listen(PORT, () => {
  console.log(`Server running at http://localhost:${PORT}`);
});
```

🗎 `package.json`

```
{
  "name": "nodejs-profile-lab",
  "version": "1.0.0",
  "main": "app.js",
  "scripts": {
    "start": "node app.js"
  },
```

```
  "dependencies": {}
}
```

🗎 Dockerfile

```
FROM node:18-alpine
WORKDIR /app
COPY package.json .
RUN npm install
COPY . .
CMD ["npm", "start"]
```

🗎 docker-compose.yml

```
services:
  nodeapp:
    build: .
    ports:
      - "3000:3000"
    profiles:
      - prod

  dev-debug:
    image: alpine
    command: sleep 3600
    profiles:
      - debug
```

Run

```
$ docker compose --profile prod up
```

Or with debug

```
$ docker compose --profile prod --profile debug up
```

Open `http://localhost:3000` in your browser.

Output:

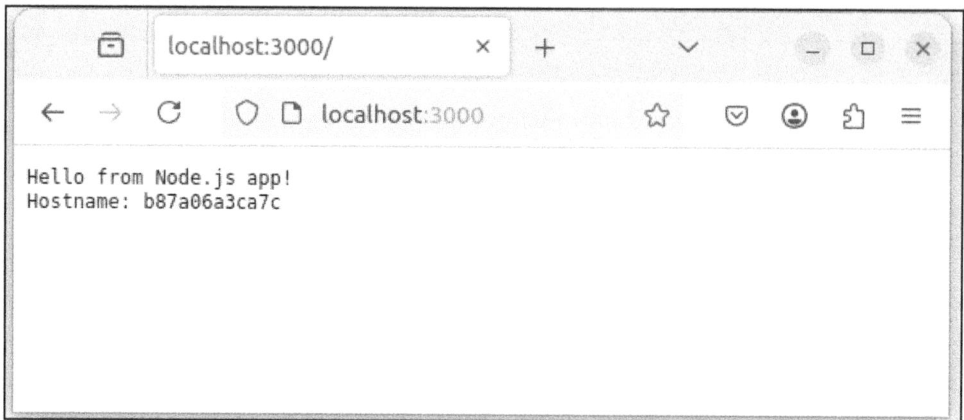

Figure 8.4: Access Node.js App with Profiles

Summary

In this chapter, you learned how to:

- Use multiple Compose files for different environments
- Add health checks and restart policies
- Build images in parallel and pass build-time arguments
- Secure configurations using .env files
- Integrate Compose into CI/CD pipelines
- Use profiles to dynamically include/exclude services
- Use Compose in staging or production setups

Key Takeaways

In this chapter, you mastered advanced Docker Compose techniques — including profile-based service activation, multi-file orchestration for dev and prod, CI/CD pipeline integration with GitHub Actions, health checks, restart policies, secret management, and scalable architecture patterns for real-world deployments.

Knowledge Check

1. **What does the `build:` keyword in a Compose file define?**
   A) Image name
   B) Location of Dockerfile or build context
   C) Run command
   D) Volume mount
2. **Which version of Docker Compose supports long syntax like `deploy:` and `resources:`?**
   A) v1 only
   B) v2 only
   C) v3 and above
   D) All versions
3. **What is the purpose of `docker-compose.override.yml`?**
   A) Stores override logic for deployments
   B) Used to override service definitions in docker-compose.yml
   C) Overrides the Dockerfile
   D) Overrides CLI options
4. **Which keyword sets memory limits in a Compose service?**
   A) `cpu_quota`
   B) `mem_limit`
   C) `deploy.resources.limits.memory`
   D) `runtime.memory`
5. **In Compose v3+, which deployment mode supports scaling?**
   A) single
   B) global
   C) replicated
   D) rolling
6. **How do you define a shared network in Compose?**
   A) Inside `services:` only
   B) In `networks:` root section
   C) With `dns:` tag
   D) Using `cluster:` option
7. **What flag can you use with `docker compose` to apply multiple YAML files?**
   A) `-file`
   B) `-config`
   C) `-compose`
   D) `--context`
8. **Which Compose feature allows environment substitution like `${PORT}`?**
   A) Interpolation

B) Parameter injection
C) Dynamic binding
D) Container templating

9. **What is the function of secrets: in Docker Compose?**
A) Secure shell access
B) Build environment injection
C) Secure distribution of sensitive data like passwords
D) Encrypt Docker volumes

10. **Which of these is NOT a supported key under `deploy:` in Compose v3?**
A) `mode`
B) `resources`
C) `restart`
D) `placement`

11. **Which are valid ways to scale services in Compose?**
- ☐ Use `--scale` with `docker compose up`
- ☐ Define `deploy.replicas` in YAML
- ☐ Add `replicas:` under volumes:
- ☐ Use `--replicate` flag

12. **In advanced Compose networking, what can you define per service?**
- ☐ Static IP within subnet
- ☐ Network alias
- ☐ Custom bridge
- ☐ Router table routes

13. **How can Compose improve environment management?**
- ☐ `.env` file support
- ☐ Per-service environment: blocks
- ☐ Variable substitution using `${}`
- ☐ Terraform integration

14. **What are the benefits of using named volumes in Compose?**
- ☐ Data persistence
- ☐ Reusability across services
- ☐ GPU acceleration
- ☐ Volume lifecycle control

15. **Which deployment-related fields exist in Compose v3 Swarm mode?**
- ☐ `restart_policy`
- ☐ `placement.constraints`
- ☐ `update_config`

- ▢ `rollback_delay`

16. Which features can be layered via multiple Compose files?

- ▢ Development overrides
- ▢ CI/CD adjustments
- ▢ Dynamic port mappings
- ▢ Kernel-level parameters

17. What advanced features can you enable under `build:` in Compose?

- ▢ Context path
- ▢ Target stage (multi-stage build)
- ▢ Dockerfile name
- ▢ Kernel swap control

18. What's true about `external:` in `volumes:` or `networks:`?

- ▢ It links to a pre-existing resource
- ▢ It always creates a new volume
- ▢ Can be shared across Compose projects
- ▢ Required in all cases

19. What happens when two Compose files defines the same service?

- ▢ Fields are merged with override preference
- ▢ Both services are ignored
- ▢ Compose crashes
- ▢ Last defined file has higher precedence

20. What options are available to run different environments using Compose?

- ▢ Use `-f` to load different YAML files
- ▢ Inject different `.env` files
- ▢ Use profiles (v3.9+)
- ▢ Use BIOS firmware tagging

Answers

Q#	Correct Answer	Explanation
1	B	`build:` defines the Dockerfile path or context for image build.
2	C	Compose v3+ supports `deploy, resources,` and Swarm-only keys.
3	B	Override files merge with base Compose files to change service definitions.
4	C	Resource limits like memory are set under `deploy.resources.limits.`
5	C	`replicated` mode allows defining replicas for a service in Swarm.
6	B	Networks must be defined globally in the root-level `networks:` section.
7	A	Use `-f file1.yml -f file2.yml` to apply multiple Compose files.
8	A	Environment variable interpolation uses `${}` syntax from `.env` or system envs.
9	C	`secrets:` securely injects sensitive values like passwords.
10	C	`restart:` is not allowed inside the `deploy:` block in Compose v3.

Q11. Which are valid ways to scale services in Compose?

- **[√]** Use `--scale` with `docker compose up`
- **[√]** Define `deploy.replicas` in YAML
- **[X]** Add `replicas:` under `volumes:`
- **[X]** Use `--replicate` flag

  Explanation: Only `--scale` CLI and `deploy.replicas` in YAML are valid.

Q12. In advanced Compose networking, what can you define per service?

- **[√]** Static IP within subnet
- **[√]** Network alias
- **[√]** Custom bridge
- **[X]** Router table routes

  Explanation: Docker allows IP, aliases, and driver options but not host-level routing.

Q13. How can Compose improve environment management?

- **[√]** `.env` file support
- **[√]** Per-service environment: blocks
- **[√]** Variable substitution using `${}`

- [X] Terraform integration
  Explanation: Compose supports multiple environment approaches, not direct Terraform.

Q14. What are the benefits of using named volumes in Compose?

- [✓] Data persistence
- [✓] Reusability across services
- [X] GPU acceleration
- [✓] Volume lifecycle control
  Explanation: Named volumes are essential for persistent and shared storage.

Q15. Which deployment-related fields exist in Compose v3 Swarm mode?

- [✓] `restart_policy`
- [✓] `placement.constraints`
- [✓] `update_config`
- [✓] `rollback_delay`
  Explanation: Swarm services support placement, restart, and update control.

Q16. Which features can be layered via multiple Compose files?

- [✓] Development overrides
- [✓] CI/CD adjustments
- [✓] Dynamic port mappings
- [X] Kernel-level parameters
  Explanation: Docker Compose supports configuration layering.

Q17. What advanced features can you enable under build: in Compose?

- [✓] Context path
- [✓] Target stage (multi-stage build)
- [✓] Dockerfile name
- [X] Kernel swap control
  Explanation: Advanced builds can define context, target, and Dockerfile override.

Q18. What's true about `external:` in `volumes:` or `networks:`?

- [✓] It links to a pre-existing resource
- [✓] It always creates a new volume
- [✓] Can be shared across Compose projects
- [X] Required in all cases
  Explanation: `external: true` attaches to an existing object (volume/network).

Q19. What happens when two Compose files defines the same service?

- [✓] Fields are merged with override preference
- [X] Both services are ignored
- [X] Compose crashes

- **[√]** Last defined file has higher precedence
  Explanation: Later files override fields from earlier ones.

Q20. What options are available to run different environments using Compose?

- **[√]** Use `-f` to load different YAML files
- **[√]** Inject different `.env` files
- **[√]** Use profiles (v3.9+)
- **[X]** Use BIOS firmware tagging
  Explanation: Compose supports custom profiles and file chaining for different environments.

Chapter 9: Docker in Production – Hardening, Scaling & Zero-Downtime Deployments

Deploying Dockerized applications in production isn't just about running `docker compose up -d`. It involves security hardening, automated deployment, fault tolerance, monitoring, and careful volume and network configuration. This chapter walks you through deploying resilient, scalable, and secure applications using Docker.

Preparing Images for Production

Use Lightweight Base Images

Use minimal images like `alpine` to reduce image size and attack surface.

Instead of:

```
FROM python:3.11
```

Use:

```
FROM python:3.11-alpine
```

Remove Build Dependencies

Use **multi-stage builds** to remove tools used only during build time.

Example: Dockerfile

```
# Stage 1: Build
FROM node:18 as build
WORKDIR /app
COPY . .
RUN npm install && npm run build

# Stage 2: Serve
FROM nginx:alpine
COPY --from=build /app/dist /usr/share/nginx/html
```

Securing Containers in Production

Principle of Least Privilege (Dockerfile)

- Avoid running apps as `root` inside containers.

- Create a dedicated user:

```
RUN addgroup -S app && adduser -S app -G app
USER app
```

Limit Capabilities

Drop Linux capabilities not needed

```
$ docker run --cap-drop=ALL --cap-add=NET_BIND_SERVICE myapp
```

Read-Only Filesystems

Prevent file tampering

```
$ docker run --read-only -v /app/uploads myapp
```

Scan Images for Vulnerabilities

Use tools like:

- `docker scout` (uses Snyk)
- Trivy

Before proceeding you need to install docker scout, Docker Desktop, Trivy.

Install Docker Scout v1.17.1 on Ubuntu 22.04

1. Create the plugin folder

```
$ mkdir -p ~/.docker/scout
$ cd ~/.docker/scout
```

2. Download and extract the binary

```
$ curl -LO https://github.com/docker/scout-
cli/releases/download/v1.17.1/docker-scout_1.17.1_linux_amd64.tar.gz

$ tar -xzf docker-scout_1.17.1_linux_amd64.tar.gz
```

This will extract a binary named `docker-scout`.

3. Make it executable

```
$ chmod +x docker-scout
```

4. Add plugin path to Docker config

Edit `~/.docker/config.json` or create it if it doesn't exist

```
$ nano ~/.docker/config.json
```

Add the `scout` directory to your `.docker/config.json` as a plugin directory

- `$HOME/.docker/config.json` on *Linux* and *macOS*
- Add the `cliPluginsExtraDirs` property to the `config.json` file

```
{
  "cliPluginsExtraDirs": [
    "/home/sudipta/.docker/scout"
  ]
}
```

Make sure it's valid JSON (you can validate it via `jq . ~/.docker/config.json`)
If `jq` is not installed in your system install it via command "`sudo apt  install jq`"

5. Verify Docker Scout is working

```
$ docker scout version
```

You should see:

```
$ docker scout version
```

Output:

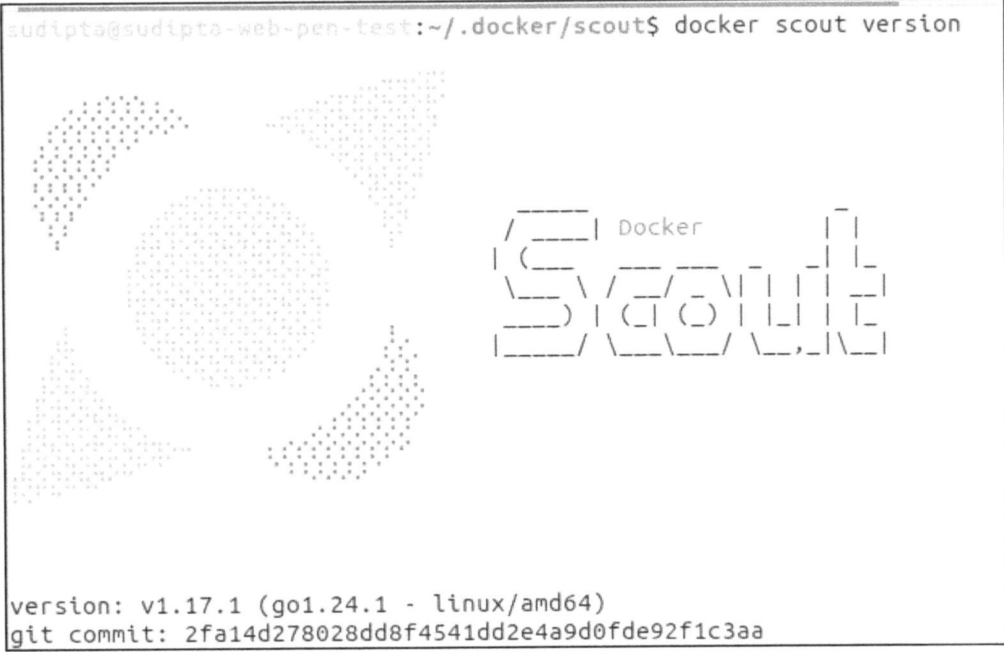

Figure 9.1: Scout version

Now ready to scan images:

```
$ docker scout quickview nginx:alpine
```

NOTE: To scan the image, you need to login to Docker Hub with your Docker ID or email address to use `docker scout`.

```
sudipta@docker:~/.docker/scout$ docker login

USING WEB-BASED LOGIN

i Info → To sign in with credentials on the command line, use 'docker login
-u <username>'


Your one-time device confirmation code is: ABCD-MNOP
Press ENTER to open your browser or submit your device code here:
https://login.docker.com/activate

Waiting for authentication in the browser…
```

Now scan the images

```
$ docker scout quickview nginx:alpine
$ scout cves nginx:alpine
$ docker scout cves nginx:alpine
```

Lab: Vulnerability & Metadata Analysis Using Docker Scout (Free Tier)

Hands-on lab for using **Docker Scout** with a **free Docker Hub account (no organization needed)**. It focuses on publicly available images and does **not** require paid features or organizational setup.

Difficulty Level: Basic

Objective:

Analyze public Docker images using Docker Scout, explore SBOM, CVEs, image lineage, and base image recommendations.

Pre-requisites:

- ☑ Docker Engine installed (v24+ recommended)

☑ Docker CLI available

☑ Docker Scout CLI installed at: `~/.docker/cli-plugins/docker-scout`

☑ Logged in to Docker Hub: `docker login`

Step 1: Pull Some Public Images

```
$ docker pull ubuntu:22.04
$ docker pull python:3.11
$ docker pull node:18
$ docker pull nginx:alpine
```

Step 2: Run Quick Metadata Overview

Use `quickview` to get SBOM and provenance:

```
$ docker scout quickview ubuntu:22.04
$ docker scout quickview python:3.11
$ docker scout quickview node:18
$ docker scout quickview nginx:alpine
```

You'll see:

- ✓ SBOM from attestation
- ✓ Provenance details
- ✓ Base image lineage

Step 3: Scan CVEs in the Images

```
$ docker scout cves ubuntu:22.04
$ docker scout cves python:3.11
$ docker scout cves node:18
$ docker scout cves nginx:alpine
```

You'll get:

- CVE IDs
- Affected packages
- Severity ratings (Low to Critical)
- Fix availability

Step 4: View Recommendations (Safer Base Images)

```
$ docker scout recommendations ubuntu:22.04
$ docker scout recommendations python:3.11
$ docker scout recommendations node:18
```

```
$ docker scout recommendations nginx:alpine
```

You have learned:

- What base image you're currently using
- Which newer/safer one you can switch to (e.g., `slim`, `alpine` variants)
- Vulnerability reductions

🗎 Script for `quickview`, `cves`, `recommendations` and HTML Report

```
#!/bin/bash

# Define list of images
IMAGES=("ubuntu:22.04" "python:3.11" "node:18" "nginx:alpine")

# Output directory
OUTPUT_DIR="scout-reports"
mkdir -p "$OUTPUT_DIR"

# Loop through images
for image in "${IMAGES[@]}"; do
  safe_name=$(echo "$image" | tr ':/' '_')
  report_file="${OUTPUT_DIR}/${safe_name}.html"

  echo " Processing $image"
  echo "<html><head><title>Docker Scout Report -
$image</title></head><body>" > "$report_file"
  echo "<h1>Docker Scout Report for <code>$image</code></h1>" >>
"$report_file"

  # QUICKVIEW
  echo "<h2> Quickview</h2><pre>" >> "$report_file"
  docker scout quickview "$image" 2>&1 >> "$report_file"
  echo "</pre>" >> "$report_file"

  # CVEs
  echo "<h2> CVEs</h2><pre>" >> "$report_file"
  docker scout cves "$image" 2>&1 >> "$report_file"
  echo "</pre>" >> "$report_file"

  # Recommendations
  echo "<h2> Recommendations</h2><pre>" >> "$report_file"
```

```
  docker scout recommendations "$image" 2>&1 >> "$report_file"
  echo "</pre>" >> "$report_file"

  echo "</body></html>" >> "$report_file"
  echo " Report saved: $report_file"
done

echo -e "\n All reports generated inside: $OUTPUT_DIR/"
```

Save it as `scout-scan.sh`, then run

```
$ chmod +x scout-scan.sh
$ ./scout-scan.sh
```

Lab Summary

Feature	Supported in Free Tier
SBOM metadata	☑ Yes
CVE Scan	☑ Yes
Base updates	☑ Yes

Now we will move to vulnerability scan of the images

- Snyk
- Trivy

Docker Image Vulnerability Scanning

1. Snyk CLI

Installation

```
$ curl -Lo snyk https://downloads.snyk.io/cli/v1.1296.2/snyk-linux
```

Make it executable

```
$ chmod +x snyk
```

Move it to a directory in your PATH

```
$ sudo mv snyk /usr/local/bin/
```

Verify

```
$ snyk --version
```

Authenticate

```
$ snyk auth
```

It will open a browser window to authorize.

Scan with Snyk

```
$ snyk test --docker ubuntu:22.04
$ snyk test --docker python:3.11
$ snyk test --docker node:18
$ snyk test --docker nginx:alpine
```

To save JSON reports

```
$ snyk test --docker python:3.11 --json > python_snyk.json
```

2. Trivy

Installation

```
$ wget
https://github.com/aquasecurity/trivy/releases/download/v0.61.1/trivy_0.61.1
_Linux-64bit.deb
$ sudo dpkg -i trivy_0.61.1_Linux-64bit.deb
```

Verify

```
$ trivy –version
```

Scan with Trivy

```
$ trivy image ubuntu:22.04
$ trivy image python:3.11
$ trivy image node:18
$ trivy image nginx:alpine
```

To save JSON output

```
$ trivy image --format json -o ubuntu_trivy.json ubuntu:22.04
```

Reverse Proxy with SSL

In production, your app should never be exposed directly. Use **NGINX** or **Traefik** as a reverse proxy.

NGINX as Reverse Proxy

```
server {
  listen 443 ssl;
  server_name myapp.com;

  ssl_certificate /etc/ssl/certs/myapp.pem;
  ssl_certificate_key /etc/ssl/private/myapp.key;

  location / {
    proxy_pass http://localhost:3000;
  }
}
```

Use Docker volumes to mount certs into NGINX.

Complete Lab on Node.js App + NGINX Reverse Proxy + Certbot (HTTPS), refer to **Appendix B**

Lab: Real-World Deployment: Node.js App + NGINX + Certbot (HTTPS) with Auto-Renewal

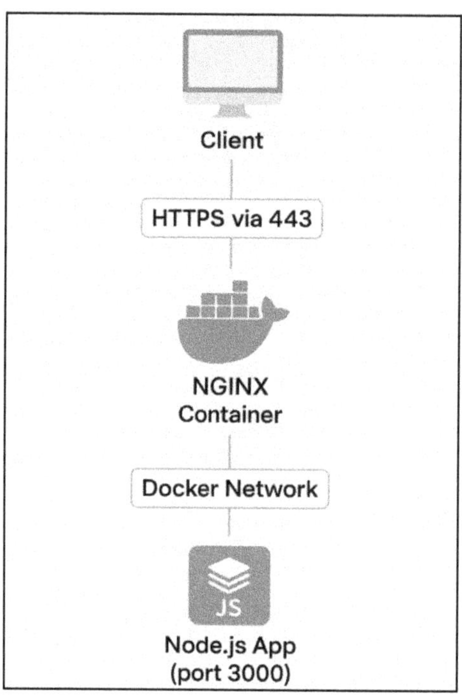

Figure 9.2: Secure Docker Deployment with NGINX Reverse Proxy and HTTPS

This architecture illustrates how a client connects via HTTPS to a NGINX container, which forwards requests to a Node.js app running in the same Docker network

Difficulty Level: Advanced

🗁 Folder Structure:

```
/production-app/
├── docker-compose.prod.yml
├── nginx.conf
├── certs/        (Certbot will place SSL certs here)
├── nodeapp/
│   ├── Dockerfile
│   ├── app.js
│   └── package.json
├── renew_certbot_and_reload.sh
```

🖹 docker-compose.prod.yml

```
services:
  nodeapp:
```

```
    build: ./nodeapp
    restart: always
    environment:
      - NODE_ENV=production
    expose:
      - "3000"     # Internal port, no direct external mapping
    networks:
      - webnet

  nginx:
    image: nginx:latest
    volumes:
      - ./nginx.conf:/etc/nginx/nginx.conf:ro
      - ./certs:/etc/ssl:ro
    ports:
      - "80:80"
      - "443:443"
    depends_on:
      - nodeapp
    networks:
      - webnet

networks:
  webnet:
    driver: bridge
```

Production-Ready NGINX Config

- Auto **HTTP → HTTPS redirection**
- **Strong SSL ciphers**
- **HSTS** security header
- Proxy to **Node.js** app running inside Docker
- Proper **timeouts** and **headers**

🗎 nginx.conf

```
events {
  worker_connections 1024;
}

http {
  include       mime.types;
```

```
  default_type  application/octet-stream;

  sendfile        on;
  keepalive_timeout  65;

  # Redirect all HTTP traffic to HTTPS
  server {
    listen 80;
    server_name itbestpractice.net www.itbestpractice.net;

    # Redirect to HTTPS
    return 301 https://$host$request_uri;
  }

  server {
    listen 443 ssl http2;
    server_name itbestpractice.net www.itbestpractice.net;

    # SSL Certificates (mounted inside /etc/ssl/)
    ssl_certificate /etc/ssl/live/itbestpractice.net/fullchain.pem;
    ssl_certificate_key /etc/ssl/live/itbestpractice.net/privkey.pem;

    # SSL Protocols and Ciphers
    ssl_protocols TLSv1.2 TLSv1.3;
    ssl_prefer_server_ciphers on;
    ssl_ciphers "ECDHE-ECDSA-AES128-GCM-SHA256:ECDHE-RSA-AES128-GCM-SHA256:
                 ECDHE-ECDSA-AES256-GCM-SHA384:ECDHE-RSA-AES256-GCM-SHA384:
                 ECDHE-ECDSA-CHACHA20-POLY1305:ECDHE-RSA-CHACHA20-POLY1305";

    # Security Headers
     add_header Strict-Transport-Security "max-age=31536000;
includeSubDomains; preload" always;
     add_header X-Frame-Options DENY always;
     add_header X-Content-Type-Options nosniff always;
     add_header X-XSS-Protection "1; mode=block" always;
     add_header Referrer-Policy "strict-origin-when-cross-origin" always;
   add_header Content-Security-Policy "default-src 'self'; script-src
'self'; style-src 'self' fonts.googleapis.com; font-src fonts.gstatic.com;
img-src 'self' data:; object-src 'none'; frame-ancestors 'none'; upgrade-
insecure-requests;" always;
```

```
    add_header Permissions-Policy "geolocation=(), microphone=(), camera=()"
always;

    # SSL Session Cache (performance)
    ssl_session_cache shared:SSL:10m;
    ssl_session_timeout 10m;

    # Logging
    access_log /var/log/nginx/access.log;
    error_log /var/log/nginx/error.log;

    # Proxy Settings to Node.js (container)
    location / {
      proxy_pass http://nodeapp:3000;
      proxy_http_version 1.1;
      proxy_set_header Upgrade $http_upgrade;
      proxy_set_header Connection 'upgrade';
      proxy_set_header Host $host;
      proxy_cache_bypass $http_upgrade;
    }

    # Healthcheck Endpoint (Optional)
    location /health {
      proxy_pass http://nodeapp:3000/health;
    }
  }
}
```

Notes:

- First server block redirects HTTP (port 80) to HTTPS (port 443).
- Second server block handles HTTPS traffic to the Node.js app.
- SSL certs will be mounted via /etc/ssl/ path.

Setting up Certbot (Let's Encrypt SSL Certificates)

Use Certbot in **standalone** or **Docker mode** to generate SSL certs.

Install Certbot (host machine or separate container):

```
$ sudo apt install certbot
```

Generate certs manually:

```
$ sudo certbot certonly --standalone -d itbestpractice.net
```

➔ Certs will typically be saved under `/etc/letsencrypt/live/itbestpractice.net /`

Copy certs (or mount them) to `./certs` folder.

Example

```
$ sudo cp -r /etc/letsencrypt/live/itbestpractice.net ./certs/
```

Now NGINX will have correct SSL certificates inside `/etc/ssl` path when containers run.

DNS Based (Optional in case port 80/tcp is blocked)

```
$ sudo certbot certonly --manual --preferred-challenges=dns -d
itbestpractice.net
```

Building and Running in Production

Go to project root

```
$ cd /production-app/
```

Build and start services

```
$ docker compose -f docker-compose.prod.yml up -d --build
```

Services:

- Node.js App → Exposed inside network only (port 3000 internal)
- NGINX → Front-facing server (ports 80 and 443)
- Certs → SSL secured HTTPS traffic

Add Host Entry `/etc/hosts` and save it, to access it from your local system

```
$ sudo nano /etc/hosts
127.0.0.1   itbestpractice.net
```

Access the app from your local system web browser

`https://itbestpractice.net/`

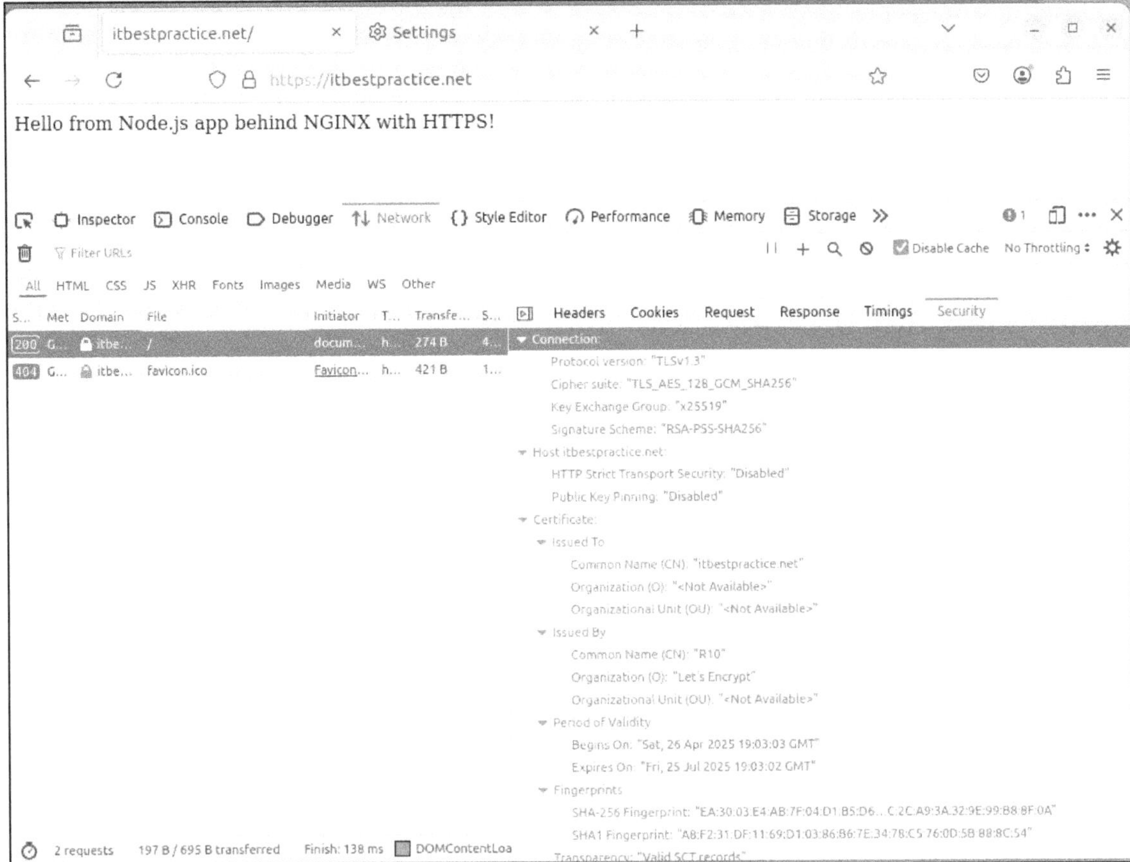

Figure 9.3: Dockerized HTTPS Deployment using NGINX and Certbot

Auto-Renew Certbot Script-Certificate Renewal

Create a bash script to **auto-renew certificates** and **reload NGINX**:

🗎 renew_certbot_and_reload.sh

```
#!/bin/bash

echo "Starting Let's Encrypt Certificate Renewal..."

# Renew certificates
sudo certbot renew --quiet --no-self-upgrade

# If renewal happened, reload NGINX
if [ $? -eq 0 ]; then
    echo "Certificates renewed successfully."
    echo "Reloading NGINX..."
    docker-compose restart nginx
```

```
else
    echo "Certificate renewal failed."
fi
```

Make it executable

```
$ chmod +x renew_certbot_and_reload.sh
```

Setup Auto-Cronjob (Optional but recommended)

Schedule it via `cron` (runs daily at 2:30 AM)

```
$ crontab -e
```

Add below lines for auto renewal (give the correct path of the scripts `renew_certbot_and_reload.sh`)

```
30 2 * * * /home/yourusername/production-app /renew_certbot_and_reload.sh >>
/home/yourusername/certbot_renew.log 2>&1
```

Production Optimization Recommendations

Area	Suggestion
Auto Renew SSL	Use a Certbot cron job or Docker Certbot container for auto-renewal every 60 days
Security Headers	Add `Strict-Transport-Security` and `X-Frame-Options` in NGINX
Logging	Mount log volumes (`/var/log/nginx/`) for persistent logs
Scaling Node App	Add Docker Swarm service or Kubernetes Deployment later
Backup Certs	Regular backup of `/certs/` folder

HTTP Security Header (OWASP Top 10 Recommended)

Header	Purpose
`Strict-Transport-Security`	Enforce HTTPS, prevent SSL strip
`X-Frame-Options`	Block Clickjacking
`X-Content-Type-Options`	Stop MIME sniffing
`X-XSS-Protection`	Prevent legacy XSS attacks
`Referrer-Policy`	Control information leakage
`Content-Security-Policy`	Block XSS, secure resource loading

Header	Purpose
`Permissions-Policy`	Disable dangerous browser APIs

Quick Reference Commands

Task	Command
View running containers	`docker ps`
Restart NGINX service	`docker compose restart nginx`
View NGINX logs	`docker logs <nginx_container_id>`
Renew cert manually	`sudo certbot renew`
Update app	`docker compose up -d --build`

Monitoring and Logging

Metrics Tools

- **Prometheus**: Scrapes container metrics
- **Grafana**: Dashboards
- **cAdvisor**: Per-container resource stats
- **Node Exporter**: Host metrics

Logging Strategies

- Use logging drivers:

```
$ docker run --log-driver=json-file ...
```

- Aggregate logs using:
  - ELK Stack (Elasticsearch + Logstash + Kibana)
  - Fluentd
  - Loki + Grafana

Centralize Logs with Volumes

```
$ docker run -v /var/log:/logs myapp
```

Complete Lab on **Docker Monitoring + Logging with Prometheus, Grafana, Loki, Fluent-Bit with Node.js Application** refer to **Appendix B**

Zero-Downtime Deployments with Compose

Docker Compose doesn't support **rolling updates** natively like Kubernetes or Swarm, but you can:

1. Spin up a new version on another port
2. Point the reverse proxy to the new container
3. Stop the old one

Or use tools like **Watchtower** to automatically pull and restart updated images.

```
$ docker run -d \
  --name watchtower \
  -v /var/run/docker.sock:/var/run/docker.sock \
  containrrr/watchtower
```

Scaling Docker Services

You can scale stateless services using:

```
$ docker compose up --scale web=3
```

Then use **NGINX** or **HAProxy** as a load balancer.

CI/CD Example: GitLab CI + Docker Compose

🗎 `.gitlab-ci.yml`

```
stages:
  - test
  - deploy

services:
  - docker:dind

before_script:
  - docker info

test:
  stage: test
  script:
    - docker compose up -d
    - docker compose exec -T web npm test
    - docker compose down

deploy:
  stage: deploy
  script:
```

```
    - docker compose -f docker compose.yml -f docker-compose.prod.yml up -d
```

Best Practices for Production-Ready Docker

Category	Best Practice
Images	Use slim/minimal images, clean up build deps, pin versions
Security	Run as non-root, scan images, limit capabilities
Logging	Use centralized logging drivers, volume logs
Monitoring	Use Prometheus, cAdvisor, or Datadog
Secrets	Use environment variables, avoid hardcoding in Compose
Scaling	Use `--scale`, reverse proxies, and rolling updates

Summary

In this chapter, you learned how to:

- Harden and optimize Docker images for production use
- Run containers securely with limited privileges
- Add HTTPS using reverse proxies like NGINX and Traefik
- Collect logs and metrics using tools like ELK and Prometheus
- Automate CI/CD pipelines with Docker Compose
- Use Watchtower or blue/green methods for zero-downtime deployment
- Scale and orchestrate services using Compose or Swarm

Key Takeaways

In this chapter, you mastered how to securely deploy Docker apps in production environments. You learned to reduce image size and vulnerabilities with multi-stage builds, enforce runtime security via read-only filesystems and limited privileges, set up HTTPS using NGINX and Certbot, and integrate Docker into GitLab CI/CD workflows. Finally, you explored logging, monitoring, and scaling patterns, enabling zero-downtime deployments and long-term service resilience.

Knowledge Check

1. **What is a common method to limit CPU usage for a production container?**
   A) `--cpu-cores`
   B) `–cpus`
   C) `--cpu-limit`
   D) `--cores`
2. **Which logging driver would you typically use for production observability?**
   A) `json-file`
   B) `none`
   C) `syslog`
   D) `random`
3. **What command ensures a container restart automatically in production?**
   A) `--keep-alive`
   B) `--restart always`
   C) `–loop`
   D) `--resurrect`
4. **Which of these should be avoided in production Dockerfiles?**
   A) `FROM alpine`
   B) `COPY . .` without `.dockerignore`
   C) `RUN apk add`
   D) `EXPOSE 443`
5. **What is the benefit of multi-stage builds in production?**
   A) Faster run time
   B) Auto-scaling
   C) Smaller final image size
   D) Reduced network latency
6. **What is the purpose of a read-only root filesystem for containers?**
   A) Prevent container logs
   B) Increase CPU performance
   C) Improve security by restricting write access
   D) Disable container access
7. **What does the `docker stats` command show?**
   A) Volume usage
   B) Network errors
   C) Live resource usage of running containers
   D) Build history
8. **Which of these is NOT a recommended way to store secrets in production?**

A) Environment variables
B) Docker Swarm secrets
C) Docker Volumes
D) Hardcoded in Dockerfile

9. **What happens when you use `docker system prune` in production?**
   A) Restarts the container
   B) Cleans all unused data (containers, networks, images)
   C) Installs updates
   D) Performs backup
10. **Which component is most commonly used for container orchestration in production?**
   A) Docker Compose
   B) Kubernetes
   C) GitHub
   D) Jenkins
11. **Which practices help reduce Docker image size?**
   - [ ] Use Alpine or minimal base images
   - [ ] Combine RUN instructions
   - [ ] Clean up unnecessary packages
   - [ ] Store data in container rootfs
12. **Which restart policies are valid for production containers?**
   - [ ] `always`
   - [ ] `unless-stopped`
   - [ ] `on-failure`
   - [ ] `on-success`
13. **What should be monitored continuously in Docker production environments?**
   - [ ] CPU and memory usage
   - [ ] Container health status
   - [ ] Container logs
   - [ ] Docker Desktop license
14. **What is some container hardening practices?**
   - [ ] Run containers as non-root
   - [ ] Limit capabilities
   - [ ] Use read-only filesystem
   - [ ] Mount / from host
15. **What options are available to log Docker container activity?**

- ▢ Use `docker logs`
- ▢ Redirect logs to `fluentd, ELK`, or `Loki`
- ▢ Embed logs in images
- ▢ Use centralized log drivers

16. What does `docker update --memory` allow you to do?

- ▢ Change container memory limit
- ▢ Restart the container
- ▢ Remove all volumes
- ▢ Apply runtime memory updates

17. What mechanisms can prevent container compromise?

- ▢ Seccomp profiles
- ▢ AppArmor/SELinux policies
- ▢ Read-only mounts
- ▢ Allowing all capabilities

18. Where should image scanning be done in CI/CD pipelines?

- ▢ Before pushing to registry
- ▢ Before production deploy
- ▢ After rollout
- ▢ As a security gate

19. Why is `docker image prune` dangerous in production?

- ▢ Can delete unused but needed images
- ▢ Stops all containers
- ▢ May break builds or rollbacks
- ▢ Deletes host OS

20. What are some production-ready logging best practices?

- ▢ Use centralized log collectors
- ▢ Add labels for log filtering
- ▢ Use structured logs (JSON)
- ▢ Pipe logs to `/dev/null`

Answers

Q#	Correct Answer	Explanation
1	B	Use `--cpus` to control the number of CPU cores used by the container.
2	C	`syslog, fluentd`, and others are recommended over `json-file` for production.
3	B	The `--restart always` policy ensures automatic restarts after failure.
4	B	Without a `.dockerignore`, your image may include unnecessary files.
5	C	Multi-stage builds strip unnecessary build-time layers for leaner images.
6	C	A read-only root FS prevents unauthorized write access inside containers.
7	C	`docker stats` show live CPU, memory, and IO usage stats.
8	D	Secrets should never be hardcoded in a Dockerfile.
9	B	`docker system prune` deletes unused images, containers, and volumes.
10	B	Kubernetes is the industry standard orchestration tool for production.

Q11. Which practices help reduce Docker image size?

- [✓] Use Alpine or minimal base images
- [✓] Combine `RUN` instructions
- [✓] Clean up unnecessary packages
- [X] Store data in container `rootfs`

  Explanation: Reducing layers and cleaning temp files leads to smaller images.

Q12. Which restart policies are valid for production containers?

- [✓] `always`
- [✓] `unless-stopped`
- [✓] `on-failure`
- [X] `on-success`

  Explanation: Docker supports three restart options for fault tolerance.

Q13. What should be monitored continuously in Docker production environments?

- [✓] CPU and memory usage
- [✓] Container health status
- [✓] Container logs
- [X] Docker Desktop license

  Explanation: Resource usage and logs help detect failures and optimize operations.

Q14. What is some container hardening practices?

- [✓] Run containers as non-root
- [✓] Limit capabilities
- [✓] Use read-only filesystem
- [X] Mount / from host

  Explanation: Dropping privileges and filesystem lockdowns reduce attack surface.

Q15. What options are available to log Docker container activity?

- [✓] Use `docker logs`
- [✓] Redirect logs to `fluentd, ELK,` or `Loki`
- [X] Embed logs in images
- [✓] Use centralized log drivers

  Explanation: Production setups require external log aggregation.

Q16. What does `docker update --memory` allow you to do?

- [✓] Change container memory limit
- [X] Restart the container
- [X] Remove all volumes
- [✓] Apply runtime memory updates

  Explanation: `docker update` adjusts container resource limits.

Q17. What mechanisms can prevent container compromise?

- [✓] Seccomp profiles
- [✓] AppArmor/SELinux policies
- [✓] Read-only mounts
- [X] Allowing all capabilities

  Explanation: Security modules like seccomp/AppArmor enforce strict access control.

Q18. Where should image scanning be done in CI/CD pipelines?

- [✓] Before pushing to registry
- [✓] Before production deploy
- [X] After rollout

- [✓] As a security gate
  Explanation: Image scanning should occur early to catch vulnerabilities before deploying.

Q19. Why is docker image prune dangerous in production?

- [✓] Can delete unused but needed images
- [X] Stops all containers
- [✓] May break builds or rollbacks
- [X] Deletes host OS
  Explanation: You risk removing images that aren't tagged but still in use.

Q20. What is some production-ready logging best practices?

- [✓] Use centralized log collectors
- [✓] Add labels for log filtering
- [✓] Use structured logs (JSON)
- [X] Pipe logs to /dev/null
  Explanation: Logging should be secure, searchable, and structured.

Chapter 10: Advanced Docker — Internals, Orchestration, and Secure Multi-Host Deployments

By now, you've mastered Docker's core features. In this chapter, we'll open the hood and examine the engine that powers containers, giving you insights into low-level features like namespaces, cgroups, advanced networking setups, and container orchestration models like Docker Swarm and Kubernetes.

How Containers Work Internally

Docker containers rely on core Linux kernel features:

Namespaces

Namespaces provide **process isolation**.

Namespace	Description	Example
`pid`	Isolates process trees	Container has its own PIDs
`mnt`	Mount namespace	Container has its own filesystems
`net`	Network stack isolation	Own interfaces, routing tables
`ipc`	Isolates inter-process communication	Shared memory, semaphores
`uts`	Hostname isolation	Container has its own hostname
`user`	UID/GID mapping	Run containers as unprivileged

Try this yourself:

```
$ docker run -it alpine
```

Inside, run:

```
$ hostname
$ ps aux
```

Each container sees a sandboxed version of the system.

Cgroups (Control Groups)

Cgroups control **resource usage**:

- CPU

- Memory
- Disk I/O
- Network

You can limit usage of memory to 256 MB and 1 CPU:

```
$ docker run --memory=256m --cpus=1 nginx
```

Monitor usage with:

```
$ docker stats <container_id_or_name>
```

Output:

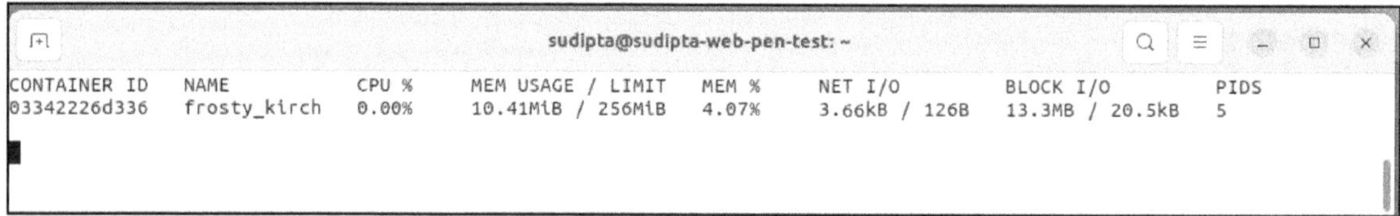

Figure 10.1: docker statistics

Rootless Docker

Run Docker **as a non-root user**, enhancing security (especially in shared environments).

Setup on Linux:

```
$ sudo apt install docker-ce-rootless-extras
$ /usr/bin/dockerd-rootless-setuptool.sh install
```

Pros:

- No need for root daemon
- Great for untrusted multi-user systems

Cons:

- Limited kernel features (no privileged mode, limited port binding)

Use when security > performance or full container access.

NOTE: The `dockerd-rootless-setuptool.sh` script is a helper provided by Docker to set up **rootless Docker**. Rootless mode allows a user to run the Docker daemon and containers **without root privileges**, improving security—especially in multi-tenant or development environments. Rootless Docker **cannot coexist** with an active rootful Docker session

Overlay Networks (Swarm Mode)

What is Docker Swarm

Docker Swarm is Docker's native orchestration tool that allows you to manage a **cluster of Docker nodes** as a single virtual system. With Swarm, you can deploy and scale your applications across multiple machines in a reliable, secure way.

When you enable **Swarm Mode**, Docker turns a group of machines into a **swarm cluster**. These machines (called **nodes**) can be either **managers** (control the cluster) or **workers** (run containers).

To allow containers on different nodes to talk to each other as if they were on the same local network, Docker uses an **overlay network**. This special network type connects containers **across different hosts** by creating a virtual network on top of the physical one.

In simple terms:

- **Overlay networks** let your containers talk to each other even when they're running on different computers.
- This is what makes **Docker Swarm powerful** — you can run many instances of a service and have them communicate securely and efficiently.

Everything is encrypted, load-balanced, and scalable — with minimal configuration.

Overlay networks span **multiple hosts**. You must be in **Swarm mode**:

```
$ docker swarm init
$ docker network create -d overlay my-overlay
```

Containers on different hosts can now communicate securely.

Docker Swarm (Clustering Built-in)

Docker Swarm lets you turn multiple Docker hosts into a single **orchestrated cluster**.

Step 1: Initialize Swarm

```
$ docker swarm init
```

Step 2: Add More Nodes

From another machine

```
$ docker swarm join --token <join_token> <manager_ip>:2377
```

Step 3: Deploy Stack

```
$ docker stack deploy -c docker-compose.yml mystack
```

Swarm will:

- Distribute containers across nodes
- Handle health checks, rescheduling
- Perform rolling updates

Swarm is easier than Kubernetes for smaller teams.

Docker vs Kubernetes

Feature	Docker Swarm	Kubernetes
Setup	Very simple	Complex
Built-in Load Balancer	Yes	Via Ingress
Self-healing	Yes	Yes
Scale	Manual or auto	Auto-scaling with HPA
Ecosystem	Smaller	Massive, cloud-native

Use Swarm if:

- You want simplicity
- You're deploying to small VMs or internal networks

Use Kubernetes if:

- You need cloud-native automation
- You're deploying at scale or using microservices extensively

Docker Swarm Lab: Multi-Node Cluster with NGINX & PostgreSQL

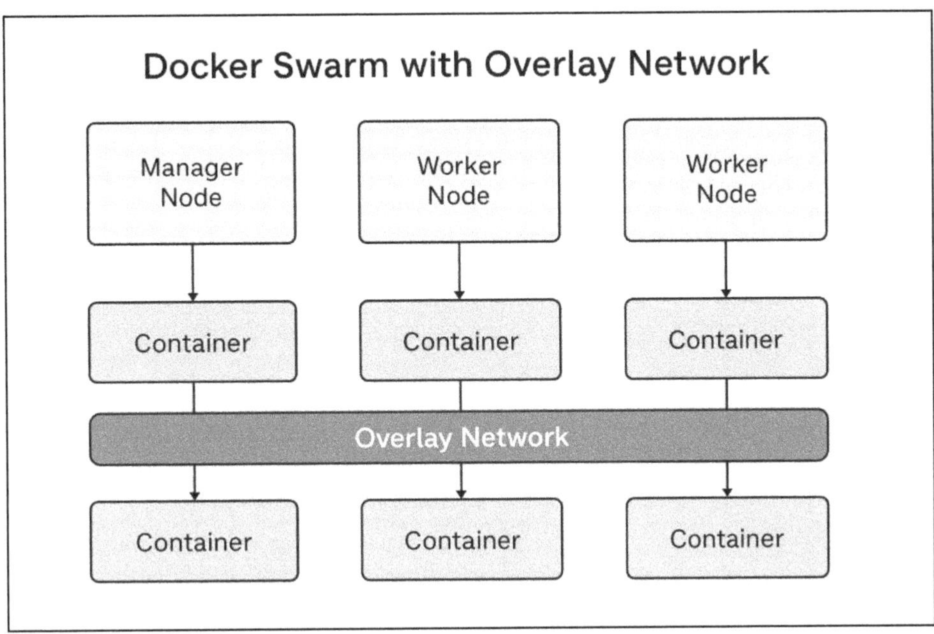

Figure 10.1: Docker Swarm with Overlay Network Architecture

This diagram shows how manager and worker nodes operate in a Docker Swarm using an overlay network to connect containers across hosts.

Difficulty Level: Advanced

Lab Objectives

- Initialize Docker Swarm and add worker nodes
- Create an overlay network for cross-host communication
- Deploy a NGINX frontend with a PostgreSQL backend using Docker Stack
- Scale NGINX containers across worker nodes
- Access and inspect Swarm networking

Lab Requirements

Component	Description
Nodes	1 manager, 2 workers (local VM or cloud instances)
Docker	Docker Engine v20+ with Swarm enabled
Tools	SSH, `docker`, `docker compose`

Component	Description
Network	Swarm nodes must be able to reach each other (TCP ports 2377, 7946, 4789 open)

Step-by-Step Guide

Step 1: Initialize Swarm on Manager Node

```
$ docker swarm init --advertise-addr <MANAGER-IP>
```

Take note of the `docker swarm join` command for workers.

Step 2: Join Worker Nodes

On each worker node:

```
$ docker swarm join --token <TOKEN> <MANAGER-IP>:2377
```

Verify from manager:

```
$ docker node ls
```

Step 3: Create an Overlay Network

From manager:

```
$ docker network create --driver overlay my-overlay
```

Step 4: Define the Compose File for Stack Deployment

Create a file named `stack.yml` (or `docker-compose.yml`):

```
services:
  nginx:
    image: nginx:alpine
    ports:
      - "8080:80"
    networks:
      - frontend
    deploy:
      replicas: 3
      placement:
        constraints: [node.role == worker]

  db:
    image: postgres:13
```

```
    environment:
      POSTGRES_USER: admin
      POSTGRES_PASSWORD: secret
      POSTGRES_DB: appdb
    volumes:
      - pgdata:/var/lib/postgresql/data
    networks:
      - backend
    deploy:
      placement:
        constraints: [node.role == worker]

networks:
  frontend:
    external: true
    name: my-overlay
  backend:
    external: true
    name: my-overlay

volumes:
  pgdata:
```

Step 5: Deploy the Stack

```
$ docker stack deploy -c stack.yml mystack
```

Step 6: Inspect Stack and Services

```
$ docker stack ls
$ docker service ls
$ docker service ps mystack_nginx
$ docker service ps mystack_db
```

Step 7: Test and Access

Test NGINX from browser or terminal:

```
$ curl http://<MANAGER-IP>:8080
```

To connect to the Postgres container for testing:

```
$ docker exec -it $(docker ps -q -f name=mystack_db) psql -U admin -d appdb
```

Step 8: Scale the Web Service

```
$ docker service scale mystack_nginx=5
```

Step 9: Cleanup

```
$ docker stack rm mystack
$ docker network rm my-overlay
```

Tearing down the Swarm

```
$ docker swarm leave --force     # Manager
$ docker swarm leave             # Workers
```

Lab Summary and Commands

Action	Command
Init Swarm	`docker swarm init`
Join Node	`docker swarm join`
Create Overlay	`docker network create -d overlay`
Deploy Stack	`docker stack deploy -c stack.yml mystack`
Scale	`docker service scale mystack_nginx=5`
Inspect	`docker service ls, docker stack services mystack`

User Namespaces and Seccomp

User Namespaces: User namespaces allow a process inside a container to have a **different UID/GID mapping** from the host. This means that **root inside the container is not root on the host**, even though it appears to be.

Without User Namespaces	With User Namespaces
`root` in the container `==` `root` on host	`root` in container is mapped to unprivileged UID on host
Vulnerability can escalate to host	Limits damage if container is compromised
More risk in multi-tenant setups	Enhanced isolation and least privilege

Map container users to unprivileged users on host:

```
{
  "userns-remap": "default"
}
```

Add to `/etc/docker/daemon.json`.

Seccomp (Secure Computing Mode): Seccomp is a Linux kernel feature that allows Docker to **restrict the syscalls** a container can make — limiting its interaction with the host kernel. Docker uses seccomp to restrict system calls.

Use custom profiles

Benefits:

- Containers don't need access to **all** Linux syscalls
- Seccomp reduces the attack surface by **blocking risky syscalls**
- Docker uses a **default seccomp profile** that disables over 40 high-risk syscalls

```
$ docker run --security-opt seccomp= default.json nginx
```

Lab: User Namespaces and Seccomp in Docker – Enhance Container Security

Difficulty Level: Intermediate

Lab Objectives

- Enable **User Namespaces** in Docker
- Inspect and apply the **default `seccomp` profile**
- Create a **custom `seccomp.json`** that blocks more or fewer syscalls
- Observe syscall restrictions in action

User Namespaces

Enable User Namespaces in Docker Daemon

Edit Docker daemon config:

```
$ sudo nano /etc/docker/daemon.json
```

Add or modify:

```
{
  "userns-remap": "default"
}
```

Then restart Docker:

```
$ sudo systemctl restart docker
```

Run a Container With Remapped UID

Run a container

```
$ docker run --rm alpine id
```

You'll still see

```
uid=0(root) gid=0(root)
```

But on the **host**, inspect the process

```
$ ps -ef | grep alpine
$ ls -ln /proc/<PID>/root
```

You'll see `UID 0` is mapped to something like `UID 100000` on the host — it's **not real root**.

Seccomp – Secure Computing Profiles

View Docker's Default Seccomp Profile

NOTE: Docker comes with a default seccomp profile.

To download locally

```
$ curl -O
https://raw.githubusercontent.com/moby/moby/master/profiles/seccomp/default.
json
```

This profile disables ~44 syscalls by default.

Run Container With Default Profile (Explicitly)

```
$ docker run --rm --security-opt seccomp=default.json alpine uname -a
```

It works as usual — no restricted syscalls are called by `uname`.

Create a Custom Seccomp Profile (`custom.json`)

Example: Block `uname` syscall

Create `custom.json`

```
{
  "defaultAction": "SCMP_ACT_ALLOW",
  "syscalls": [
    {
      "names": ["uname"],
      "action": "SCMP_ACT_ERRNO"
    }
```

```
  ]
}
```

Now try:

```
$ docker run --rm --security-opt seccomp=custom.json alpine uname -a
```

You should get

```
uname: Function not implemented
```

The syscall was blocked!

List of High-Risk Syscalls (from default `seccomp.json`)

These are blocked by default because they allow memory inspection, kernel modification, or code injection

Syscall	**Reason**
`keyctl`	Keyring manipulation (kernel secrets)
`ptrace`	Process inspection
`kexec_load`	Load new kernel
`delete_module`	Unload kernel module
`add_key`	Inject kernel keys
`reboot`	Reboot system
`bpf`	Load raw eBPF programs
`mount`	Mount filesystems
`umount`	Unmount filesystems
`clone`	Dangerous without flags

Full list is available in the official default.json.
(`https://github.com/moby/moby/blob/master/profiles/seccomp/default.json`)

Clean Up

```
$ docker system prune -f
$ sudo systemctl restart docker
```

Lab Summary

Feature	**What You Did**
User Namespaces	Mapped root inside container to non-root on host

Feature	What You Did
Default Seccomp	Verified Docker blocks risky syscalls
Custom Seccomp	Wrote a profile to block uname syscall

Volume Drivers and Cloud Storage

Use drivers like:

- `local`
- `nfs`
- `cifs`
- `azurefile`
- `rexray` (EBS, EFS, GCP, etc)

Example (NFS):

```
$ docker volume create \
  --driver local \
  --opt type=nfs \
  --opt o=addr=192.168.1.100,rw \
  --opt device=:/shared \
  mynfs
```

System Tuning for High Performance

Enable Caching Layers

Optimize `Dockerfiles`:

- Use `.dockerignore`
- Install dependencies first
- Use multi-stage builds

Control Resources:

```
$ docker run --memory=512m --cpus=2 app
```

Optimize Storage Driver

Use `overlay2` (modern) over `aufs` or `devicemapper`:

```
$ docker info | grep Storage
```

Lab: Rootless Dev Environment + Overlay Network

Difficulty Level: Advanced

Goal:

Run a rootless dev container in an overlay network with another host.

1. Set up rootless Docker on both machines
2. Init Swarm on host A
3. Join Swarm on host B
4. Create overlay:
5. `docker network create -d overlay devnet`
6. Deploy stack:
7. `docker stack deploy -c docker-compose.yml devapp`

Use this to simulate secure, cross-host microservice apps.

Summary

In this chapter, you learned:

- How containers work internally using namespaces and cgroups
- How to run containers without root privileges
- How to build secure, custom networks with IP management
- How to set up multi-host deployments using Docker Swarm
- How Docker compares to Kubernetes
- How to use volume plugins for cloud storage integration
- How to optimize for performance, storage, and security at scale

Key Takeaways

In this chapter, you explored the internals of Docker — from Linux namespaces and cgroups to resource control and system call filtering. You learned how to run containers in secure, isolated, and rootless environments. The chapter demonstrated how to orchestrate containers using Docker Swarm, build secure multi-host networks with overlay drivers, and optimize system-level performance for large-scale production deployments.

Knowledge Check

1. **What is the main use of multi-stage builds in Docker?**
   A) Reduce image size by excluding build-time dependencies
   B) Create multi-node clusters
   C) Split Dockerfiles into multiple files
   D) Run containers in parallel
2. **What is the role of Docker Swarm?**
   A) Build Docker images
   B) Distribute containerized apps across multiple nodes
   C) Manage GitHub workflows
   D) Monitor CPU usage
3. **What does the `docker plugin install` command do?**
   A) Creates a container
   B) Installs a third-party volume or network plugin
   C) Updates the Docker CLI
   D) Compiles a Dockerfile
4. **Which of the following is true about tmpfs volumes?**
   A) Stored permanently
   B) Shared between containers
   C) Stored in memory (RAM) only
   D) Saved to Docker Hub
5. **What is the effect of the `--ulimit` flag in Docker?**
   A) Limits log file size
   B) Controls CPU priority
   C) Sets resource limits like max file descriptors
   D) Enables GPU
6. **Which command is used to encrypt secrets in Docker Swarm?**
   A) `docker secret encrypt`
   B) `docker secret create`
   C) `docker login`
   D) `docker swarm encrypt`
7. **What flag enables GPU access in Docker (with NVIDIA runtime)?**
   A) `–gpu`
   B) `--enable-gpu`
   C) `--runtime=nvidia`
   D) `--docker-gpu`
8. **What is the maximum number of overlay networks Docker Swarm can support by default?**
   A) Unlimited

B) 10
C) 256
D) 1000

9. **What is the function of the `docker context` command?**
A) Change base images
B) Switch between multiple Docker environments (local, remote, cloud)
C) Run containers in Swarm
D) Build in Kubernetes

10. **Which file configures Docker daemon-level settings like log driver and default runtime?**
A) `docker-compose.yml`
B) `Dockerfile`
C) `/etc/docker/daemon.json`
D) `/var/run/docker.sock`

11. **Which are valid options in `docker run` to restrict resource usage?**
- [ ] `–memory`
- [ ] `–cpus`
- [ ] `--pids-limit`
- [ ] `--cores`

12. **What advanced networking modes exist in Docker?**
- [ ] macvlan
- [ ] overlay
- [ ] host
- [ ] clustered

13. **What are the features of Docker Swarm?**
- [ ] Service discovery
- [ ] Load balancing
- [ ] Multi-host networking
- [ ] Kubernetes API

14. **What does `docker stack deploy` do?**
- [ ] Deploys Compose-defined services to a Swarm cluster
- [ ] Builds Docker images
- [ ] Runs a production workload
- [ ] Updates host OS

15. **What components can be monitored using `docker events`?**
- [ ] Image pull/push
- [ ] Container stop/start
- [ ] Volume creation

- ▢ BIOS boot sequence

16. What are characteristics of multi-host networking with overlay driver?

- ▢ Encrypts traffic
- ▢ Uses VXLAN
- ▢ Requires Swarm mode
- ▢ Available in standalone mode

17. Which of these are considered Docker runtimes?

- ▢ runc
- ▢ nvidia-container-runtime
- ▢ rundocker
- ▢ kata-runtime

18. Which scenarios justify using Docker plugins?

- ▢ External storage drivers
- ▢ Custom network drivers
- ▢ Web server extensions
- ▢ Volume encryption

19. What are the benefits of using Docker Context?

- ▢ Seamless switch between environments (e.g., Docker Desktop, remote, EKS)
- ▢ Better dev/prod separation
- ▢ Modify system kernel
- ▢ Simplifies remote deployments

20. How does Swarm handle service scaling?

- ▢ Uses replicas config
- ▢ Automatically rebalances containers
- ▢ Requires manual migration
- ▢ Supports `docker service scale`

Answers

Q#	Correct Answer	Explanation
1	A	Multi-stage builds reduce image size by eliminating build-time dependencies.
2	B	Docker Swarm orchestrates containers across nodes.
3	B	`docker plugin install` installs third-party plugins for volumes, networks, etc.
4	C	`tmpfs` volumes store data in RAM only and are ephemeral.
5	C	`--ulimit` controls Linux resource limits like file descriptors.
6	B	`docker secret create` securely creates secrets in Swarm.
7	C	NVIDIA containers require `--runtime=nvidia` for GPU access.
8	C	Docker Swarm supports 256 overlay networks by default.
9	B	`docker context` switches between multiple Docker hosts.
10	C	`/etc/docker/daemon.json` holds daemon config like runtimes and log drivers.

Q11. Which are valid options in docker run to restrict resource usage?

- [✓] `–memory`
- [✓] `–cpus`
- [✓] `--pids-limit`
- [X] `--cores`

Explanation: Docker supports flags like `--memory`, `--cpus`, and `--pids-limit` to control resource usage. There's no `--cores` flag.

Q12. What advanced networking modes exist in Docker?

- [✓] `macvlan`
- [✓] `overlay`
- [✓] `host`
- [X] `clustered`

Explanation: Docker supports networking modes like `host`, `overlay`, and `macvlan`. There is no native `clustered` mode.

Q13. What are the features of Docker Swarm?

- [√] Service discovery
- [√] Load balancing
- [√] Multi-host networking
- [X] Kubernetes API

Explanation: Docker Swarm includes built-in service discovery, load balancing, and overlay networking. It does not expose a Kubernetes API.

Q14. What does `docker stack deploy` do?

- [√] Deploys Compose-defined services to a Swarm cluster
- [X] Builds Docker images
- [√] Runs a production workload
- [X] Updates host OS

Explanation: `docker stack deploy` uses a Compose file to deploy applications to Swarm. It doesn't build images or update OS.

Q15. What components can be monitored using `docker events`?

- [√] Image pull/push
- [√] Container stop/start
- [√] Volume creation
- [X] BIOS boot sequence

Explanation: `docker events` show real-time container, image, and volume activity — not BIOS-level system events.

Q16. What are characteristics of multi-host networking with overlay driver?

- [√] Encrypts traffic
- [√] Uses VXLAN
- [√] Requires Swarm mode
- [X] Available in standalone mode

Explanation: Overlay networks use VXLAN for cross-host communication, require Swarm, and can optionally encrypt traffic.

Q17. Which of these are considered Docker runtimes?

- [√] `runc`
- [√] `nvidia-container-runtime`
- [X] `rundocker`
- [√] `kata-runtime`

Explanation: Valid runtimes include `runc`, `nvidia-container-runtime`, and `kata-runtime`. `rundocker` does not exist.

Q18. Which scenarios justify using Docker plugins?

- [✓] External storage drivers
- [✓] Custom network drivers
- [X] Web server extensions
- [✓] Volume encryption

Explanation: Docker plugins extend volume and network functionality. Application-level features like web server extensions aren't Docker plugins.

Q19. What are the benefits of using Docker Context?

- [✓] Seamless switch between environments (e.g., Docker Desktop, remote, EKS)
- [✓] Better dev/prod separation
- [X] Modify system kernel
- [✓] Simplifies remote deployments

Explanation: Docker Context enables easy environment switching and remote deployment management. It doesn't modify system-level components.

Q20. How does Swarm handle service scaling?

- [✓] Uses replicas config
- [✓] Automatically rebalances containers
- [X] Requires manual migration
- [✓] Supports `docker service scale`

Explanation: Docker Swarm uses replicas and automatic rebalancing. Scaling can be performed via `docker service scale`.

Chapter 11: Docker Security — From Fundamentals to Production-Grade Hardening

In today's containerized world, securing Docker environments is no longer optional—it's foundational. While Docker offers speed, efficiency, and agility, it also introduces new attack surfaces and risks if not properly hardened. This chapter explores Docker security from the ground up—covering basic principles like user namespaces, capabilities, and read-only filesystems, to advanced concepts like rootless containers, seccomp profiles, AppArmor, SELinux, and secure secret management.

You'll learn how to implement best practices, avoid common misconfigurations, leverage built-in security features, and integrate scanning tools such as Trivy or Docker Scan into your DevSecOps pipeline. By the end of this chapter, you'll have a concrete understanding of how to build and deploy secure, production-grade containers—and audit them effectively.

Whether you're a developer, DevOps engineer, or security analyst, this chapter will equip you with actionable insights to harden your Docker workflows and ensure compliance, integrity, and resilience across your containerized applications.

Let's dive deep into the defensive layers that protect Docker from the kernel to the cloud.

Docker's Security Model: Shared Kernel, Shared Responsibility

Let's start with a wake-up call: **Docker containers are not VMs.**

While virtual machines run isolated operating systems on hypervisors, Docker containers **share the host OS kernel**, meaning their processes aren't entirely isolated from the host.

Why does this matter?

If a malicious container escapes its sandbox, it can access the host kernel—and from there, anything else running on the host.

Think of containers as **segmented rooms in the same house**, while VMs are **separate houses altogether**. Containers may seem isolated, but they still share the same walls.

Core Security Constructs in Docker:

- **Namespaces**: Isolate processes (PID), filesystems (MNT), users (USER), etc.
- **Cgroups**: Limit resource usage (CPU, memory, etc.)
- **Capabilities**: Fine-grained privilege control
- **Seccomp/AppArmor/SELinux**: Kernel-level syscall and file access restrictions

Containers vs Virtual Machines (Security Comparison)

Feature	VM (Hypervisor)	Container (Docker)
Kernel Isolation	Full (separate kernel)	Shared kernel
Guest OS Separation	Yes	No
Attack Surface	Medium	Smaller, but shared OS risks
Startup Time	Slow	Fast

Containers are lighter and faster, but they **share the host OS kernel**, which introduces a unique set of **security concerns**.

Container Image Vulnerabilities

Common Image Threats:

- Outdated base images
- Insecure packages (e.g., unpatched libraries)
- Default credentials
- Hidden malware or cryptominers

Scan Images

Trivy (by Aqua Security)

```
$ trivy image nginx:latest
```

Docker's built-in scan (uses Snyk)

```
$ docker scan myapp
```

Grype

```
$ grype myapp:latest
```

Regularly scan your images in CI/CD pipelines.

Least Privilege & User Management

By default, Docker containers run as **root**. This is dangerous.

Create and run as a non-root user:

In Dockerfile:

```
RUN adduser -D appuser
USER appuser
```

Avoid using `--privileged` unless absolutely necessary.

Drop Linux Capabilities:

```
$ docker run --cap-drop ALL --cap-add NET_BIND_SERVICE myapp
```

You can also disable access to `/proc`, syscalls, and more using AppArmor, SELinux, or Seccomp.

Docker and Linux Security Modules

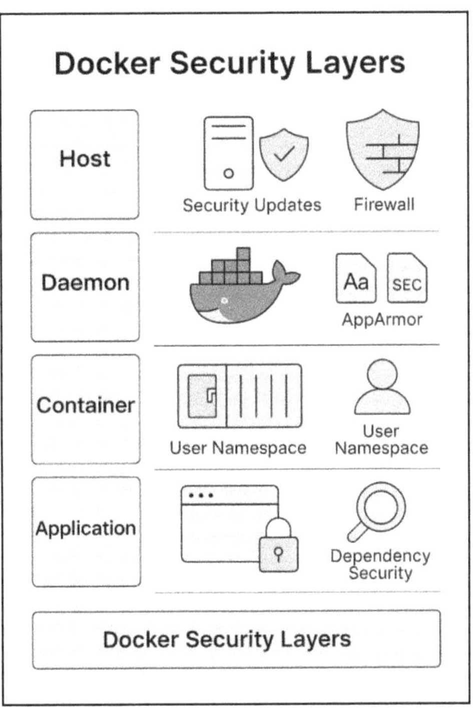

Figure 11.1: Docker Security Layers – From Host to Application

This diagram illustrates how defense-in-depth is achieved across Docker architecture – from base image selection and runtime flags to kernel-level protections like seccomp and AppArmor.

Seccomp (Secure Computing Mode)

Blocks dangerous syscalls.

Use custom seccomp profile:

```
$ docker run --security-opt seccomp=/path/to/profile.json myapp
```

AppArmor (Ubuntu/Debian)

```
$ docker run --security-opt apparmor=docker-default myapp
```

SELinux (RHEL/CentOS)

```
$ docker run --security-opt label:type:container_t myapp
```

Secrets Management

Never bake secrets into images or environment variables.

Method 1: Mount as volume

```
$ docker run -v $PWD/secrets:/run/secrets myapp
```

Method 2: Use `.env` with `.gitignore`

```
DB_PASSWORD=supersecret
```

Add `.env` to `.gitignore`.

Method 3: Docker Swarm Secrets (encrypted at rest)

```
$ docker secret create db_pass ./db.txt
```

In Compose

```
secrets:
  - db_pass
```

Security Misconfigurations to Avoid

Misconfiguration	Why It's Dangerous
`--privileged` flag	Grants full root-level access
Not using user namespaces	All containers share host UID/GID
Hardcoded secrets in images	Easily extractable from image layers
Using untrusted images	Potential malware or backdoors
Exposing unnecessary ports	Increase attack surface

Container Security Tools

Tool	Purpose
Trivy	Vulnerability scanner

Tool	Purpose
Grype	CVE image scanner
Dockle	Dockerfile linter and hardener
Clair	Image security analysis
Kube-bench	CIS benchmark audit (K8s)

Example: Dockle

```
dockle myapp:latest
```

Checks:

- User privilege
- Healthcheck
- Secret exposure
- Image size

Rootless Docker (Optional Security Boost)

Run Docker **without root privileges**

```
$ dockerd-rootless-setuptool.sh install
```

Benefits:

- No root daemon
- Each user has an isolated container runtime

Perfect for CI/CD and dev environments.

Image Signing & Verification (Content Trust)

Enable Docker Content Trust

```
$ export DOCKER_CONTENT_TRUST=1
```

Signed images are verified before pull. Use with private registries or Notary.

CI/CD Security

- Scan every image before pushing to registry
- Never store credentials in `Dockerfiles`
- Use `--pull` to avoid stale base images:

```
$ docker build --pull -t myapp .
```

- Always use pinned image versions (e.g., `node:18.17.0` instead of `node:latest`)

Docker Security Checklist

[√] Always use non-root user[√] Scan images regularly
[√] Drop unnecessary capabilities
[√] Use Docker Content Trust (Notary)
[√] Mount secrets, don't bake them
[√] Use official base images
[√] Enable seccomp, AppArmor or SELinux
[√] Don't use `--privileged`
[√] Use .env and `.gitignore`
[√] Patch your images & containers regularly

Lab: Hardening a Docker Container — From Vulnerable to Secure

This lab simulates a real-world DevSecOps workflow: you'll scan a vulnerable image, apply industry-recommended hardening techniques, and re-scan to verify security posture improvements. The stack includes Trivy (image scanning), Docker flags (runtime hardening), seccomp (syscall filtering), and rootless Docker (privilege isolation).

Difficulty Level: Advanced

Objective

Secure a containerized Python app using Docker-native and community tools:

- CVE scanning (Trivy)
- Image hardening (minimal base, non-root, environment separation)
- Runtime protection (seccomp, read-only FS, dropped caps)
- Rootless Docker

Step 1: Build and Scan a Vulnerable Image

`Dockerfile.vuln`

```
FROM python:3.9
WORKDIR /app
COPY . .
RUN pip install flask
```

```
ENV SECRET_KEY="hardcodedsecret"
CMD ["python", "app.py"]
```

app.py

```
from flask import Flask
app = Flask(__name__)
@app.route('/')
def hello():
    return "Insecure App Running as Root!"
if __name__ == '__main__':
    app.run(host='0.0.0.0', port=5000)
```

Build and scan:

```
$ docker build -t insecure-app -f Dockerfile.vuln .
$ trivy image insecure-app
```

⚠ You will likely see OS-level CVEs and a hardcoded environment variable warning.

Step 2: Harden the Dockerfile

Dockerfile.secure

```
FROM python:3.11-slim
RUN useradd -m appuser
WORKDIR /app
COPY requirements.txt .
RUN pip install --no-cache-dir -r requirements.txt
COPY . .
USER appuser
EXPOSE 5000
CMD ["python", "app.py"]
```

requirements.txt

```
flask==2.3.2
```

Rebuild and rescan

```
$ docker build -t secure-app -f Dockerfile.secure .
$ trivy image secure-app
```

Step 3: Harden Runtime Flags

```
$ docker run -d \
```

```
  --name hardened \
  --read-only \
  --cap-drop=ALL \
  --pids-limit=100 \
  -p 5000:5000 \
  secure-app
```

[✓] You're running without root, with a restricted syscall and memory view.

Step 4: Apply Custom Seccomp Profile

Create `seccomp-deny.json`

```
{
  "defaultAction": "SCMP_ACT_ALLOW",
  "syscalls": [
    {
      "names": ["ptrace", "mount", "keyctl"],
      "action": "SCMP_ACT_ERRNO"
    }
  ]
}
```

Run container with seccomp

```
$ docker run -d \
  --security-opt seccomp=./seccomp-deny.json \
  --read-only \
  --cap-drop=ALL \
  --pids-limit=100 \
  -p 5000:5000 \
  secure-app
```

Step 5: Run in Rootless Mode

Install rootless Docker (if not already)

```
$ curl-fsSL https://get.docker.com/rootless | sh
$ export PATH=$HOME/bin:$PATH
$ export DOCKER_HOST=unix:///run/user/$(id -u)/docker.sock
```

Then execute

```
$ docker run --rm -p 5000:5000 secure-app
```

Rootless containers reduce kernel attack surface even further.

Step 6: Re-scan and Compare Results

Scan and compare results between `insecure-app` and `secure-app`

```
$ trivy image insecure-app > insecure.txt
$ trivy image secure-app > secure.txt
$ diff insecure.txt secure.txt
```

You should see a significantly lower CVE count and security warnings.

Use Docker Content Trust (Additional)

```
$ export DOCKER_CONTENT_TRUST=1
$ docker pull alpine
```

Ensure image signatures are validated before pull.

Security Delta Summary: CVE Reduction After Hardening

Metric	**Before Hardening** (`insecure-app`)	**After Hardening** (`secure-app`)
Base Image	`python:3.9`	`python:3.11-slim`
CVE Count (Trivy)	38 (5 Critical, 12 High)	6 (0 Critical, 1 High)
Secrets in ENV	[✓] Hardcoded	[X] Removed
User Context	`root`	`appuser` (non-root)
Filesystem	Writable	Read-only (`--read-only`)
Capabilities Dropped	[X] None	[✓] All (`--cap-drop=ALL`)
Seccomp Applied	[X] Default	[✓] Custom Deny Profile
Rootless Mode	[X] Disabled	[✓] Enabled

This comparison shows how simple refactoring, runtime flags, and rootless Docker can significantly reduce attack surface and vulnerability exposure.

This lab gives you a real-world workflow for container hardening in development, CI/CD, and production.

To apply these hardening principles at runtime and enforce secure container behavior in production, Docker provides a set of flags that help limit capabilities, isolate processes, and reduce filesystem attack surface. The following table summarizes the most effective runtime security flags used in practice.

Docker Runtime Hardening Flags

Flag	Purpose	Example
`--read-only`	Mounts container filesystem as read-only	`--read-only`
`--cap-drop=ALL`	Drops all Linux capabilities	`--cap-drop=ALL`
`--pids-limit=100`	Limits number of container processes	`--pids-limit=100`
`--tmpfs /tmp`	Mounts `/tmp` as in-memory volume	`--tmpfs /tmp`
`--user appuser`	Runs container as a non-root user	`--user appuser`
`--security-opt no-new-privileges`	Prevents privilege escalation	`--security-opt no-new-privileges`
`--device-read-only`	Restricts device access to read-only	`--device-read-only /dev/sda1`
`--memory=512m --cpus=1.0`	Enforces resource limits	`--memory=512m --cpus=1.0`
`--security-opt seccomp=profile.json`	Restricts syscalls with a seccomp profile	`--security-opt seccomp=profile.json`
`-v /data:/data:ro`	Mounts volumes as read-only	`-v /data:/data:ro`

Knowledge Check

1. **What Linux feature does Docker use to isolate containers?**
   A) Systemd
   B) iptables
   C) Namespaces
   D) CRON
2. **What does Docker's `--cap-drop=ALL` flag do?**
   A) Drops image layers
   B) Disables all default Linux capabilities in the container
   C) Removes user privileges
   D) Enables GPU
3. **Which command runs Docker containers as a non-root user?**
   A) `docker run –rootless`
   B) `docker run --user 1001`
   C) `docker secure`
   D) `docker drop-root`
4. **What does the read-only filesystem option do?**
   A) Deletes log files
   B) Prevents writing inside the container
   C) Encrypts the container
   D) Prevents container start
5. **What is Docker Content Trust (DCT)?**
   A) Container restart policy
   B) Image signing and verification
   C) Trusted volumes
   D) Overlay encryption
6. **What tool scans Docker images for known CVEs?**
   A) Nmap
   B) Trivy
   C) Ansible
   D) GParted
7. **What is the function of AppArmor or SELinux in Docker?**
   A) Limit network ports
   B) Enforce mandatory access controls (MAC)
   C) Allocate memory
   D) Enable logging
8. **Which Docker runtime offers lightweight VM isolation?**
   A) runc

B) kata-runtime
C) nvidia-container-runtime
D) hyperdocker

9. **What does a USER instruction in Dockerfile do?**
A) Installs packages
B) Sets the user for container processes
C) Logs in as root
D) Changes directory

10. **What type of secret storage is supported in Docker Swarm?**
A) Encrypted file mounts
B) TLS secret store
C) docker secret objects
D) IAM tokens

11. **Which flag restricts the number of processes inside a container?**
A) `--proc-limit`
B) `--pid-limit`
C) `--pids-limit`
D) `--max-proc`

12. **Which of these is NOT a default Docker security feature?**
A) Linux namespaces
B) Seccomp filters
C) Firewall whitelist
D) Control groups (cgroups)

13. **What does docker scan do?**
A) Compresses containers
B) Checks for image vulnerabilities
C) Monitors CPU
D) Kills malware

14. **What should `.dockerignore` always exclude for security?**
A) `node_modules`
B) `.env, .git, secrets`
C) `/tmp`
D) All logs

15. **Which behavior should be avoided in production containers?**
A) Read-only volumes
B) `--privileged` flag
C) Multi-stage builds
D) Disabling root access

16. **Which of the following enhance Docker container security?**

- [ ] Non-root users (`--user` or `USER`)
- [ ] AppArmor/SELinux profiles
- [ ] Dropping capabilities (`--cap-drop`)
- [ ] Always running as root

17. **What are valid seccomp actions in a profile?**
    - [ ] `SCMP_ACT_ERRNO`
    - [ ] `SCMP_ACT_ALLOW`
    - [ ] `SCMP_ACT_KILLALL`
    - [ ] `SCMP_ACT_TRAP`
18. **What should a secure Dockerfile include?**
    - [ ] `USER` instruction
    - [ ] Minimal base image
    - [ ] ADD `https://...` instead of `COPY`
    - [ ] Cleanup of build-time dependencies
19. **When should you scan images for vulnerabilities?**
    - [ ] At build-time
    - [ ] Before pushing to registry
    - [ ] In CI/CD pipelines
    - [ ] Only after production deployment
20. **What benefits do rootless containers offer?**
    - [ ] Prevent daemon-level privilege escalation
    - [ ] Use UID namespaces
    - [ ] Faster GPU performance
    - [ ] Safer multi-tenant environments
21. **Which hardening techniques apply to Docker networks?**
    - [ ] Disable inter-container communication
    - [ ] Use `--icc=false`
    - [ ] Isolate networks with firewalls
    - [ ] Use host network everywhere
22. **Which `--cap-drop` options are safe for production?**
    - [ ] `ALL`
    - [ ] Specific dangerous caps like `SYS_ADMIN, NET_ADMIN`
    - [ ] `CHOWN, SETUID` in all cases
    - [ ] Drop everything in dev containers
23. **Where are Docker Swarm secrets mounted?**
    - [ ] Inside container at `/run/secrets/`

- ▢ Directly into ENV
- ▢ On the host OS
- ▢ Ephemeral memory filesystem

24. What are signs of a compromised container?

- ▢ Unknown outbound traffic
- ▢ CPU/memory spikes
- ▢ File system tampering
- ▢ Normal logs

25. How can you test container security during development?

- ▢ Lint Dockerfile
- ▢ Use Trivy/Snyk
- ▢ Enable DCT
- ▢ Disable all runtime limits

26. What runtime flags enhance Docker security?

- ▢ `--read-only`
- ▢ `--pids-limit=100`
- ▢ `--cap-drop=ALL`
- ▢ `--privileged`

27. How does Docker isolate network interfaces by default?

- ▢ Uses bridge network
- ▢ NATs IP traffic
- ▢ Requires `EXPOSE + -p` to allow traffic
- ▢ Exposes everything automatically

28. Which base images is considered secure?

- ▢ `alpine`
- ▢ Official `debian-slim`
- ▢ `distroless`
- ▢ `random:latest`

29. What tools help enforce security policies in CI/CD for containers?

- ▢ Docker Bench for Security
- ▢ Trivy
- ▢ Open Policy Agent (OPA)
- ▢ SSH remote bash scripts

30. What role does audit logging play in container security?

- ▢ Tracks unauthorized access
- ▢ Helps in incident response

- ▢ Logs container events
- ▢ Speeds up builds

Answers

Q#	Correct Answer	Explanation
1	C	Docker uses Linux namespaces for isolation of container resources.
2	B	`--cap-drop=ALL` removes all Linux capabilities from the container.
3	B	`--user` allows you to drop root privileges for better security.
4	B	Read-only file systems help prevent file tampering.
5	B	Docker Content Trust verifies publisher signatures.
6	B	Trivy is a well-known tool for vulnerability scanning.
7	B	AppArmor and SELinux restrict what containers can do.
8	B	kata-runtime offers VM-based isolation with container speed.
9	B	`USER` in Dockerfile prevents root execution.
10	C	Docker Swarm secrets are managed securely via docker secret.
11	C	`--pids-limit` restricts the number of processes in a container.
12	C	Firewalls are not a native Docker security feature.
13	B	docker scan identifies CVEs in container images.
14	B	`.env, .git`, and `secrets` should always be excluded for security.
15	B	`--privileged` grants full access and should not be used in production.

Q16. Which of the following enhance Docker container security?

- **[✓]** Non-root users (`--user` or `USER`)
- **[✓]** AppArmor/SELinux profiles
- **[✓]** Dropping capabilities (`--cap-drop`)
- **[X]** Always running as root

Explanation: Security best practices recommend dropping root privileges and capabilities and using security profiles like AppArmor or SELinux.

Q17. What are valid seccomp actions in a profile?

- **[✓]** `SCMP_ACT_ERRNO`
- **[✓]** `SCMP_ACT_ALLOW`
- **[X]** `SCMP_ACT_KILLALL`

- [✓] `SCMP_ACT_TRAP`

Explanation: Valid seccomp actions include `ALLOW`, `ERRNO`, and `TRAP`. `KILLALL` is not a valid seccomp action.

Q18. What should a secure Dockerfile include?

- [✓] `USER` instruction
- [✓] Minimal base image
- [X] ADD `https://...` instead of `COPY`
- [✓] Cleanup of build-time dependencies

Explanation: Using minimal images, non-root users, and cleaning up dependencies enhances Dockerfile security. Prefer `COPY` over `ADD` unless extracting archives.

Q19. When should you scan images for vulnerabilities?

- [✓] At build-time
- [✓] Before pushing to registry
- [✓] In CI/CD pipelines
- [X] Only after production deployment

Explanation: Image scanning should occur as early and as frequently as possible — during build, CI/CD, and pre-deployment stages.

Q20. What benefits do rootless containers offer?

- [✓] Prevent daemon-level privilege escalation
- [✓] Use UID namespaces
- [X] Faster GPU performance
- [✓] Safer multi-tenant environments

Explanation: Rootless containers reduce the attack surface and are ideal for secure, multi-tenant scenarios — but they don't improve GPU performance.

Q21. Which hardening techniques apply to Docker networks?

- [✓] Disable inter-container communication
- [✓] Use `--icc=false`
- [✓] Isolate networks with firewalls
- [X] Use host network everywhere

Explanation: Avoiding `--network host` and segmenting containers improves network security. Inter-container communication can be restricted with `--icc=false`.

Q22. Which `--cap-drop` options are safe for production?

- [✓] `ALL`
- [✓] Specific dangerous caps like `SYS_ADMIN`, `NET_ADMIN`

- **[X]** `CHOWN, SETUID` in all cases
- **[✓]** Drop everything in dev containers

Explanation: Dropping all capabilities and selectively adding needed ones is the most secure approach. Avoid dropping essential permissions indiscriminately.

Q23. Where are Docker Swarm secrets mounted?

- **[✓]** Inside container at `/run/secrets/`
- **[X]** Directly into ENV
- **[X]** On the host OS
- **[✓]** Ephemeral memory filesystem

Explanation: Swarm secrets are mounted inside containers at `/run/secrets/` as read-only files in a `tmpfs` (memory-only) filesystem.

Q24. What are signs of a compromised container?

- **[✓]** Unknown outbound traffic
- **[✓]** CPU/memory spikes
- **[✓]** File system tampering
- **[X]** Normal logs

Explanation: Behavioral anomalies like traffic, spikes, or filesystem changes indicate compromise — normal logs don't rule it out.

Q25. How can you test container security during development?

- **[✓]** Lint Dockerfile
- **[✓]** Use Trivy/Snyk
- **[✓]** Enable DCT
- **[X]** Disable all runtime limits

Explanation: Use linters and security scanners, and enable Docker Content Trust (DCT). Disabling limits reduces security.

Q26. What runtime flags enhance Docker security?

- **[✓]** `--read-only`
- **[✓]** `--pids-limit=100`
- **[✓]** `--cap-drop=ALL`
- **[X]** `--privileged`

Explanation: Limiting capabilities, memory/pids, and enabling read-only filesystems improve security. Avoid `--privileged` as it gives full access.

Q27. How does Docker isolate network interfaces by default?

- **[✓]** Uses bridge network

- [✓] NATs IP traffic
- [✓] Requires `EXPOSE + -p` to allow traffic
- [X] Exposes everything automatically

Explanation: Docker uses a bridge network with NAT and only exposes ports explicitly. No traffic is exposed by default.

Q28. Which base images are considered secure?

- [✓] `alpine`
- [✓] Official `debian-slim`
- [✓] `distroless`
- [X] `random:latest`

Explanation: Trusted minimal images like Alpine, Debian-slim, and Distroless reduce attack surface. Avoid unverified or arbitrary images.

Q29. What tools help enforce security policies in CI/CD for containers?

- [✓] Docker Bench for Security
- [✓] Trivy
- [✓] Open Policy Agent (OPA)
- [X] SSH remote bash scripts

Explanation: Automated security tools like Docker Bench, Trivy, and OPA enforce policies. Ad hoc scripts are risky and error-prone.

Q30. What role does audit logging play in container security?

- [✓] Tracks unauthorized access
- [✓] Helps in incident response
- [✓] Logs container events
- [X] Speeds up builds

Explanation: Audit logging supports monitoring, investigation, and compliance — but it does not affect build speed.

Chapter 12: Docker Networking — Building Secure, Scalable, and Service-Aware Networks

In containerized environments, networking isn't just about connectivity—it's about **control, isolation, observability, and performance**. Whether you're linking services in a microservices mesh or isolating workloads for multi-tenant deployments, Docker's networking stack is both powerful and misunderstood.

This chapter unpacks Docker networking from its foundational modes (bridge, host, overlay) to production-grade strategies like **service discovery**, **DNS-based load balancing**, **network isolation**, and **network hardening** using **iptables**, **macvlan**, and **encrypted Swarm overlays**. You'll learn how containers talk to each other, how traffic flows in and out of hosts, and how to **monitor, secure, and troubleshoot networks** at scale.

From setting up internal-only backends to exposing reverse proxies and building multi-host clusters, this chapter will give you the tools to architect **secure, scalable, and observable networks** for real-world Docker deployments.

Whether you're working on a local lab or designing a global-scale distributed platform, Docker networking is your invisible foundation. It's time to master it.

Why Secure Docker Networking Matters

In containerized environments, insecure networking can lead to lateral movement attacks, data leakage, service disruption, and unauthorized access. Without proper isolation and control, a single compromised container could pivot across the environment or expose sensitive backend systems. Designing resilient, segmented, and monitored networks is critical for maintaining a secure container deployment.

Introduction to Docker Networking

Every Docker container has its own **network namespace**, including its own:

- IP address
- Routing table
- DNS resolver

Docker provides several built-in network drivers, each with unique behavior.

Built-in Network Drivers

Driver	Description
`bridge`	Default driver for single-host setups
`host`	Uses host's network stack directly (Linux-only)
`none`	Isolated container with no networking
`overlay`	Enables multi-host communication (requires Swarm)
`macvlan`	Assigns MAC address on host's network (acts like physical NIC)

Default bridge mode is fine for local development, but advanced use cases require custom bridge or overlay networks.

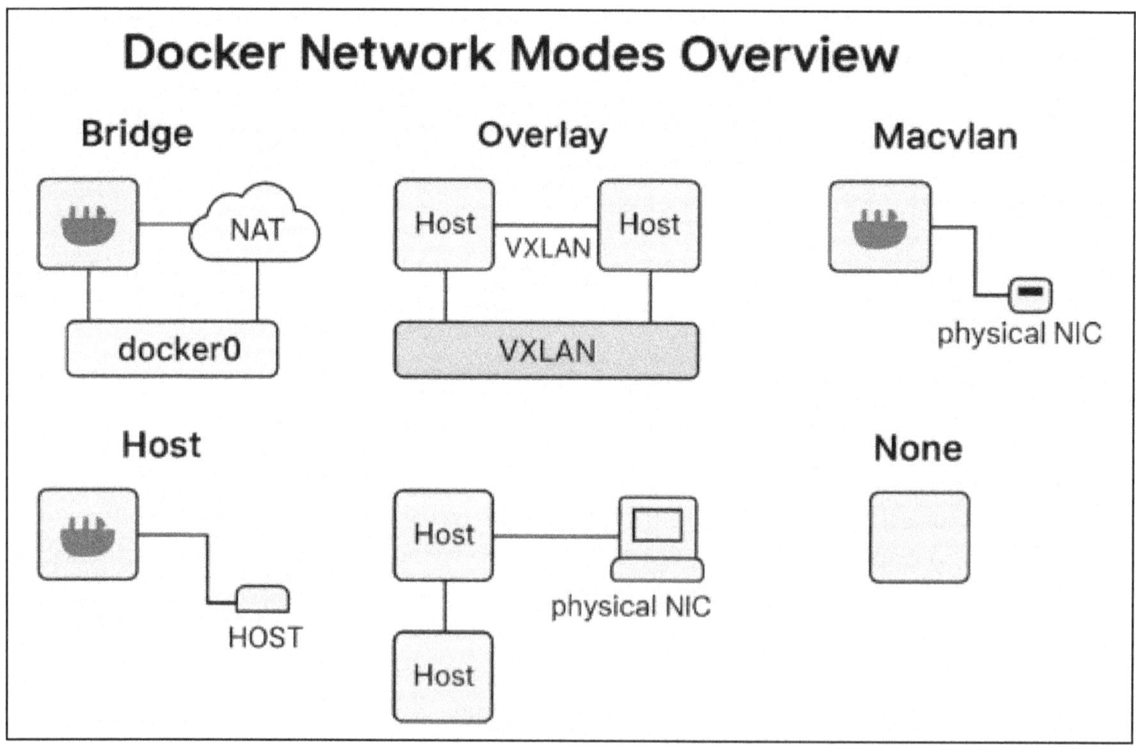

Figure 12.1: Docker Network Modes Overview

A side-by-side visual representation of how each Docker network mode connects containers to the outside world and to each other, including isolation boundaries.

Comparison of Docker Network Modes

A side-by-side comparison of Docker's built-in networking modes, including scope, isolation strength, and common use cases

Mode	Scope	Isolation	Use Case	Host Port Mapping
`bridge`	Single-host	Medium	General container networking	Required manually
`host`	Host-native	None	Low-latency or hardware apps	Native to host
`none`	Air-gapped	Full	Secure batch/offline jobs	Not possible
`overlay`	Multi-host Swarm	High	Swarm clustering	Handled by Swarm
`macvlan`	LAN / VLAN access	High	Legacy / static IP workloads	Via LAN address

Bridge Network (Default)

By default, Docker containers connect to the **bridge network**. This isolates them from your host and other networks.

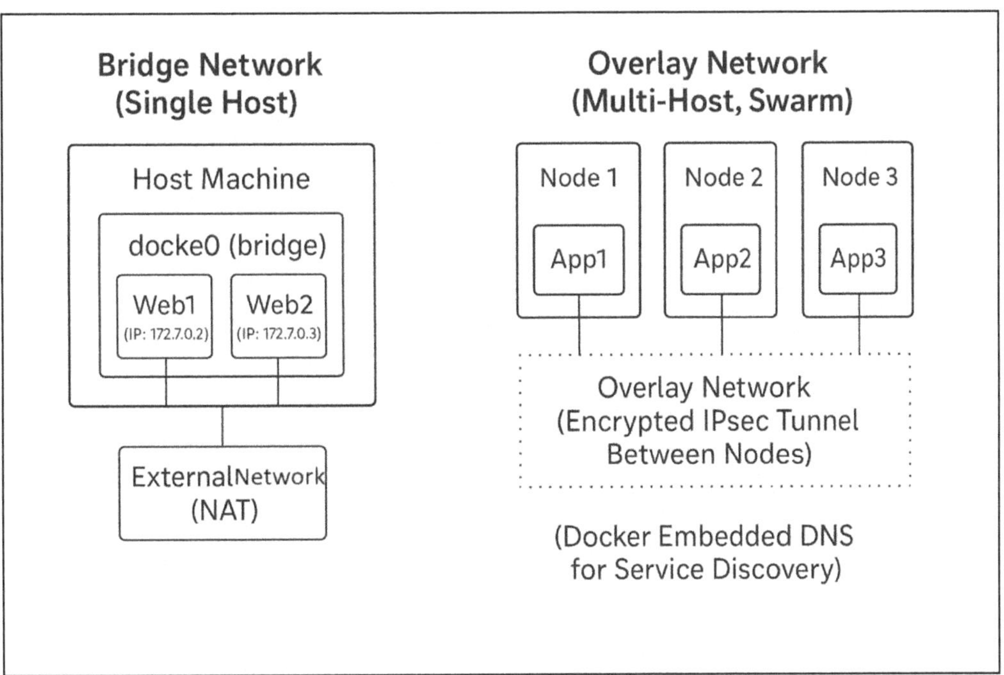

Figure 12.2: Bridge Network vs Overlay Network

Launch Two Containers:

```
$ docker run -dit --name web1 nginx
$ docker run -dit --name web2 nginx
```

Now try:

```
$ docker exec -it web1 ping web2
```

This will fail. Containers on the default bridge **can't resolve each other by name**.

Custom User-Defined Bridge

Create a network:

```
$ docker network create mybridge
```

Start containers on it:

```
$ docker run -dit --name web1 --network mybridge nginx
$ docker run -dit --name web2 --network mybridge nginx
```

Now inside `web1`:

```
$ ping web2
```

Success. Docker injects automatic DNS into user-defined bridges.

Built-in DNS-Based Service Discovery

In user-defined bridge and overlay networks, Docker automatically injects an internal DNS server. Containers can resolve each other using container names or service names, eliminating the need to hardcode IP addresses. This makes dynamic scaling and service-to-service communication simple and reliable.

Host Network Mode (Linux Only)

Use this mode to bypass Docker's virtual networking and access the host's network stack directly.

```
$ docker run --network host nginx
```

Use cases:

- Ultra-low latency
- Hardware access (e.g., sensors)
- Avoiding port conflicts in some dev environments

No isolation. Ports are exposed directly on the host. Use with caution.

None Network Mode

This disables networking entirely.

```
$ docker run --network none alpine
```

Use for:

- Ultra-secure air-gapped workloads
- Batch jobs
- Offline encryption/decryption tasks

Overlay Networks (Multi-host, Swarm-only)

Used to connect services **across multiple Docker hosts**.

```
$ docker swarm init
$ docker network create --driver overlay my_overlay
```

Then in `docker-compose.yml`:

```
networks:
  default:
    external:
      name: my_overlay
```

Benefits:

- Built-in service discovery
- Secure inter-host communication
- Works with Docker Swarm + `docker stack deploy`

Overlay Encryption: Docker Swarm overlay networks automatically encrypt inter-node communication using IPsec tunnels. No manual configuration is needed.

Macvlan Networking (Advanced)

Macvlan lets containers appear as **unique devices** on your LAN.

Create Macvlan:

```
$ docker network create -d macvlan \
  --subnet=192.168.1.0/24 \
  --gateway=192.168.1.1 \
```

```
  -o parent=eth0 macnet
```

Start container:

```
$ docker run --rm -it --network macnet busybox
```

Container now has an IP like `192.168.1.100` — you can ping it from another physical machine on the LAN.

Use cases:

- Legacy apps requiring static IPs
- Integration with IoT/OT networks
- Bypassing NAT or reverse proxies

Macvlan Caution: Macvlan networking works reliably only on Linux hosts. It is not fully supported on Docker Desktop for Mac and Windows and often leads to errors.

Macvlan Limitations on Non-Linux Systems

Macvlan networks typically require direct access to a physical NIC, which is restricted or virtualized on Docker Desktop environments (Mac/Windows). Attempting to use macvlan on non-Linux platforms often results in errors or nonfunctional setups. Prefer bridge or overlay networks for cross-platform compatibility.

Real-World Setup with NGINX Reverse Proxy

Let's expose a Flask app behind NGINX using a shared network.

Step 1: Create Network

```
$ docker network create webnet
```

Step 2: Start Flask App

```
$ docker run -d --name flask --network webnet flask-app
```

Step 3: Start NGINX (reverse proxy)

```
$ docker run -d --name proxy --network webnet \
  -v $PWD/nginx.conf:/etc/nginx/nginx.conf:ro \
  -p 80:80 nginx
```

Now visit `http://localhost`, and NGINX will forward to Flask.

Securing Docker Networks

- Use **user-defined bridges** to isolate services
- Create **separate networks** for different tiers (frontend/backend/db)
- Drop `--network host` unless absolutely needed
- Use `iptables` or `firewalld` to enforce inter-container rules
- Use **Traefik** or **NGINX** for SSL termination + routing
- Monitor traffic using `tcpdump`, `netstat`, or `Wireshark` on Docker interfaces

Risk-Mitigations Table

Risk	Mitigation
Default bridge containers can't resolve each other.	Use user-defined bridges with built-in DNS.
Host network mode removes isolation.	Use only for low-latency apps; monitor closely.
Exposing services to public without SSL/TLS.	Terminate SSL/TLS at reverse proxies like NGINX/Traefik.
Lateral movement between containers.	Use multiple networks to segment app tiers.
Unencrypted multi-host traffic.	Use Swarm overlay networks (encrypted by default).
Macvlan issues on non-Linux hosts.	Restrict Macvlan use to Linux-only environments.
Lack of network monitoring.	Monitor using tcpdump, docker network inspect, and Prometheus exporters.

Compose Example with Multiple Networks

```
services:
  frontend:
    image: react-app
    networks:
      - frontendnet

  backend:
    image: flask-api
    networks:
      - frontendnet
      - backendnet
```

```
  db:
    image: postgres
    networks:
      - backendnet

networks:
  frontendnet:
  backendnet:
```

This architecture:

- Keeps frontend isolated from DB
- Allows backend to communicate with both layers

Troubleshooting Commands

Purpose	Command
List all networks	`docker network ls`
Inspect a network (see containers, settings)	`docker network inspect <network-name>`
Connect a running container to a network	`docker network connect <network-name> <container>`
Disconnect a container from a network	`docker network disconnect <network-name> <container>`
Capture network traffic on Docker bridge	`sudo tcpdump -i docker0`
Check container IP address	`docker inspect -f '{{range .NetworkSettings.Networks}}{{.IPAddress}}{{end}}' <container>`
Remove an unused network	`docker network rm <network-name>`
List open ports on Docker host	`sudo netstat -tuln or ss -tuln`
View real-time Docker events (including network)	`docker events`

Docker Networking Best Practices – Quick Recap

1. Use User-Defined Networks

- Always prefer **user-defined bridge** or **overlay networks** over the **default bridge**.
- Enables automatic DNS-based service discovery.
- Improves isolation and flexibility.

2. Segment Applications by Network

- Create separate networks for each app tier:
  - Frontend → Backend → Database
- Enforce **Zero Trust principles**: only allow necessary communications.
- Example: Frontend should not directly talk to DB.

3. Minimize Host Network Usage

- Use `--network host` only when absolutely required (e.g., ultra-low latency apps).
- Host mode removes container isolation — increases security risks.

4. Secure Ingress and Egress

- Use reverse proxies like **NGINX** or **Traefik** to control and secure incoming traffic.
- Apply SSL/TLS at the proxy layer.
- Restricts egress traffic from containers using firewall rules (`iptables, firewalld`).

5. Use Overlay Networks for Multi-Host Clusters

- In Docker Swarm mode, **overlay networks** enable seamless multi-node service communication.
- Built-in encryption secures inter-node traffic.

6. Monitor Network Traffic and Events

- Use tools like:
  - `docker network inspect`
  - `tcpdump` on Docker interfaces
  - `docker events` for real-time network monitoring
- Consider deploying cAdvisor, Weave Scope, or Prometheus exporters.

7. Apply Firewalling and ACLs

- Define strict `iptables` rules between containers if needed.
- Use Docker's embedded IP filtering options (in `docker network create`).

8. Macvlan Only for Special Use Cases

- Use **macvlan networks** when containers must appear as separate devices on the physical network.
- Avoid using macvlan on non-Linux systems (limited compatibility).

9. Understand DNS-Based Service Discovery

- Containers on the same network can resolve each other by **service name**.
- No need to hardcode IP addresses.
- Use service names in app configuration whenever possible.

10. Stay Updated and Test Regularly

- Docker networking behavior evolves (e.g., changes between Docker CE versions).
- Regularly test network connectivity, DNS, service exposure, and firewall policies after upgrades.

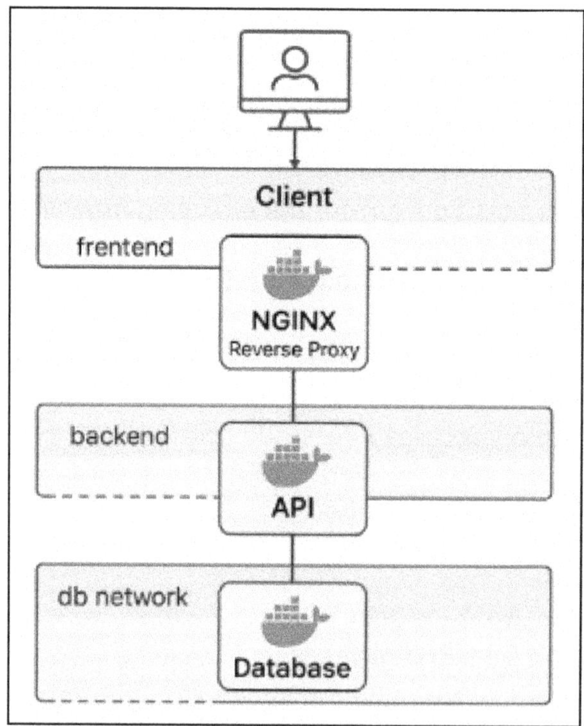

Figure 12.3: Multi-Network Tiered Docker Architecture

This diagram illustrates a secure three-tier deployment using Docker: frontend services (NGINX) communicate only with the backend API; the API connects to the database on an isolated network.

Let's apply these concepts in practice by designing real-world architecture with a frontend reverse proxy, backend API, and an isolated database — all running across multiple Docker networks.

Lab: Multi-Tier Docker Networking with Service Isolation and Reverse Proxy

Difficulty Level: Intermediate

Purpose:

Implement a **frontend → backend → database** architecture with:

- DNS-based service discovery
- Internal-only access to DB
- Reverse proxy SSL termination
- Use of multiple user-defined networks

Step 1: Create Networks

```
$ docker network create frontend_net
$ docker network create backend_net
```

Step 2: Run Postgres DB

```
$ docker run -d \
  --name db \
  --network backend_net \
  -e POSTGRES_USER=admin \
  -e POSTGRES_PASSWORD=secret \
  postgres:15
```

Step 3: Run Flask API (backend)

```
$ docker run -d \
  --name api \
  --network frontend_net \
  --network-alias api \
  --network backend_net \
  flask-api-image
```

Step 4: Run NGINX Reverse Proxy

```
$ docker run -d \
  --name proxy \
  --network frontend_net \
  -v $PWD/nginx.conf:/etc/nginx/nginx.conf:ro \
  -p 443:443 \
  nginx
```

Step 5: Validate

- Ensure NGINX forwards to Flask
- Flask connects to Postgres via service name `db`

Lab: Using `--internal` for Isolated DB Networks in Docker

This lab demonstrates how to create a **fully isolated internal Docker network** using the `--internal` flag. This prevents external containers or hosts from reaching sensitive services like databases, a crucial measure in secure CI/CD or production environments.

Difficulty Level: Advanced

Objective

- Create an internal network that blocks all outgoing internet access.
- Run a PostgreSQL database inside it.
- Add frontend/backend services on separate networks that route traffic to this isolated DB.
- Validate network isolation and connectivity across tiers.

Step 1: Create Networks

```
$ docker network create --driver bridge --internal internal_net
$ docker network create frontend_net
$ docker network create backend_net
```

Step 2: Run PostgreSQL on the Internal Network

```
$ docker run -d \
  --name isolated-db \
  --network internal_net \
  -e POSTGRES_USER=admin \
  -e POSTGRES_PASSWORD=secret \
  postgres:15
```

Step 3: Run Backend API with Dual Networks

Assuming `flask-api-image` connects to DB using hostname `isolated-db`:

```
$ docker run -d \
```

```
  --name backend-api \
  --network backend_net \
  --network-alias api \
  --network internal_net \
  flask-api-image
```

[✓] This backend can access the DB internally but is not exposed externally.

Step 4: Run Frontend Proxy on Frontend Network

```
$ docker run -d \
  --name reverse-proxy \
  --network frontend_net \
  -v $PWD/nginx.conf:/etc/nginx/nginx.conf:ro \
  -p 443:443 \
  nginx
```

The NGINX container reverse proxies to `api`, which exists on both frontend and backend networks.

Step 5: Validate Tiered Isolation

- `reverse-proxy` → can reach `backend-api`
- `backend-api` → can reach `isolated-db`
- `reverse-proxy` → cannot reach `isolated-db`
- Host → cannot reach any internal services

Summary Table

Component	Networks	Internet Access	Access to DB	Exposed to Host
`isolated-db`	`internal_net`	[X]	[✓] internal only	[X]
`backend-api`	`backend_net,` `internal_net`	[X]	[✓]	[X]
`reverse-proxy`	`frontend_net`	[✓] (via port 443)	[X]	[✓]

Use Case

This setup mirrors a **real production microservices stack** with enforced separation:

- Sensitive services (DB) on isolated `--internal` networks
- Middleware (API) on dual networks with limited exposure

- Edge services (proxy/frontend) on public networks only

You can easily define this architecture in `docker-compose.yml` with `networks:` and `depends_on:` for service wiring. Below is the `docker-compose.yml` file

Docker Compose File for Isolated Tiered Architecture `docker-compose.yml`

```
services:
  db:
    image: postgres:15
    environment:
      POSTGRES_USER: admin
      POSTGRES_PASSWORD: secret
    networks:
      - internal_net
    restart: unless-stopped

  backend:
    image: flask-api-image
    depends_on:
      - db
    networks:
      - backend_net
      - internal_net
    restart: unless-stopped

  reverse-proxy:
    image: nginx
    volumes:
      - ./nginx.conf:/etc/nginx/nginx.conf:ro
    ports:
      - "443:443"
    depends_on:
      - backend
    networks:
      - frontend_net
    restart: unless-stopped

networks:
  internal_net:
```

```
    driver: bridge
    internal: true

  backend_net:
    driver: bridge

  frontend_net:
    driver: bridge
```

Summary

- Use user-defined bridge networks (not default)
- Create separate networks for app tiers
- Avoid using `--network host` unless required
- Secure public-facing services with reverse proxies
- Use overlay networks for multi-host setups
- Use Macvlan for LAN IP needs
- Monitor traffic with `tcpdump` or `docker network inspect`

Key Takeaways

In this chapter, you explored Docker's flexible and powerful networking architecture, covering single-host and multi-host setups. From bridge and overlay to macvlan and host networks, you learned how to segment traffic, build secure service tiers, and monitor container-to-container communication. Armed with CLI tools, best practices, and real-world deployment strategies, you are now equipped to build scalable and secure networks across local and distributed environments.

Knowledge Check

1. **What is Docker's default network driver?**
   A) host
   B) overlay
   C) bridge
   D) none
2. **What does the `docker network ls` command do?**
   A) Shows connected volumes
   B) Lists all Docker networks
   C) Displays current container Ips
   D) Starts the network service
3. **What does the `--network=host` flag do?**
   A) Assigns an external IP
   B) Binds container directly to the host network stack
   C) Blocks all networking
   D) Creates a virtual bridge
4. **What is required to create a custom bridge network?**
   A) `docker network create --driver bridge <name>`
   B) Use the host's IP
   C) Edit `/etc/docker/bridge.conf`
   D) Compose override file
5. **Which network mode provides container-level isolation?**
   A) host
   B) none
   C) bridge
   D) overlay
6. **What is the purpose of `docker inspect <network>`?**
   A) Create VLANs
   B) Show DNS cache
   C) Display network details in JSON
   D) Delete subnets
7. **How can you connect a container to multiple networks?**
   A) Define `–multinet`
   B) Use `docker network connect`
   C) Use `--multi` on run
   D) Use Dockerfile
8. **Which Docker network allows containers on different hosts to communicate?**
   A) bridge

B) host
C) overlay
D) none

9. **What is the default subnet for Docker's bridge network?**
   A) 172.17.0.0/16
   B) 10.0.0.0/8
   C) 192.168.0.0/16
   D) 127.0.0.0/8
10. **What does the `--publish` flag do when running a container?**
   A) Connects to Swarm
   B) Assigns container to a named network
   C) Exposes container ports to the host
   D) Pushes to Docker Hub
11. **Which DNS method does Docker use by default?**
   A) External system resolver
   B) Container-level `/etc/hosts`
   C) Embedded DNS server (127.0.0.11)
   D) Google DNS
12. **What is the function of the `--internal` flag when creating networks?**
   A) Allows access to the internet
   B) Disables inter-container communication
   C) Restricts network to internal communication only
   D) Connects to the default bridge
13. **What happens when you don't expose any ports in Docker?**
   A) Container is unreachable externally
   B) All ports are open
   C) Container is assigned random ports
   D) Docker opens ports automatically
14. **What Docker command creates an overlay network?**
   A) `docker network deploy`
   B) `docker network create --driver overlay`
   C) `docker bridge overlay`
   D) `docker overlay enable`
15. **What driver connects a container directly to a physical interface?**
   A) host
   B) bridge
   C) macvlan
   D) overlay
16. **Which of the following are Docker network drivers**

- ▢ bridge
- ▢ overlay
- ▢ macvlan
- ▢ tunnel

17. What are valid port publishing formats?

- ▢ `-p 80:80`
- ▢ `--publish 443:8443`
- ▢ `-p 127.0.0.1:8080:80`
- ▢ `--expose-port 80`

18. Which tools help monitor Docker networking in production?

- ▢ `docker network inspect`
- ▢ `netstat, ss`
- ▢ `cAdvisor`
- ▢ `nano`

19. Which Swarm network features are enabled by default in overlay mode?

- ▢ Service discovery
- ▢ Built-in DNS resolution
- ▢ Multi-host encrypted traffic
- ▢ External NAT routing

20. When is host networking useful?

- ▢ For performance-critical workloads
- ▢ When exact host port access is needed
- ▢ When multi-tenancy is needed
- ▢ When isolation is critical

21. Which `docker-compose.yml` fields support network configuration?

- ▢ `networks:` (root section)
- ▢ `services:<svc>.networks:`
- ▢ `services:<svc>.bridge:`
- ▢ `driver:` under `networks`

22. What can `docker network disconnect` be used for?

- ☐ Detach a container from a network
- ☐ Block IP traffic
- ☐ Change container's active network
- ☐ Attach container to a volume

23. What limitations exist for macvlan networks?

- ☐ Works only with static Ips
- ☐ Not available on Docker Desktop by default
- ☐ Requires physical NIC or bridge
- ☐ Supports Swarm overlay

24. What makes overlay network secure for production?

- ☐ Encrypted VXLAN tunnels
- ☐ Mutual TLS between nodes
- ☐ Firewall bypass
- ☐ DNS-based service discovery

25. What flags are used with `docker run` for networking?

- ☐ `--network=host`
- ☐ `--network=none`
- ☐ `–ip`
- ☐ `--vlan`

26. Which components use embedded DNS in Docker?

- ☐ Containers on user-defined bridge networks
- ☐ Swarm services
- ☐ Overlay networks
- ☐ Containers on legacy bridge

27. What can go wrong with duplicated port mappings?

- ☐ Conflict errors
- ☐ Container start failures
- ☐ Silent pass-through
- ☐ Port collision on host

28. What are signs of network misconfiguration in Docker?

- ▢ Containers can't resolve names
- ▢ DNS failures
- ▢ Unreachable containers across nodes
- ▢ Running logs only

29. How do containers communicate across custom networks?

- ▢ By name (Docker DNS)
- ▢ Via IP
- ▢ MAC-only
- ▢ If on the same user-defined network

30. Which Compose version supports advanced network config?

- ▢ v2.1+
- ▢ v3+ (for Swarm)
- ▢ v1.0 only
- ▢ v3.8 for profiles

Answers

Q#	Correct Answer	Explanation
1	C	Docker uses the bridge network driver by default for standalone containers.
2	B	`docker network ls` lists all locally available Docker networks.
3	B	`--network=host` attaches the container directly to the host's network stack.
4	A	You must specify the `--driver bridge` flag to create a custom bridge network.
5	C	The bridge network isolates containers from the host and other networks by default.
6	C	`docker inspect <network>` returns JSON metadata about the network configuration.
7	B	Use `docker network connect` to attach a container to multiple networks.
8	C	The overlay driver allows container communication across Docker hosts in Swarm mode.
9	A	Docker's default bridge network uses the `172.17.0.0/16` subnet.
10	C	The --publish or `-p` flag maps container ports to host machine ports.
11	C	Docker uses an embedded DNS server (`127.0.0.11`) in user-defined networks.
12	C	The `--internal` flag prevents external access to containers in that network.
13	A	Containers without exposed ports are not reachable from outside the host.
14	B	Use `docker network create --driver overlay` to define overlay networks in Swarm.
15	C	`macvlan` enables containers to be assigned MAC addresses and connect directly to the physical network.

Q16. Which of the following are Docker network drivers?

- [✓] bridge
- [✓] overlay
- [✓] macvlan

- [X] tunnel

Explanation: Native Docker network drivers include `bridge`, `overlay`, and `macvlan`. There is no `tunnel` driver in Docker.

Q17. What are valid port publishing formats?

- [✓] `-p 80:80`
- [✓] `--publish 443:8443`
- [✓] `-p 127.0.0.1:8080:80`
- [X] `--expose-port 80`

Explanation: Docker supports publishing ports using `-p` and `--publish`. `--expose-port` is not a valid flag.

Q18. Which tools help monitor Docker networking in production?

- [✓] `docker network inspect`
- [✓] `netstat, ss`
- [✓] `cAdvisor`
- [X] `nano`

Explanation: Monitoring tools like `inspect`, `cAdvisor`, and OS-level utilities help ensure Docker network visibility and health.

Q19. Which Swarm network features are enabled by default in overlay mode?

- [✓] Service discovery
- [✓] Built-in DNS resolution
- [✓] Multi-host encrypted traffic
- [X] External NAT routing

Explanation: Overlay networks in Swarm support encrypted communications and service discovery across nodes. NAT is handled internally.

Q20. When is host networking useful?

- [✓] For performance-critical workloads
- [✓] When exact host port access is needed
- [X] When multi-tenancy is needed
- [X] When isolation is critical

Explanation: `host` mode removes isolation but boosts performance and reduces network stack overhead.

Q21. Which docker-compose.yml fields support network configuration?

- [✓] `networks:` (root section)
- [✓] `services:<svc>.networks:`

- [X] `services:<svc>.bridge:`
- [√] `driver:` under `networks`

Explanation: Compose supports defining networks at the root and service level, including driver types like `bridge` or `overlay`.

Q22. What can `docker network disconnect` be used for?

- [√] Detach a container from a network
- [X] Block IP traffic
- [√] Change container's active network
- [X] Attach container to a volume

Explanation: This command removes a container from a specific network, useful during runtime topology changes.

Q23. What limitations exist for macvlan networks?

- [√] Works only with static Ips
- [√] Not available on Docker Desktop by default
- [√] Requires physical NIC or bridge
- [X] Supports Swarm overlay

Explanation: `macvlan` allows containers to appear on LAN but has hardware and platform limitations and is not supported in Swarm overlay mode.

Q24. What makes overlay network secure for production?

- [√] Encrypted VXLAN tunnels
- [√] Mutual TLS between nodes
- [X] Firewall bypass
- [√] DNS-based service discovery

Explanation: Overlay networks encrypt traffic between nodes using VXLAN and enable secure, DNS-based service lookups.

Q25. What flags are used with docker run for networking?

- [√] `--network=host`
- [√] `--network=none`
- [√] `-ip`
- [X] `--vlan`

Explanation: Docker supports setting network modes and static IPs, but not VLANs directly via `docker run`.

Q26. Which components use embedded DNS in Docker?

- [√] Containers on user-defined bridge networks

- **[√]** Swarm services
- **[√]** Overlay networks
- **[X]** Containers on legacy bridge

Explanation: Docker's embedded DNS works in user-defined networks and Swarm, but not in the default legacy `bridge` network.

Q27. What can go wrong with duplicated port mappings?

- **[√]** Conflict errors
- **[√]** Container start failures
- **[X]** Silent pass-through
- **[√]** Port collision on host

Explanation: Docker will throw errors or block container startup if port mappings conflict on the host machine.

Q28. What are signs of network misconfiguration in Docker?

- **[√]** Containers can't resolve names
- **[√]** DNS failures
- **[√]** Unreachable containers across nodes
- **[X]** Running logs only

Explanation: DNS and routing failures are typical symptoms of misconfigured Docker networks, especially in Swarm.

Q29. How do containers communicate across custom networks?

- **[√]** By name (Docker DNS)
- **[√]** Via IP
- **[X]** MAC-only
- **[√]** If on the same user-defined network

Explanation: Docker uses an internal DNS for name resolution, but containers must be on the same user-defined network.

Q30. Which Compose version supports advanced network config?

- **[√]** v2.1+
- **[√]** v3+ (for Swarm)
- **[X]** v1.0 only
- **[√]** v3.8 for profiles

Explanation: Network capabilities evolved in Compose from v2.1 onward. v3+ supports Swarm mode; v3.8 adds advanced features like profiles.

Chapter 13: Best Practices and Container Hardening — Securing Containers by Design

Containers are fast, efficient, and flexible—but they are not inherently secure. Without careful configuration, even the smallest container image can become a **launchpad for lateral movement, data exfiltration, or privilege escalation**.

This chapter distils years of real-world experience into actionable **best practices and hardening strategies** that help you **build secure containers by design**—not by chance. You'll learn to minimize attack surfaces, strip unnecessary privileges, lock down runtime behavior, and enforce secure defaults through automation and policy-as-code.

We'll cover everything from:

- Secure Dockerfile patterns
- Read-only file systems and tmpfs
- Capability dropping and seccomp tuning
- Minimal images and multi-stage builds
- Runtime defenses like AppArmor and rootless containers
- Defense-in-depth workflows for DevSecOps and CI/CD pipelines

Whether you're developing on your laptop, deploying to Kubernetes, or managing containers in production at scale, these best practices will help you ensure that **every container is hardened, auditable, and resilient by default**.

By the end of this chapter, container security will no longer feel like a bolt-on—it'll be baked into everything you build.

Building Better Images

Your container is only as secure and efficient as the image it runs on. Here's how to get it right. Use Minimal Base Images Start with the smallest image possible to reduce attack surface and size.

Use alpine, distroless, or slim variants:

```
FROM python:3.11-alpine
```

Pin Image Versions Avoid using latest, which changes over time and may break builds.

```
FROM node:18.17.1
```

Clean Up After Yourself Every RUN creates a layer. Minimize leftover packages and caches:

```
RUN apt update && apt install -y curl && \
    apt clean && rm -rf /var/lib/apt/lists/*
```

Layer Optimization & Caching

Docker uses a layered filesystem — ordering matters.

Copy `package.json` First

```
COPY package*.json ./
RUN npm install
COPY . .
```

Changes to source files won't invalidate dependency cache if you keep them after install steps.

Use `.dockerignore`

Avoid sending unnecessary files to the Docker daemon

```
.git
node_modules
.env
*.log
Dockerfile.old
```

This improves build time and keeps your image clean.

Security Hardening

Avoid Root User

```
RUN adduser --disabled-password myuser
USER myuser
```

Drop Capabilities

```
$ docker run --cap-drop=ALL --cap-add=NET_BIND_SERVICE myapp
```

Read-Only Filesystem

```
$ docker run --read-only -v /app/uploads myapp
```

Health Checks

Health checks let Docker know when your service is ready or unhealthy.

```
HEALTHCHECK CMD curl --fail http://localhost:3000 || exit
```

In Compose:

```
healthcheck:
  test: ["CMD", "curl", "-f", "http://localhost"]
  interval: 30s
  timeout: 10s
  retries: 3
```

Logging and Monitoring

Centralized Logging Use docker logs, but prefer centralized logging:

- Fluentd
- ELK stack (Elasticsearch + Logstash + Kibana)
- Loki + Grafana Example

```
$ docker run --log-driver=fluentd myapp
```

Use `docker stats` View real-time CPU/memory usage:

```
$ docker stats
```

Network Segmentation

Separate your services by network:

- `frontendnet` for UI
- `backendnet` for APIs
- `dbnet` for databases

Only expose what's necessary to each tier:

```
networks:
  frontendnet:
  backendnet:
    internal: true
```

Secrets Management

Never Bake Secrets into Images Instead, use:

- `.env` files (ignore in Git)
- Docker secrets (Swarm)
- Kubernetes secrets (if using K8s)

Real-World Dockerfile Before vs After

Before:

```
FROM node:latest
COPY . .
RUN npm install
CMD ["npm", "start"]
```

After:

```
FROM node:18.17.0-alpine
WORKDIR /app
COPY package*.json ./
RUN npm install --production
COPY . .
USER node
EXPOSE 3000
CMD ["node", "index.js"]
```

Development vs Production Images

Use separate `Dockerfiles` or Compose overrides.

- `Dockerfile.dev`: Includes dev tools, debuggers, hot reloaders
- `Dockerfile.prod`: Clean, optimized, no dev dependencies

CI/CD Best Practices

- Always build fresh images (`--pull`)
- Scan images in pipeline (trivy, grype)
- Push to private registries (Harbor, GitHub Packages, GitLab)
- Automatically tag images with SHA or semver

Supply Chain & Signature Verification

Use docker trust (Notary) or Sigstore to verify images before running them.

Enable Docker Content Trust:

```
export DOCKER_CONTENT_TRUST=1
```

Only verified images will be allowed.

Tools You Should Use

Tool	Purpose
Hadolint	Linter for Dockerfiles
Dockle	Dockerfile security checker
Trivy	CVE scanner for images and repos
Dive	Inspect image layers and sizes
Snyk	Commercial vuln scanner

Container Hardening

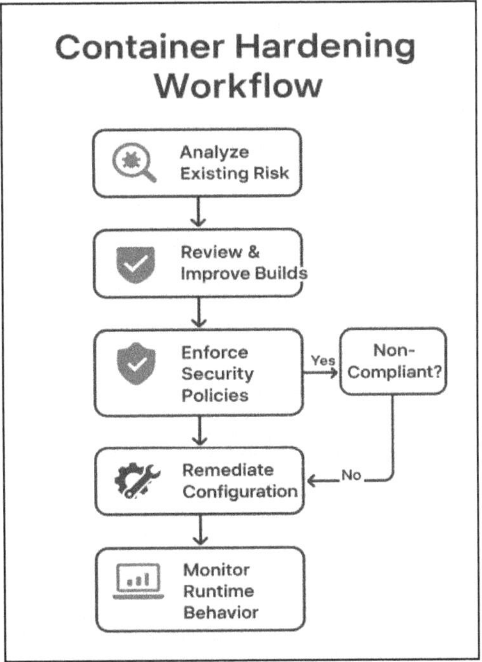

Figure 13.1 Container Hardening Workflow

Defense-in-Depth for Containers — 4 Security Layers

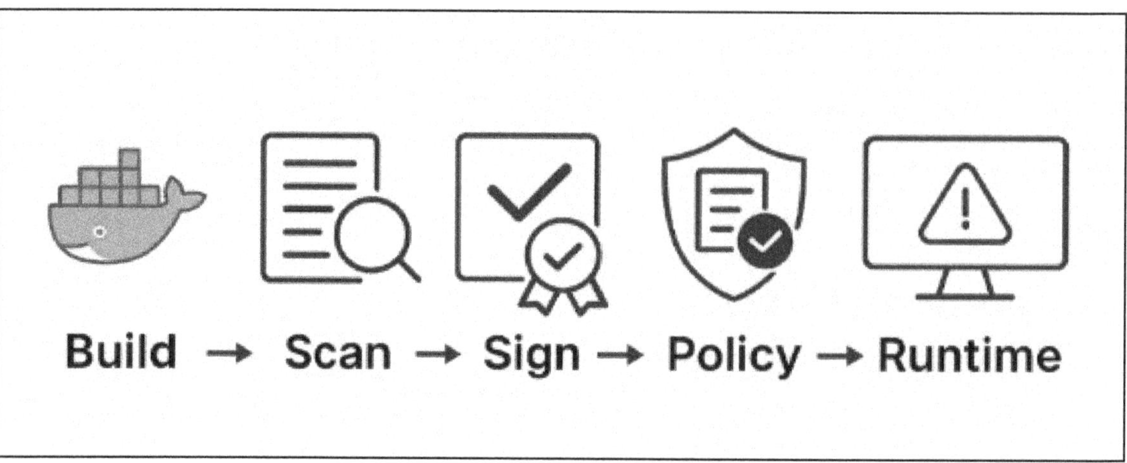

Figure 13.2: Defense-in-Depth for Secure Containers

Security Layer	Tools	Purpose
Image Hardening	Hadolint, Trivy, Grype, Dockle	Scan, lint, and harden container images before deployment.
Runtime Monitoring	Falco, Tetragon	Detect suspicious container behaviors at runtime (e.g., unexpected syscalls, file access, shell spawns).
Policy Enforcement	Open Policy Agent (OPA), Gatekeeper	Enforce security rules like non-root containers, signed images, mandatory health checks.
Supply Chain Integrity	Cosign, Rekor, Docker Content Trust (DCT)	Sign images, verify authenticity, and maintain audit logs for trusted deployments.

🔒 ***Pro Tip:*** A truly secure containerized environment covers all four layers — from build to deploy to runtime.

Container Hardening Checklist

[√]	Task
☐	Use **minimal base images** (Alpine, Distroless) to reduce attack surface.
☐	**Drop root privileges** — run containers as non-root users wherever possible.
☐	**Scan container images regularly** with tools like Trivy, Grype, or Dockle during CI/CD.

[✓]	Task
▢	**Use multi-stage builds** to create clean, optimized production images.
▢	**Do not expose unused ports** – explicitly expose only necessary ones.
▢	**Add health checks** in Dockerfile or Compose files to monitor container health.
▢	**Separate secrets and configuration** using Secrets management (Docker Secrets, Vault, Kubernetes Secrets).
▢	**Use `--read-only` filesystem** to prevent unwanted filesystem changes inside containers.
▢	**Use strict `.dockerignore`** to minimize the build context and reduce attack surface.
▢	**Enable image signing and trust validation** (Cosign, Docker Content Trust) to ensure authenticity.

🔒 ***Pro Tip:*** *Combine the hardening checklist with:*

Layer	Tools	Purpose
Runtime Monitoring	Falco, Tetragon	Detect container runtime anomalies.
Policy Enforcement	OPA, Gatekeeper	Enforce security policies (e.g., no root containers, mandatory healthchecks).
Signature Verification	Cosign, Rekor	Validate the authenticity and integrity of container images.

Achieving **Defense in Depth** ensures containers are secure **by design**, **by runtime**, and **by supply chain**.

Rootless Docker and UID Namespacing

Running Docker in rootless mode or using user namespace remapping is one of the most effective ways to reduce the impact of container compromise.

```
$ dockerd-rootless-setuptool.sh install
```

Alternatively, enable UID remapping in `daemon.json`:

```
{
  "userns-remap": "default"
}
```

This ensures container root maps to an unprivileged user on the host, minimizing risks.

Custom Seccomp, AppArmor, and SELinux Profiles

Apply minimal syscall profiles using seccomp to restrict containers:

```
$ docker run --security-opt seccomp=/path/seccomp-profile.json myapp
```

Use `AppArmor` (Ubuntu) or `SELinux` (RHEL) to enforce access control on files, processes, and devices. Hardened policies can prevent common exploits and container escapes.

Immutable Containers and Filesystem Lockdown

Containers should be treated as immutable. Combine `--read-only` with `tmpfs` for temp writes:

```
$ docker run --read-only --tmpfs /tmp -v /data/uploads myapp
```

Rebuild containers with updated code instead of patching inside.

Runtime Monitoring with Falco and Tetragon

Use tools like Falco and Tetragon to detect suspicious behavior such as shell execution or unexpected file access inside containers:

```
$ falco -r rules.yaml
```

These tools add real-time visibility and are ideal for production observability.

Policy Enforcement via OPA

Open Policy Agent (OPA) and Gatekeeper can enforce security policies:

- Disallow containers running as root
- Require signed images
- Enforce healthchecks OPA is ideal in Kubernetes but also works with admission controllers and CI/CD.

Security Policy Sample – OPA Rego Example

```
package docker.security

deny[msg] {
  input.request.object.spec.securityContext.runAsUser == 0
  msg := "Running containers as root is forbidden. Please use a non-root
user."
```

```
}
```

This OPA policy denies any container deployment if `runAsUser` is set to `0` (root). You can integrate this with Kubernetes Admission Controllers or CI/CD pipelines to automatically enforce least privilege.

Multi-Arch Builds and Secure Cross-Platform

Build images for multiple architectures securely:

```
$ docker buildx build --platform linux/amd64,linux/arm64 -t myapp .
```

Supports edge deployments and hybrid infrastructure while maintaining consistency and security.

Advanced SBOM + Sigstore Supply Chain Security

Generate SBOMs using Syft:

```
$ syft myapp:latest -o cyclonedx-json > sbom.json
```

Then scan with Grype:

```
$ grype sbom:sbom.json
```

Sign your image with Cosign:

```
$ cosign sign myapp:latest
```

Verify signatures and log metadata in Rekor for attestation.

Deep Network Isolation and mTLS

Use multiple Docker networks with `internal: true`, disable inter-container communication (`--icc=false`), and use service mesh or mTLS for encrypted container-to-container traffic.

Security Anti-Patterns and Red Flags

- Running with `--privileged`
- Mounting host `/var/run/docker.sock`
- Using `latest` image tags in production
- Including tools like `curl, git, bash` in production builds
- Baking secrets into layers or ENV

Avoid these to reduce blast radius and comply with security standards.

Quick Remediation Tips – Anti-Patterns ➔ Immediate Fixes

Anti-Pattern	Best Practice (Fix)
Running with `--privileged`	Drop all capabilities, add back only needed ones (use `--cap-drop=ALL --cap-add=NET_BIND_SERVICE`).
Mounting `/var/run/docker.sock`	Avoid unless absolutely necessary; use remote API proxy if needed.
Using `latest` image tag	Pin specific versions (`python:3.11-alpine`), use Git SHA or SemVer tags.
Including curl, git, bash in prod builds	Remove all build/development tools in final multi-stage build.
Baking secrets into images or ENV	Use Docker Secrets, Kubernetes Secrets, or Vault injection during runtime.
No healthchecks	Add HEALTHCHECK instruction in Dockerfile or Compose file to monitor service health.
No resource limits (CPU/memory)	Define resource limits (`--memory, --cpus`) for containers to prevent abuse.

CIS Docker Benchmarking & Compliance Checklist

Run Docker Bench for Security to check CIS compliance:

```
$ git clone https://github.com/docker/docker-bench-security.git
$ cd docker-bench-security && ./docker-bench-security.sh
```

Covers best practices from the Center for Internet Security (CIS) across image, runtime, and daemon security.

Production Security in Action

You've seen best practices across Dockerfiles, image minimization, runtime enforcement, and supply chain security.
To reinforce these concepts practically, revisit the full lab in **Chapter 11**, **"Lab: Hardening a Docker Container — From Vulnerable to Secure"** where we transform a vulnerable container into a hardened, production-ready service using:

- ☑ Non-root execution
- ☑ Capabilities dropping
- ☑ Read-only filesystem

☑ Seccomp policy
☑ CVE scanning
☑ Signature and trust

That lab ties together the layered security techniques discussed here, giving you a complete baseline for real-world deployments.

Lab: Secure Supply Chain & Policy Enforcement with Cosign, OPA, Falco

This lab builds on the foundation from Chapter 11 by focusing on **container supply chain security**, **runtime policy enforcement**, and **behavioral monitoring** to move from "secure by config" to **secure by design and continuous enforcement**.

Difficulty Level: Advanced

Objective:

- Generate an SBOM (Software Bill of Materials)
- Sign container images using Cosign
- Enforce runtime policy using OPA Gatekeeper
- Monitor container behavior with Falco

Step 1: Generate a Software Bill of Materials (SBOM)

Use **Syft** (by Anchore):

```
$ syft docker:secure-app -o table
$ syft docker:secure-app -o spdx-json > sbom-secure-app.json
```

[✓] Helps with vulnerability and license tracking.

Step 2: Sign the Image Using Cosign

Create key pair:

```
$ cosign generate-key-pair
```

Sign the image:

```
$ cosign sign --key cosign.key secure-app
```

Verify the signature:

```
$ cosign verify --key cosign.pub secure-app
```

[√] Prevents tampering and ensures provenance in CI/CD.

Step 3: Define Runtime Policy with OPA Gatekeeper (Kubernetes)

Install OPA Gatekeeper (if on K8s):

```
$ kubectl apply -f https://raw.githubusercontent.com/open-policy-agent/gatekeeper/release-3.12/deploy/gatekeeper.yaml
```

Create a constraint template to **block containers running as root**:

```
apiVersion: templates.gatekeeper.sh/v1beta1
kind: ConstraintTemplate
metadata:
  name: k8srequiredrunasnonroot
spec:
  crd:
    spec:
      names:
        kind: K8sRequiredRunAsNonRoot
  targets:
    - target: admission.k8s.gatekeeper.sh
      rego: |
        package k8srequiredrunasnonroot
        violation["Containers must not run as root"] {
          container := input.review.object.spec.containers[_]
          not container.securityContext.runAsNonRoot
        }
```

Apply it:

```
$ kubectl apply -f <constraint-template.yaml>
```

[√] Blocks policy-violating deployments before they reach runtime.

Step 4: Monitor Runtime Behavior with Falco

Install Falco:

```
$ curl -s https://falco.org/install.sh | sudo bash
```

Start monitoring:

```
$ sudo falco
```

Run a suspicious container (test):

```
$ docker run -it --privileged alpine sh -c 'apk add curl && curl
http://malicious-site.com'
```

ALERT: Falco should alert on unexpected `curl` activity inside container.

Summary Table

Component	Tool	Purpose
SBOM	Syft	Tracks packages and dependencies
Signature	Cosign	Validates image integrity & provenance
Policy Control	OPA	Blocks insecure container configurations
Runtime Alerts	Falco	Monitors for behavioral security anomalies

Use Case

This lab upgrades Chapter 11's hardening techniques by integrating tools that provide **continuous assurance**, **auditable compliance**, and **zero-trust deployment validation**.

You can now:

- Detect what's inside your containers (SBOM)
- Trust only signed containers (Cosign)
- Prevent insecure deployments (OPA)
- Detect runtime anomalies (Falco)

Summary

- Introduced secure-by-default container design practices aligned with real-world production needs.
- Showed how to build **minimal, non-root Docker images** using slim base images and `.dockerignore`.
- Explored **runtime hardening flags** like `--read-only`, `--cap-drop=ALL`, and `--pids-limit`.
- Explained how to apply and enforce **custom Seccomp profiles** for syscall control.
- Compared insecure vs secure builds with a **CVE delta summary** using Trivy.
- Discussed **image signing with Cosign** and **SBOM generation** using Syft.
- Demonstrated the importance of **rootless Docker**, **AppArmor**, and **OPA/Gatekeeper**.
- Integrated **Falco** and **Tetragon** for live container behavior monitoring.
- Provided optimization strategies for reproducible and compliant production images.
- Delivered a **Bonus Lab** covering supply chain and runtime enforcement practices.

Key Takeaways

In this chapter, you mastered the foundational and advanced practices for container hardening in production environments. From Dockerfile best practices to runtime restrictions, image signing, SBOM generation, and behavior monitoring, you learned how to shift security left and enforce defense-in-depth. By combining static analysis tools, policy engines, and runtime protections, you're now equipped to build, sign, run, and monitor containers that are secure by design and resilient in real-world deployments.

Knowledge Check

1. **What is the recommended base image type for secure, minimal containers?**
   A) Ubuntu Full
   B) Node:latest
   C) Alpine or Distroless
   D) ArchLinux
2. **Why should you avoid using latest as the image tag in production?**
   A) It is faster
   B) `latest` is not always predictable
   C) It breaks volume mounts
   D) It increases container size
3. **What is the purpose of `.dockerignore` in image builds?**
   A) Prevent secrets and unnecessary files from entering images
   B) Mount volumes
   C) Add metadata
   D) Define user accounts
4. **What is one benefit of combining RUN commands in Dockerfile?**
   A) Lower container port
   B) Fewer image layers
   C) Adds logging
   D) Supports GPU
5. **What's the risk of leaving a container with root privileges?**
   A) None
   B) It can escape and control host resources
   C) It consumes more memory
   D) It disables DNS
6. **Which instruction in Dockerfile switches from root to non-root user?**
   A) `LOGIN`
   B) `USER`
   C) `RUN drop-root`
   D) `CMD`
7. **What should be done with unused Docker images on production hosts?**
   A) Retag them
   B) Leave them for backups
   C) Prune or remove them
   D) Export as tar
8. **What Dockerfile instruction is preferred over ADD for copying files?**
   A) `RUN`

B) `COPY`
C) `EXPOSE`
D) `USER`

9. What is a container "healthcheck"?
A) Checks memory limits
B) Defines a command that determines container's health
C) Launches the container
D) Prunes images

10. Why should you scan images in CI/CD pipelines?
A) To check performance
B) To reduce logging
C) To detect known vulnerabilities before deployment
D) To install Docker

11. What does the `--read-only` flag do at container runtime?
A) Enables DNS
B) Prevents write access inside container
C) Deletes volumes
D) Sets restart policy

12. Why is multi-stage Dockerfile better in production?
A) Automatically creates containers
B) Reduces image size by separating build-time and run-time environments
C) Allows multiple ports
D) Builds in RAM

13. What is the role of a non-root user in container hardening?
A) Saves memory
B) Reduces access to host system resources
C) Speeds up startup
D) Disables container logs

14. What should be done with sensitive environment variables in Docker?
A) Hardcode in Dockerfile
B) Use `.env` and inject at runtime
C) Publish in `README`
D) Ignore them

15. What is the benefit of labels in Dockerfiles and containers?
A) GPU support
B) Better UI
C) Metadata tagging for tracking, scanning, automation
D) Networking

16. What improves image build performance and security?
- [ ] Using multi-stage builds

- ▢ Using `COPY` instead of `ADD`
- ▢ Clean up build tools with `RUN apt-get remove`
- ▢ Installing build dependencies at runtime

17. **What are valid flags for limiting container resources?**
    - ▢ `--memory=512m`
    - ▢ `--cpus=1.5`
    - ▢ `--pids-limit=100`
    - ▢ `--disk-speed=fast`
18. **What are effects of `--cap-drop=ALL`?**
    - ▢ Removes all Linux kernel capabilities
    - ▢ Improves isolation
    - ▢ Grants root by default
    - ▢ You can selectively re-add only what's required
19. **What causes image bloat in Dockerfiles?**
    - ▢ Unnecessary dependencies
    - ▢ Copying large files
    - ▢ Specifying ENTRYPOINT
    - ▢ Failing to clean package manager caches
20. **What are examples of sensitive files that must be in `.dockerignore`?**
    - ▢ `.env`
    - ▢ `.git/`
    - ▢ `id_rsa` or SSH keys
    - ▢ `README.md`
21. **What security scanners are available for Docker images?**
    - ▢ Trivy
    - ▢ Grype
    - ▢ Docker Scan (Snyk)
    - ▢ tcpdump
22. **Why should containers be ephemeral?**
    - ▢ To simplify lifecycle and avoid state management
    - ▢ To speed up the internet
    - ▢ Stateless design improves scalability
    - ▢ To allow privilege escalation
23. **Which instructions should be minimized or avoided in Dockerfiles?**
    - ▢ `ADD` (unless required)
    - ▢ `RUN apt-get upgrade -y`

- ▢ `RUN curl | bash`
- ▢ `USER appuser`

24. What behaviors reduce container attack surface?

- ▢ Remove unnecessary tools
- ▢ Use Distroless base images
- ▢ Enable seccomp or AppArmor
- ▢ Allow `--privileged` flag

25. Where should image vulnerabilities be fixed?

- ▢ In base image updates
- ▢ In app dependencies
- ▢ By removing outdated packages
- ▢ Ignored until incidents

26. What are best practices for volumes?

- ▢ Mount only what's needed
- ▢ Avoid writing to root filesystem
- ▢ Restrict volume access
- ▢ Use host root (/) as bind mount

27. Which are safe practices for credentials?

- ▢ Use secrets managers (Vault, Swarm Secrets)
- ▢ Inject at runtime
- ▢ Add via `ENV` in Dockerfile
- ▢ Rotate secrets regularly

28. What can be audited using `docker events` or logs?

- ▢ Image pulls
- ▢ Container starts/stops
- ▢ Volume usage
- ▢ Kernel logins

29. What are common hardening steps for production containers?

- ▢ Disable inter-container traffic
- ▢ Use minimal images
- ▢ Use non-root users
- ▢ Enable SSH inside containers

30. What are goals of container hardening?

- ▢ Reduce attack surface
- ▢ Ensure runtime integrity
- ▢ Enforce least privilege

- [ ] Increase image size

Answer

Q#	Correct Answer	Explanation
1	C	Alpine and Distroless are minimal and reduce surface area.
2	B	`latest` tags can change without notice and break production.
3	A	`.dockerignore` prevents secrets from being added to the image.
4	B	Combining `RUN` steps reduces layers and builds time.
5	B	Containers running as root can potentially escape and harm the host.
6	B	`USER` sets UID/GID inside the container.
7	C	Prune unused images to avoid clutter and reduce attack risk.
8	B	`COPY` is safer and more predictable than `ADD`.
9	B	Healthchecks help monitor container availability.
10	C	CI/CD image scanning detects CVEs early.
11	B	--read-only prevents filesystem writes and enhances security.
12	B	Multi-stage builds optimize size and split build/runtime concerns.
13	B	Non-root reduces privilege escalation risks.
14	B	Use `.env` or secrets injection at runtime — avoid Dockerfile `ENV`.
15	C	Labels help automation, asset tracking, and vulnerability scanning.

Q16. What improves image build performance and security?

- **[✓]** Using multi-stage builds
- **[✓]** Using `COPY` instead of `ADD`
- **[✓]** Clean up build tools with `RUN apt-get remove`
- **[X]** Installing build dependencies at runtime

Explanation: Multi-stage builds reduce final image size. COPY is safer than ADD. Cleaning build tools prevents unnecessary bloat and vulnerabilities. Avoid runtime installations.

Q17. What are valid flags for limiting container resources?

- **[✓]** `--memory=512m`
- **[✓]** `--cpus=1.5`
- **[✓]** `--pids-limit=100`
- **[X]** `--disk-speed=fast`

Explanation: Docker supports memory, CPU, and PIDs limits. There is no flag for disk speed throttling.

Q18. What are effects of `--cap-drop=ALL`?

- **[√]** Removes all Linux kernel capabilities
- **[√]** Improves isolation
- **[X]** Grants root by default
- **[√]** You can selectively re-add only what's required

Explanation: `-cap-drop=ALL` removes all default capabilities, enforcing least privilege. Capabilities can be re-added using `--cap-add`.

Q19. What causes image bloat in Dockerfiles?

- **[√]** Unnecessary dependencies
- **[√]** Copying large files
- **[X]** Specifying ENTRYPOINT
- **[√]** Failing to clean package manager caches

Explanation: Large files and leftover cache increase image size. ENTRYPOINT doesn't cause bloat.

Q20. What are examples of sensitive files that must be in `.dockerignore`?

- **[√]** `.env`
- **[√]** `.git/`
- **[√]** `id_rsa` or SSH keys
- **[X]** `README.md`

Explanation: Sensitive files like credentials, git history, and SSH keys must be excluded. README is not sensitive.

Q21. What security scanners are available for Docker images?

- **[√]** Trivy
- **[√]** Grype
- **[√]** Docker Scan (Snyk)
- **[X]** tcpdump

Explanation: Trivy, Grype, and Docker Scan check image vulnerabilities. Tcpdump is a network sniffer, not a security scanner.

Q22. Why should containers be ephemeral?

- **[√]** To simplify lifecycle and avoid state management
- **[X]** To speed up the internet
- **[√]** Stateless design improves scalability

- **[X]** To allow privilege escalation

Explanation: Ephemeral, stateless containers are easier to manage, replicate, and scale. They also improve resilience.

Q23. Which instructions should be minimized or avoided in Dockerfiles?

- **[✓]** `ADD` (unless required)
- **[✓]** `RUN apt-get upgrade -y`
- **[✓]** `RUN curl | bash`
- **[X]** `USER appuser`

Explanation: Avoid unsafe or non-reproducible instructions. USER is the best practice, not a risk.

Q24. What behaviors reduce container attack surface?

- **[✓]** Remove unnecessary tools
- **[✓]** Use Distroless base images
- **[✓]** Enable seccomp or AppArmor
- **[X]** Allow `--privileged` flag

Explanation: Minimal images and security profiles reduce risk. `--privileged` increases it significantly.

Q25. Where should image vulnerabilities be fixed?

- **[✓]** In base image updates
- **[✓]** In app dependencies
- **[✓]** By removing outdated packages
- **[X]** Ignored until incidents

Explanation: All layers should be patched. Ignoring vulnerabilities invites attacks.

Q26. What are best practices for volumes?

- **[✓]** Mount only what's needed
- **[✓]** Avoid writing to root filesystem
- **[✓]** Restrict volume access
- **[X]** Use host root (/) as bind mount

Explanation: Limit volume scope and privileges. Binding the full root path is a major risk.

Q27. Which are safe practices for credentials?

- **[✓]** Use secrets managers (Vault, Swarm Secrets)
- **[✓]** Inject at runtime
- **[X]** Add via `ENV` in Dockerfile
- **[✓]** Rotate secrets regularly

Explanation: Explanation: Secrets should be dynamic and injected securely. `ENV` exposes them in image layers.

Q28. What can be audited using `docker events` or logs?

- [✓] Image pulls
- [✓] Container starts/stops
- [✓] Volume usage
- [X] Kernel logins

Explanation: Docker logs and events capture activity related to containers, images, and volumes — not OS-level logins.

Q29. What are common hardening steps for production containers?

- [✓] Disable inter-container traffic
- [✓] Use minimal images
- [✓] Use non-root users
- [X] Enable SSH inside containers

Explanation: Containers shouldn't run SSH. Use orchestration tools and logging for access instead.

Q30. What are goals of container hardening?

- [✓] Reduce attack surface
- [✓] Ensure runtime integrity
- [✓] Enforce least privilege
- [X] Increase image size

Explanation: Hardening focuses on making containers lean, secure, and resistant to compromise — not on bloating them.

Chapter 14: Docker Backup and Recovery – Strategies for Resilience and Continuity

Containers are often considered "stateless" by design—but the reality is more nuanced. Your containers may be ephemeral, but the **data they handle is not**. From database volumes to logs, configs, uploads, and secrets, protecting that data is crucial for **business continuity, disaster recovery, and audit compliance**.

This chapter dives deep into **backup and recovery strategies for Dockerized environments**, including:

- Backing up named volumes and bind mounts
- Snapshotting container data and image layers
- Versioning and restoring with Docker CLI and automation
- Disaster recovery planning across dev, staging, and production
- Backup best practices for databases like PostgreSQL, MySQL, and MongoDB in containers
- Cloud-native backup options and CI/CD-integrated recovery jobs

Whether you're backing up a simple web app or a multi-node containerized infrastructure, this chapter helps you build a **resilient, restorable Docker environment** that can recover from hardware failure, data corruption, accidental deletion, or total cluster loss.

Remember: *if you don't test your backups, you don't have them.*

Why Backup Matters in Docker

Containers are ephemeral, but data isn't.
Things you should be backing up:

- Volumes (e.g., databases, file uploads)
- Container configs and .env
- Dockerfiles, Compose files
- Custom networks or volume plugins
- Secrets or TLS certs
- Container state (only for stateful services)

Types of Docker Data to Backup

Type	Description	Backup Method
Named Volumes	Persistent storage managed by Docker	docker volume + tar
Bind Mounts	Host directories mounted into container	OS-native file backups
Container State	Data inside the container FS	docker export/commit
Compose Files	Infra-as-code	Version control (Git)
Secrets & Certs	Sensitive configuration	Encrypted storage

Backup a Named Volume

Step 1: Create a Test Volume

```
$ docker volume create mydata
$ docker run -v mydata:/data busybox sh -c "echo hello > /data/file.txt"
```

Step 2: Backup the Volume to a Tarball

```
$ docker run --rm -v mydata:/data -v $PWD:/backup busybox \
  tar czvf /backup/mydata-backup.tar.gz /data
```

Restore a Docker Volume

Step 1: Create a New Volume

```
$ docker volume create restored
```

Step 2: Restore From the Tarball

```
$ docker run --rm -v restored:/data -v $PWD:/backup busybox \
  tar xzvf /backup/mydata-backup.tar.gz -C /
```

Validate:

```
$ docker run --rm -v restored:/data busybox cat /data/file.txt
```

Backup and Restore Entire Containers (with FS)

- Export a container:

```
$ docker export container_id > mycontainer.tar
```

- Import:

```
$ cat mycontainer.tar | docker import - mycontainer-restored
```

⚠ Does not preserve container metadata or history.

Automating Volume Backups (Cron + Script)

backup.sh

```
#!/bin/bash
DATE=$(date +%Y%m%d_%H%M)
VOLUME=mydata
BACKUP=./backups/${VOLUME}_$DATE.tar.gz

docker run --rm \
  -v $VOLUME:/data \
  -v $PWD/backups:/backup \
  busybox \
  tar czvf /backup/$(basename $BACKUP) /data
```

Cron Job:

```
$ crontab -e
0 2 * * * /home/user/backup.sh
```

Backing Up to Cloud or Remote Servers

- `rclone` for Google Drive, S3, Dropbox, etc.
- `rsync` or `scp` for Linux-to-Linux
- Restic for incremental encrypted backups

Example with rclone:

```
$ rclone copy /backups remote:s3bucket/docker-backups
```

Using Docker Volume Plugins (for Cloud/Remote Storage)

Plugin	Backend
`local-persist`	Host filesystem
`rexray/ebs`	AWS EBS
`vieux/sshfs`	SSHFS
`azurefile`	Azure File Storage
`glusterfs`	Distributed filesystems

Example (SSHFS):

```
$ docker plugin install vieux/sshfs
$ docker volume create \
  -d vieux/sshfs \
  -o sshcmd=user@host:/backup \
  -o password=secret \
  Sshvolume
```

Now mount it:

```
$ docker run -v sshvolume:/data myapp
```

Full Stack Recovery with Compose

Step 1: Backup All Volumes:

```
$ docker volume ls
$ docker run -v postgres-data:/data -v $PWD:/backup busybox \
  tar czvf /backup/pgdata.tar.gz /data
```

Also back up:

- `docker-compose.yml`
- `.env`
- `TLS certs`
- `Custom configs`

Step 2: Recovery:

```
$ docker volume create postgres-data
$ docker run -v postgres-data:/data -v $PWD:/backup busybox \
  tar xzvf /backup/pgdata.tar.gz -C /

$ docker compose up
```

Protecting Backups

Backups are a lifeline—but without protection, they become a liability. Whether you're dealing with ransomware threats, insider misuse, or accidental exposure, your backup strategy must also include **security, access control, and resilience**.

Encrypt your backups using tools like `gpg`, `openssl`, or `age`

Example:

```
$ gpg -c pgdata.tar.gz
$ openssl enc -aes-256-cbc -in pgdata.tar.gz -out pgdata.enc
```

Recommended Practices

1. **Use secure transfer protocols** for remote or cloud uploads
   - Prefer `rsync over SSH, rclone with encrypted config`, or SFTP
   - Ensure you never send secrets over plaintext
2. **Store backups off-site and off-network**
   - Use cloud storage (S3, B2, Azure Blob)
   - Maintain separate backup nodes in isolated networks
3. **Enable versioning** in your cloud storage buckets
   - Prevents overwriting or accidental deletion
   - Allows rollback to any point-in-time snapshot
4. **Restrict backup access with minimal privileges**
   - Backup folders and vaults should be readable only by automation or backup operators
   - Rotate access tokens and keys regularly
5. **Monitor backup size and health**
   - Validate that backup size matches expected output
   - Use checksums (`sha256sum, md5sum`) to verify integrity
6. **Use immutable or WORM storage options**
   - S3 Object Lock, Glacier Vault Lock, or append-only filesystems (ZFS, Btrfs)
7. **Avoid storing sensitive .env, secrets, or private keys unencrypted**
   - If you must include them, encrypt that section separately or use Vault integrations

🔒 **Pro Tip:** *Treat your backups like crown jewels—***encrypt, isolate, and guard them** *as you would production credentials.*

Disaster Recovery Playbook

Disaster recovery is not just about backups—it's about a **repeatable and time-tested process** to restore business operations with minimal downtime and maximum clarity.

Here's a sample Docker-centric recovery playbook for your ready reference you can customize based on your environment:

1. **Detect the Incident**
   - ⇥ Identify container or service failures through logs, alerts, healthchecks
   - ⇥ Examples: "PostgreSQL won't start," "File uploads corrupted," "Volumes deleted"

2. **Stop All Affected Containers**
   - Avoid further write or data corruption
   - Prevent clients from interacting with the damaged state
3. **Confirm the Root Cause**
   - Was it accidental deletion, corrupted data, filesystem issue, or malicious activity?
   - Audit logs and event timelines
4. **Locate the Last Known-Good Backup**
   - Use checksum-verified backups from your volume or DB snapshot
   - Always prefer **logical DB dumps** (e.g., `pg_dump`) if available
5. **Restore the Affected Data**
   - Recreate the volume or target mount
   - Use `tar, rsync`, or DB restore commands
   - Reapply Kubernetes PersistentVolumeClaims if using K8s
6. **Restart the Stack or Container**
   - Use `docker compose up` or redeploy using GitOps/CI pipeline
   - Monitor startup logs for integrity errors or connection failures
7. **Run Post-Restore Validation Checks**
   - Confirm DB queries return expected data
   - Run application-level smoke tests
   - Check logs, metrics, and availability dashboards
8. **Communicate with Stakeholders**
   - Inform engineering, support, business, and customers
   - Update incident channels and escalation status
9. **Document the Incident and Lessons Learned**
   - Include timestamps, backups used, steps taken
   - Update your internal runbook or DR wiki
10. **Patch the Root Cause**
    - If caused by config drift, missing automation, or human error—fix it permanently

Practice Regular DR Drills: *Recovery is not just a plan—it's a muscle. Exercise it before you need it.*

Database-Aware Container Backups (PostgreSQL, MySQL, MongoDB)

- Avoid relying solely on volume snapshots — may cause data corruption
- Use database-native tools:

```
# PostgreSQL
```

```
$ docker exec db pg_dumpall -U postgres > backup.sql

# MySQL
$ docker exec db mysqldump -u root -p mydb > backup.sql

# MongoDB
$ docker exec mongodb mongodump --out /data/dump
```

- Use database-specific restore tools (`psql`, `mysql`, `mongorestore`)

GitOps for Backup Definitions

Embracing GitOps principles for backup and recovery allows you to **treat backups as code**, improving traceability, repeatability, and auditability.

1. **Store all backup configuration files and scripts in Git**
   ⇥ Include `.sh` scripts, `cron` jobs, Compose overrides, and helper YAMLs
2. **Version control your backup logic and frequency**
   ⇥ Know exactly when and how backups are running
   ⇥ Roll back to known working logic if needed
3. **Use declarative files like** `backup.yaml` **or** `restore.yaml`
   ⇥ Define services, volumes, frequency, retention
   ⇥ Enables automation through GitOps tools like Flux, Argo CD, or CI/CD
4. **Audit-ready pipelines**
   ⇥ Every backup job is logged, reviewed, and reproducible
   ⇥ Ideal for regulated environments and enterprise compliance

Backup Automation via CI/CD Pipelines

Automation is key for ensuring reliable, repeatable, and continuous backup processes. CI/CD systems can be used to schedule, execute, and monitor backups.

1. **Automate backups in your CI/CD pipeline**
   ⇥ Use GitHub Actions, GitLab CI, Jenkins, or Bitbucket Pipelines
   ⇥ Trigger backups on schedule or on tag/release
2. **Store backup results securely**
   ⇥ Upload to S3, GCS, Azure Blob, or a remote backup host
   ⇥ Tag with timestamp, service name, and commit SHA
3. **Example: GitHub Action for daily PostgreSQL dump to S3**
   ⇥ Use `cron` trigger with environment secrets

- Run `pg_dump` and push to S3 using `aws-cli` or `rclone`
- Add restore validation jobs to test backup integrity

4. **Integrate restore validation jobs**
   - Spin up a non-prod environment using the latest backup
   - Run automated tests to verify backup quality

Example: GitHub Action for daily PostgreSQL dump:

```
# .github/workflows/db-backup.yml
name: Postgres Daily Backup
on:
  schedule:
    - cron: '0 3 * * *'  # Runs daily at 3 AM UTC
jobs:
  backup:
    runs-on: ubuntu-latest
    steps:
      - name: Dump Postgres Database
        run: |
          docker exec postgres pg_dumpall -U postgres > pg_backup.sql
      - name: Upload to S3 (using AWS CLI)
        env:
          AWS_ACCESS_KEY_ID: ${{ secrets.AWS_ACCESS_KEY_ID }}
          AWS_SECRET_ACCESS_KEY: ${{ secrets.AWS_SECRET_ACCESS_KEY }}
        run: |
          aws s3 cp pg_backup.sql s3://my-backups/postgres/pg_backup_$(date
+%F).sql
```

🔒 **Pro Tip:** *Add backup job summaries to your CI/CD dashboard or pull request checks.*

Monitoring and Validating Backup Health

Creating backups is only half the battle—**ensuring they complete successfully and remain restorable** is just as critical. A silent backup failure can go unnoticed until disaster strikes. This section focuses on building confidence in your backup pipeline through proactive monitoring and validation.

1. **Track backup script exit codes** using automation or CI pipelines
   - Always capture success/failure codes (0 = success)
   - Send status to monitoring dashboards or logs
2. **Validate integrity with checksums after each backup**

- Use `sha256sum`, `md5sum`, or `blake2` to generate and compare hashes
- Store checksum files alongside the backup archives

3. **Log backup activity centrally for visibility and auditing**
   - Forward logs to a central system like:
     - **Loki + Grafana**
     - **ELK/EFK stack (Elasticsearch, Fluentd/Logstash, Kibana)**
   - Include backup name, timestamp, size, and status
4. **Send real-time alerts on failures or anomalies**
   - Use alerting tools such as:
     - Slack (via webhook)
     - Email (via cron or SMTP)
     - PagerDuty (for SRE escalation)
   - Trigger alerts if:
     - A backup fails
     - File size is unexpectedly small
     - No backup was created in X hours
5. **Visualize backup history** with dashboards
   - Create a Grafana panel that shows:
     - Last successful backup timestamp
     - File size trends over time
     - Failure counts by service/volume

🔒 **Pro Tip:** *Log and alert not only failures—but* **silence**, *which often means automation has quietly failed.*

Air-Gapped and Encrypted Restore Strategies

In highly secure or compliance-driven environments, you may need to store or restore backups in **air-gapped systems**—systems disconnected from external networks.

1. **Use removable or portable storage**
   - Store critical backups on encrypted USB drives or offline disks
   - Use `rsync` or `dd` for copying to air-gapped environments
2. **Encrypt backups before transfer**

GPG (recommended):

```
$ gpg -c mydata.tar.gz
```

- `OpenSSL` or `age` for lightweight encryption

3. **Store encryption keys separately from backup data**

- Never bundle encryption keys with the encrypted archive
- Use hardware tokens, HSMs, or Vault to store keys securely

4. **Perform offline restore drills periodically**
    - Test decrypting and restoring without internet access
    - Simulate ransomware or cloud outage scenarios

Security Tip: *Air-gapped restores should be part of your ransomware and nation-state threat models.*

Immutable and Tamper-Proof Backup Storage

To ensure your backups can't be altered or deleted—accidentally or maliciously—adopt **immutable and tamper-resistant storage solutions**. These measures are especially important in environments concerned with **ransomware, insider threats, or regulatory compliance**.

1. **Use object lock or WORM (Write Once, Read Many) storage**
    - Supported by AWS S3 (Object Lock), Backblaze B2, Azure Immutable Blob Storage
    - Enforces write-once behavior—data cannot be deleted or changed for a defined retention period
2. **Prevent backup deletion or overwrite using lifecycle rules**
    - Lock critical buckets or folders
    - Disable delete APIs or enable delete protection where supported
3. **Implement append-only backup mechanisms**
    - Use **ZFS** or **Btrfs snapshots** for incremental, versioned backups
    - For object storage, configure **immutable buckets** or use third-party bucket locking features
4. **Protect backup systems against ransomware**
    - Isolate backup infrastructure from general access
    - Prevent lateral movement by running backup jobs under minimal privileges
    - Monitor for abnormal deletion behavior in cloud logs

Best Practice: *Store immutable backups in a* ***separate account or project*** *with minimal cross-access from production systems.*

Cold Storage and Backup Lifecycle Management

Storing every backup forever is unsustainable. Instead, adopt a **tiered backup strategy** that balances cost, access speed, and data retention policies.

1. **Define storage tiers based on frequency and access needs:**
    - **Hot storage**:
        1. Daily or recent backups
        2. Fast recovery required
        3. Use: S3 Standard, GCS Standard, Azure Hot Blob
    - **Warm storage**:
        1. Weekly or older data
        2. Access is occasional
        3. Use: S3 Infrequent Access, Azure Cool Tier, B2 Lifecycle
    - **Cold storage**:
        1. Monthly, quarterly, or compliance archives
        2. Long retrieval times acceptable
        3. Use: S3 Glacier, Glacier Deep Archive, Azure Archive, B2 Cold
2. **Automate lifecycle transitions**
    - Use cloud-native lifecycle policies to move older backups between storage tiers automatically
    - Example: move backups older than 30 days to Warm, and after 90 days to Cold
3. **Manage transitions with tools like `rclone`, Terraform, or SDKs**
    - Schedule transitions in CI/CD
    - Validate retrieval logic from cold tiers

🔒 **Pro Tip:** *Cold storage can reduce long-term costs by 80–90%, but* **test restore speeds** *and access limitations before relying on it.*

Testing and Verifying Backups Automatically

A backup is worthless if it can't be restored. **Automatic backup testing** ensures your data is truly recoverable—and builds trust in your DR plan.

1. **Run restore tests as part of CI/CD or cron jobs**
    - Spin up a container using the latest backup volume
    - Validate that the container boots and data loads successfully
2. **Check for data and service consistency post-restore**
    - Run database queries, API health checks, or checksum validations
    - Ensure file structures and configs match expected state
3. **Schedule automated test runs weekly or monthly**
    - Tag test results with success/failure status
    - Log and alert failed restores just like failed backups
4. **Treat restore testing as a production-grade responsibility**

- Backups must be **provable and repeatable**, not just assumed

Golden Rule: "No tested backup = no backup." *Trust only what you can restore.*

Sample backup.yaml and restore.yaml Templates

`backup.yaml`

```
name: daily-docker-backup
volume: mydata
frequency: daily
retention: 7
storage:
  type: s3
  bucket: docker-backups
  encryption: true
```

`restore.yaml`

```
name: restore-mydata
from_backup: s3://docker-backups/mydata_20240328.tar.gz
target_volume: mydata-restored
validate: true
auto_start: false
```

These YAML templates can be consumed by CI/CD pipelines or backup agents for declarative backup and recovery processes.

Summary — Docker Backup & Recovery Checklist

Checkpoint	Description
Backup named volumes	Use `tar`, `rsync`, or `docker cp` to archive data
Automate backup scheduling	Use `cron`, CI/CD pipelines, or backup containers
Encrypt sensitive backup data	Protect secrets, DB dumps, and `.env` files with `gpg`, `openssl`, or `age`
Store backups off-site or in cloud	Use `rclone`, S3, Backblaze, Dropbox, or remote servers
Enable backup versioning	Avoid accidental overwrites and allow point-in-time restore
Use secure transfer protocols	Transfer over SSH, HTTPS, or encrypted APIs

Checkpoint	Description
Limit access to backup storage	Apply principle of least privilege; restrict access to automation only
Monitor backup success/failure	Log results, alert on failure, and audit backup size
Validate backup integrity	Use checksums (`sha256sum, md5sum`) to verify backup completeness
Regularly test restore process	Simulate full or partial restores in staging environments
Backup Compose files and configs	Store `docker-compose.yml, .env,` and secrets in version control
Maintain disaster recovery playbook	Include detection, response, restoration, validation, and communication steps
Use volume plugins or CSI drivers	Back up cloud and distributed volumes (e.g., EBS, NFS, GlusterFS)
Tag backups consistently	Use timestamp, Git SHA, or service name in backup filenames
Avoid storing secrets unencrypted	Do not bake secrets into backups or Docker layers
Implement retention policies	Prune outdated backups automatically based on age or priority
Test edge-case recovery scenarios	Practice cold restores, corrupt volume restores, and cross-host recovery

Labs: Docker Backup, Restore, and Disaster Recovery Simulation

Introduction:

In this hands-on lab series, you'll simulate a full backup and disaster recovery lifecycle for Docker volumes.

You'll create critical data, back it up securely, automate backups, simulate a real disaster (data loss), and restore your system — building true resilience and confidence in your infrastructure.

Each lab builds on the previous —like a disaster recovery plan step by step process

Difficulty Level: Advanced

Lab Flow Overview

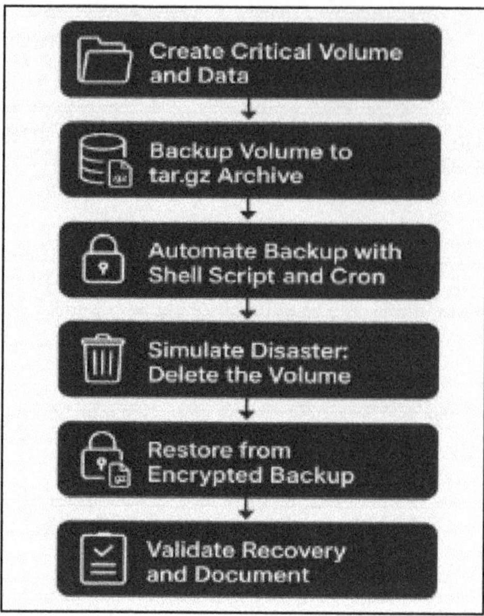

Lab 1:Create a Critical Docker Volume with Important Data

Goal: Create a persistent volume and simulate important business data inside it.

Why? In real systems, volumes hold critical information — databases, uploads, configs.

Steps:

1. Create a Docker volume:

```
$ docker volume create criticaldata
```

2. Create a container and write data:

```
$ docker run --rm -v criticaldata:/data busybox sh -c "echo 'This is
mission-critical data!' > /data/important.txt"
```

3. Verify the data exists:

```
$ docker run --rm -v criticaldata:/data busybox cat /data/important.txt
```

[✓] You now have a live volume with critical information.

Lab 2: Backup the Docker Volume

Goal: Backup the important data to an archive file (.tar.gz).

Why? If the volume is lost, we can use this archive to recover.

Steps:

1. Create a backup folder:

```
$ mkdir -p backups
```

2. Backup the volume:

```
$ docker run --rm -v criticaldata:/data -v $(pwd)/backups:/backup busybox
tar czvf /backup/criticaldata-backup_$(date +%Y%m%d_%H%M).tar.gz /data
```

3. Confirm the backup exists:

```
$ ls -lh backups/
```

[✓] You now have a complete volume backup saved on disk.

Lab 3: Encrypt the Backup for Security

Goal: Encrypt the backup file using GPG.

Why? Unencrypted backups are a security risk (compliance failure, insider threats, ransomware).

Steps:

1. Encrypt the backup:

```
$ gpg -c backups/criticaldata-backup.tar.gz
```

◉ ***Note:*** If filename includes a dynamic date, update it accordingly.

2. Remove the original plaintext backup (Optional):

```
$ rm backups/criticaldata-backup.tar.gz
```

[✓] Your backup is now safely encrypted. Only those with the password can restore it.

Lab 4: Automate Backups with Shell Script and Cron

Goal: Create an automated, daily encrypted backup system.

Why? Manual backups are unreliable. Automation ensures resilience.

Steps:

1. Create a backup script:

```
$ mkdir -p backup-scripts
$ nano backup-scripts/backup.sh
```

2. Script contents (`backup.sh`):

```
#!/bin/bash
cd "$(dirname "$0")/.."  # navigate to root of project (adjust if needed)
DATE=$(date +%Y%m%d_%H%M)
docker run --rm -v criticaldata:/data -v $(pwd)/backups:/backup busybox \
tar czvf /backup/criticaldata-backup_$DATE.tar.gz /data

gpg -c backups/criticaldata-backup_$DATE.tar.gz
rm backups/criticaldata-backup_$DATE.tar.gz
```

3. Make the script executable:

```
$ chmod +x backup-scripts/backup.sh
```

4. Set up a daily cron job:

```
$ crontab -e
```

5. Add:

```
0 2 * * * /absolute/path/to/backup-scripts/backup.sh
```

[✓] Now your volume is backed up and automatically encrypted every day.

Lab 5: Simulate a Disaster (Volume Loss)

Goal: Simulate accidental deletion of critical data.

Why? Real-world disasters — human error, disk failure, ransomware — often involve volume loss.

Steps:

1. Delete the critical volume:

```
$ docker volume rm criticaldata
```

2. Confirm it's deleted:

```
$ docker volume ls

$ docker volume inspect criticaldata || echo "Volume successfully removed."
```

[✓] Your critical data is gone — simulating a real incident.

Lab 6: Restore from Encrypted Backup

Goal: Recover your system from the encrypted backup.

Why? A backup is only useful if restoration works smoothly.

Steps:

1. **Decrypt the latest backup:**

```
$ gpg backups/criticaldata-backup_YYYYMMDD_HHMM.tar.gz.gpg
```

   (Enter the passphrase you set earlier)

2. **Create a new volume for restoration:**

```
$ docker volume create criticaldata-restored
```

3. **Restore backup into the volume:**

```
$ docker run --rm -v criticaldata-restored:/data -v $(pwd)/backups:/backup
busybox \
tar xzvf /backup/criticaldata-backup_YYYYMMDD_HHMM.tar.gz -C /
```

4. **Verify the file:**

```
$ docker run --rm -v criticaldata-restored:/data busybox cat
/data/important.txt
```

[✓] Congratulations — you have successfully restored critical data from an encrypted backup.

Lab 7: Validate the Recovery and Document

Goal: Validate the system and document the recovery process.

Why? Post-recovery validation ensures business operations can resume safely.

Steps:

1. Confirm critical files are accessible and correct.

2. Create a recovery incident log, e.g.:

```
1. - Incident: Critical volume loss
2. - Time detected: 04/29/2025 02:15 UTC
3. - Backup used: criticaldata-backup_20250429_0200.tar.gz.gpg
4. - Recovery time: 18 minutes
5. - Recovery success: Yes
6. - Post-recovery validation: File contents intact
7. - Lessons learned: Add backup size monitoring
```

[✓] You have completed a full disaster recovery simulation — just like a real platform team.

Why These Labs Matter

Practicing backup and recovery in realistic scenarios is essential.

Theory is easy — but in real-world production systems, only **tested, automated, encrypted, and monitored** backups ensure true resilience.

These labs train you to think like a platform engineer:

- *Not just backup — but also validate.*
- *Not just automate — but also secure.*
- *Not just restore — but also document and learn.*

*[✓] **Congratulations** — you are now ready to design and defend resilient Dockerized systems!*

Labs Checklist

Lab	Task	Completed ([✓])
1	Created critical volume and data	▢
2	Backed up volume to archive	▢
3	Encrypted backup	▢
4	Automated backup with cron	▢
5	Simulated disaster (volume loss)	▢
6	Decrypted and restored backup	▢
7	Validated and documented recovery	▢

Summary

- Docker containers may be stateless, but **persistent data (volumes, databases, configs)** must be backed up for operational continuity.
- You explored **volume backup strategies** using `docker cp`, `tar`, `rsync`, `docker save/load`, and `docker export/import`.
- **Cloud and plugin-based storage solutions** (e.g., NFS, S3 via REX-Ray, Flocker) enable offsite and scalable backup strategies.
- You learned to implement **encryption-at-rest** using GPG and compress backups to optimize storage costs.
- **Cold storage tiers** like Amazon Glacier provide long-term, immutable backups suitable for compliance-driven environments.
- The chapter introduced **automated backup and restore pipelines** using `cron`, `rclone`, and CI tools like GitHub Actions.
- A **disaster recovery (DR) simulation lab** was provided to test real-world restoration from backup in a production-like failure scenario.
- The importance of **validating backups, maintaining playbooks**, and monitoring backup failures was emphasized as essential to reliable recovery.

Key Takeaways

In this chapter, you gained deep insight into Docker backup strategies, tools, and real-world disaster recovery workflows. From local volume snapshots to cloud-native encrypted backups, and from automation with CI pipelines to air-gapped cold restores, you now have a production-ready understanding of how to safeguard your containerized infrastructure with resilience and repeatability.

Knowledge Check

1. **Which Docker component requires backup to preserve container state?**
   A) Dockerfile
   B) Image tags
   C) Volumes
   D) Bridge network
2. **What command is used to export a running container's filesystem?**
   A) `docker backup`
   B) `docker export`
   C) `docker save`
   D) `docker archive`
3. **Which Docker command is used to back up an image for transport?**
   A) `docker export`
   B) `docker load`
   C) `docker save`
   D) `docker pull`
4. **What's the primary difference between `docker export` and `docker save`?**
   A) `export` backs up volumes
   B) `save` includes image history and layers; export is for containers only
   C) `save` compresses logs
   D) `export` is used for clusters
5. **What tool is recommended to back up Docker volumes?**
   A) `rsync, tar`, or volume plugins
   B) `docker save`
   C) `docker diff`
   D) `df -h`
6. **Which folder stores Docker volume data by default on Linux?**
   A) `/home/docker`
   B) `/var/docker/volumes`
   C) `/var/lib/docker/volumes/`
   D) `/etc/docker/`
7. **Which command allows you to restore an exported container image?**
   A) `docker restore`
   B) `docker run`
   C) `docker import`
   D) `docker start`
8. **Which command loads a saved image back into Docker?**

A) `docker build`
B) `docker import`
C) `docker run`
D) `docker load`

9. **What's a common use case for docker commit in backups?**
A) Capture live state of a running container as a new image
B) Version control
C) Back up logs
D) Schedule jobs

10. **Why are bind mounts difficult to back up?**
A) Not persistent
B) Tied to host path structure
C) Encrypted
D) Use secrets

11. **What are recommended best practices for Docker backup?**
A) Automate, test restores, encrypt archives
B) Manual copy/paste
C) Only back up logs
D) Restart containers daily

12. **Which file types should NOT be included in image backups?**
A) `.env, .pem`
B) Secrets
C) Config files
D) Application binaries

13. **In Docker Swarm, how are secrets backed up?**
A) Using docker secret backup
B) Via docker inspect
C) Secrets are not retrievable—must be re-created
D) docker cp

14. **What is the purpose of snapshotting Docker volumes?**
A) Shrink size
B) Real-time backups for rollback
C) Reduce RAM
D) Clone image

15. **Why is it important to backup `docker-compose.yml` files?**
A) They store logs
B) They define infrastructure and state
C) They're encrypted
D) They replace Dockerfile

16. **What are reliable ways to back up Docker volumes?**
    - ▢ Use docker run with volume bind and tar
    - ▢ Use rsync to archive the volume path
    - ▢ Use Docker Volume plugins (e.g., Convoy, NetApp)
    - ▢ Use docker save
17. **What are the limitations of docker export?**
    - ▢ It doesn't save volumes
    - ▢ It doesn't preserve history/layers
    - ▢ It saves logs
    - ▢ It includes secrets
18. **What are features of docker save/docker load?**
    - ▢ Saves full image and metadata
    - ▢ Can be used across air-gapped systems
    - ▢ Supports offline transfer
    - ▢ Stores container logs
19. **When should you use docker commit?**
    - ▢ Emergency snapshot of container
    - ▢ Regular CI builds
    - ▢ Testing intermediate states
    - ▢ Replace Dockerfile entirely
20. **What should be included in disaster recovery plans?**
    - ▢ Volume backup strategy
    - ▢ Image registry redundancy
    - ▢ Compose/YAML/Infra as code
    - ▢ Random image pulls
21. **What file format results from docker save?**
    - ▢ `.tar`
    - ▢ `.img`
    - ▢ `Compressed tarball`
    - ▢ `.yml`
22. **What happens if you lose** `/var/lib/docker` **entirely?**
    - ▢ Images, volumes, containers, and networks are lost
    - ▢ Only logs disappear
    - ▢ Auto-recovers from cloud

- ▢ Requires full restore

23. What are benefits of automatic backup scheduling for Docker?

- ▢ Reduced data loss
- ▢ Regular rollback points
- ▢ Supports compliance
- ▢ Slower containers

24. What is a safe way to move a volume to another host?

- ▢ Tar and transfer `/var/lib/docker/volumes/`
- ▢ Use volume plugins with remote support
- ▢ Use `docker push`
- ▢ Use `docker cp`

25. What should be tested during backup validation?

- ▢ Can it be restored?
- ▢ Data integrity (e.g., checksum)
- ▢ Application boot post-restore
- ▢ Only file count

26. What tools support backup automation for Docker?

- ▢ cron + bash scripts
- ▢ Restic, Duplicity, Velero
- ▢ CI/CD jobs
- ▢ docker logs

27. Which of the following are common causes of data loss in Docker environments?

- ▢ Unmounted volumes
- ▢ Bind mounts pointing to wrong path
- ▢ No backup before container rebuild
- ▢ Having multiple `.env` files

28. When backing up a live database volume, what should you do?

- ▢ Lock or snapshot the DB
- ▢ Use `mysqldump` or DB-native tools
- ▢ Backup during low-traffic times
- ▢ Use `docker cp` blindly

29. Where can you store Docker image backups securely?

- ▢ S3 or MinIO

- ▢ Encrypted drives
- ▢ Cloud object storage
- ▢ Public GitHub repos

30. What defines a successful Docker recovery process?

- ▢ Data integrity
- ▢ Minimal downtime
- ▢ Repeatable restoration steps
- ▢ Changing image IDs

Answers

Q#	Correct Answer	Explanation
1	C	Volumes hold data and must be backed up.
2	B	`docker export` exports container FS to tar.
3	C	`docker save` exports an image and its layers.
4	B	`save` includes image history; `export` doesn't.
5	A	Use tar, rsync, or volume plugins for volume backup.
6	C	Default Docker volume path is `/var/lib/docker/volumes/`.
7	C	`docker import` restores a tar-exported container.
8	D	Use `docker load` to import a saved image.
9	A	`docker commit` captures a container's current state.
10	B	Bind mounts are host-path dependent, harder to port.
11	A	Always automate and test Docker backups.
12	B	Secrets should never be included in images.
13	C	Swarm secrets are write-only; they must be re-created.
14	B	Snapshots enable rollback by freezing state.
15	B	Compose files define services, volumes, and infra.

Q16. What are valid strategies for backing up Docker volumes?

- [✓] Use `docker run` with volume bind and `tar`
- [✓] Use `rsync` to archive the volume path
- [✓] Use Docker Volume plugins (e.g., Convoy, NetApp)
- [X] `docker save` is for images, not volumes

Explanation: Volume backups require file-level tools like `tar`, `rsync`, or plugins. `docker save` backs up images, not volume data.

Q17. What are limitations of `docker commit`?

- [✓] It doesn't save volumes
- [✓] It doesn't preserve history/layers
- [X] It saves logs
- [X] It includes secrets

Explanation: `docker commit` snapshots container state but omits volumes, logs, and historical metadata.

Q18. What are benefits of using `docker save`?

- [✓] Saves full image and metadata
- [✓] Can be used across air-gapped systems
- [✓] Supports offline transfer
- [X] Does not include container logs

Explanation: `docker save` is used to archive and move images but does not contain logs or runtime states.

Q19. When might you use `docker commit`?

- [✓] Emergency snapshot of container
- [✓] Testing intermediate states
- [X] Not meant for regular CI or replacing Dockerfiles

Explanation: `docker commit` helps in capturing ad-hoc changes but isn't a CI/CD best practice.

Q20. What enhances backup resilience in Docker environments?

- [✓] Volume backup strategy
- [✓] Image registry redundancy
- [✓] Compose/YAML/Infra as code
- [X] Avoid random image pulls

Explanation: Structured infra, redundancy, and controlled image management ensure secure backups and restores.

Q21. What are valid formats for Docker image or volume backups?

- [✓] `.tar`
- [✓] Compressed tarball
- [X] `.img` and `.yml` are invalid for this use case

Explanation: Docker images/volumes are commonly exported as `.tar.gz` or `.tar` archives.

Q22. What happens if you delete Docker's `/var/lib/docker` without a backup?

- **[√]** Images, volumes, containers, and networks are lost
- **[√]** Requires full restore
- **[X]** Docker cannot auto-recover from this

Explanation: Deleting Docker's core storage path removes all artifacts; restore requires external backup.

Q23. What are the advantages of periodic volume backups?

- **[√]** Reduced data loss
- **[√]** Regular rollback points
- **[√]** Supports compliance
- **[X]** No performance hit from backup automation

Explanation: Backups support resilience and compliance but may affect performance if not optimized.

Q24. How can you migrate Docker volumes across systems?

- **[√]** Tar and transfer volume directory
- **[√]** Use remote volume plugins
- **[X]** docker push and `docker cp` don't work with volumes

Explanation: Volumes require filesystem-level transfer or plugin-based replication — not `docker push`.

Q25. What should be validated in a Docker volume backup?

- **[√]** Can it be restored?
- **[√]** Integrity check (checksums)
- **[√]** Boot and test restored apps
- **[X]** File count doesn't prove validity

Explanation: Restores must be tested, and checksums confirm integrity — file count alone is not proof.

Q26. What tools can automate Docker backup workflows?

- **[√]** `cron` + bash
- **[√]** Restic, Duplicity, Velero
- **[√]** CI/CD pipelines
- **[X]** `docker logs` isn't a backup tool

Explanation: Reliable backups can be scheduled and tested via cron jobs or integrated CI pipelines.

Q27. What scenarios can result in Docker volume data loss?

- [✓] Unmounted volumes
- [✓] Wrong bind paths
- [✓] No backups before rebuild
- [X] Multiple `.env` files don't cause data loss directly

Explanation: Misconfigured paths and lack of backups are common causes of data loss — not `.env` files.

Q28. How should you back up live databases in Docker containers?

- [✓] Lock DB or take snapshot
- [✓] Use `mysqldump` or native tools
- [✓] Backup during idle time
- [X] Avoid `docker cp` on live DBs

Explanation: Use database-native backups to avoid corruption — `docker cp` is unsafe for live DBs.

Q29. What are secure storage options for container backups?

- [✓] S3/MinIO
- [✓] Encrypted drives
- [✓] Secure cloud object stores
- [X] Never use public GitHub for backups

Explanation: Backups should be encrypted and stored securely — public GitHub is not a valid option.

Q30. What are goals of a good Docker backup strategy?

- [✓] Data integrity
- [✓] Minimal downtime
- [✓] Repeatable recovery steps
- [X] Changing image IDs is not desired

Explanation: Backups should ensure consistency and rapid recovery — changing image IDs can break reproducibility.

Chapter 15: Troubleshooting Docker — Logs, Crashes, and Real-World Debugging Tactics

Know the Lifecycle — Where Things Can Fail

When a container doesn't behave as expected, the problem could be in:

1. **The Image** (bad base image, incorrect CMD, missing dependencies)
2. **The Container** (crashes, hangs, misconfigurations)
3. **The Network** (service not reachable, port conflicts, DNS)
4. **The Volumes** (missing data, permission errors)
5. **The Host** (insufficient memory/CPU, full disk, systemd limits)

Let's dive into the tools and techniques that help pinpoint the root cause.

Diagnosing Container Failures

Container Exits Immediately?

Check the exit code:

```
$ docker ps -a
```

Then inspect:

```
$ docker inspect <container_id> --format='{{.State.ExitCode}}'
```

Use `docker logs` to see last output:

```
$ docker logs <container_name>
```

Common exit codes:

- `0:` Normal exit
- `1:` Application crash
- `137:` Killed (OOM or SIGKILL)
- `139:` Segfault
- `143:` SIGTERM (e.g., `docker stop`)

Debugging Live Containers

Open an interactive shell:

```
$ docker exec -it <container> sh       # Alpine/busybox
$ docker exec -it <container> bash     # Ubuntu/Debian
```

Inspect files and logs:

```
$ cat /var/log/nginx/error.log
$ ls -la /app
env
```

Check environment inside container:

```
$ printenv
```

Analyzing Logs

View logs of a container:

```
$ docker logs <container>
```

Follow logs live:

```
$ docker logs -f <container>
```

Filter logs with grep:

```
$ docker logs <container> | grep ERROR
```

For multi-service apps, use centralized log tools (Loki, ELK, Fluentd)

Debugging Build Failures

Use `--progress=plain` for full output:

```
$ docker build --progress=plain -t myapp .
```

Use `--no-cache` to skip layer cache:

```
$ docker build --no-cache -t myapp .
```

Add debug lines in Dockerfile:

```
RUN echo "Step reached" && ls -la /app
```

Network Troubleshooting

List Networks:

```
$ docker network ls
```

Inspect Network:

```
$ docker network inspect <network>
```

Test DNS/Connectivity from inside:

```
$ docker exec -it <container> ping redis
$ docker exec -it <container> nslookup redis
```

Check open ports:

```
$ docker port <container>
```

Monitoring Resources

Live resource stats:

```
$ docker stats
```

System-wide resource usage:

```
$ htop
$ df -h
$ free -m
```

Inspect container metrics:

```
$ docker inspect <container> | jq '.[0].HostConfig.Memory'
```

Common Errors & Fixes

Problem	Fix
`OCI runtime error`	Check Docker version, restart daemon
`No space left on device`	Clear unused volumes/images: `docker system prune`
`Port already in use`	Use `lsof -i :<port>` to find conflict
`Permission denied`	Check volume permissions; use non-root user
Container restarts loop	Check logs + health check config
App can't reach DB	Ensure same network; use service name not IP in connection

Useful Debugging Tools

Tool	Use Case
`strace`	Trace syscalls inside container
`curl`	Check internal HTTP connections
`iftop`	Real-time network monitoring
`tcpdump`	Capture network traffic
`netstat`	View open ports
`ps aux`	View processes in container

Example:

```
$ docker exec -it <container> curl http://localhost:5000
$ docker exec -it <container> strace -p 1
```

Troubleshooting Docker Compose

Service won't start?

```
$ docker compose logs <service>
```

Rebuild without cache:

```
$ docker compose build --no-cache
```

Restart and recreate services:

```
$ docker compose up --force-recreate -build
```

Service unreachable?

- Ensure both are in same network
- Use service name, not IP (`db:5432` instead of `172.x.x.x`)
- Add health checks to wait before startup

When All Else Fails

Export Container for Postmortem:

```
$ docker export <container> > debug.tar
```

View Full Inspection:

```
$ docker inspect <container> | less
```

Snapshot running container as image:

```
$ docker commit <container> debug-image
$ docker run -it debug-image /bin/bash
```

Docker Daemon Diagnostics

Check daemon logs:

```
$ journalctl -u docker
```

Restart Docker safely:

```
$ sudo systemctl restart docker
```

Troubleshooting Checklist

- ☐ Check container logs
- ☐ Use `docker exec` to inspect runtime state
- ☐ Inspect networks and ports
- ☐ Monitor resource usage
- ☐ Use Compose logs to debug service issues
- ☐ Export container if needed for deeper analysis
- ☐ Restart Docker daemon only as last resort
- ☐ Use `--no-cache` and `--progress=plain` when rebuilding
- ☐ Add health checks to prevent loops and flapping

Lab: Diagnosing and Fixing a Failing Docker Service

This hands-on lab walks you through a full cycle of troubleshooting and recovering a failing Docker container using real tools. It simulates a crash scenario, helps you investigate with CLI commands, and guides you to a successful fix.

Difficulty Level: Advanced

Objective

- Deploy a broken container (Python Flask app)
- Investigate the failure using `docker logs, inspect`, and `stats`
- Simulate a DNS/network issue and fix it
- Explore container exit codes and system-level problems
- Apply a fix and validate the recovered app

Step 1: Create the Broken Flask App

app.py

```
from flask import Flask
import sys

app = Flask(__name__)

@app.route('/')
def home():
    return "This app will crash immediately!"

if __name__ == '__main__':
    sys.exit(1)  # Simulates a failure
```

Dockerfile

```
FROM python:3.11-slim
WORKDIR /app
COPY app.py .
RUN pip install flask
CMD ["python", "app.py"]
```

Step 2: Build the Docker Image

```
$ docker build -t crash-app .
```

Step 3: Run the Container

```
$ docker run -d --name crash-test crash-app
```

Verify it's not running:

```
$ docker ps -a
```

You should see `Exited (1)` or `Exited (137)`.

Step 4: Investigate the Logs

```
$ docker logs crash-test
```

Check exit code:

```
$ docker inspect crash-test --format='{{.State.ExitCode}}'
```

Use `docker events` to see system events:

```
$ docker events --filter container=crash-test &
```

Step 5: Simulate and Fix a Network Issue

Try pinging Google DNS:

```
$ docker run -it busybox ping 8.8.8.8
```

Then:

```
$ docker network inspect bridge
```

If DNS fails, try manually setting a DNS:

```
$ docker run --dns=8.8.8.8 busybox nslookup google.com
```

You can use this to fix services failing due to DNS issues.

Step 6: Explore Resource Constraints

Run a resource-heavy container:

```
$ docker run -d --memory=64m --name stress-container busybox sh -c "yes >
/dev/null"
```

Then inspect:

```
$ docker stats stress-container
```

Exit code `137` indicates an out-of-memory kill by the kernel.

Step 7: Fix the Crash

Edit `app.py` to remove the crash:

```
from flask import Flask
app = Flask(__name__)

@app.route('/')
def home():
    return "App running normally!"

if __name__ == '__main__':
    app.run(host='0.0.0.0', port=5000)
```

Rebuild and re-run:

```
$ docker build -t crash-app-fixed .
$ docker run -d -p 5000:5000 --name stable-app crash-app-fixed
```

Test in browser:

```
$ curl http://localhost:5000
```

Summary

Symptom	Diagnostic Tool	Fix or Outcome
App exited	`docker logs`	Exit code showed crash
DNS resolution fail	`nslookup, inspect`	Use `--dns` or fix `/etc/resolv.conf`
Memory kill (137)	`docker stats`, OOM log	Increase limits or reduce load
Crash on start	`logs, exit` code	Fix `app.py` logic

This lab mimics a full postmortem recovery and equips you with the commands needed to triage failures in real-world containerized deployments.

Troubleshooting Workshop Series: Real-World Scenarios & Fixes

Difficulty Level: Intermediate–Advanced

These hands-on labs are designed to simulate real-world issues encountered in DevOps pipelines, CI/CD workflows, and production environments. Each lab includes a problem statement, symptoms, root cause analysis, and resolution.

Workshop Lab 1: Container CrashLoopBackOff / Exit Immediately

Symptoms:

`$ docker ps -a` shows container exits with code `0 or 137` immediately.

Commands to Diagnose:

```
$ docker logs <container_id>
$ docker inspect <container_id>
```

Cause:

ENTRYPOINT or CMD process terminates too quickly (e.g., `CMD ["bash"]` without interactive mode).

Fix:

Use interactive shell or correct entrypoint.

```
$ docker run -it ubuntu bash
```

Workshop Lab 2: Docker Daemon Not Starting (Linux)

Symptoms:

`$ systemctl status` docker shows `failed` or `inactive`.

Diagnosis:

```
$ journalctl -xeu docker
$ docker info
```

Common Causes:

- Corrupted `/var/lib/docker`
- Overlay filesystem issues
- Misconfigured `daemon.json`

Fix:

```
$ sudo mv /var/lib/docker /var/lib/docker.bak
$ sudo systemctl restart docker
```

Workshop Lab 3: Container Can't Reach Internet

Symptoms:
`$ apt-get update` fails inside container.

Diagnosis:

```
$ docker run busybox ping 8.8.8.8
```

Cause:
Docker bridge network not configured, or host firewall is blocking.

Fix:
Restart Docker, reset iptables:

```
$ sudo iptables -P FORWARD ACCEPT
$ sudo systemctl restart docker
```

Workshop Lab 4: Volume Mount Permission Errors

Symptoms:
`Permission denied` errors when accessing mounted files.

Cause:
Host path ownership mismatch. Docker maps host UID/GID to container UID.

Fix:

```
$ sudo chown -R 1000:1000 /host/volume/path
```

Workshop Lab 5: Docker Login Failures in CI/CD

Symptoms:

GitHub Actions / Jenkins fails during `docker login` with:
`Error saving credentials` or `unauthorized: incorrect username/password.`

Diagnosis:

- Check DockerHub token expiration.
- Use secrets securely.

Fix (GitHub Actions):

yaml

```
- name: Docker Login
  run: echo "${{ secrets.DOCKER_PASSWORD }}" | docker login -u "${{
secrets.DOCKER_USERNAME }}" --password-stdin
```

Workshop Lab 6: Docker Compose Service Hangs on `starting`

Symptoms:

After running `docker-compose up`, a service hangs indefinitely in `starting` state.
Logs show:

```
Starting <service_name> ...
```

but the container never transitions to `healthy`.

Diagnosis:

Inspect healthcheck settings in `docker-compose.yml`

Run:

```
$ docker inspect <container_id> | jq '.[0].State'
$ docker logs <container_id>
```

Common Causes:

- Misconfigured `healthcheck` (e.g., incorrect `test`, `interval`, or `timeout`)
- Dependency container not available yet
- `depends_on` not using `condition: service_healthy`

Fix:

- Ensure dependent services expose ports properly
- Example healthcheck fix:

```
healthcheck:
  test: ["CMD", "curl", "-f", "http://localhost:8080/health"]
  interval: 10s
  timeout: 3s
 retries: 3
```

- Use `condition: service_healthy` for `depends_on` where applicable.

Workshop Lab 7: Swarm Node State = "Down" After Reboot

Symptoms:

After a reboot, one or more nodes in your Swarm cluster appear as `Down` in:

```
$ docker node ls
```

Diagnosis:

- Check logs:
  - `$ journalctl -u docker`
  - `$ docker info`
- Validate docker swarm join-token was not reset
- Confirm if clock skew or IP changes occurred

Common Causes:

- Docker daemon not restarted on reboot
- IP address changed due to DHCP
- Firewall blocking ports (`2377`, `7946`, `4789`)
- Clock drift causing TLS certificate mismatch

Fix:

```
$ systemctl restart docker
$ docker swarm join --token <...> <manager_ip>:2377
```

- Use static IPs for nodes
- Enable NTP to prevent clock skew
- Make sure firewall allows:
  - `TCP 2377 (cluster management)`
  - `TCP/UDP 7946 (node communication)`
  - `UDP 4789 (overlay network)`

Workshop Lab 8: Docker Registry Push Fails – `413 Payload Too Large`

Symptoms:

You attempt to `docker push` a large image to a private registry and receive:

- `413 Request Entity Too Large`

Diagnosis:

- Review registry reverse proxy configuration (e.g., nginx, Traefik)
- Check Content-Length headers in logs:
    - $ curl -v -X PUT --data-binary @<layer.tar> http://registry.local:5000

Common Causes:

- Nginx client_max_body_size too low
- HTTP proxy like Apache limits payload
- Registry service buffer limit reached

Fix (Nginx Example):

```
server {
    ...
    client_max_body_size 1G;
    ...
}
```

Restart services after update:

```
$ sudo systemctl reload nginx
```

Alternative: Split large base image into smaller layers using multistage builds.

These real-world troubleshooting workshops simulate what SREs, DevOps engineers, and support teams face daily. Practice resolving these to develop production-grade confidence with Docker deployments.

Monitoring and Observability: When CLI Debugging Isn't Enough

While docker logs, inspect, and exec provide powerful command-line debugging tools, modern container infrastructure often requires real-time observability. When diagnosing production issues, especially intermittent failures or performance bottlenecks, CLI tools alone may not provide enough context.

For a more holistic view, tools like **Prometheus (metrics collection)**, **Grafana (dashboarding)**, and **Loki (centralized log aggregation)** offer significant advantages:

- 💹 **Prometheus** tracks CPU, memory, network, and container uptime metrics.
- 📊 **Grafana** visualizes trends and alert thresholds.
- 🗃 **Loki** centralizes logs from multiple containers, with filtering and querying.

These tools are discussed in **Chapter 9: Docker in Production – Hardening, Scaling & Zero-Downtime Deployments** and implemented hands-on in **Chapter 13: Best Practices and Container Hardening – Securing Containers by Design**. If you're debugging a distributed microservices system or managing live environments, integrating them into your troubleshooting workflow is essential.

🔒 **Pro Tip:** *Pair Prometheus metrics (e.g., container CPU spikes) with correlated logs from Loki to pinpoint root causes faster.*

Summary

- Diagnosing Docker issues starts by pinpointing whether the problem is in the image, container, network, volume, or host.
- Tools like `docker logs, ps -a, inspect`, and `events` are critical to understanding container lifecycle and failure points.
- Runtime debugging with `exec, strace, curl`, and `htop` helps assess container internals.
- Network problems can be isolated using `ping, nslookup, docker network inspect`, and `tcpdump`.
- Docker Compose failures are often caused by bad `depends_on` logic, service order, or missing health checks.
- System-level constraints (memory, disk, ports) and file permissions are common causes of crashes.
- The checklist and command toolbox enable quick triage under pressure.

Key Takeaways

In this chapter, you explored the full lifecycle of troubleshooting Docker—from detecting container failures and analyzing logs to inspecting live containers and resolving build or network issues. Equipped with CLI tools, real-time diagnostics, and systematic triage techniques, you are now ready to debug containers, resolve flapping services, and restore confidence in production-grade deployments

Knowledge Check

1. **What command shows the live logs of a running container?**
   A) `docker monitor`
   B) `docker logs`
   C) `docker watch`
   D) `docker debug`
2. **What flag follows logs in real-time?**
   A) `–stream`
   B) `-f` or `–follow`
   C) `–tail`
   D) `--monitor`
3. **What command enters an interactive shell in a running container?**
   A) `docker ssh`
   B) `docker access`
   C) `docker exec -it sh`
   D) `docker run --debug`
4. **Which command lists all running containers?**
   A) `docker show`
   B) `docker ps`
   C) `docker ls`
   D) `docker status`
5. **What command shows system-wide resource usage by containers?**
   A) `docker inspect`
   B) `docker stats`
   C) `docker logs`
   D) `docker resource`
6. **How do you find the IP address of a running container?**
   A) `docker ip`
   B) `docker inspect`
   C) `docker address`
   D) `docker net ip`
7. **What Docker command shows detailed info about a container, network, or volume?**
   A) `docker logs`
   B) `docker system`
   C) `docker inspect`
   D) `docker config`
8. **What tool shows low-level Docker host info?**
   A) `docker sysinfo`

B) `docker system info`
C) `docker info`
D) `docker version`

9. **What is the effect of docker events?**
A) Shows log history
B) Starts audit logging
C) Streams real-time Docker event messages (e.g., start/stop)
D) Rebuilds container

10. **What's a common reason a container exits immediately?**
A) Image not pulled
B) No volume mounted
C) Entrypoint or CMD exits after execution
D) Logs are full

11. **What happens if you use an incorrect port with `-p`?**
A) Nothing happens
B) Container crashes
C) Port binding error
D) Volume disappears

12. **How do you restart a stopped container?**
A) `docker start`
B) `docker reset`
C) `docker up`
D) `docker relaunch`

13. **Which command shows the last exit code of a container?**
A) `docker logs`
B) `docker inspect`
C) `docker ps -a`
D) `docker restart`

14. **Which Dockerfile mistake commonly causes build failures?**
A) Multiple COPY instructions
B) Not specifying FROM as the first line
C) Having comments
D) Using lowercase keywords

15. **What does `docker compose logs` do?**
A) Shows container metadata
B) Launches containers
C) Displays logs from all services in Compose
D) Restores volumes

16. **What are reasons a container becomes unresponsive?**

- ▢ Exceeded memory limit
- ▢ App crashed inside
- ▢ Unused volume
- ▢ Port conflict

17. What steps help debug a broken container?

- ▢ `docker logs`
- ▢ `docker exec into it`
- ▢ Inspect exit code via `docker ps -a`
- ▢ Delete and recreate immediately

18. What can you find in docker inspect output?

- ▢ IP address
- ▢ Mounts and volumes
- ▢ Entry point
- ▢ Terminal logs

19. Which of these can be analyzed using docker stats?

- ▢ CPU %
- ▢ Memory usage
- ▢ Network throughput
- ▢ Dockerfile content

20. What causes Image not found errors?

- ▢ Image doesn't exist locally or in registry
- ▢ Image tag is incorrect
- ▢ Host is offline
- ▢ Registry requires login

21. How can you troubleshoot DNS resolution in containers?

- ▢ Use `docker exec + nslookup`
- ▢ Check embedded DNS (127.0.0.11)
- ▢ Restart the Docker daemon blindly
- ▢ Inspect `/etc/resolv.conf` inside the container

22. What are signs of a failing container healthcheck?

- ▢ STATUS: unhealthy
- ▢ Repeated restarts
- ▢ Healthcheck log output
- ▢ High CPU

23. What commands help identify container crashes?

- ▢ `docker logs`

- ▢ `docker ps -a`
- ▢ `docker inspect`
- ▢ `docker build`

24. What causes permission denied errors in containers?

- ▢ Wrong UID/GID
- ▢ Files copied as root
- ▢ Read-only filesystem
- ▢ Correct volume name

25. Which flags make docker run helpful for debugging?

- ▢ `-it`
- ▢ `-rm`
- ▢ `--entrypoint /bin/sh`
- ▢ `--detach`

26. When would docker events be useful?

- ▢ Trace container lifecycle
- ▢ Audit network changes
- ▢ View CPU usage
- ▢ Track restart loops

27. What problems might incorrect bind mounts cause?

- ▢ App can't find files
- ▢ Permission errors
- ▢ Network latency
- ▢ Overwrite host paths

28. What is the output of `docker system df`?

- ▢ Image and volume disk usage
- ▢ Total reclaimable space
- ▢ Container storage
- ▢ File descriptor leaks

29. What happens if you restart the Docker daemon?

- ▢ Running containers continue
- ▢ Docker resets internal state
- ▢ All volumes are deleted
- ▢ May clear logs depending on driver

30. What can help identify Docker network issues?

- ▢ `docker network inspect`
- ▢ `docker exec ping`

▢ `tcpdump` inside the container

▢ Only `docker ps`

Answer

Q#	Correct Answer	Explanation
1	B	`docker logs` displays container stdout/stderr.
2	B	`-f` or `--follow` streams logs in real time.
3	C	`docker exec -it <container> sh` starts an interactive shell.
4	B	`docker ps` lists running containers.
5	B	`docker stats` shows live resource usage.
6	B	Use `docker inspect` to view container IP.
7	C	`docker inspect` returns detailed metadata in JSON.
8	C	`docker info` shows host and daemon details.
9	C	`docker events` streams container lifecycle events.
10	C	Containers exit when the main process finishes.
11	C	Port conflicts result in binding errors.
12	A	Use `docker start` to restart stopped containers.
13	C	Exit code is visible via `docker ps -a`.
14	B	Dockerfiles must begin with a `FROM` instruction.
15	C	`docker compose logs` aggregates logs across all services.

Q16. What are reasons a container becomes unresponsive?

- [✓] Exceeded memory limit
- [✓] App crashed inside
- [X] Unused volume
- [✓] Port conflict

Explanation: Containers can hang or fail if they hit resource limits, the app crashes, or ports clash.

Q17. What steps help debug a broken container?

- [✓] `docker logs`
- [✓] `docker exec` into it
- [✓] Inspect exit code via `docker ps -a`

- [X] Delete and recreate immediately

Explanation: Logs, inspection, and live exec provide critical context before restarting or deleting.

Q18. What can you find in `docker inspect` output?

- [✓] IP address
- [✓] Mounts and volumes
- [✓] Entry point
- [X] Terminal logs

Explanation: `docker inspect` shows metadata like network info, mounts, and commands — not stdout logs.

Q19. Which of these can be analyzed using docker stats?

- [✓] CPU %
- [✓] Memory usage
- [✓] Network throughput
- [X] Dockerfile content

Explanation: `docker stats` tracks live resource consumption — not image/Dockerfile details.

Q20. What causes "Image not found" errors?

- [✓] Image doesn't exist locally or in registry
- [✓] Image tag is incorrect
- [✓] Host is offline
- [✓] Registry requires login

Explanation: Image errors stem from bad tags, missing registries, or auth/network issues.

Q21. How can you troubleshoot DNS resolution in containers?

- [✓] Use `docker exec + nslookup`
- [✓] Check embedded DNS (`127.0.0.11`)
- [X] Restart the Docker daemon blindly
- [✓] Inspect `/etc/resolv.conf` inside the container

Explanation: Use live container inspection and internal tools; daemon restarts are last-resort.

Q22. What are signs of a failing container healthcheck?

- [✓] `STATUS: unhealthy`
- [✓] Repeated restarts
- [✓] Healthcheck log output

- [X] High CPU

Explanation: Health status and logs signal healthcheck failure — high CPU may be unrelated.

Q23. What commands help identify container crashes?

- [√] `docker logs`
- [√] `docker ps -a`
- [√] `docker inspect`
- [X] `docker build`

Explanation: Logs, history, and inspection reveal crash causes — build relates to image creation.

Q24. What causes "permission denied" errors in containers?

- [√] Wrong UID/GID
- [√] Files copied as root
- [√] Read-only filesystem
- [X] Correct volume name

Explanation: Permissions depend on UID/GID and filesystem mode, not volume name correctness.

Q25. Which flags make `docker run` helpful for debugging?

- [√] `-it`
- [√] `-rm`
- [√] `--entrypoint /bin/sh`
- [X] `-detach`

Explanation: Interactive mode, shell entry, and auto-cleanup are debugging essentials — detached mode hides logs.

Q26. When would `docker events` be useful?

- [√] Trace container lifecycle
- [√] Audit network changes
- [X] View CPU usage
- [√] Track restart loops

Explanation: Events provide a real-time stream of Docker activity, not performance metrics.

Q27. What problems might incorrect bind mounts cause?

- [√] App can't find files
- [√] Permission errors
- [X] Network latency
- [√] Overwrite host paths

Explanation: Misconfigured mounts lead to missing or inaccessible files, or unintentional data overwrite.

Q28. What is the output of `docker system df`?

- [✓] Image and volume disk usage
- [✓] Total reclaimable space
- [✓] Container storage
- [X] File descriptor leaks

Explanation: `system df` shows disk usage insights — not low-level OS or runtime metrics.

Q29. What happens if you restart the Docker daemon?

- [✓] Running containers continue
- [✓] Docker resets internal state
- [X] All volumes are deleted
- [✓] May clear logs depending on driver

Explanation: Containers persist unless specifically configured otherwise. Logging behavior depends on driver.

Q30. What can help identify Docker network issues?

- [✓] `docker network inspect`
- [✓] `docker exec ping`
- [✓] `tcpdump` inside the container
- [X] Only `docker ps`

Explanation: Active inspection, ping testing, and traffic capture help troubleshoot Docker networking.

Chapter 16: CI/CD Pipeline with GitHub Actions + DockerHub

Introduction

In the world of containerized applications, building and pushing Docker images manually is not scalable. This is where CI/CD comes in. In this chapter, we'll build a complete CI/CD pipeline that:

- Automatically builds Docker images when code is pushed to GitHub
- Running tests before deployment
- Pushes tagged images to DockerHub
- Optionally deploys to staging or production using secrets

We'll be using **GitHub Actions** for the pipeline and **DockerHub** as the image registry.

CI/CD Pipeline Architecture

Components

Tool	Purpose
GitHub	Source code version control and CI/CD triggers
GitHub Actions	Automated workflows (CI/CD)
Docker	Containerization
DockerHub	Image registry (hosted or private)
Secrets	GitHub Encrypted Secrets for security

Flow

- Developer pushes code → GitHub
- GitHub Actions is triggered → Runs pipeline
- Tests run → Docker image built
- If successful → Image pushed to DockerHub
- Deployment workflow triggered (optional)

Project Structure

Example repo layout:

```
/myapp
  ├── app/
```

```
├── Dockerfile
├── docker-compose.yml
├── .github/workflows/
│   └── docker-ci.yml
├── requirements.txt
└── README.md
```

GitHub Actions Workflow: `docker-ci.yml`

```
name: CI/CD Pipeline

on:
  push:
    branches: [ main ]
  pull_request:
    branches: [ main ]

jobs:
  build:
    runs-on: ubuntu-latest

    steps:
    - name: Checkout Code
      uses: actions/checkout@v3

    - name: Set up Docker Buildx
      uses: docker/setup-buildx-action@v2

    - name: Login to DockerHub
      uses: docker/login-action@v2
      with:
        username: ${{ secrets.DOCKERHUB_USERNAME }}
        password: ${{ secrets.DOCKERHUB_TOKEN }}

    - name: Build and Push Docker Image
      uses: docker/build-push-action@v5
      with:
        context: .
        push: true
```

```
        tags: ${{ secrets.DOCKERHUB_USERNAME }}/myapp:latest

    - name: Optional Test Step
      run: |
        echo "Run your tests here, e.g., pytest"
        # pytest tests/
```

Setting Up GitHub Secrets

Navigate to your GitHub repository → Settings → Secrets → Actions.

Add the following:

Secret Name	Description
DOCKERHUB_USERNAME	Your DockerHub username
DOCKERHUB_TOKEN	DockerHub personal access token

Optional: Tag-Based Deployment

Modify the on section to trigger on new tags:

```
on:
  push:
    tags:
      - 'v*'
```

Then in `docker/build-push-action`, use:

```
tags: ${{ secrets.DOCKERHUB_USERNAME }}/myapp:${{ github.ref_name }}
```

This way, every time you push a tag like `v1.0.0`, it builds and pushes that version to DockerHub.

Optional: Auto Deploy to Server (SSH)

Add this step at the end (only if needed):

```
- name: Deploy to Server
  uses: appleboy/ssh-action@master
  with:
    host: ${{ secrets.SERVER_IP }}
    username: ${{ secrets.SSH_USER }}
    key: ${{ secrets.SSH_PRIVATE_KEY }}
```

```
    script: |
      docker pull myuser/myapp:latest
      docker stop myapp || true
      docker rm myapp || true
      docker run -d --name myapp -p 80:80 myuser/myapp:latest
```

Benefits of This Pipeline

Feature	**Benefit**
Automated Builds	Faster release cycles
Secrets Management	Secure credentials
DockerHub Integration	Versioned, portable images
Customizable	Add tests, notifications, deploy scripts
Scalable	Use for monorepos, microservices, staging/prod

Tips and Best Practices

- Use **multi-stage Dockerfiles** to reduce image size
- Automatically **scan images** using Trivy in the pipeline
- Add **Slack notifications** for success/failure
- Use **branch protection rules** to ensure only reviewed code is deployed
- Version your **Docker tags** (e.g., `v1.2.3`, not just `latest`)

Lab: CI/CD with GitHub Actions — Build, Scan, and Push Secure Docker Images

Difficulty Level: Advanced

Objective

Automate Docker image builds, scan them with Trivy for vulnerabilities, and securely push to DockerHub upon each commit to the main branch or new version tag.

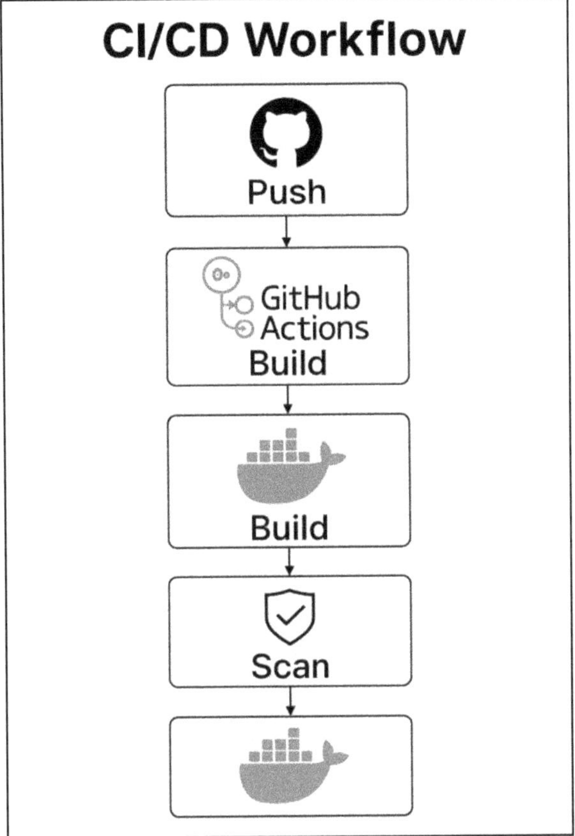

Figure 16.1: CI/CD Workflow Diagram

📂 File Structure

```
.github/
└── workflows/
    └── docker-ci.yml
Dockerfile
app/
└── app.py
```

📄 `docker-ci.yml` (GitHub Actions Workflow)

```
name: Secure CI/CD Pipeline


on:
  push:
    branches: [ main ]
    tags: [ 'v*' ]


jobs:
  build-and-push:
```

```
    runs-on: ubuntu-latest
    steps:
    - name: Checkout source code
      uses: actions/checkout@v3

    - name: Set up Docker Buildx
      uses: docker/setup-buildx-action@v2

    - name: Run Trivy Scan
      uses: aquasecurity/trivy-action@v0.12.0
      with:
        image-ref: '.'
        format: 'table'

    - name: Login to DockerHub
      uses: docker/login-action@v2
      with:
        username: ${{ secrets.DOCKERHUB_USERNAME }}
        password: ${{ secrets.DOCKERHUB_TOKEN }}

    - name: Build and Push Docker Image
      uses: docker/build-push-action@v5
      with:
        context: .
        push: true
        tags: yourname/yourapp:latest, yourname/yourapp:${{ github.ref_name
}}
```

■ `Dockerfile` (for Flask App)

```
FROM python:3.11-slim
WORKDIR /app
COPY . .
RUN pip install flask
CMD ["python", "app.py"]
```

■ `app/app.py`

```
from flask import Flask
app = Flask(__name__)

@app.route('/')
def home():
```

```
    return "Hello from CI/CD Pipeline!"

if __name__ == '__main__':
    app.run(host='0.0.0.0', port=5000)
```

`.dockerignore` (optional but recommended)

```
__pycache__/
.git/
.dockerignore
*.pyc
```

Lab Summary Table

Step	Action	Tool/Command	Purpose
1	Trigger Workflow	`on: push / on: tags`	Automatically initiates pipeline on code change
2	Checkout Code	`actions/checkout@v3`	Retrieves repository code
3	Setup Docker Builder	`docker/setup-buildx-action@v2`	Enables multi-platform builds and caching
4	Scan Image for Vulnerabilities	`aquasecurity/trivy-action@v0.12.0`	Ensures image security before push
5	Authenticate with DockerHub	`docker/login-action@v2`	Secure credential injection
6	Build and Push Image	`docker/build-push-action@v5`	Builds image and pushes to registry
7 (Opt.)	Deploy to Server/Registry/K8s	`docker run, ssh, or kubectl`	Optional post-push deployment

Summary

- CI/CD pipelines eliminate manual Docker image builds and deployments.
- GitHub Actions automates image building, scanning, tagging, and deployment.
- Secrets management with GitHub protects DockerHub credentials.
- You can trigger workflows based on branches, tags, or schedules.
- Best practices include multi-stage builds, semantic tagging, and Trivy scans.
- Optional SSH-based deployment lets you auto-pull to production servers.
- The included workflow supports modern DevOps pipelines across all environments.

Key Takeaways

This chapter taught you to automate Docker image lifecycles using GitHub Actions and DockerHub. By integrating builds, scans, pushes, and deployments into secure workflows, you learned to build reliable, repeatable CI/CD pipelines suitable for both open-source and enterprise-grade applications.

Knowledge Check

1. **What is the purpose of GitHub Actions in a CI/CD pipeline?**
   A) Store Docker images
   B) Manage cloud hosting
   C) Automate workflows such as testing, building, and deploying
   D) View Docker logs
2. **What GitHub file triggers a Docker build and push workflow?**
   A) `.dockerignore`
   B) `dockerfile.yml`
   C) `.github/workflows/.yml`
   D) `docker-compose.yml`
3. **What is required to push to DockerHub from GitHub Actions?**
   A) Dockerfile in a repo
   B) Manual login
   C) DockerHub credentials stored as GitHub secrets
   D) Kubernetes YAML
4. **What command logs into DockerHub in GitHub Actions workflows?**
   A) `docker login -u $USER -p $PASS`
   B) `gh login docker`
   C) `kubectl push`
   D) `dockerhub login`
5. **What GitHub Action step builds the Docker image?**
   A) `run: make docker`
   B) `run: docker build -t your-image-name .`
   C) `image: build`
   D) `build: docker.yml`
6. **Which of the following is a valid GitHub Action trigger for CI/CD?**
   A) on: push
   B) on: pull_request
   C) on: schedule
   D) All of the above
7. **What is the benefit of multi-stage Docker builds in CI/CD pipelines?**
   A) Supports Kubernetes
   B) Reduces image size
   C) Auto-deploys YAMLs
   D) Adds health checks
8. **What GitHub Action keyword is used to define secrets?**
   A) `env:`

B) `with:`
C) `secrets:`
D) `docker:`

9. **What is the purpose of the uses: keyword in GitHub Actions?**
A) Run shell script
B) Invoke an existing GitHub Action or Docker action
C) Pull image
D) Create a new branch

10. **What step ensures your image is pushed to DockerHub only on main branch commits?**
A) `if: github.ref == 'refs/heads/main'`
B) `run: git branch`
C) `trigger: manual`
D) `docker: validate`

11. **What does jobs: define in a workflow file?**
A) Git branches
B) Job names, steps, environments
C) YAML syntax
D) Deployment region

12. **What action does docker/build-push-action perform?**
A) Creates Dockerfile
B) Builds and optionally pushes Docker image
C) Runs shell
D) Adds logging

13. **Which base image is recommended for GitHub Actions Docker builds?**
A) `ubuntu-latest`
B) `debian`
C) `node`
D) `github/image`

14. **Which file should NOT be pushed to DockerHub?**
A) Secrets
B) .dockerignore
C) Dockerfile
D) App source

15. **What happens if you don't log in to DockerHub before docker push?**
A) Docker auto-authenticates
B) Image is saved locally
C) Push fails with 401 Unauthorized
D) GitHub builds a new token

16. What are examples of GitHub Actions runners?

- ▢ `ubuntu-latest`
- ▢ `windows-latest`
- ▢ `macos-latest`
- ▢ `centos-legacy`

17. What are key elements of a DockerHub CI/CD pipeline?

- ▢ Build image
- ▢ Tag version
- ▢ Push to registry
- ▢ Secure credentials

18. What steps improve security in GitHub Action pipelines? ▢ Store secrets securely

- ▢ Avoid printing secrets in logs
- ▢ Validate base images
- ▢ Hardcode credentials

19. What are common triggers for DockerHub CI/CD pipelines?

- ▢ Push to main
- ▢ Pull request to dev
- ▢ Cron job for nightly build
- ▢ Merge conflict

20. What's the purpose of semantic versioning in CI/CD image tagging?

- ▢ Helps trace build version
- ▢ Supports rollback
- ▢ Improves automation
- ▢ Makes image heavier

21. What are valid GitHub Actions best practices?

- ▢ Reuse actions from marketplace
- ▢ Use cache for dependencies
- ▢ Pin action versions
- ▢ Store workflows in /home

22. What tools can enhance Docker CI/CD debugging?

- ▢ act (local GitHub Action runner)
- ▢ docker logs
- ▢ set -x in shell steps
- ▢ Disable logging

23. What is a multi-tag DockerHub push useful for?

- ▢ Tagging latest and v1.0.1
- ▢ Identifying environments (e.g., dev, prod)
- ▢ Easier rollbacks
- ▢ Duplicate storage

24. What happens if you omit the Dockerfile path in the docker build step?

- ▢ Build fails
- ▢ Defaults to ./Dockerfile
- ▢ Builds from scratch
- ▢ Picks up latest cached layer

25. What does GITHUB_REF contain?

- ▢ Branch or tag ref
- ▢ Full git ref string
- ▢ Docker image ID
- ▢ Used for tagging builds

26. Why use docker tag before pushing in CI/CD?

- ▢ Define proper versioning
- ▢ Tag image with latest
- ▢ Push multiple tags
- ▢ Remove base layers

27. What are valid registry destinations for GitHub Docker workflows?

- ▢ DockerHub
- ▢ GitHub Container Registry
- ▢ Amazon ECR
- ▢ Adobe Cloud

28. What are ways to trigger image build when Dockerfile changes?

- ▢ on: push to Dockerfile path
- ▢ Use path filter in GitHub Actions
- ▢ Trigger on pull requests
- ▢ Only merge tags

29. What should you validate post-push in DockerHub?

- ▢ Tags exist
- ▢ Pull works
- ▢ Image scan passed

- [ ] GitHub PR closed

30. What makes a CI/CD Docker pipeline production-grade?

- [ ] Automated builds
- [ ] Secure credential handling
- [ ] Image validation/scanning
- [ ] Logging secrets

Answer

Q#	Correct Answer	Explanation
1	C	GitHub Actions automate CI/CD tasks based on Git events.
2	C	Workflows reside under `.github/workflows/`.
3	C	Use encrypted GitHub secrets for DockerHub auth.
4	A	`docker login` uses secrets passed via GitHub.
5	B	`docker build` command creates the image.
6	D	All listed triggers are valid.
7	B	Multi-stage builds reduce size and improve speed.
8	C	`secrets:` passes credentials securely.
9	B	`uses:` loads external GitHub actions.
10	A	Limits the push step to main branch commits.
11	B	`jobs:` declares stages and steps in workflows.
12	B	Official action to build and push Docker images.
13	A	`ubuntu-latest` is the default GitHub-hosted runner.
14	A	Secrets should never be stored in DockerHub.
15	C	Push fails with 401 without login.

Q16. What are examples of GitHub Actions runners?

- [✓] `ubuntu-latest`
- [✓] `windows-latest`
- [✓] `macos-latest`
- [X] `centos-legacy`

Explanation: GitHub Actions officially supports runners like `ubuntu-latest, windows-latest,` and `macos-latest. centos-legacy` is not a supported runner.

Q17. What are key elements of a DockerHub CI/CD pipeline?

- [√] Build image
- [√] Tag version
- [√] Push to registry
- [√] Secure credentials

Explanation: A secure and functional DockerHub CI/CD pipeline includes building, tagging, pushing images, and securing secrets.

Q18. What steps improve security in GitHub Action pipelines?

- [√] Store secrets securely
- [√] Avoid printing secrets in logs
- [√] Validate base images
- [X] Hardcode credentials

Explanation: Secrets should be stored in GitHub's secure store and never hardcoded or logged. Image validation helps prevent supply chain risks.

Q19. What are common triggers for DockerHub CI/CD pipelines?

- [√] Push to main
- [√] Pull request to dev
- [√] Cron job for nightly build
- [X] Merge conflict

Explanation: Valid triggers include pushes, PRs, and scheduled jobs. Merge conflicts are not triggers — they block automation.

Q20. What's the purpose of semantic versioning in CI/CD image tagging?

- [√] Helps trace build version
- [√] Supports rollback
- [√] Improves automation
- [X] Makes image heavier

Explanation: Semantic versioning makes builds traceable and manageable but does not affect image size.

Q21. What are valid GitHub Actions best practices?

- [√] Reuse actions from marketplace
- [√] Use cache for dependencies
- [√] Pin action versions
- [X] Store workflows in `/home`

Explanation: Best practices include reusability, caching, and pinning versions. Workflow files belong in `.github/workflows`.

Q22. What tools can enhance Docker CI/CD debugging?

- **[√]** `act` (local GitHub Action runner)
- **[√]** `docker logs`
- **[√]** `set -x` in shell steps
- **[X]** Disable logging

Explanation: Debugging tools help trace problems — disabling logs removes visibility, which hinders debugging.

Q23. What is a multi-tag DockerHub push useful for?

- **[√]** Tagging `latest` and `v1.0.1`
- **[√]** Identifying environments (e.g., dev, prod)
- **[√]** Easier rollbacks
- **[X]** Duplicate storag

Explanation: Multi-tagging supports versioning, environments, and rollback. Docker optimizes storage for tags.

Q24. What happens if you omit the Dockerfile path in the docker build step?

- **[X]** Build fails
- **[√]** Defaults to `./Dockerfile`
- **[X]** Builds from scratch
- **[X]** Picks up latest cached layer

Explanation: If path is omitted, Docker uses `./Dockerfile` by default. Build only fails if the file isn't found.

Q25. What does `GITHUB_REF` contain?

- **[√]** Branch or tag ref
- **[√]** Full git ref string
- **[X]** Docker image ID• **[√]** Used for tagging builds

Explanation: `GITHUB_REF` contains the full ref like `refs/heads/main`, useful for CI-based tagging logic.

Q26. Why use `docker tag` before pushing in CI/CD?

- **[√]** Define proper versioning
- **[√]** Tag image with `latest`
- **[√]** Push multiple tags
- **[X]** Remove base layers

Explanation: `docker tag` applies semantic tags and allows multi-tag pushes — it doesn't alter base layers.

Q27. What are valid registry destinations for GitHub Docker workflows?

- **[√]** DockerHub
- **[√]** GitHub Container Registry
- **[√]** Amazon ECR
- **[X]** Adobe Cloud

Explanation: Popular container registries include DockerHub, GHCR, and ECR. Adobe Cloud is not a container registry.

Q28. What are ways to trigger image builds when the Dockerfile changes?

- **[√]** `on: push` to Dockerfile path
- **[√]** Use path filter in GitHub Actions
- **[√]** Trigger on pull requests
- **[X]** Only merge tags

Explanation: GitHub Actions supports path-based triggers for Dockerfiles. Merge tags alone won't detect file changes.

Q29. What should you validate post-push in DockerHub?

- **[√]** Tags exist
- **[√]** Pull works
- **[√]** Image scan passed
- **[X]** GitHub PR closed

Explanation: Post-push checks should verify tag availability, scan results, and pullability — PR state is unrelated.

Q30. What makes a CI/CD Docker pipeline production-grade?

- **[√]** Automated builds
- **[√]** Secure credential handling
- **[√]** Image validation/scanning
- **[X]** Logging secrets

Explanation: Secure and automated pipelines ensure quality and compliance — logging secrets is a serious vulnerability.

Chapter 17: Mastering DockerHub — From Basics to Expert Use

DockerHub is the most widely used container registry for sharing, storing, and automating container images. Whether you're a solo developer or running production infrastructure at scale, understanding DockerHub—from basic usage to advanced integration—is essential. This chapter covers everything from image creation to advanced security, automation, and enterprise-grade practices with DockerHub.

Introduction to DockerHub

DockerHub is a cloud-based repository that allows you to store, manage, and share container images. It's the default registry for Docker CLI and supports both public and private repositories. It allows users to:

- Push and pull images
- Automate builds via GitHub/GitLab integrations
- Share images across teams or communities
- Set up CI/CD pipelines using DockerHub triggers
- Scan images for vulnerabilities

📝 DockerHub is to Docker what GitHub is to Git: a collaborative, versioned, and cloud-accessible platform.

Creating and Managing Repositories

Creating a DockerHub Account

Sign up at https://hub.docker.com. A free account provides public repos and limited private repos. Paid plans allow increased rate limits, more collaborators, and private repos.

Creating a Repository

To create a repo:

1. Go to "Repositories" > "Create Repository"
2. Choose public/private
3. Give it a name and optional description
4. Optionally link it to GitHub/GitLab

Naming Convention

Docker images follow this structure:

```
docker.io/username/repository:tag
```

Example:

```
$ docker pull username/myapp:latest
```

Tags like `:latest`, `:v1.0.1`, `:prod`, and `:dev` help distinguish versions.

Pushing and Pulling Images

Tagging Images

Before pushing, tag the local image:

```
$ docker tag myapp:latest username/myapp:v1.0.0
```

Authenticating with DockerHub

Login via the CLI:

```
$ docker login
```

Or in GitHub Actions:

```
- run: echo "${{ secrets.DOCKER_PASSWORD }}" | docker login -u ${{
secrets.DOCKER_USERNAME }} --password-stdin
```

Pushing and Pulling

```
$ docker push username/myapp:v1.0.0
$ docker pull username/myapp:v1.0.0
```

Pushes upload the image; pulls retrieve it from the registry.

Lab: Create a Custom App (`myapp`) and Push to Docker Hub

Difficulty Level: Basic

Lab Objectives

- Build a basic Python-based Docker app
- Create a Dockerfile
- Tag and push the image to Docker Hub
- Run and test the image from another machine

🗁 Folder Structure

```
myapp/
├── app.py
└── Dockerfile
```

Step 1: Create the App

🖹 app.py

```
import time

print("Running myapp...")
time.sleep(99999)
```

🖹 Dockerfile

```
# Use Python base image
FROM python:3.11-slim

# Set working directory
WORKDIR /app

# Copy app
COPY app.py .

# Run the app
CMD ["python", "app.py"]
```

Step 2: Build the Docker Image

Navigate to the project folder:

```
$ cd ~/myapp
$ docker build -t yourdockerhubusername/myapp:latest .
```

[✓] Replace `yourdockerhubusername` with your Docker Hub ID.

Step 3: Login to Docker Hub

```
$ docker login
```

Enter your **Docker Hub username and password**.

Step 4: Push the Image to Docker Hub

```
$ docker push yourdockerhubusername/myapp:latest
```

If successful, you'll see something like:

```
latest: digest: sha256:xxxx size: 1572
```

[✓] Now your image is available at:

```
https://hub.docker.com/r/yourdockerhubusername/myapp
```

Step 5: Pull and Run from Any System

On another machine:

```
$ docker pull yourdockerhubusername/myapp:latest
$ docker run -d --name testmyapp yourdockerhubusername/myapp
```

Check:

```
$ docker ps
```

You should see the container **running in the background**.

Cleanup (Optional)

```
$ docker stop myapp
$ docker rm myapp
$ docker rmi yourdockerhubusername/myapp:latest
```

Lab Summary

Task	Command
Build image	`docker build -t yourhub/myapp .`
Login	`docker login`
Push image	`docker push yourhub/myapp`
Pull & run	`docker run -d yourhub/myapp`

Automating Builds

DockerHub supports automatic builds from GitHub or Bitbucket.

Setup:

1. Link GitHub in DockerHub account settings.
2. Under your repository, choose "Configure Automated Builds."
3. Select repo and Dockerfile path.
4. Define build rules per branch/tag.

Benefits

- No local Docker install needed
- Build triggers on git commits

- Automatically tags based on branches or tags
- Great for open-source projects

DockerHub Webhooks

You can configure DockerHub webhooks to notify external systems (e.g., CI/CD, Slack, Kubernetes, Jenkins) when an image is pushed.

Example Use Cases:

- Trigger Kubernetes rollout after image push
- Notify Slack of deployment
- Sync image to another registry

DockerHub Security Features

Security is critical for any registry, and DockerHub provides several tools and best practices.

Private Repositories

Mark repositories as private to restrict access. You can control who sees or pulls the image.

Image Scanning

DockerHub integrates with Snyk to scan for vulnerabilities.

- Automatically scans pushed images
- Shows CVEs and risk level
- Lists remediation steps

Scanning requires enabling it per repo.

Two-Factor Authentication (2FA)

Enable 2FA to protect your DockerHub account from unauthorized access. Required for CLI operations if using personal access tokens (PATs).

Teams and Organizations

Organizations

An organization is a shared account to manage access and collaboration.

- Add multiple collaborators
- Assign roles: Owner, Maintainer, Member
- Share image repositories securely

Teams

Within orgs, teams allow granular control.

- Limit push/pull/delete to specific repos
- Useful in large teams with Dev, QA, Prod segregation

Rate Limits and Authentication Tokens

DockerHub enforces pull rate limits for anonymous and free-tier users:

Account Type	Anonymous	Authenticated
Free	100 pulls/6hr	200 pulls/6hr
Pro/Team	Unlimited	Unlimited

Use access tokens or PATs for secure, revocable CLI authentication.

Advanced Tagging and Versioning

Use semantic versioning and multi-tag strategies for professional image management:

```
$ docker tag myapp myapp:1.0.3
$ docker tag myapp myapp:prod
$ docker push myapp:1.0.3
$ docker push myapp:prod
```

Avoid using `:latest` for production.

Image Signing and Content Trust

Enable **Docker Content Trust (DCT)** to enforce signed image pulling:

```
$ export DOCKER_CONTENT_TRUST=1
$ docker pull myorg/app:v1.0.0
```

- Ensures authenticity
- Only pulls images with signed metadata

DockerHub CLI Alternatives

While `docker` CLI is most common, others include:

- `skopeo`: Copies images between registries
- `crane`: Inspects and deletes images
- `regctl`: Advanced Docker registry CLI tool

Example:

```
$ skopeo copy docker://docker.io/sudipta/app:latest dir:/backup/
```

Mirroring and Caching

In enterprise networks, DockerHub proxies or mirrors help reduce pull latency and handle rate limits.

Solutions:

- Docker Registry Mirror
- Harbor as caching proxy
- Nexus/Artifactory as Docker registry

Using DockerHub with CI/CD

DockerHub integrates seamlessly with:

- GitHub Actions
- GitLab CI/CD
- Jenkins
- CircleCI

Sample GitHub Action Workflow:

```
name: Build and Push Docker Image
on:
  push:
    branches: [ main ]
jobs:
  docker:
    runs-on: ubuntu-latest
    steps:
    - uses: actions/checkout@v2
    - run: docker build -t myorg/app:${{ github.sha }} .
    - run: echo "${{ secrets.DOCKER_PASSWORD }}" | docker login -u ${{
secrets.DOCKER_USERNAME }} --password-stdin
    - run: docker push myorg/app:${{ github.sha }}
```

Best Practices for DockerHub Usage

[√] Always tag images explicitly
[√] Use `.dockerignore` to avoid uploading secrets
[√] Scan images on push
[√] Use multi-stage builds to keep images lean
[√] Rotate access tokens regularly
[√] Enable DCT for critical environments
[√] Avoid pushing unnecessary images or using :latest
[√] Automate pushes via CI/CD
[√] Track vulnerability trends and apply patches
[√] Clean up unused images to reduce clutter

Key Takeaways

DockerHub remains a cornerstone of modern container workflows. While it provides simple push-and-pull functionality, its full power lies in automation, security, team collaboration, and CI/CD integration. From basic usage to expert-level practices like image signing, vulnerability scanning, and access control, mastering DockerHub unlocks a reliable, secure, and efficient container delivery pipeline.

Knowledge Check

1. **What is DockerHub primarily used for?**
   A) Log management
   B) Container orchestration
   C) Hosting and sharing Docker images
   D) Managing Kubernetes clusters
2. **What does the `docker push` command do?**
   A) Pulls an image from DockerHub
   B) Pushes an image to DockerHub
   C) Scans the local image
   D) Removes an image from the registry
3. **What is required before pushing an image to DockerHub?**
   A) SSH key
   B) Signed certificate
   C) Docker login using your DockerHub credentials
   D) GitHub token
4. **What is the purpose of DockerHub organizations?**
   A) To monitor system memory
   B) To group users and manage access to repositories
   C) To run Kubernetes clusters
   D) To run serverless functions
5. **Which access control level is NOT available in DockerHub?**
   A) Admin
   B) Read-only
   C) Write
   D) Observer
6. **What is a DockerHub automated build?**
   A) A remote server backup process
   B) A trigger-based image build process connected to GitHub or Bitbucket
   C) A Kubernetes pod template
   D) A container runtime setting
7. **What tag does DockerHub apply to an image if none is specified?**
   A) edge
   B) stable
   C) beta
   D) latest
8. **What is the purpose of a "verified publisher" badge on DockerHub?**
   A) Tracks CI/CD pipelines

B) Authenticates image downloads
C) Shows that the image comes from a trusted and verified organization
D) Increases image performance

9. **What does DockerHub's rate limit apply to?**
A) CLI logs
B) Push frequency
C) Number of public pulls per IP
D) File size

10. **What is the default visibility of a newly created repository on DockerHub?**
A) Public
B) Encrypted
C) Archived
D) Private

11. **What does DockerHub support as image sources for automated builds?**
- ☐ GitHub
- ☐ GitLab
- ☐ Bitbucket
- ☐ FTP server

12. **What metadata can be defined in DockerHub repositories?**
- ☐ Short and full descriptions
- ☐ README in Markdown
- ☐ Tags and labels
- ☐ Webhooks.

13. **What benefits come with DockerHub Pro or Team plans?**
- ☐ Unlimited private repos
- ☐ Increased pull rate limits
- ☐ Audit logs and team management
- ☐ Guaranteed image verification

14. **How can DockerHub enhance CI/CD workflows?**
- ☐ Host build cache layers
- ☐ Push versioned images post-test
- ☐ Trigger downstream automation
- ☐ Manage multi-arch images

15. **What are ways to manage image security in DockerHub?**
- ☐ Use signed images
- ☐ Enable 2FA on accounts

- ▢ Use Docker Content Trust
- ▢ Rely only on random:latest

16. **What does a DockerHub webhook do?**
    - ▢ Sends a request when an image is pushed
    - ▢ Tracks downloads
    - ▢ Blocks unverified pulls
    - ▢ Backs up container logs
17. **What's the best way to support multi-architecture builds on DockerHub?**
    - ▢ Use Buildx
    - ▢ Use Docker Compose
    - ▢ Use raw shell scripts
    - ▢ Rename tags manually
18. **What are best practices for tagging DockerHub images?**
    - ▢ Use semantic versioning (v1.2.3)
    - ▢ Use git commit hashes
    - ▢ Use "latest" cautiously
    - ▢ Overwrite tags randomly
19. **What DockerHub feature helps monitor repository activity?**
    - ▢ Insights
    - ▢ Webhooks
    - ▢ Rate limits
    - ▢ CLI ping
20. **How can teams collaborate on DockerHub securely?**
    - ▢ Assign roles in organizations
    - ▢ Share credentials publicly
    - ▢ Use signed images and private repos
    - ▢ Maintain one shared root account

Answer

Q#	Correct Answer	Explanation
1	C	DockerHub is a central registry for container images.
2	B	`docker push` sends your image to the remote DockerHub registry.
3	C	Authentication is required before any image can be pushed.
4	B	Organizations allow multi-user management and access control.
5	D	DockerHub offers Admin, Write, and Read-only, not "Observer".
6	B	Automated builds use connected repositories to trigger builds.
7	D	The `latest` tag is default if none is specified.
8	C	Verified publishers are trusted sources of official images.
9	C	Rate limits apply to pull requests from unauthenticated IPs.
10	A	Repositories are public by default unless set to private.

Q11. What does DockerHub support as image sources for automated builds?

- **[✓]** GitHub
- **[✓]** GitLab
- **[✓]** Bitbucket
- **[X]** FTP server

Explanation: DockerHub supports Git-based version control systems like GitHub, GitLab, and Bitbucket for automated builds — not FTP.

Q12. What metadata can be defined in DockerHub repositories?

- **[✓]** Short and full descriptions
- **[✓]** README in Markdown
- **[✓]** Tags and labels
- **[✓]** Webhooks

Explanation: DockerHub repositories can be enriched with Markdown-based documentation, labels, and webhook integration.

Q13. What benefits come with DockerHub Pro or Team plans?

- **[✓]** Unlimited private repos
- **[✓]** Increased pull rate limits
- **[✓]** Audit logs and team management
- **[X]** Guaranteed image verification

Explanation: Paid plans offer more features like team roles, logging, and limits — but not guaranteed verification.

Q14. How can DockerHub enhance CI/CD workflows?

- [✓] Host build cache layers
- [✓] Push versioned images post-test
- [✓] Trigger downstream automation
- [✓] Manage multi-arch images

Explanation: DockerHub acts as the final delivery stage for image publishing, cache handling, and architecture management.

Q15. What are ways to manage image security in DockerHub?

- [✓] Use signed images
- [✓] Enable 2FA on accounts
- [✓] Use Docker Content Trust
- [X] Rely only on random:latest

Explanation: Secure practices include trust verification and authentication; random:latest is unreliable and insecure.

Q16. What does a DockerHub webhook do?

- [✓] Sends a request when an image is pushed
- [X] Tracks downloads
- [X] Blocks unverified pulls
- [X] Backs up container logs

Explanation: Webhooks notify external systems (like CI/CD tools) when new images are pushed to the repo.

Q17. What's the best way to support multi-architecture builds on DockerHub?

- [✓] Use Buildx
- [X] Use Docker Compose
- [X] Use raw shell scripts
- [X] Rename tags manually

Explanation: Buildx supports building and pushing cross-platform (multi-arch) images using manifest lists.

Q18. What are best practices for tagging DockerHub images?

- [✓] Use semantic versioning (v1.2.3)
- [✓] Use git commit hashes
- [✓] Use latest cautiously

- **[X]** Overwrite tags randomly

Explanation: Tags should be meaningful and traceable. Avoid arbitrary overwrites to prevent confusion and deployment errors.

Q19. What DockerHub feature helps monitor repository activity?

- **[√]** Insights
- **[√]** Webhooks
- **[X]** Rate limits
- **[X]** CLI ping

Explanation: DockerHub Insights show usage analytics. Webhooks can trigger logs — but CLI ping and rate limits are unrelated.

Q20. How can teams collaborate on DockerHub securely?

- **[√]** Assign roles in organizations
- **[X]** Share credentials publicly
- **[√]** Use signed images and private repos
- **[X]** Maintain one shared root account

Explanation: Secure collaboration requires clear roles, secret handling, and private/signed assets — not shared credentials.

Chapter 18: Docker Alternatives Overview (Podman, Buildah)

This chapter introduces advanced readers to **Docker-compatible alternatives** – especially relevant for those in enterprise, rootless, or Red Hat environments. We'll compare tools like:

- **Podman** (daemonless container engine)
- **Buildah** (image builder for OCI-compliant containers)

Why Look Beyond Docker?

While Docker remains dominant, modern container ecosystems are expanding due to:

- Security requirements (e.g., rootless containers)
- Daemonless architecture preference
- Kubernetes-native workflows
- Systemd integration on Linux
- OCI-compliance and scripting flexibility

Podman: Drop-in Docker Replacement

Feature	**Description**
Daemonless	Runs as a CLI tool without a persistent daemon
Rootless	Supports unprivileged users for improved security
Docker CLI Compatible	Run `alias docker=podman` in many use cases
Systemd Integration	Generate systemd units from containers
Supports Pods	Native pod concept like Kubernetes

Example: Running a container with Podman

```
$ podman run -d -p 8080:80 nginx
```

Create systemd unit:

```
$ podman generate systemd --name myapp > ~/.config/systemd/user/myapp.service
```

Perfect for:

- Secure multi-user Linux environments
- Red Hat, Fedora, CentOS users
- Kubernetes devs preferring kube-style pods

Buildah: Lightweight Dockerfile-Free Image Builder

Feature	Description
No Dockerfile Required	Script-driven container building
No Daemon	Build process happens entirely in CLI
Rootless Support	Build images as unprivileged user
OCI-Compatible	Outputs standard OCI container images

Example: Build image using shell script

```
$ buildah from ubuntu
$ buildah run ubuntu-working-container apt update
$ buildah commit ubuntu-working-container my-ubuntu-img
```

Ideal for:

- Automated CI pipelines
- Environments without Docker
- Secure build processes (no daemon escalation)

Podman vs Buildah vs Docker – Comparison Table

Feature	Docker	Podman	Buildah
Requires Daemon	[√] Yes	[X] No	[X] No
Rootless Support	🟡 Limited	[√] Full	[√] Full
Dockerfile Support	[√] Yes	[√] Yes	🟡 Optional
Systemd Integration	[X] No	[√] Yes	[X] No
Kubernetes Pod Model	[X] No	[√] Yes (native)	[X] No
OCI Image Format	[√] Yes	[√] Yes	[√] Yes
CI/CD Friendly	[√] Yes	[√] Yes	[√] Yes
Available on Windows	[√] Yes	[X] Linux-only	[X] Linux-only

When Should You Use These?

Scenario	Suggested Tool
Security-hardened Linux servers	Podman
Image build automation (CI pipelines)	Buildah
Systemd-based container lifecycle	Podman
Learning Kubernetes pods locally	Podman
Cross-platform dev (Windows/Mac)	Docker (for now)

Docker vs Podman vs Buildah vs containerd – Command Comparison

Action	Docker	Podman	Buildah	containerd / ctr
Pull image	`docker pull nginx`	`podman pull nginx`	`buildah pull nginx`	`ctr image pull docker.io/library/nginx`
Run container	`docker run -d nginx`	`podman run -d nginx`	N/A (Buildah is build-only)	`ctr run -d --rm nginx mynginx`
Build image	`docker build -t myapp .`	`podman build -t myapp .`	`buildah bud -t myapp .`	Use `buildkit`, not direct in `ctr`
Push image	`docker push myapp`	`podman push myapp`	`buildah push myapp`	`ctr image push docker.io/yourrepo/myapp`
View running containers	`docker ps`	`podman ps`	N/A	`ctr containers list`
Inspect image/container	`docker inspect myapp`	`podman inspect myapp`	`buildah inspect myapp`	`ctr image info myapp`

Action	Docker	Podman	Buildah	containerd / ctr
Remove container	`docker rm container_id`	`podman rm container_id`	N/A	`ctr container rm container_id`
Remove image	`docker rmi myapp`	`podman rmi myapp`	`buildah rmi myapp`	`ctr image rm myapp`
Compose-like support	`docker-compose up`	`podman-compose up` *(limited)*	N/A	N/A
Rootless support	Limited (Docker daemon required)	[√] Full rootless support	[√] Full rootless support	Partial / Advanced config required
Daemon required	[√] Yes (`dockerd`)	[X] No	[X] No	[√] Requires `containerd` service

Chapter 19: Kubernetes Crash-Course — From Docker to K8s

Why Kubernetes? From Single-Host Containers to Cloud-Native Orchestration

Containers revolutionized application development by making it possible to package an application and all its dependencies into a single portable unit. Tools like Docker made it effortless to build and run containers. However, when organizations tried to move from a single server to multiple servers — or needed high availability, self-healing, seamless upgrades, and scalability — the limitations of Docker alone became apparent.

Imagine an e-commerce startup deploying its first application with Docker:

- A few `docker run` commands launch the app.
- A manual `docker ps` check ensures containers are running.
- If a container crashes, someone must manually restart it.
- Scaling the app during Black Friday sales means manually spinning up new containers and wiring load balancers by hand.

This model quickly falls apart at scale. What if a container dies at 3 a.m.? What if an update breaks the app? What if different containers need to find each other dynamically? What if traffic doubles overnight?

Kubernetes is solution for such problems.

Kubernetes (abbreviated as **K8s**) is an open-source platform for **automating deployment, scaling, management, and recovery** of containerized applications. Originally developed at Google based on their internal cluster management system called **Borg**, Kubernetes abstracts the underlying infrastructure so you can focus on your applications — not the servers.

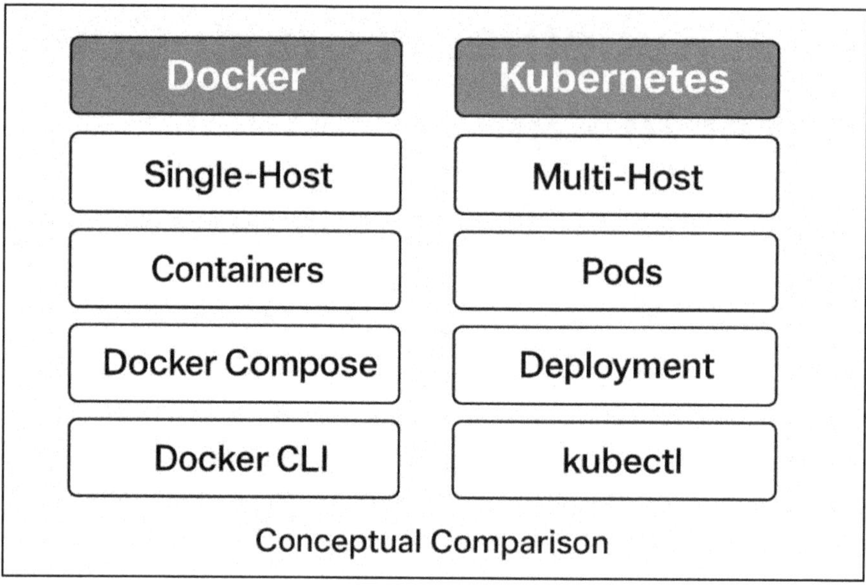

Figure 19.1: Docker vs Kubernetes — Conceptual Comparison

Why Kubernetes?

- **Scaling**: Automatically adds or removes application instances based on demand (manual, scheduled, or automatic scaling).
- **Self-Healing**: Detects container or node failures and restarts or reschedules containers automatically.
- **Service Discovery & Load Balancing**: Exposes containers through stable network identities (DNS names) and balances traffic.
- **Rolling Updates & Rollbacks**: Updates applications with zero downtime and can roll back automatically if problems occur.
- **Resource Optimization**: Efficiently packs applications onto nodes based on CPU and memory needs.
- **Infrastructure Abstraction**: Run apps across different environments — laptops, on-premises datacentres, or multiple clouds — with the same APIs.

Capability	Docker Standalone	Kubernetes
Cluster Management	Manual	Automated
Health Check & Restart	Partial	Full Self-Healing
Service Discovery	External Tools	Native DNS-based
Load Balancing	Manual/Nginx	Built-in via Services
Auto-Scaling	Scripts	Built-in (HPA/VPA)
Secrets Management	Basic support	Native Secrets with Encryption

Capability	Docker Standalone	Kubernetes
High Availability (HA)	Complex	Built-in multi-master

🔒 **Pro Tip:** *Kubernetes is not a replacement for Docker — it* **builds on top** *of container technology. Kubernetes still runs containers under the hood but manages them* **at scale**.

Over time, Kubernetes has become the **industry standard** for cloud-native computing. All major cloud providers (AWS, Azure, GCP) offer managed Kubernetes services like EKS, AKS, and GKE. Kubernetes has a rich ecosystem with thousands of tools, extensions, and operators making it the foundation of modern infrastructure.

Understanding Kubernetes Architecture

Kubernetes has a **modular, distributed architecture** designed for scalability, fault tolerance, and automation. The architecture is divided into two main layers:

- **Control Plane** (Master Components)
- **Worker Nodes** (Nodes where applications run)

Understanding this architecture is essential for both developers deploying applications and DevOps teams maintaining clusters.

Control Plane Components

The Control Plane is the **brain** of Kubernetes. It makes global decisions (e.g., scheduling) and detects/responds to cluster events (e.g., restarting a failed pod).

Main Control Plane Components:

- **kube-apiserver**
  The API server is the front end of the Kubernetes control plane.
  → It handles all REST API requests, validates them, and updates the cluster state.
  → It talks securely (mutual TLS) to all other components.
- **etcd**
  A highly available key-value store that persists all cluster configuration and state.
  → Think of it as Kubernetes' database.
  → If etcd is corrupted or lost, the cluster data is gone – backups are critical.
- **kube-scheduler**
  Assigns Pods to Nodes based on resource availability, affinity/anti-affinity rules,

taints/tolerations, and policies.

➔ It watches unassigned Pods and picks optimal Nodes.

- **kube-controller-manager**
  Runs controllers (logic loops) that regulate cluster state:
  ➔ Node Controller, Deployment Controller, ReplicaSet Controller, Service Account Controller, etc.
- **cloud-controller-manager** (optional)
  Integrates Kubernetes with underlying cloud providers for managing load balancers, storage, routes.

Production Tip: *Always set up the Control Plane in* ***high availability (HA)*** *mode with* ***multi-master nodes*** *to eliminate single points of failure. Use an external etcd cluster and load-balanced API servers.*

Worker Node Components

Worker Nodes are where your actual applications (containers) run.

Main Worker Node Components:

- **kubelet**
  An agent running on every Node.
  ➔ It reads Pod specs from the API server and ensures the containers are healthy and running as specified.
- **kube-proxy**
  Maintains network rules on Nodes.
  ➔ Handles routing traffic to Pods, service discovery, and sometimes NAT.
- **Container Runtime**
  The software that runs containers.
  ➔ Examples: **Docker, containerd, CRI-O**.
  ➔ Kubernetes supports multiple runtimes via the Container Runtime Interface (CRI).

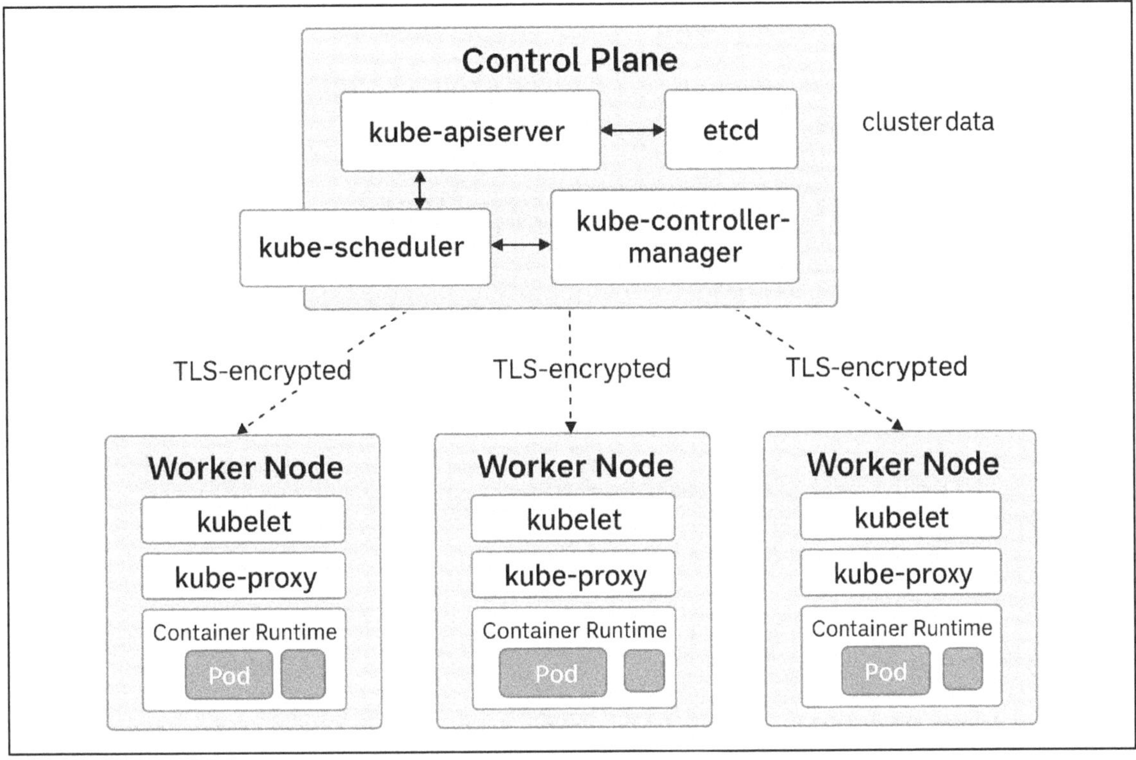

Figure 19.2 – Kubernetes Architecture Overview

- Show **Control Plane** (kube-apiserver, etcd, scheduler, controller manager).
- Connected to multiple **Worker Nodes** (each running kubelet, kube-proxy, runtime).
- Traffic flow from kubectl → API Server → cluster.

Traffic Flow inside Kubernetes

1. User sends a command via `kubectl`.
2. `kubectl` sends an HTTPS request to the **kube-apiserver**.
3. **kube-apiserver** authenticates, validates, and updates **etcd**.
4. Scheduler and Controllers react to changes in etcd.
5. **kubelet** on Worker Nodes pulls updated specs and manages containers accordingly.

Everything is **declarative**: you declare the desired state, and Kubernetes constantly tries to **reconcile** reality to match your intention.

Hardening Control Plane for Production

- Enable **TLS encryption** between all components.
- Use **Role-Based Access Control (RBAC)** strictly.
- Audit logs of API server requests for forensics.
- Limit etcd access only to API servers.

- Implement **Pod Security Standards (PSS)** cluster-wide.

🔒 **Pro Tip:** *Even in non-production labs, get into the habit of treating your Kubernetes Control Plane as critical infrastructure. Always think "security first".*

Core Kubernetes Concepts (Deep Dive)

To truly work with Kubernetes — not just copy-paste YAML files — you must **understand** its core objects and how they **interact**. Kubernetes introduces a **set of primitives** that model your infrastructure and applications declaratively.

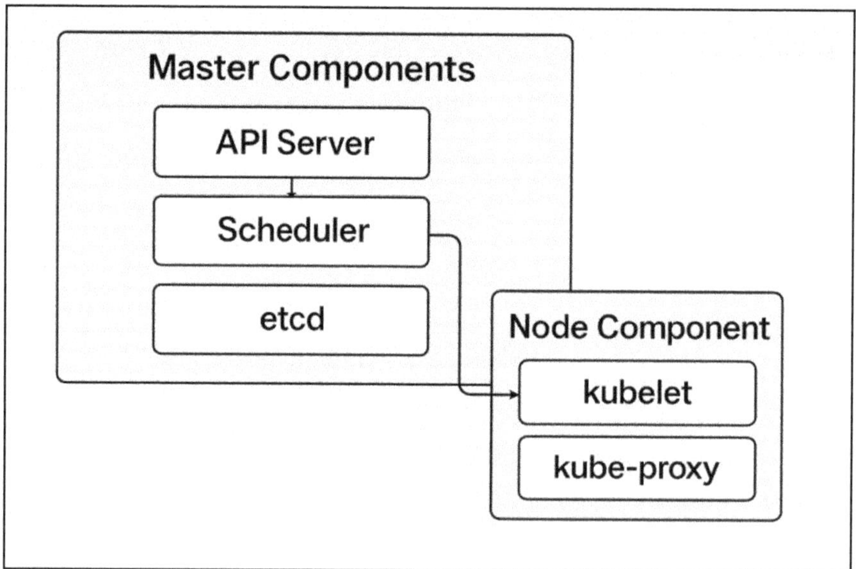

Figure 19.2: Kubernetes Core Architecture

Let's explore these essentials:

Pods: The Smallest Deployable Unit

A **Pod** is the fundamental building block in Kubernetes.

- It represents **one or more containers** that share:
  - The same network namespace (they can talk via localhost).
  - The same storage volumes (shared filesystem access).
  - The same lifecycle (they start, stop, and restart together).

Why Pods?

Kubernetes abstracts away individual containers because in real-world scenarios, a container often needs sidekick processes.

Example:

- A main **Nginx** server container + a **Fluent Bit** sidecar container for logging.

Important: In most cases, you will have **one main container per Pod**, but Kubernetes allows multiple (sidecars, helpers).

Deployments and ReplicaSets: Managing Pods at Scale

You don't manually create Pods in production – you manage them with higher-level objects like **Deployments**.

- **Deployment** defines the **desired state**:
    - What image to run
    - How many replicas
    - How to upgrade (rolling updates)
- Kubernetes uses a **ReplicaSet** behind the scenes to maintain the correct number of Pods.

Workflow:
You create a **Deployment**, which owns a **ReplicaSet**, which manages the actual **Pods**.

Services: Stable Networking for Pods

Pods are **ephemeral** – they can die and get replaced, changing IPs.
To ensure reliable communication:

- **Services** provide a **stable DNS name** and **virtual IP**.
- Services automatically **load balance** traffic across healthy Pods.
- Services decouple consumers from the dynamic nature of Pods.

Types of Services:

Type	Description	Scope	Public Access
ClusterIP (default)	Exposes service on internal cluster IP.	Within Cluster	[X]
NodePort	Exposes service on each Node's IP at a static port.	Outside via NodeIP:Port	⚠ (Exposed)
LoadBalancer	Provisions an external load balancer (cloud environments).	Public	[✓]

Type	Description	Scope	Public Access
ExternalName	Maps the service to an external DNS name.	External DNS	[✓]

Production Tip: *In cloud-native environments, use LoadBalancer for exposing apps externally; otherwise, set up Ingress.*

Namespaces: Logical Clusters inside a Cluster

Namespaces allow you to divide a Kubernetes cluster into **virtual partitions**.

Use Cases:

- Separate dev, staging, and production environments.
- Control access with RBAC per namespace.
- Limit resource usage (CPU/memory quotas) per team.

By default, Kubernetes has these namespaces:

- `default`
- `kube-system` (for Kubernetes components)
- `kube-public` (accessible publicly, minimal use)

ConfigMaps and Secrets: Externalizing Configurations

ConfigMaps and **Secrets** inject externalized data into Pods.

- **ConfigMaps**: Non-sensitive configurations like app settings.
- **Secrets**: Sensitive data like passwords, API keys.

Tip: *Avoid hard-coding configs inside containers. Use ConfigMaps/Secrets for 12-Factor App compliance.*

Example:

- Mount a ConfigMap as environment variables.
- Mount a Secret as a file inside a Pod.

Volumes: Persistent Storage for Containers

Containers are **ephemeral**. If a container crashes, any data inside it is lost. **Volumes** solve this by attaching **persistent storage** to Pods.

Common Kubernetes Volumes:

- **emptyDir**: Temporary storage shared between containers in a Pod.
- **hostPath**: Mounts a file/directory from Node filesystem (use carefully).
- **PersistentVolume (PV) / PersistentVolumeClaim (PVC)**: Abstracts storage like NFS, EBS, or Ceph.

🔒 **Pro Tip:** *Always prefer managed storage solutions (like EBS in AWS) for critical applications rather than hostPath.*

StatefulSets, DaemonSets, Jobs, and CronJobs

Beyond Deployments, Kubernetes offers specialized workload controllers:

Object	Purpose
StatefulSet	For applications requiring stable network IDs and persistent storage (e.g., Databases).
DaemonSet	Ensures one Pod per Node. Useful for monitoring/logging agents.
Job	Executes a task once to completion (e.g., database migration).
CronJob	Schedules jobs at specific times (like Unix cron tasks).

Example: Deploy Fluent Bit as a DaemonSet to collect Node logs.

Ingress: Exposing Services via HTTP/S

An **Ingress** manages external access to internal services.

- Acts as an HTTP load balancer inside the cluster.
- Supports URL routing, SSL/TLS termination.
- Needs an Ingress Controller (e.g., Nginx Ingress Controller).

Ingress Example:

- Route `/api` to your backend API Service.
- Route `/web` to your frontend Service.

Production Tip: *Always use TLS with Ingress to encrypt traffic end-to-end.*

Recommendations

- Use **Namespaces** per team/project for isolation.
- Enforce **Resource Quotas** to prevent noisy neighbor problems.

- Deploy **Ingress Controllers** with Let's Encrypt integration for automatic SSL certificates.
- Use **Secrets encryption** at rest with Kubernetes providers (KMS/Azure Key Vault).

Setting Up Kubernetes Labs (Practical Guide)

Before managing production clusters, it's crucial to **practice hands-on** with Kubernetes. Fortunately, several tools make it easy to set up **local** or **online** Kubernetes labs.

In this section, we'll walk through **four lab setups**:

1. **Minikube** – Run Kubernetes locally inside a VM or container.
2. **Kind** – Kubernetes IN Docker (lightweight clusters inside containers).
3. **k3d** – Lightweight Kubernetes (k3s) clusters in Docker.
4. **Play With Kubernetes (PWK)** – Free online interactive playground.

Each has its own benefits depending on your resources, goals, and environment.

Lab Option 1: Minikube (Local Single-Node Kubernetes)

Minikube is the most popular beginner tool to run Kubernetes on a laptop.

Requirements:

- 2 CPU cores (minimum)
- 2 GB RAM
- Docker installed (or VirtualBox/VMware for VM drivers)

Install Minikube:

```
$ curl -LO https://storage.googleapis.com/minikube/releases/latest/minikube-
linux-amd64
$ sudo install minikube-linux-amd64 /usr/local/bin/minikube
```

Start Minikube Cluster:

```
$ minikube start
```

🔒 **Pro Tip:** *Use Docker as a driver for faster startup:*

```
$ minikube start --driver=docker
```

Check Cluster Status:

```
$ kubectl get nodes
```

Expected output:

```
NAME        STATUS    ROLES            AGE    VERSION
minikube    Ready     control-plane    2m     v1.28.0
```

Access the Kubernetes Dashboard (GUI):

```
$ minikube dashboard
```

It opens a browser window where you can see running Pods, Deployments, Services visually.

Lab Option 2: Kind (Kubernetes in Docker)

Kind is a fast way to spin up Kubernetes clusters **inside Docker containers**.

Install Kind:

```
$ curl -Lo ./kind https://kind.sigs.k8s.io/dl/latest/kind-linux-amd64
$ chmod +x ./kind
$ sudo mv ./kind /usr/local/bin/kind
```

Create a Cluster:

```
$ kind create cluster --name kind-lab
```

View Nodes:

```
$ kubectl get nodes
```

Kind Advantages:

- Lightweight
- Multi-node cluster simulation (good for production topology testing)
- No need for a hypervisor/VM

Lab Option 3: k3d (k3s Lightweight Kubernetes in Docker)

k3d runs lightweight Kubernetes (k3s) inside Docker containers.

Install k3d:

```
$ curl -s https://raw.githubusercontent.com/k3d-io/k3d/main/install.sh |
bash
```

Create a Cluster:

```
$ k3d cluster create k3d-lab
```

k3d Highlights:

- Extremely fast (cluster starts in seconds)
- Low memory and CPU footprint
- Useful for IoT, edge, and small device testing

Lab Option 4: Play With Kubernetes (PWK) – Online Free Labs

Website: https://labs.play-with-k8s.com/

- Spin up 3–5 nodes in a temporary Kubernetes cluster.
- No installation required.
- Great for trying Kubernetes on the go or in restricted environments.

Limitations:

- Free labs expire after 4 hours.
- Limited cluster size/resources.
- Not suitable for long-running projects.

Lab Setup Best Practices (Production Style)

Even when experimenting locally, follow these **good habits**:

Practice	Why It Matters
Use `kubectl config get-contexts`	Manage multiple clusters without confusion.
Practice Role-Based Access Control (RBAC)	Don't always work as cluster-admin.
Enable Metrics Server	For resource monitoring and autoscaling demos.
Simulate Node Failures	Test application resiliency by shutting down nodes.
Use Namespaces	Separate applications logically even in test clusters.
Deploy Ingress Controller	Practice exposing HTTP/S services cleanly.

Recommendations

In production environments:

- Always separate Control Plane and Worker Nodes.
- Set resource quotas for Namespaces to avoid "noisy neighbors".
- Use network policies (e.g., Calico) to restrict Pod communications.

- Implement Pod Disruption Budgets (PDBs) to maintain application availability during upgrades

Kubernetes Hands-on Commands and Operations (Deep Dive)

Once your lab cluster is running, interacting with Kubernetes efficiently requires mastering `kubectl` – the Kubernetes command-line tool.

`kubectl` is powerful, flexible, and sometimes overwhelming at first.
This section focuses on real-world **production-like `kubectl` usage**, not just basic commands.

Managing Resources with `kubectl`

Task	Command
List all Pods in a Namespace	`kubectl get pods -n <namespace>`
List all Services across Namespaces	`kubectl get services --all-namespaces`
List all Deployments	`kubectl get deployments`
Create a resource from YAML	`kubectl apply -f deployment.yaml`
Delete a Pod	`kubectl delete pod pod-name`

Tip: Always use `-o wide` for detailed output.

Example:

```
$ kubectl get pods -o wide
```

Observability and Live Monitoring

Observe cluster events **in real time**:

```
$ kubectl get events --sort-by='.metadata.creationTimestamp'
```

Live watch resource changes:

```
$ kubectl get pods -w
```

The `-w` flag keeps output streaming.

Check top resource consumption (after Metrics Server installed):

```
$ kubectl top nodes
$ kubectl top pods
```

View node details including labels, taints, conditions:

```
$ kubectl describe node node-name
```

Debugging Applications

Inspect a Pod in detail:

```
$ kubectl describe pod pod-name
```

Stream logs:

```
$ kubectl logs -f pod-name
```

Exec into a running container:

```
$ kubectl exec -it pod-name -- bash
```

🔒 **Pro Tip:** *Always* `describe` *before* `logs` *when troubleshooting — Pod events often tell you more than application logs.*

Advanced `kubectl` Usages

Explain any resource:

```
$ kubectl explain deployment.spec
```

Gives schema and documentation.

Edit a live resource (opens in your default editor):

```
$ kubectl edit deployment deployment-name
```

Scale deployments manually:

```
$ kubectl scale deployment deployment-name --replicas=10
```

Set environment variables dynamically:

```
$ kubectl set env deployment/my-deployment ENV_VAR_NAME=value
```

Rollout status for tracking updates:

```
$ kubectl rollout status deployment/deployment-name
```

Rollback to previous version:

```
$ kubectl rollout undo deployment/deployment-name
```

Real-World Use Cases

- **Scenario 1:** Pod keeps restarting
  - Check logs → `kubectl logs pod-name`
  - Describe Pod → `kubectl describe pod pod-name`
  - Verify events for crash reasons (OOMKilled, ImagePullBackOff).
- **Scenario 2:** Application is slow
  - Use `kubectl top pods` to check resource consumption.
  - Check node saturation with `kubectl top nodes`.
- **Scenario 3: Service is unreachable**
  - Verify Service endpoints: `kubectl get endpoints`
  - Check DNS resolution inside a Pod using `nslookup service-name`.

Pro Tips for Production `kubectl` Usage

- Use **resource labels** consistently (e.g., `app=frontend`) to group and filter resources.
- Always set resource **requests and limits** for Pods.
- Regularly prune old, unused objects:
  - `kubectl delete pod --field-selector=status.phase=Succeeded`
- Implement **kubectl plugins** (e.g., `kubectl tree`, `kubectl neat`) for better UX.
- Script daily operations with `bash + kubectl` pipelines for efficiency.

Recommendations

In production-grade clusters:

- Operators often use `kubectl get pods --field-selector=status.phase!=Running` to spot failing applications.
- **Audit logging** of all `kubectl` activities via API Server audit logs is recommended.
- Combine `kubectl port-forward` with security best practices when troubleshooting exposed Pods.

Deploying Applications on Kubernetes – Practical Scenarios

Deploying applications on Kubernetes is much more than just launching a container. A real-world deployment includes:

- Defining the app image and ports
- Setting resource requests and limits

- Wiring in ConfigMaps and Secrets
- Exposing the application safely
- Ensuring health monitoring
- Preparing for seamless scaling and upgrades

In this section, we'll **practically build** and **deploy** real-world examples step-by-step.

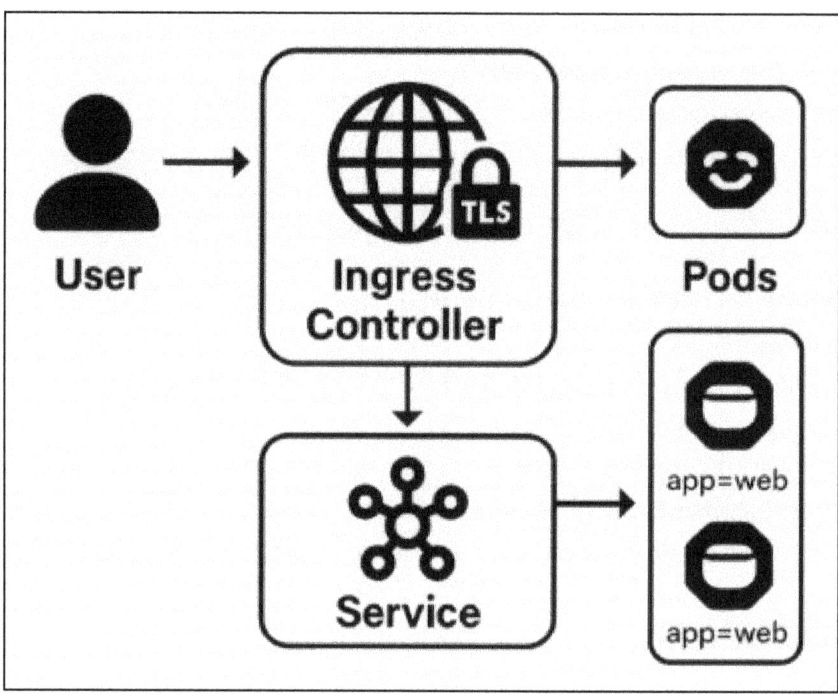

Figure 19.4: Ingress Controller Traffic Flow

Building a Basic Deployment: Nginx Web Server

Step 1: Create Deployment YAML

```
apiVersion: apps/v1
kind: Deployment
metadata:
  name: nginx-deployment
spec:
  replicas: 3
  selector:
    matchLabels:
      app: nginx
  template:
    metadata:
      labels:
```

```
        app: nginx
    spec:
      containers:
      - name: nginx
        image: nginx:1.25
        ports:
        - containerPort: 80
        resources:
          requests:
            cpu: "100m"
            memory: "128Mi"
          limits:
            cpu: "500m"
            memory: "512Mi"
```

Apply Deployment:

```
$ kubectl apply -f nginx-deployment.yaml
```

Step 2: Expose Deployment with a Service

```
$ kubectl expose deployment nginx-deployment --type=NodePort --port=80
```

This will:

- Create a Service
- Expose the Pods on a Node IP and specific port (e.g., `30008`)

Get NodePort:

```
$ kubectl get svc
```

Access the app by visiting:

```
http://<NodeIP>:<NodePort>
```

🔒 **Pro Tip:** *In Minikube, use* `minikube service nginx-deployment --url` *to get the URL directly.*

Adding Health Checks (Liveness and Readiness Probes)

In production, Kubernetes needs to know if a container is alive and ready to serve traffic.

Update Deployment YAML:

```
livenessProbe:
  httpGet:
    path: /
    port: 80
  initialDelaySeconds: 30
  periodSeconds: 10
readinessProbe:
  httpGet:
    path: /
    port: 80
  initialDelaySeconds: 5
  periodSeconds: 5
```

Liveness Probe: Checks if the container is still running. If not, it restarts it.

Readiness Probe: Checks if the app is ready to serve traffic.

Patch Deployment with Probes:

```
$ kubectl apply -f nginx-deployment.yaml
```

Deploying a Multi-Container Pod

Sometimes you need sidecar containers — for logging, authentication proxies, etc.

Example YAML:

```
apiVersion: v1
kind: Pod
metadata:
  name: nginx-sidecar-pod
spec:
  containers:
  - name: nginx
    image: nginx
    ports:
    - containerPort: 80
  - name: sidecar
    image: busybox
    command: ["sh", "-c", "while true; do echo hello; sleep 10;done"]
```

Here:

- The main container is `nginx`.

- The sidecar is a `busybox` container generating logs.

Production Tip: *Always separate business logic (app container) from operational logic (sidecar container).*

Real-World Deployment Example: Python Flask API

Imagine you are deploying a Flask API server behind Kubernetes.

Deployment YAML:

```
apiVersion: apps/v1
kind: Deployment
metadata:
  name: flask-api
spec:
  replicas: 2
  selector:
    matchLabels:
      app: flask-api
  template:
    metadata:
      labels:
        app: flask-api
    spec:
      containers:
      - name: flask
        image: yourdockerhub/flask-api:latest
        ports:
        - containerPort: 5000
        envFrom:
        - configMapRef:
            name: flask-config
        - secretRef:
            name: flask-secrets
```

Service YAML:

```
apiVersion: v1
kind: Service
metadata:
  name: flask-service
spec:
```

```
  type: ClusterIP
  selector:
    app: flask-api
  ports:
    - port: 80
      targetPort: 5000
```

Ingress YAML (Optional):

```
apiVersion: networking.k8s.io/v1
kind: Ingress
metadata:
  name: flask-ingress
spec:
  rules:
  - host: flask.yourdomain.com
    http:
      paths:
      - path: /
        pathType: Prefix
        backend:
          service:
            name: flask-service
            port:
              number: 80
```

Summary of Deployment Steps (DevOps Checklist)

Step	Action
1	Create Deployment with resource requests/limits.
2	Attach Liveness and Readiness probes.
3	Expose Deployment via Service (ClusterIP, NodePort, LoadBalancer).
4	Secure communication via Ingress + TLS certificates.
5	Monitor resource usage with Metrics Server.
6	Set up Horizontal Pod Autoscaler (HPA) if needed.
7	Set Pod Disruption Budgets (PDB) for controlled rolling updates.

Recommendations

- Always version-control your Kubernetes YAML files (GitOps).
- Never expose Services directly with NodePorts to the public; use Ingress or External Load Balancer.
- Validate YAMLs before applying using:
    - `kubectl apply --dry-run=client -f file.yaml`
- Annotate critical Deployments for easy tracking:
    - `metadata:`
        - `annotations:`
        - `owner: devops-team`
        - `environment: production`

Kubernetes Networking Deep Dive

Networking in Kubernetes can seem magical at first: every Pod gets its own IP address, services automatically find each other, and traffic load-balances across Pods seamlessly.

But behind the scenes, Kubernetes networking is carefully engineered — and understanding it is critical for **real-world troubleshooting, security, and scaling**.

Key Principles of Kubernetes Networking

- **Pod-to-Pod Communication:** Every Pod gets a unique IP address. Pods can communicate directly with each other across Nodes without NAT (Network Address Translation).
- **Service-to-Pod Communication:** Services act as stable network frontends for groups of dynamic Pods. DNS records are automatically created for each Service.
- **External Traffic Ingress:** External clients can access applications inside the cluster via **NodePorts**, **LoadBalancers**, or **Ingress Controllers**.
- **Flat Network Space:** All Pods see a single, flat IP address space. There is no IP masquerading between Pods on the same network.

🔒 **Pro Tip:** *Kubernetes networking assumes a non-firewalled environment internally. You must explicitly secure communication via Network Policies!*

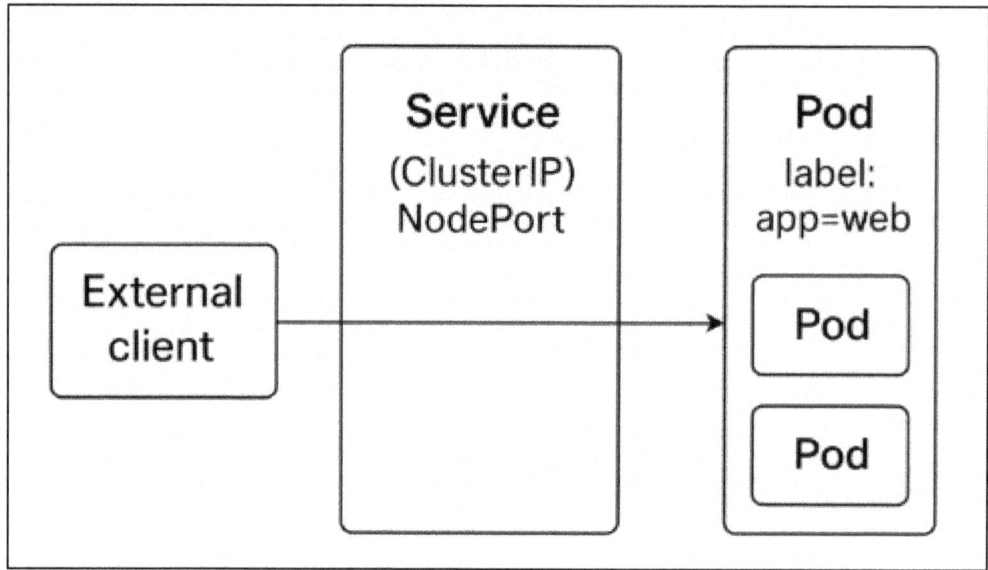

Figure 19.3: Pod and Service Networking Flow

Container Network Interface (CNI) Plugins

Kubernetes relies on CNI plugins to implement networking. The CNI plugin assigns IP addresses to Pods, sets up routes, and manages network security.

Popular CNI plugins:

Plugin	Description
Flannel	Simple overlay network; great for beginners.
Calico	Powerful networking + Network Policy enforcement.
Weave Net	Automatic peer discovery, encryption by default.
Cilium	eBPF-based, high-performance networking and security.

Example: Using Calico for production:

- Enables fine-grained Network Policies.
- Provides security between Pods.
- Supports BGP for highly scalable networking.

Production Tip: *Always deploy a CNI that supports Network Policies (Calico or Cilium recommended for serious workloads).*

Kubernetes Service Networking

When you create a Service in Kubernetes:

- It gets a **ClusterIP** (virtual IP).
- Kubernetes configures iptables or IPVS rules on the Nodes.
- Traffic sent to the Service IP is **load-balanced** across healthy Pods behind it.

Example:

```
$ kubectl get svc
```

Output:

```
NAME           TYPE         CLUSTER-IP    EXTERNAL-IP   PORT(S)   AGE
flask-service  ClusterIP    10.96.0.42    <none>        80/TCP    10m
```

Pods connecting to flask-service on port 80 are automatically routed to one of the backend Pods.

DNS in Kubernetes

DNS is automatically set up inside the cluster:

- **kube-dns** or **CoreDNS** is deployed by default.
- Services get DNS names like `<service>.<namespace>.svc.cluster.local`.

Example:

- A Pod can `curl http://flask-service.default.svc.cluster.local` without worrying about IPs.

DNS also handles headless Services (`ClusterIP: None`), which resolve to a list of Pod IPs directly.

Ingress Controllers and Traffic Routing

For HTTP/HTTPS traffic from outside the cluster, you typically use an **Ingress Controller**.

Popular Ingress Controllers:

Ingress Controller	Description
Nginx Ingress Controller	Most popular, easy to configure.
Traefik	Lightweight, dynamic, good for microservices.
HAProxy Ingress	Highly optimized for performance.
Istio Gateway	Used in service mesh deployments.

Typical Production Architecture:

External DNS → Cloud Load Balancer → Ingress Controller → Kubernetes Services → Pods

TLS Termination at Ingress

Modern applications must use HTTPS. Kubernetes Ingress controllers can **terminate TLS** connections:

- Serve HTTPS traffic to users.
- Forward plain HTTP traffic inside the cluster (or mutual TLS inside if needed).

Example TLS-enabled Ingress YAML:

```
apiVersion: networking.k8s.io/v1
kind: Ingress
metadata:
  name: secure-ingress
  annotations:
    nginx.ingress.kubernetes.io/ssl-redirect: "true"
spec:
  tls:
  - hosts:
    - myapp.example.com
    secretName: my-tls-secret
  rules:
  - host: myapp.example.com
    http:
      paths:
      - path: /
        pathType: Prefix
        backend:
          service:
            name: myapp-service
            port:
              number: 80
```

Recommendations

- Always use **Ingress with TLS** enabled for production apps.
- Use tools like **cert-manager** to automate SSL certificates from Let's Encrypt.
- Deploy Network Policies to restrict Pod-to-Pod communication and enforce **zero trust** internally.

Configuration and Secrets Management Deep Dive

Modern cloud-native applications must be **configurable** without rebuilding containers and must **securely** handle sensitive information like passwords, API keys, and tokens.

Kubernetes provides two core objects for this:

- **ConfigMaps**: For non-sensitive configurations (settings, environment variables).
- **Secrets**: For sensitive data (passwords, private keys, certificates).

Mastering these is crucial for production-grade deployments.

ConfigMaps: Injecting Externalized Configuration

ConfigMaps allow you to decouple configuration artifacts from container images, following the 12-Factor App methodology.

Create a ConfigMap:

From literal key-value pairs:

```
$ kubectl create configmap app-config --from-literal=ENV=production --from-literal=LOG_LEVEL=info
```

From a file:

```
$ kubectl create configmap app-config --from-file=config.properties
```

Using ConfigMaps in Pods (YAML example):

```
apiVersion: v1
kind: Pod
metadata:
  name: configmap-demo
spec:
  containers:
  - name: app
    image: my-app-image
    env:
    - name: ENV
      valueFrom:
        configMapKeyRef:
          name: app-config
          key: ENV
```

Best Practices for ConfigMaps:

- Separate configs from code.
- Version your ConfigMaps alongside app releases.
- Use application reload patterns (e.g., SIGHUP) if config changes dynamically.
- Validate ConfigMap references with liveness/readiness probes.

Secrets: Securely Managing Sensitive Information

Secrets are designed to store sensitive data, like:

- Database passwords
- API tokens
- SSH keys
- TLS certificates

Create a Secret:

From literal:

```
$ kubectl create secret generic db-secret --from-
literal=password=MySecretPassword
```

From file:

```
$ kubectl create secret generic tls-secret --from-file=cert.crt --from-
file=cert.key
```

Using Secrets in Pods (YAML example):

```
apiVersion: v1
kind: Pod
metadata:
  name: secret-demo
spec:
  containers:
  - name: app
    image: my-app-image
    env:
    - name: DB_PASSWORD
      valueFrom:
        secretKeyRef:
          name: db-secret
          key: password
```

Secrets Management Challenges

By default, Kubernetes Secrets are **Base64-encoded**, not encrypted.
While this prevents casual reading, it **is not sufficient** against serious threats.

Ways to secure Secrets:

- Enable **Secrets Encryption at Rest** using KMS plugins.
- Use **RBAC policies** to restrict who can view Secrets (`kubectl get secrets`).
- Leverage external tools like:
  - **HashiCorp Vault**
  - **AWS Secrets Manager**
  - **Sealed Secrets (Bitnami project)**
  - **SOPS (Secrets OPerationS) by Mozilla**

Real-World Secrets Workflow Example

In a production application:

- Store database credentials in a Kubernetes Secret.
- Configure app Deployment to load credentials from the Secret.
- Restrict secret access only to application ServiceAccount via RBAC.
- Rotate secrets periodically (automated pipeline or manual trigger).
- Audit secret access via Kubernetes API Server logs.

Sample RBAC Policy:

```
apiVersion: rbac.authorization.k8s.io/v1
kind: Role
metadata:
  namespace: production
  name: secret-reader
rules:
- apiGroups: [""]
  resources: ["secrets"]
  verbs: ["get"]
```

🔒 **Pro Tip:** *Never give* `list` *or* `watch` *permissions on secrets unless absolutely necessary.*

Limit to `get` and **scope to a namespace** whenever possible.

Secrets in CI/CD Pipelines

When integrating Kubernetes with Continuous Deployment systems (e.g., ArgoCD, GitLab CI, Jenkins X):

- Never store raw secrets in Git.
- Use encrypted GitOps tools (e.g., Sealed Secrets + ArgoCD).
- Store sensitive credentials in the CI/CD vault, not in plaintext YAMLs.
- Deploy secrets via automation, not manual `kubectl create secret`.

Recommendations

- Encrypt Secrets at Rest at the cluster level.
- Scan secrets for over-permissive access during security reviews.
- Rotate secrets at least every 90 days (or as per compliance policy).
- Use distinct secrets per application, avoid secret sharing across apps.

Scaling and Auto-Healing in Kubernetes (Deep + Real-World)

One of Kubernetes' most powerful features is **automatic scaling and healing** of applications. Instead of hiring an engineer to monitor workloads 24x7, Kubernetes dynamically adjusts resources based on demand and recovers from failures without manual intervention.

Let's explore how it works in both **manual** and **automated** ways.

Manual Scaling of Deployments

You can manually scale Deployments up or down using simple `kubectl` commands.

Example:

```
$ kubectl scale deployment nginx-deployment --replicas=5
```

This command tells Kubernetes to run exactly **5 replicas** of the Pods defined in `nginx-deployment`.

Kubernetes will **add or remove Pods** until the desired replica count is met.

Best Practices for Manual Scaling:

- Always scale **during low-traffic windows** when possible.
- **Monitor CPU/memory usage** during scale-outs to ensure cluster has enough headroom.

- **Set Pod Disruption Budgets (PDBs)** to protect against excessive simultaneous evictions during scale-ins.

Horizontal Pod Autoscaler (HPA)

In production, we don't want to manually monitor and scale workloads all the time. **Horizontal Pod Autoscaler (HPA)** automates scaling based on CPU usage or custom metrics.

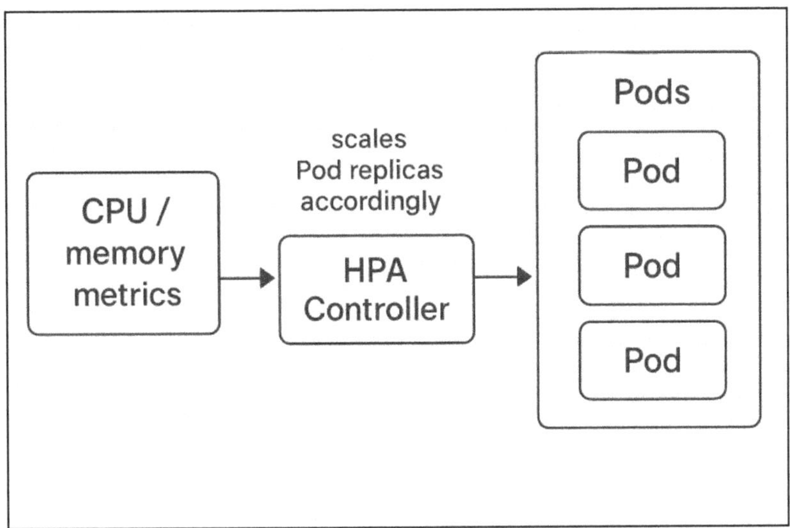

Figure 19.6: Horizontal Pod Autoscaler (HPA) Flow

Enable Metrics Server first:

```
$ minikube addons enable metrics-server
```

Create an HPA

```
$ kubectl autoscale deployment nginx-deployment --cpu-percent=50 --min=2 --
max=10
```

- If the average CPU usage across Pods exceeds 50%, Kubernetes will automatically scale up.
- If CPU usage drops, Kubernetes will scale Pods down.

YAML-based HPA Example

```
apiVersion: autoscaling/v2
kind: HorizontalPodAutoscaler
metadata:
  name: nginx-hpa
spec:
  scaleTargetRef:
```

```
    apiVersion: apps/v1
    kind: Deployment
    name: nginx-deployment
  minReplicas: 2
  maxReplicas: 10
  metrics:
  - type: Resource
    resource:
      name: cpu
      target:
        type: Utilization
        averageUtilization: 50
```

🔒 **Pro Tip:** *Always test your HPA behavior by simulating load during pre-production stages.*

Vertical Pod Autoscaler (VPA)

VPA automatically adjusts resource **requests** and **limits** for Pods based on actual usage.

Use cases:

- Applications with unpredictable memory/CPU needs.
- Optimization of resource usage across the cluster.

VPA Modes:

- `Off`: Only recommend resources.
- `Initial`: Apply recommendations on Pod startup.
- `Auto`: Apply recommendations during runtime (may restart Pods).

Production Tip: *Use HPA for scaling replicas horizontally.*

Use VPA cautiously — avoid dynamic resource resizing during critical production hours unless explicitly validated.

Kubernetes Self-Healing Demonstration

Scenario:
Suppose a Pod crashes due to an internal error.

Kubernetes Automatically:

- Detects that the Pod is unhealthy.
- Terminates and removes the failed Pod.
- Creates a new Pod to meet the Deployment replica count.

Try it in lab:

Manually delete a running Pod:

```
$ kubectl delete pod <pod-name>
```

Immediately check:

```
$ kubectl get pods
```

You'll see Kubernetes **creates a new Pod** automatically to maintain the desired replica count.

🔒 ***Pro Tip:*** *This* **self-healing behavior** *extends to node failures, container crashes, and even network partitions if properly configured.*

Resource Requests, Limits, and Eviction Policies

Kubernetes needs to schedule workloads intelligently based on resource availability.

- **Requests**: Minimum guaranteed resources (for scheduling).
- **Limits**: Maximum allowable resources (to avoid overuse).

Example Deployment Snippet:

```
resources:
  requests:
    cpu: "200m"
    memory: "256Mi"
  limits:
    cpu: "500m"
    memory: "512Mi"
```

If a Pod exceeds its memory **limit**, Kubernetes may **kill and restart** it (`OOMKilled`). If the node itself runs out of memory or disk, Kubernetes evicts the least critical Pods first, based on priorities and QoS classes.

Pod Disruption Budgets (PDBs)

PDBs define **how many Pods must stay available** during voluntary disruptions (like node upgrades, cluster maintenance).

Example PDB YAML:

```
apiVersion: policy/v1
kind: PodDisruptionBudget
metadata:
  name: nginx-pdb
spec:
  minAvailable: 2
  selector:
    matchLabels:
      app: nginx
```

In this example:

- At least **2 Pods** must be available at all times.
- Kubernetes will refuse to evict more Pods during maintenance if it would violate the PDB.

Recommendations

- Always configure **resource requests and limits** for every production workload.
- Test HPA/VPA behavior during non-peak times.
- Use PDBs to maintain high availability during cluster upgrades or node drains.
- Implement **cluster autoscaler** if using cloud-managed Kubernetes to dynamically add/remove nodes based on Pod needs.

Rolling Updates, Rollbacks, and Deployment Strategies

One of Kubernetes' most powerful features is the ability to **upgrade applications** without downtime.
Kubernetes supports **rolling updates** natively — gracefully updating Pods one at a time — and allows easy **rollback** if something goes wrong.

But real-world deployments need more than basic upgrades: techniques like **Blue-Green Deployments** and **Canary Releases** are critical for minimizing risk during production updates.

Let's go deep into how Kubernetes handles updates safely.

Rolling Updates (Default Strategy)

When you change a Deployment (new image, new config, etc.), Kubernetes by default performs a **Rolling Update**:

- It slowly **terminates old Pods** and **creates new ones**.

- It **always ensures a minimum number of healthy Pods** (controlled by `maxUnavailable`).
- It avoids downtime.

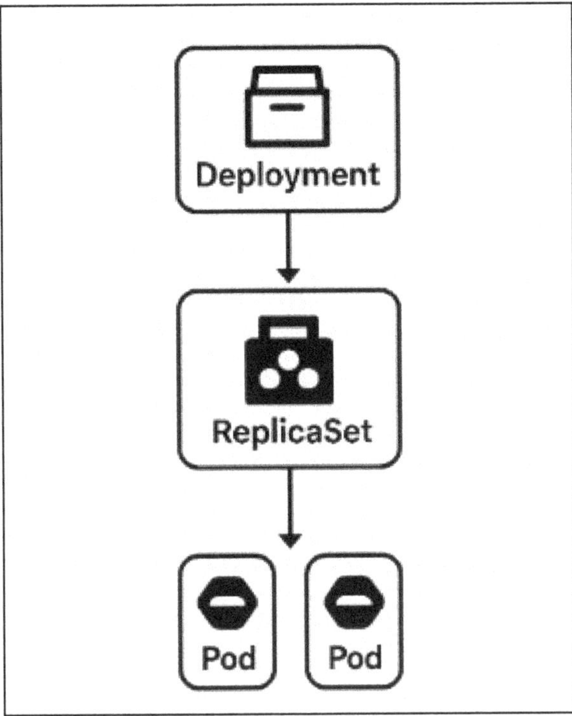

Figure 19.5: Kubernetes Object Lifecycle

Example:

Update an image:

```
$ kubectl set image deployment/nginx-deployment nginx=nginx:1.26
```

Check rollout status:

```
$ kubectl rollout status deployment/nginx-deployment
```

Rollback if something breaks:

```
$ kubectl rollout undo deployment/nginx-deployment
```

Tuning Rolling Update Parameters

Inside a Deployment YAML, you can fine-tune the Rolling Update behavior.

```
strategy:
  type: RollingUpdate
  rollingUpdate:
    maxUnavailable: 1
    maxSurge: 2
```

Parameter	Meaning
`maxUnavailable`	How many Pods can be down during update (absolute number or percentage).
`maxSurge`	How many extra Pods can be created temporarily above desired replicas.

Production Tip: *Setting* `maxUnavailable: 0` *ensures* ***zero downtime*** *during updates but requires extra resources temporarily.*

Rollbacks

If a rollout fails, Kubernetes maintains the previous ReplicaSet. You can easily rollback.

Rollback example:

```
$ kubectl rollout undo deployment/nginx-deployment
```

You can also see rollout history:

```
$ kubectl rollout history deployment/nginx-deployment
```

Rollbacks are fast, reliable, and fully automated — critical for production safety.

Blue-Green Deployments

In **Blue-Green Deployment**, you maintain two environments:

- **Blue**: Stable production version.
- **Green**: New version being tested.

When Green is fully validated, traffic is switched from Blue to Green instantly.

In Kubernetes:

- Deploy two versions of your app (e.g., `blue`, and `green` Deployments).
- Use a Service to **point traffic** to the active Deployment.
- Update Service selectors during cutover.

Example:

Initially:

```
selector:
  app: blue-app
```

After successful testing:

```
selector:
  app: green-app
```

🔒 **Pro Tip:** *This allows* **instant rollback** *simply by switching Service back to the Blue Deployment.*

Canary Releases

Canary Deployment is a progressive rollout where:

- Only a **small percentage** of users see the new version initially.
- Gradually increase exposure if no problems detected.

In Kubernetes:

- Deploy new version alongside old version with **different labels**.
- Use advanced Ingress rules or Service mesh (like Istio, Linkerd) to split traffic (e.g., 90% old, 10% new).

Canary Workflow:

1. Deploy version `v2` alongside stable `v1`.
2. Route 5–10% of traffic to `v2`.
3. Monitor metrics, error rates, latency.
4. If stable, shift more traffic.
5. Complete cutover.

Production Tip: *Always monitor* **application health**, **error budgets**, *and* **SLOs** *during canary phases. Automate rollbacks if thresholds breached.*

Best Practices for Safe Application Updates

Practice	Why It Matters
Use RollingUpdates	Avoid downtime.
Set Readiness Probes	Ensure only healthy Pods receive traffic.
Use HorizontalPodAutoscaler (HPA)	Maintain service responsiveness during rollout surges.
Monitor Rollouts	Integrate rollout status into your CI/CD pipelines.
Automate Rollbacks	Implement metrics-driven automatic rollbacks with Argo Rollouts or Flagger.

Recommendations

- Always **deploy Readiness Probes** to avoid sending traffic to Pods that are still starting up.
- In production, **monitor deployments in real time** using tools like Prometheus, Grafana, ArgoCD.
- Prefer **progressive delivery** techniques (Canary/Blue-Green) over blind rolling updates for mission-critical systems.
- Validate rollback procedures **regularly**, not just in theory.

Observability, Monitoring, and Troubleshooting Kubernetes Applications

Running a Kubernetes cluster without monitoring is like flying an airplane with no cockpit instruments. You **won't know** if your application is healthy, if nodes are overburdened, or if subtle problems are building up until it's too late.

In real-world Kubernetes operations, **observability** (metrics, logs, events, traces) is absolutely critical for **operational excellence**.

Let's dive deep into how we monitor, debug, and troubleshoot Kubernetes like a professional.

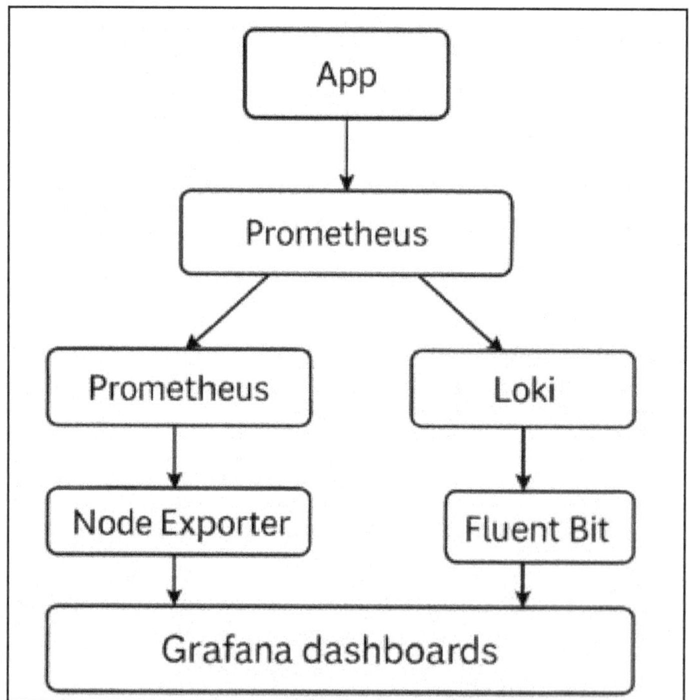

Figure 19.7: Monitoring Stack with Prometheus, Grafana, Loki

Core Observability Components in Kubernetes

Metrics: Quantitative values over time (CPU usage, request rates, memory consumption).

Logs: Text output from applications or system components, important for root cause analysis.

Events: Cluster-level lifecycle notifications — what happened, when, and why.

Tracing (Advanced): Correlates multiple microservices across requests to track distributed operations.

Metrics Collection and Monitoring

Kubernetes-native metrics are exposed via the **Metrics Server**:

- CPU and memory consumption per Pod/Node.
- Pod startup times.
- Node resource saturation.

Install Metrics Server (if not already present):

```
$ minikube addons enable metrics-server
```

Useful Commands:

- Node-level resource usage:
  - `$ kubectl top nodes`
- Pod-level resource usage:
  - `$ kubectl top pods`

Advanced Metrics: Prometheus and Grafana

Prometheus is the de facto standard for Kubernetes monitoring.

Setup Overview:

- Prometheus scrapes metrics from Kubernetes components and Pods.
- Grafana visualizes Prometheus metrics with beautiful dashboards.

Typical Stack:

- Prometheus Operator (for easy install/management)
- Grafana Dashboards for:
  - Node health
  - Pod CPU/memory
  - HPA behavior
  - API server latencies

  - Ingress controller metrics

Example Dashboard Metrics:

- Pod restarts over time
- CPU throttling events
- 99th percentile API response times
- Ingress error rates

Production Tip:
Always monitor:

- Pod Restart Counts
- Node Disk Pressure
- API Server Error Rates
- Application-specific RED metrics (Rate, Errors, Duration)

Centralized Logging

Logs are just as important as metrics — often even more critical for deep debugging.

Centralized Logging Architecture in Kubernetes:

Component	Purpose
Fluent Bit / Fluentd	Collect logs from all Pods/Nodes.
Loki	Lightweight log aggregation backend (Grafana Labs).
Elasticsearch	Full-text search, indexing, and querying for logs.
Kibana	Dashboard for Elasticsearch logs.
Grafana Loki	Visualizes logs efficiently alongside metrics.

Typical Flow:

1. Fluent Bit reads logs from container runtime (e.g., containerd or Docker).
2. Fluent Bit forwards logs to Loki.
3. Grafana queries Loki to display logs.

Benefits:

- Search logs across all Pods instantly.
- Correlate metrics + logs in single dashboard.
- Retain logs for audits and security investigations.

Common Failure Cases and Troubleshooting Techniques

Symptom	Probable Cause	Troubleshooting Steps
Pod stuck in Pending	Resource shortage, node taints	`kubectl describe pod` and `kubectl get nodes`
Pod CrashLoopBackOff	App crash, bad config	`kubectl logs` and inspect readiness/liveness probes
ImagePullBackOff	Image name typo, auth issues	`kubectl describe pod`, check event logs
Node Not Ready	Network/storage failures	`kubectl describe node`, inspect kubelet and containerd logs
Service Unreachable	Wrong selector, network policies	Check Service endpoints, DNS resolution inside Pods

Real-World Debugging Workflow

Scenario: API application Pods crash repeatedly.

Step-by-step:

1. `kubectl get pods` ➔ Find crash-looping Pod.
2. `kubectl describe pod` ➔ View lifecycle events.
3. `kubectl logs pod-name` ➔ Look for stack traces or error messages.
4. `kubectl get deployment` ➔ Check number of replicas vs. ready replicas.
5. Validate ConfigMaps, Secrets, and environment variables.
6. Use a busybox Pod to debug DNS, network access: `kubectl run -it busybox --image=busybox --restart=Never -- sh`

🔒 ***Pro Tip:*** *Always start with* `kubectl describe`*, not just* `kubectl logs`.
Many operational issues (e.g., bad configs, node capacity problems) appear first in Pod events, not in application logs.

Recommendations

- Tag all Prometheus alerts with severity levels (critical, warning, info).
- Build Grafana dashboards focusing on application SLIs (Service Level Indicators).
- Alert on **symptoms** (error rates, latency spikes) — not only on resource metrics.
- Retain centralized logs for **at least 30–90 days** depending on compliance requirements.

Real-World Kubernetes Use Cases and Final Production Best Practices

Now that you have learned how Kubernetes works, how to deploy applications, scale, heal, monitor, and troubleshoot — it's time to zoom out and look at **real-world adoption scenarios**.

Enterprises across industries have used Kubernetes to solve major challenges of scale, agility, and operational excellence.

Let's explore how.

Common Enterprise Use Cases for Kubernetes

Industry	Kubernetes Use Case
Banking	Secure, scalable deployment of microservices for online banking apps, fraud detection systems.
Retail / E-Commerce	Elastic web servers, flash sale event scaling, recommendation engines.
Healthcare	Hosting sensitive patient data apps (HIPAA compliant) with isolated multi-tenant environments.
Media & Streaming	Dynamic scaling of video transcoding services and content delivery platforms.
Telecom	5G network functions virtualization (NFV) and edge computing with lightweight K8s (k3s).
SaaS Companies	Multi-region, multi-cloud service hosting, with CI/CD pipelines pushing hundreds of deployments daily.

Real Case Example: A large fintech company runs **over 10,000 Pods** daily across 3 public clouds using Kubernetes, with automatic failover, encrypted secrets management, and progressive canary releases monitored via Prometheus and Grafana.

Kubernetes Deployment Models

Kubernetes offers flexible deployment architectures depending on business needs:

Model	Description
Self-Managed Cluster	Install and manage K8s yourself on VMs/bare-metal (maximum control, maximum complexity).

Model	Description
Managed Kubernetes	Cloud providers manage the Control Plane for you (e.g., AWS EKS, Azure AKS, GCP GKE).
Hybrid / Multi-Cloud	Kubernetes clusters span across multiple clouds or datacenters for redundancy.
Edge Deployments	Lightweight Kubernetes (k3s) clusters run at the edge (e.g., retail stores, remote offices).

Production Tip: *Start with managed Kubernetes (EKS/AKS/GKE) unless you have strong platform engineering capabilities in-house. Operating Kubernetes yourself involves upgrading clusters, patching CVEs, etc., which is* ***non-trivial****.*

Key Components for a Production-Grade Kubernetes Platform

If you're building Kubernetes clusters for production use, your checklist should include:

[√] Monitoring and Alerting

- Prometheus
- Grafana
- Loki (for logs)

[√] Secure Networking

- CNI Plugin (Calico, Cilium)
- Network Policies

[√] Secrets Management

- Kubernetes Secrets encrypted at rest
- External Secret Stores (Vault, AWS Secrets Manager)

[√] CI/CD Pipelines

- GitOps (ArgoCD, Flux)
- Progressive delivery with canaries and blue-green rollouts

[√] Auto-Scaling

- Horizontal and Vertical Pod Autoscalers
- Cluster Autoscaler (for cloud-native dynamic node scaling)

[√] Disaster Recovery and Backups

- etcd backups
- Application backup using Velero or Stash

[√] Role-Based Access Control (RBAC) and Security Hardening

- Fine-grained access control
- Pod Security Standards (baseline/restricted)

[√] Multi-Environment Management

- Dev/Staging/Production namespace isolation
- Promotion pipelines between environments

Design Patterns for Kubernetes Success

Pattern	What It Solves
Sidecar Pattern	Enhances applications without code changes (e.g., service mesh proxy injection).
Ambassador Pattern	API Gateway-style proxy for microservices.
Adapter Pattern	Format-shifting logs or metrics before external transmission.
Operator Pattern	Encapsulate domain knowledge into controllers (e.g., database operators managing backups automatically).

Final Production Best Practices

- **Treat Infrastructure as Code**: Use GitOps to manage YAMLs and cluster configurations.
- **Prefer Immutable Deployments**: Avoid patching live containers; replace Pods with updated ones.
- **Use Namespaces Effectively**: Isolate teams and environments.
- **Set Resource Requests/Limits**: Prevent CPU/memory resource starvation.
- **Implement Readiness/Liveness Probes**: Essential for service availability.
- **Secure Your API Server**: Limit public exposure, use firewalling or VPC-only access.
- **Encrypt Secrets at Rest and In-Transit**: Never assume cluster internals are secure without encryption.
- **Audit and Rotate Certificates Regularly**: Kubernetes certificates expire; manage lifecycle proactively.

- **Automate Everything**: Use Terraform, Crossplane, Cluster API for infrastructure automation.
- **Chaos Test Your Cluster**: Simulate node failures and see how your system recovers.

Kubernetes Future Trends (2025+)

- **AI/ML Workloads on Kubernetes**: Kubernetes is now the default platform for AI model training and serving.
- **Edge Kubernetes Growth**: K3s and lightweight clusters spread to retail, manufacturing, and telecom industries.
- **Zero Trust Architectures**: Deep integration with identity, service mesh, and encryption technologies.
- **Serverless Kubernetes (Knative, Keda)**: Automatic scale-to-zero workloads.
- **Platform Engineering Revolution**: Building Internal Developer Platforms (IDPs) powered by Kubernetes APIs.

Kubernetes is not "just another tool." It's a new **operating system for the cloud** — abstracting infrastructure and letting developers and businesses focus purely on building value.

Let's Practice What You've Learned

Now that you've explored the core concepts of Kubernetes — from Pods and Deployments to Services, ConfigMaps, and Autoscaling — it's time to put that knowledge into practice. In the following hands-on lab, you'll simulate a real-world microservice deployment using Kubernetes. This lab reinforces key skills like deploying applications, exposing services, configuring environment variables, setting up health checks, and implementing autoscaling.

Hands-On Lab: Kubernetes Deployment with Auto-Scaling and Health Checks

Difficulty Level: Intermediate-Advanced

Objective:

Deploy a production-like Python web app on Kubernetes with:

- Deployment + Service + ConfigMap
- Horizontal Pod Autoscaling (HPA)
- Health checks (readiness & liveness)
- Resource limits and labels

📁 Folder Structure:

```
/k8s-lab/
├── app/
│   ├── app.py
│   ├── Dockerfile
├── manifests/
│   ├── deployment.yaml
│   ├── service.yaml
│   ├── configmap.yaml
│   ├── hpa.yaml
│   ├── readiness-probe.yaml
│   ├── resource-limits.yaml
└── load-test/
    └── hey-test.sh
```

Step-by-Step Lab

1. Build the Docker App

📜 app/app.py

```
from flask import Flask
import os
app = Flask(__name__)

@app.route('/')
def home():
    return f"App is running in ENV={os.environ.get('ENV', 'not set')}"

if __name__ == "__main__":
    app.run(host="0.0.0.0", port=5000)
```

📜 app/Dockerfile

```
FROM python:3.10-slim
WORKDIR /app
COPY app.py .
RUN pip install flask
ENV ENV=production
CMD ["python", "app.py"]
```

2. Push Image

```
$ docker build -t yourdockerhub/k8s-demo-app:latest ./app
$ docker push yourdockerhub/k8s-demo-app:latest
```

3. Apply K8s Manifests

📜 manifests/deployment.yaml

```
apiVersion: apps/v1
kind: Deployment
metadata:
  name: k8s-demo
spec:
  replicas: 2
  selector:
    matchLabels:
      app: demo
  template:
    metadata:
      labels:
        app: demo
    spec:
      containers:
      - name: web
        image: yourdockerhub/k8s-demo-app:latest
        ports:
        - containerPort: 5000
        env:
        - name: ENV
          valueFrom:
            configMapKeyRef:
              name: app-config
              key: ENV
```

📜 manifests/service.yaml

```
apiVersion: v1
kind: Service
metadata:
  name: k8s-demo-svc
spec:
  selector:
    app: demo
  ports:
    - protocol: TCP
      port: 80
      targetPort: 5000
  type: LoadBalancer
```

📜 manifests/configmap.yaml

```
apiVersion: v1
kind: ConfigMap
metadata:
  name: app-config
```

```
data:
  ENV: staging
```

Apply the above:

```
$ kubectl apply -f manifests/
```

4. Add Probes and Resources

📜 `manifests/readiness-probe.yaml`

```
livenessProbe:
  httpGet:
    path: /
    port: 5000
  initialDelaySeconds: 5
  periodSeconds: 10
readinessProbe:
  httpGet:
    path: /
    port: 5000
  initialDelaySeconds: 3
  periodSeconds: 5
```

You can merge this into the container spec in `deployment.yaml`.

5. Autoscaling (HPA)

📜 `manifests/hpa.yaml`

```
apiVersion: autoscaling/v2
kind: HorizontalPodAutoscaler
metadata:
  name: hpa-demo
spec:
  scaleTargetRef:
    apiVersion: apps/v1
    kind: Deployment
    name: k8s-demo
  minReplicas: 2
  maxReplicas: 5
  metrics:
  - type: Resource
    resource:
      name: cpu
```

```
      target:
        type: Utilization
        averageUtilization: 50
```

Apply `hpa.yaml` with below command

```
$ kubectl apply -f manifests/hpa.yaml
```

6. Load Testing Script

📜 `load-test/hey-test.sh`

```
#!/bin/bash
kubectl run hey --image=rakyll/hey --restart=Never -- \
  -z 30s -c 2 http://k8s-demo-svc
```

Make executable and execute:

```
$ chmod +x load-test/hey-test.sh && ./load-test/hey-test.sh
```

7. Validate

```
$ kubectl get pods
$ kubectl describe hpa hpa-demo
$ kubectl top pods
```

- Open the LoadBalancer IP and check response
- Watch pods scale with load

8. Outcome and Understanding

- Core Kubernetes resources
- Load-balanced app deployment
- ConfigMap injection
- Auto-healing & HPA
- Real observability via `kubectl top`, `logs`, and probes

Key Takeaways

- Kubernetes is the de facto orchestration platform for containerized workloads, offering automation, self-healing, scalability, and abstraction from infrastructure.
- Unlike Docker alone, Kubernetes enables production-grade features like rolling updates, secrets management, and autoscaling natively.
- Hands-on knowledge of `kubectl` and YAML manifests is essential to operate Kubernetes effectively.
- Managed services (EKS, AKS, GKE) reduce operational complexity but still require Kubernetes expertise for application deployment and monitoring.
- Networking in Kubernetes is service-discovery driven — mastering DNS, Ingress controllers, and CNI plugins is crucial.
- Centralized observability using Prometheus, Loki, and Grafana provides deep insights and alerting capabilities.
- Real-world debugging starts with `kubectl describe`, not just logs — lifecycle events reveal more than container output.
- Use patterns like GitOps, sidecars, and operators to build maintainable and scalable K8s applications.
- Kubernetes is evolving toward zero-trust architectures, AI/ML workloads, and platform engineering via Internal Developer Platforms (IDPs).
- This chapter provides a full-stack foundation from basic deployments to advanced autoscaling, secrets, monitoring, and GitOps workflows.

Chapter 20: Docker Configuration Files and System Directories

Section 1: Core Docker Daemon & Runtime Configuration Files

This section focuses on the **core Docker daemon and runtime configuration files**, presented in full-text book style, with explanations, real-world use cases, and actual configuration examples.

The Docker daemon (dockerd) is the engine that powers container lifecycles, networking, volumes, and image management. Its behavior is governed by several key configuration files and directories that define how it starts, what defaults it enforces, where data is stored, and how it interacts with other services.

Understanding these core files is essential for configuring Docker to behave in a secure, stable, and production-ready manner.

1.1 `/etc/docker/daemon.json` — The Primary Docker Daemon Configuration File

The `/etc/docker/daemon.json` file is the **central place** to configure Docker's runtime behavior using a **declarative JSON format**. This file is read by `dockerd` on startup and overrides command-line flags passed to the systemd service.

This file controls:

- Default network bridges
- Log drivers and rotation
- Registry mirrors
- User namespace remapping
- Experimental features
- Resource limits

Purpose:

To set system-wide defaults for the Docker engine in a structured, reproducible format.

When to Use:

- Whenever you need to customize logging, networking, or security settings
- When you need persistent Docker configuration across reboots

Benefits:

- Enables clear, version-controlled Docker configuration
- Makes Docker startup behavior auditable and repeatable
- Eliminates the need to alter systemd unit files for most settings

Example: Log rotation, bridge subnet, and user namespace isolation

```
{
  "log-driver": "json-file",
  "log-opts": {
    "max-size": "10m",
    "max-file": "5"
  },
  "bip": "172.25.0.1/16",
  "userns-remap": "default",
  "live-restore": true
}
```

- `log-driver:` Sets the logging mechanism (`json-file` is default)
- `max-size / max-file:` Rotates logs after 10MB, keeps 5 files
- `bip:` Sets the IP for Docker's default bridge
- `userns-remap:` Maps containers to non-root users on the host
- `live-restore:` Prevents running containers from being stopped on daemon restart

1.2 `/var/lib/docker/` — Docker's Runtime Data Store

This is the **main working directory** for the Docker daemon. It contains all persistent data including:

- Images and layers
- Containers
- Volumes
- Network metadata
- Logs
- Overlay filesystem diffs

Purpose:

To persist Docker's runtime state between reboots and across workloads.

When to Use:

- For disaster recovery backups
- For direct inspection of container file systems
- For cleaning up orphaned layers and volumes

Benefits:

- Serves as the single source of truth for Docker's data
- Enables data migration and layered inspection

⚠ Never manually modify files in this directory. Use Docker CLI or API for safe interaction.

🗁 Example Directory Structure:

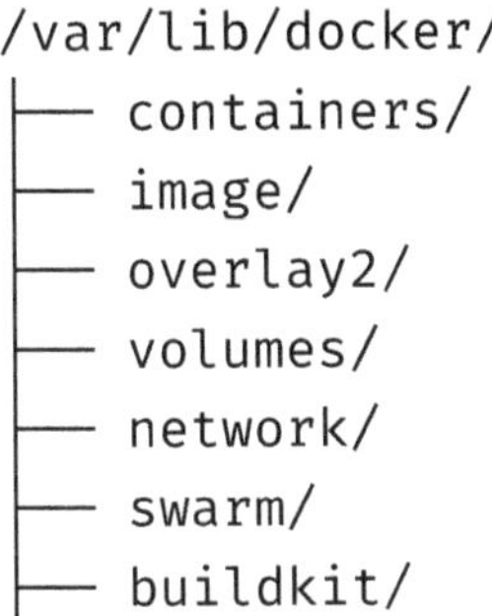

```
/var/lib/docker/
├── containers/
├── image/
├── overlay2/
├── volumes/
├── network/
├── swarm/
├── buildkit/
```

Each subdirectory holds specific runtime data:

- `containers/`: Metadata and logs for each container
- `overlay2/`: Image and container layer diffs
- `volumes/`: Named volume data
- `network/`: Persistent network configuration (including `local-kv.db`)
- `buildkit/`: BuildKit cache and metadata

1.3 `/var/run/docker.sock` — Docker's Communication Socket

This is a **UNIX domain socket** used by the Docker CLI and other clients to communicate with the Docker daemon. When you type `docker ps`, it sends a request to this socket.

Purpose:

To allow local processes to talk to the Docker daemon securely and efficiently.

When to Use:

- Always required by the Docker CLI (`docker, docker-compose`)
- Used by automation tools like Jenkins, GitLab Runners, Portainer, and Watchtower

Benefits:

- Faster than TCP communication
- Secure by default (permission-controlled)
- Required for most Docker-based workflows

⚠ **Security Warning:** Mounting this socket inside a container gives full root access to the host. Only do this in trusted scenarios (e.g., CI/CD agents with strict RBAC).

Example: Accessing Docker API via curl

```
$ curl --unix-socket /var/run/docker.sock http://localhost/containers/json
```

This mimics `docker ps` using the API directly.

1.4 `/var/lib/docker/overlay2/` — Container and Image Layer Storage

If you're using Docker's default storage driver (OverlayFS), this directory contains all of the layered filesystems for images and running containers.

Purpose:

To store union mount layer diffs and merged filesystems.

When to Use:

- Troubleshooting disk usage (`docker system df`)
- Forensic inspection of file changes across image layers

Benefits:

- Efficient CoW (Copy-on-Write) storage
- Reduces duplication across containers
- Speeds up container startup

Example: A single container's merged directory
`/var/lib/docker/overlay2/<id>/merged/`

This path represents the active, combined view of the container's filesystem.

1.5 `/var/lib/docker/containers/<container-id>/config.v2.json`

This file contains detailed metadata about a specific container: its command, entrypoint, environment variables, labels, volume mounts, networking config, and more.

Purpose:

To store container configuration state used for recreation and inspection.

When to Use:

- Troubleshooting container startup behavior
- Extracting environment or mount details from a stopped container

Benefits:

- Provides a low-level snapshot of the container's runtime configuration

Example (partial JSON snippet):

```
{
  "Config": {
    "Env": [
```

```
      "APP_ENV=production",
      "PORT=3000"
    ],
    "Cmd": ["/start.sh"],
    "Image": "myapp:latest"
  },
  "MountPoints": {
    "/data": {
      "Source": "/var/lib/docker/volumes/data_volume/_data"
    }
  }
}
```

You can use this to reconstruct or analyze how a container was launched.

Summary: Core Docker Configuration Files

File/Directory	Purpose	Example Use
`/etc/docker/daemon.json`	Configures daemon behavior	Set logging, networking, remapping
`/var/lib/docker/`	Docker's runtime state	Backup, inspect, recover
`/var/run/docker.sock`	UNIX API socket	CLI and automation integration
`/var/lib/docker/overlay2/`	Image and container layers	CoW storage and diff viewing
`/var/lib/docker/containers/<id>/config.v2.json`	Container metadata	Inspect mounts, env, commands

Section 2: Systemd, Proxy, and Environment Configuration Files

This section focuses on how **systemd**, **override files**, and **proxy configurations** influence Docker's behavior at system startup — including service customization, environment isolation, and network proxy setup. **Docker's system service, environment, and proxy integration files** that determine how Docker launches, communicates externally, and responds to changes at the OS level.

Beyond its core runtime files, the operating system's service manager governs Docker's startup behavior — typically `systemd`. This means Docker is treated like any other critical system service, complete with units, environment variables, socket dependencies, and even proxy routing logic.

In enterprise deployments and developer systems alike, these files enable Docker to launch with custom behaviors, securely route through proxies, and adapt to networking environments. Misconfigurations here often lead to startup failures, proxy-related image pull errors, or restricted service discovery.

2.1 `/lib/systemd/system/docker.service` — The Docker Systemd Service Unit

This is the **default system service definition** for Docker on Linux systems that use `systemd`. It defines how the Docker daemon is launched, which binaries are used, and what runtime options are included.

Purpose:

To control the startup and management of Docker as a system-level service.

When to Use:

- For debugging Docker startup failures
- To view default startup flags and environment integration

Benefits:

- Centralized service control with support for start, stop, reload, and restart
- Integration with logging (`journald`), proxy configuration, and user permission models

⚠ **Best Practice:** Do **not** edit this file directly. Instead, override it using a drop-in file (see next section).

Example (default service definition snippet):

```
[Unit]
Description=Docker Application Container Engine
After=network-online.target firewalld.service
```

```
Requires=docker.socket

[Service]
ExecStart=/usr/bin/dockerd
ExecReload=/bin/kill -s HUP $MAINPID
Restart=on-failure

[Install]
WantedBy=multi-user.target
```

To view it:

```
$ systemctl cat docker.service
```

2.2 `/etc/systemd/system/docker.service.d/override.conf` — Safe Docker Startup Customization

This is the **preferred and safest method** to change Docker's startup behavior. This file overrides parts of the main `docker.service` unit using systemd's drop-in mechanism.

It allows you to:

- Set proxy variables
- Change the Docker daemon binary path
- Add startup flags (e.g., custom `--bip`, `--insecure-registry`, etc.)

Purpose:

To safely override Docker's systemd service without modifying system files.

When to Use:

- To persist startup options across Docker upgrades
- To avoid manual editing of `docker.service`

Benefits:

- Clean, declarative customizations
- Does not get overwritten during upgrades
- Fully compatible with systemd tooling

Example: Enabling custom network bridge and user remap

```
[Service]
ExecStart=
```

```
ExecStart=/usr/bin/dockerd --bip=172.30.0.1/16 --userns-remap=default
```

After editing or creating this file, reload systemd and restart Docker:

```
$ sudo systemctl daemon-reexec
$ sudo systemctl restart docker
```

2.3 `/etc/systemd/system/docker.service.d/http-proxy.conf` — Proxy Settings for Docker

In many corporate environments, outbound internet access (including Docker image pulls) is restricted through an HTTP/HTTPS proxy. Docker must be explicitly told to use those proxies when connecting to the internet.

This file contains environment variables injected into Docker's systemd service to route requests properly.

Purpose:

To allow Docker to connect to the internet behind a corporate proxy firewall.

When to Use:

- When `docker pull` fails or times out due to lack of external access
- In tightly controlled enterprise or government environments

Benefits:

- Enables image pulls and registry access behind a proxy
- Respects `NO_PROXY` exceptions for internal resources

Example: Using a proxy for Docker daemon

```
[Service]
Environment="HTTP_PROXY=http://proxy.company.com:8080/"
Environment="HTTPS_PROXY=http://proxy.company.com:8080/"
Environment="NO_PROXY=localhost,127.0.0.1,docker-registry.internal"
```

Save the file at:

```
/etc/systemd/system/docker.service.d/http-proxy.conf
```

Then reload Docker:

```
$ sudo systemctl daemon-reexec
$ sudo systemctl restart docker
```

2.4 `/etc/default/docker` — Legacy Docker Environment File (Debian)

This file was used in older Docker installations (pre-systemd) to define environment variables or `DOCKER_OPTS` for startup customization.

Purpose:

To pass daemon flags and proxy variables to `dockerd`.

When to Use:

- On legacy Ubuntu or Debian systems without `systemd`
- When using older Docker Engine releases

Benefits:

- Easy override without touching systemd
- Still honored on some distros via `ExecStartPre` shell wrappers

Example:

```
DOCKER_OPTS="--dns 8.8.8.8 --log-level=warn"
```

2.5 `/etc/sysconfig/docker` — RHEL/CentOS Equivalent

Used on RHEL-based systems, this file mirrors the functionality of `/etc/default/docker`.

Purpose:

To initialize Docker environment variables and flags at startup.

When to Use:

- On CentOS, Fedora, or Red Hat systems
- For proxy configuration, DNS, or insecure registry setup

Benefits:

- Works with `sysconfig` tools and conventions
- Still supported by many systems images

Example:

```
OPTIONS="--insecure-registry=myregistry.internal:5000"
```

Summary: Systemd and Proxy Config Files

File/Path	Purpose	Use Case
`/lib/systemd/system/docker.service`	Default Docker service unit	View how Docker starts
`/etc/systemd/system/docker.service.d/override.conf`	Safe override of startup flags	Add custom options, bridge IP, remap

File/Path	Purpose	Use Case
`/etc/systemd/system/docker.service.d/http-proxy.conf`	Proxy config for Docker daemon	Corporate firewall support
`/etc/default/docker`	Legacy Debian Docker config	Older distros without systemd
`/etc/sysconfig/docker`	Legacy Red Hat Docker config	RHEL/CentOS service integration

Section 3: Security, Trust, and Rootless Docker Configuration Files

This section we will dig into how Docker enforces user namespaces, TLS communication, image signing, and syscall hardening. Focusing on Docker's **security, content trust, and rootless execution configuration files** – critical for enterprises that prioritize **isolation, image verification, and secure daemon access**.

Security is no longer optional – it's a requirement in every Docker deployment, especially in regulated industries or shared environments. Docker supports multiple security layers through user namespaces, system call restrictions, TLS-based API access, and image signing using Docker Content Trust.

This section explains how each security-related configuration file works, where to find it, and how to configure it with real examples to enforce a **zero-trust container posture**.

3.1 `/etc/docker/cert.pem, /etc/docker/key.pem, /etc/docker/ca.pem` – TLS Certificates for Secure Docker API Access

By default, the Docker daemon listens on a UNIX socket, but in distributed systems, it often needs to expose a TCP port (e.g., port 2376). When this happens, Docker **must be protected with TLS encryption** and **client-side certificate validation**.

These three files enable secure access:

- `cert.pem`: Public certificate for the Docker server
- `key.pem`: Private key for the Docker server
- `ca.pem`: Certificate Authority used to sign client certs

Purpose:

To enforce TLS-based encrypted and authenticated communication between the Docker daemon and its clients.

When to Use:

- In remote Docker environments
- When multiple nodes need to interact securely
- In CI/CD pipelines where Docker is controlled externally

Benefits:

- Protects against man-in-the-middle attacks
- Prevents unauthorized API access

- Enables secure Docker client-server architecture

Example Configuration in `/etc/docker/daemon.json`:

```
{
  "hosts": ["tcp://0.0.0.0:2376"],
  "tls": true,
  "tlsverify": true,
  "tlscacert": "/etc/docker/ca.pem",
  "tlscert": "/etc/docker/cert.pem",
  "tlskey": "/etc/docker/key.pem"
}
```

3.2 `etc/docker/certs.d/<registry>/ca.crt` — Trusted Certificate for Custom Registries

When Docker connects to a **private registry** secured with a **self-signed or internal CA certificate**, it needs to be explicitly told to trust that certificate. This is done by placing the trusted `ca.crt` file under a path that matches the registry hostname.

Purpose:

To allow Docker to pull images securely from private registries with non-public certificates.

When to Use:

- When your registry uses a self-signed certificate or internal PKI
- When `docker pull` fails with TLS-related errors

Benefits:

- Secure access to internal registries
- Prevents insecure-registry warnings
- Enables encrypted image delivery in air-gapped networks

Example Path:

```
/etc/docker/certs.d/myregistry.local:5000/ca.crt
```

The directory must exactly match the hostname and port of the registry.

3.3 `/etc/docker/key.json` — Docker Content Trust Private Key

This file stores the **private key used to sign Docker images** when Docker Content Trust (DCT) is enabled. It allows you to publish images with verifiable integrity using Notary.

Purpose:

To sign and verify Docker images using DCT and Notary.

When to Use:

- In secure CI/CD pipelines
- When promoting images across environments (e.g., dev → staging → prod)
- To verify publisher authenticity

Benefits:

- Prevents tampered images from being pulled or run
- Protects the software supply chain
- Enables signed-only policies in production

Enabling Content Trust:

```
$ export DOCKER_CONTENT_TRUST=1
$ docker push myregistry.local/myapp:latest
```

Docker will sign the image using the key stored in `key.json`.

3.4 `/etc/docker/policy.json` — Signature Verification Policy for Registries

This JSON file is used in **enterprise security models** to define signature requirements per registry or image. It allows fine-grained control over whether Docker will pull or run unsigned images.

Purpose:

To enforce trusted image policies based on image source or namespace.

When to Use:

- In regulated environments (finance, healthcare, critical infrastructure)
- To enforce "signed only" or "deny unsigned" policies

Benefits:

- Blocks unsigned or tampered images
- Allows different rules for public vs private registries
- Fully automated with DCT or Notary

Example of `policy.json`:

```
{
  "default": [
    { "type": "reject" }
  ],
  "transports": {
    "docker": {
      "myregistry.local/myapp": [
```

```
        { "type": "signedBy", "keyType": "GPGKeys", "keyPath":
"/etc/docker/gpg.key" }
      ]
    }
  }
}
```

In this config file (policy.json):

- All unsigned images are rejected by default
- The `myregistry.local/myapp` image must be signed by a trusted GPG key

3.5 `/etc/subuid` and `/etc/subgid` — Rootless Docker UID/GID Mapping

Rootless Docker allows users to run Docker **without root privileges** by using **user namespaces**. To support this, the system must reserve sub-UID and sub-GID ranges for each user.

These ranges are defined in the following two files:

- `/etc/subuid` → Sub-user ID range
- /etc/subgid → Sub-group ID range

Purpose:

To isolate users in a rootless Docker environment using user namespaces.

When to Use:

- On multi-user systems where privilege separation is critical
- In sandboxed or academic environments where users cannot have root access

Benefits:

- Least-privilege container runtime
- Better security with no daemon-level root
- Compliance with zero-trust architectures

Example `/etc/subuid` and `/etc/subgid`:

```
john:100000:65536
alice:165536:65536
```

This grants user `john` access to UID range `100000–165535`, and `alice` to `165536–231071`.

Rootless Docker will use these ranges to remap container root to non-root host users.

3.6 `/etc/docker/seccomp.json` — Custom Seccomp Security Profile

Seccomp (Secure Computing Mode) is a Linux kernel feature that restricts **which system calls (syscalls)** containers are allowed to make. Docker ships with a default profile, but you can supply a custom `seccomp.json` for finer control.

Purpose:

To limit container system call access and reduce the attack surface.

When to Use:

- In hardened environments
- When deploying sensitive workloads
- During container security audits

Benefits:

- Prevents use of dangerous syscalls (`ptrace, mount, keyctl`, etc.)
- Enforces least-privilege principles
- Mitigates kernel-level exploits

Example `seccomp.json` (partial):

```
{
  "defaultAction": "SCMP_ACT_ERRNO",
  "syscalls": [
    {
      "names": ["clone", "fork"],
      "action": "SCMP_ACT_ALLOW"
    },
    {
      "names": ["keyctl", "ptrace"],
      "action": "SCMP_ACT_ERRNO"
    }
  ]
}
```

In this profile:

- Most syscalls are blocked by default (`SCMP_ACT_ERRNO`)
- `clone` and `fork` are allowed
- Dangerous syscalls like `keyctl` and `ptrace` are explicitly blocked

You can specify this file using:

```
$ docker run --security-opt seccomp=/etc/docker/seccomp.json ...
```

Summary: Security, Trust, and Rootless Configuration Files

File	Purpose	When to Use
`/etc/docker/cert.pem, key.pem, ca.pem`	TLS encryption for Docker daemon	In remote or multi-node setups
`/etc/docker/certs.d/<registry>/ca.crt`	Trust self-signed internal registries	Air-gapped or private networks
`/etc/docker/key.json`	Image signing with Docker Content Trust	Secure CI/CD, supply chain integrity
`/etc/docker/policy.json`	Registry-level trust enforcement	Enforce signed-only policies
`/etc/subuid, /etc/subgid`	Rootless Docker UID/GID mapping	Least-privilege multi-user systems
`/etc/docker/seccomp.json`	Custom syscall filtering	Hardened security environments

By understanding these security files and properly configuring them, you can create a containerized environment that not only meets enterprise security requirements but actively prevents many common attack vectors.

Section 4: Logging, Monitoring, and Networking Configuration Files

This section will deal with how Docker logs, routes traffic and manages persistent container connectivity. Focuses on **logging, monitoring, and network configuration files** – essential for **visibility**, **troubleshooting**, and **operational control** in modern containerized environments.

Effective observability in a Dockerized environment begins with proper **logging**, **networking**, and **metric collection**. Without it, troubleshooting becomes guesswork, performance issues are hard to trace, and container-to-container communication can suffer from misconfiguration or silent failure.

4.1 /var/lib/docker/containers/<container-id>/<container-id>-json.log — Default Container Log Files

By default, Docker uses the `json-file` log driver to capture standard output (`stdout`) and standard error (`stderr`) streams from running containers. These logs are stored as newline-delimited JSON in the container's internal directory.

Purpose:

To store container logs in a human-readable format.

When to Use:

- For quick debugging without external logging tools
- When exploring how your application is behaving inside a container

Benefits:

- Simple log access via docker logs
- Easily tailable and parseable
- Rotatable using `daemon.json` config

Example Configuration in `/etc/docker/daemon.json`:

```
{
  "log-driver": "json-file",
  "log-opts": {
    "max-size": "20m",
    "max-file": "3"
  }
}
```

This will:

- Rotate logs after 20MB
- Keep the 3 most recent log files
- Prevent disk bloat due to runaway logs

Access the log directly:

```
$ cat /var/lib/docker/containers/<container-id>/<container-id>-json.log
```

Or via CLI:

```
$ docker logs <container-id>
```

4.2 `/var/lib/docker/network/files/local-kv.db` — Docker's Network Metadata Database

Docker stores its network configuration and container endpoints in an embedded **BoltDB** file. This file contains mappings for bridge, overlay, and custom user-defined networks.

Purpose:

To track active Docker networks, IP allocations, and container endpoint assignments.

When to Use:

- During network debugging (e.g., IP conflicts, unreachable containers)
- When analyzing how networks persist across restarts

Benefits:

- Atomic, lightweight internal DB
- Used by Docker CLI for `network inspect`
- Persists across daemon restarts

This file should **not be modified directly**. Always use docker network commands.

4.3 `/etc/systemd/system/docker.service.d/logging.conf` — Redirecting Logs to Journald

In many systemd-based distributions (e.g., Ubuntu, CentOS, Fedora), Docker integrates with **journald**, the system log manager. You can configure Docker to use journald instead of `json-file` by modifying the startup flags.

Purpose:

To redirect container logs to the system journal for centralized log management.

When to Use:

- When using log aggregators like Fluent Bit, Loki, or Graylog

- When systemd-based tools are used for log rotation and monitoring

Benefits:

- Leverages system-level logging
- Reduces container-specific file I/O
- Compatible with enterprise log forwarders

Example Override File:

```
/etc/systemd/system/docker.service.d/logging.conf
[Service]
ExecStart=
ExecStart=/usr/bin/dockerd --log-driver=journald
```

Remember to run:

```
$ sudo systemctl daemon-reexec
$ sudo systemctl restart docker
```

Logs can then be viewed using:

```
$ journalctl -u docker.service -f
```

4.4 `/etc/docker/daemon.json` — Global Logging Configuration (Extended)

Besides log rotation, `daemon.json` allows setting global default log drivers for **all containers**.

Purpose:

To configure consistent logging across all workloads.

When to Use:

- To enforce log format standards (e.g., JSON, journald, syslog, etc.)
- To minimize manual per-container logging settings

Benefits:

- Centralized configuration
- Easier to integrate with external log pipelines

Supported Log Drivers:

- `json-file` (default)
- `journald`
- `syslog`
- `fluentd`
- `awslogs`
- `gelf`
- `splunk`

Example:

```
{
  "log-driver": "journald"
}
```

4.5 `/etc/docker/daemon.json` — Default Address Pools for Docker Networks

Docker's user-defined networks use internal address pools by default. If you have multiple Docker hosts or networks, **IP conflicts** can occur. You can predefine pools to avoid this.

Purpose:

To avoid overlapping subnets across Docker networks.

When to Use:

- When multiple hosts run Docker (e.g., CI/CD workers, clusters)
- When integrating Docker with cloud VPCs or existing on-prem networks

Benefits:

- Prevents "host unreachable" errors
- Predictable subnet allocation

Example:

```
{
  "default-address-pools": [
    {
      "base": "172.90.0.0/16",
      "size": 24
    }
  ]
}
```

This will auto-assign `172.90.0.0/24, 172.90.1.0/24`, etc., to new custom Docker networks.

4.6 `/etc/docker/daemon.json` — Configuring DNS Servers

Docker containers, by default, inherit DNS configuration from the host. However, you can explicitly set DNS servers for all containers.

Purpose:

To override default DNS servers for outbound container resolution.

When to Use:

- When the host uses internal DNS that should not be inherited

- When containers require direct access to public DNS (e.g., 8.8.8.8)

Benefits:

- Improves name resolution speed
- Avoids DNS leaks and internal resolution issues

Example:

```
{
  "dns": ["8.8.8.8", "1.1.1.1"]
}
```

4.7 `/etc/docker/daemon.json` — Experimental Metrics & Monitoring Options

Docker offers an `experimental` flag to expose features like Prometheus-style metrics or build telemetry. This can be enabled in the daemon config file.

Purpose:

To enable monitoring endpoints for Prometheus or Docker CLI plugins.

When to Use:

- For real-time metrics collection
- When using monitoring stacks (e.g., cAdvisor, Grafana, Prometheus)

Benefits:

- Easy instrumentation of container resource usage
- Compatible with enterprise monitoring tools

Example:

```
{
  "experimental": true,
  "metrics-addr": "0.0.0.0:9323"
}
```

Access metrics via:

```
$ curl http://localhost:9323/metrics
```

Summary: Logging, Monitoring, and Network Configuration Files

File or Path	Purpose	When to Use
`/var/lib/docker/containers/<id>-json.log`	Stores logs from running containers	Local debugging
`/var/lib/docker/network/files/local-kv.db`	Stores container and network metadata	IP diagnostics

File or Path	Purpose	When to Use
`/etc/docker/daemon.json`	Global logging, DNS, metrics, IP pool settings	Consistent config
`/etc/systemd/system/docker.service.d/logging.conf`	Switch to journald or other log drivers	Centralized log pipeline
`metrics-addr` in `daemon.json`	Enable Prometheus metrics endpoint	Monitoring integration

Well configured logging and networking setup transforms Docker from a developer tool into a robust operations platform. With the right log driver, container logs become actionable insights. With predefined address pools and DNS entries, network resolution becomes predictable and conflict-free.

Section 5: BuildKit, Registry, and Image Management Configuration Files

This section covers **Docker's BuildKit engine**, private registry configuration, and trusted image management – the backbone of efficient, secure, and scalable container workflows in enterprise environments where we'll dive into image signing, private registry hosting, and advanced `buildx` capabilities

Containerization doesn't stop at runtime – it starts much earlier in the build and image distribution lifecycle. Docker provides a rich set of configuration files to control how images are built (via BuildKit), stored (via local or cloud registries), and verified (via trust policies). These configurations are essential for CI/CD pipelines, software supply chain integrity, and developer productivity.

5.1 `/etc/docker/buildkit/buildkitd.toml` – BuildKit Daemon Configuration

BuildKit is Docker's high-performance image building backend. It introduces features such as:

- Parallel build steps
- Remote cache support
- Inline secrets
- Automatic pruning

This configuration file allows you to **tune BuildKit's behavior**, such as workers, caching, registries, and concurrency.

Purpose:

To optimize and configure Docker image building workflows at scale.

When to Use:

- When building large or complex multi-stage images
- In CI/CD environments needing caching or secret handling

Benefits:

- Up to 60–70% faster builds
- Remote cache support reduces rebuilds
- Secure secret injection during build-time

Example `buildkitd.toml`:

```
[worker.oci]
  enabled = true
  gc = true
```

```
[registry."docker.io"]
  mirrors = ["https://mirror.gcr.io"]

[worker.oci.gcpolicy]
  keepBytes = 512000000
  keepDuration = "24h"
```

- Enables garbage collection (`gc`)
- Defines registry mirror for faster pulls
- Controls how long intermediate layers are cached

To run standalone BuildKit:

```
$ buildkitd --config /etc/docker/buildkit/buildkitd.toml
```

To enable BuildKit globally:

```
$ export DOCKER_BUILDKIT=1
```

5.2 `/etc/docker/daemon.json` — Enabling BuildKit in the Daemon

Instead of exporting environment variables, you can also **enable BuildKit globally** through the Docker daemon configuration.

Example:

```
{
  "features": {
    "buildkit": true
  }
}
```

Place this in `/etc/docker/daemon.json` and restart Docker

```
$ sudo systemctl restart docker
```

This enables `docker build` to automatically use BuildKit under the hood.

5.3 `/etc/docker/registry/config.yml` — Private Registry Configuration

This YAML file defines the configuration of a **Docker registry server**, typically run using the `registry:2` container image. It controls:

- Storage location (e.g., filesystem, S3)
- Auth backends
- TLS settings

- Logging and deletion policies

Purpose:

To run and manage an internal, self-hosted Docker registry.

When to Use:

- For air-gapped or secure development pipelines
- When Docker Hub rate limits are a bottleneck
- To enforce internal governance over image versions

Benefits:

- Full control over your image lifecycle
- Faster, private, and unrestricted pulls/pushes
- Enables content scanning and approval flows

Example `config.yml`**:**

```
version: 0.1
storage:
  filesystem:
    rootdirectory: /var/lib/registry
http:
  addr: :5000
  headers:
    X-Content-Type-Options: [nosniff]
```

Optional TLS section

```
http:
  tls:
    certificate: /certs/domain.crt
    key: /certs/domain.key
```

Mount and run

```
$ docker run -d -p 5000:5000 \
  -v /registry:/var/lib/registry \
  -v /certs:/certs \
  -e REGISTRY_HTTP_TLS_CERTIFICATE=/certs/domain.crt \
  -e REGISTRY_HTTP_TLS_KEY=/certs/domain.key \
  registry:2
```

5.4 `/etc/docker/registry/certs/` — TLS Certificates for the Registry

To run a secure registry over HTTPS (recommended in all production environments), Docker requires the certificate files to be available and trusted.

Purpose:

To enable TLS encryption for the Docker registry container.

When to Use:

- When serving images securely over the network
- To comply with internal security policies

Benefits:

- Prevents MITM attacks
- Ensures private image integrity

File Layout:

```
/etc/docker/registry/certs/
├── domain.crt
└── domain.key
```

Use these with environment variables

```
-e REGISTRY_HTTP_TLS_CERTIFICATE=/certs/domain.crt
-e REGISTRY_HTTP_TLS_KEY=/certs/domain.key
```

5.5 `/etc/docker/certs.d/<registry-host>/ca.crt` — Trust Configuration for Private Registries

If you're running a registry secured with a **self-signed certificate**, Docker clients need to explicitly trust it. This is done by placing the CA certificate in a directory matching the registry's host and port.

Purpose:

To avoid TLS errors when pulling from self-signed registries.

When to Use:

- In dev, staging, or secure prod networks using internal PKI

Benefits:

- Secures communication while avoiding warning bypasses
- Enables encrypted image pulls even on local networks

Example:

For a registry hosted at `myregistry.local:5000`, place:

```
/etc/docker/certs.d/myregistry.local:5000/ca.crt
```

This ensures Docker trusts the TLS certificate automatically.

5.6 `~/.docker/config.json` — Per-User Registry Authentication

This file stores **authentication credentials and configuration settings** for Docker registries.

Purpose:

To log in to Docker Hub, private registries, or cloud-based registries.

When to Use:

- For users or CI agents that need to push or pull from private registries

Benefits:

- Securely caches login tokens or credentials
- Supports different credential helpers (e.g., keychain, gcloud, AWS)

Example:

```
{
  "auths": {
    "https://index.docker.io/v1/": {
      "auth": "dXNlcjpwYXNzd29yZA=="
    }
  },
  "credsStore": "desktop"
}
```

Use `docker login` to populate this file securely.

5.7 `~/.docker/cli-plugins/` — User-Level CLI Plugin Directory

Docker CLI plugins (e.g., `docker buildx, docker scan`) are executable binaries placed in this directory. These plugins **extend Docker's CLI functionality** without modifying the core binary.

Purpose:

To provide modular CLI extensions for advanced functionality.

When to Use:

- When installing `buildx, scan`, or vendor plugins
- When customizing developer environments

Benefits:

- Lightweight extensions
- User-specific installations
- Easy to manage or disable

Plugins must follow the naming format `docker-<plugin>` and be executable.

Summary of Section 5: BuildKit and Registry Configuration Files

File or Directory	Purpose	When to Use
/etc/docker/buildkit/buildkitd.toml	Configure parallel builds, cache, workers	Advanced CI/CD builds
/etc/docker/daemon.json	Enable BuildKit, registry mirrors	Faster and reproducible builds
/etc/docker/registry/config.yml	Define self-hosted Docker registry settings	Air-gapped or enterprise environments
/etc/docker/registry/certs/	TLS certs for secure registries	HTTPS-based image distribution
/etc/docker/certs.d/<host>/ca.crt	Trust internal/self-signed registries	Private, encrypted image pulls
~/.docker/config.json	Store registry login and CLI settings	User or automation environments
~/.docker/cli-plugins/	Install optional CLI tools like buildx	Modular and pluggable CLI

With these files properly configured, Docker builds become faster, more secure, and tailored to your organization's needs. Whether you're caching layers in CI pipelines or setting up a trusted internal image supply chain, this configuration layer lays the foundation for reliable and scalable container lifecycle management.

Section 6: Plugins, Extension Points, and Runtime Integrations

This section covers Docker's **modular plugin system**, its **runtime extension points**, and its compatibility with other container runtimes such as **Podman**, **Buildah**, and **containerd** – all critical when deploying Docker in **complex, hybrid, or enterprise-scale infrastructures**.

Modern Docker is modular by design. Instead of being a monolithic binary, Docker is now a **collection of services, CLI extensions, and plugin interfaces**. Whether it's adding new build capabilities with buildx, integrating security scanning, or using volume drivers backed by NFS, Docker provides robust plugin support.

Additionally, Docker's ecosystem overlaps with other OCI-compliant tools like **Podman, CRI-O**, and **containerd**, especially in cloud-native environments or Fedora/RHEL-based systems.

This section explores how to configure these extensions, their file paths, and their purpose in multi-tool deployments.

6.1 `/etc/docker/plugins/*.json` — Volume and Network Plugin Definitions

Docker supports **volume**, **network**, and **logging** plugins through a JSON-based socket registration system. These `.json` files register the plugin's address and type with the Docker daemon.

Purpose:

To connect Docker with external storage drivers, network controllers, or log collectors.

When to Use:

- When using plugins like `rexray, flocker, fluentd`, or custom storage backends
- In enterprise storage systems with Docker integration

Benefits:

- Supports third-party and custom plugins
- Dynamically extensible Docker runtime

Example: `/etc/docker/plugins/fluentd.json`

```
{
  "Name": "fluentd",
  "Addr": "unix:///run/docker/plugins/fluentd.sock",
  "TLSConfig": {
    "InsecureSkipVerify": false
```

```
  }
}
```

Plugins must expose a UNIX socket and use the Docker plugin API.

6.2 `~/.docker/cli-plugins/` — User-Space CLI Plugin Directory

This is where **Docker CLI plugins** are installed for specific users. It includes tools like:

- `docker buildx`
- `docker scan`
- `docker compose` (v2+)
- Custom plugins by third parties or internal teams

Purpose:

To extend the CLI with modular subcommands without modifying Docker's core.

When to Use:

- To install optional functionality (e.g., security scans, enhanced builds)
- In multi-user systems with different CLI needs

Benefits:

- Modular and lightweight
- Easy to update or remove
- Does not affect system-wide Docker installation

Example Directory:

```
~/.docker/cli-plugins/
└── docker-buildx
└── docker-compose
```

Ensure binaries are executable (`chmod +x`) and match naming convention `docker-<plugin>`.

6.3 `/usr/libexec/docker/cli-plugins/` — System-Wide Plugin Directory (RPM/DEB Packages)

Linux distributions that install Docker via official RPM or DEB packages use this path to place CLI plugin binaries for **system-wide use**.

Purpose:

To expose Docker CLI plugins across all users on the system.

When to Use:

- When Docker is installed via package managers (e.g., `apt, yum`)

- When managing plugins centrally via system tools

Benefits:

- Automatically updated with system packages
- Maintains proper file system hygiene and security

6.4 `/etc/docker/cli-plugins/docker-*` — Manual Plugin Overrides

Docker also scans this directory for **plugin binaries placed explicitly** using naming conventions. This is useful for **manual deployments**, **offline installations**, or **testing newer plugin versions**.

Purpose:

To provide additional plugin discovery paths beyond the default user/system directories.

When to Use:

- For custom plugin development
- In disconnected or isolated environments

Benefits:

- Full control over plugin versioning
- Easy to deploy to controlled environments

6.5 `/etc/containers/containers.conf` — Runtime Behavior (Podman Shared)

This file is part of the **Podman/CRI-O ecosystem**, but it's worth mentioning because it is often used **alongside Docker** on hybrid systems, especially on Fedora, CentOS, and RHEL distributions.

It defines:

- Runtime engine configuration
- Default mount flags
- Networking behavior

Purpose:

To standardize container runtime behavior between Docker, Podman, and Buildah.

When to Use:

- On systems where both Docker and Podman are used
- When conforming to Open Containers Initiative (OCI) runtime standards

Benefits:

- Unified config across multiple tools
- Compatible with Kubernetes CRI runtime integrations

Example Snippet:

```
[containers]
log_driver = "journald"
pids_limit = 4096
```

6.6 `/etc/containers/storage.conf` — Unified Image and Volume Storage Configuration

This file controls how images and volumes are stored on disk for **Podman, Buildah**, and sometimes **Docker** when using `fuse-overlayfs`.

Purpose:

To define image layer storage drivers and volume options.

When to Use:

- In rootless or multi-runtime setups
- For tuning volume persistence or encryption

Benefits:

- Coexistence with Podman/Buildah
- Consistent image management backend

6.7 `/etc/containers/registries.conf` — Default Image Sources

This file defines **default registries, search order, and allowed mirrors**. It's especially useful when Docker shares a backend with Podman or when you're **blocking access to Docker Hub**.

Purpose:

To whitelist or block specific registries, define mirrors.

When to Use:

- On shared CI/CD runners
- When hardening image sources in production

Benefits:

- Improved control over image origin
- Compliance with internal governance or security policies

Example:

```
unqualified-search-registries = ["myregistry.local", "docker.io"]

[[registry]]
location = "docker.io"
insecure = false
```

Summary: Plugins, Extensions, and Integrations

File/Directory	Purpose	When to Use
`/etc/docker/plugins/*.json`	Register external volume/network plugins	Extend Docker runtime
`~/.docker/cli-plugins/`	User CLI plugin binaries	Add `buildx`, `scan`, `compose`
`/usr/libexec/docker/cli-plugins/`	System plugin path (DEB/RPM)	System-wide CLI extensions
`/etc/docker/cli-plugins/docker-*`	Manual plugin install path	Custom or air-gapped plugins
`/etc/containers/containers.conf`	Shared container runtime config	Hybrid Docker/Podman setups
`/etc/containers/storage.conf`	Storage behavior for image layers	Volume persistence, encryption
`/etc/containers/registries.conf`	Define default trusted registries	Enforce registry policies

By understanding Docker's plugin and extension architecture, you can significantly enhance your environment with custom builds, security scans, metrics collection, and alternate runtimes like Podman — all without bloating the core Docker binary.

Section 7: Rare, Legacy, and Experimental Docker Configuration Files

This section is designed to help advanced readers, platform engineers, and container architects understand lesser-known but occasionally essential configuration files that appear in edge cases, legacy systems, or future Docker proposals, where I have listed special-case files including those used in Swarm mode, rootless isolation, proposed extensions, and ephemeral runtime state.

While most Docker users interact with common configuration paths, enterprise and hybrid environments may require awareness of **uncommon, deprecated, or experimental files**. These files can surface in the following contexts:

- Advanced Swarm setups
- Disconnected environments
- Rootless daemon configurations
- Experimental builds and metrics
- Custom plugin and registry behaviors

In this section, you will walk through these files — explaining what they are, when they appear, and whether to maintain, migrate, or ignore them in your deployment strategy.

7.1 `/etc/docker/daemon-cert.pem` and `/etc/docker/daemon-key.pem` — Legacy TLS Config

Before `daemon.json` supported full TLS configuration, Docker setups often referenced these filenames directly for enabling secured API access.

Purpose:

Legacy TLS certificate and key file names for dockerd.

When to Use:

- Only in systems still using direct command-line flags like `--tls-cert` and `--tls-key`

Benefits:

- Allows backward compatibility for older orchestration scripts or legacy infra

Example (legacy flag usage):

```
$ dockerd --tlsverify \
        --tlscacert=/etc/docker/ca.pem \
        --tlscert=/etc/docker/daemon-cert.pem \
        --tlskey=/etc/docker/daemon-key.pem \
        -H=0.0.0.0:2376
```

7.2 `/etc/docker/daemon-proxy.conf` — Custom Proxy Sourcing File

In environments using automation or GitOps tooling, proxy settings are sometimes **externalized** to a separate file and sourced from `override.conf` via `EnvironmentFile`.

Purpose:

To manage proxy environment variables independently of the systemd service definition.

When to Use:

- In templated infrastructure (Terraform, Ansible, Packer, etc.)
- When Docker service proxies change between environments

Benefits:

- Central proxy config shared across multiple services
- Easy to edit without restarting systemd units

Example `daemon-proxy.conf`:

```
HTTP_PROXY=http://proxy.mycorp.com:8080/
HTTPS_PROXY=http://proxy.mycorp.com:8080/
NO_PROXY=localhost,127.0.0.1,.mycorp.local
```

7.3 `/etc/docker-init.sh` or `/etc/docker/env.sh` — Custom Bootstrapping Scripts

While not native Docker files, many advanced system administrators use wrapper scripts to preconfigure Docker settings before startup. These might:

- Populate environment variables
- Pre-pull images
- Auto-start containers
- Set kernel sysctl parameters

Purpose:

Custom automation for Docker node provisioning or hardening.

When to Use:

- When using bare-metal installs
- In cloud-init or preflight script scenarios

Benefits:

- Repeatable and scriptable configuration
- Ideal for infrastructure-as-code workflows

7.4 `/etc/docker/builder.toml` — Proposed BuildKit Config File (Experimental)

While not yet fully standardized, this file is proposed for future versions of docker buildx to support inline configuration (similar to `buildkitd.toml` but scoped for client-side control).

Purpose:

To define buildx cache strategies, export formats, and mounts.

When to Use:

- In bleeding-edge environments using `buildx bake` or build matrix orchestration

Benefits:

- Centralized build customization per project
- Replaces scattered CLI flags in CI pipelines

Currently experimental — format and support subject to change.

7.5 `/etc/docker-compose/override.yml` and `.env` — Compose Overrides

These files allow `docker-compose` projects to define **environment-specific configuration** without modifying the main `docker-compose.yml`.

Purpose:

To extend or override Docker Compose services for development, staging, or production.

When to Use:

- In multi-environment deployment pipelines
- To inject secrets, mount paths, or resource limits dynamically

Benefits:

- Clean separation between base and override settings
- Useful in GitOps/CI environments

Example `override.yml`:

```
services:
  web:
    environment:
      - DEBUG=true
    volumes:
      - ./dev-data:/data
```

7.6 `/etc/docker/daemon-health.json` — Monitoring Metadata Injection (Custom)

Some monitoring agents and exporters use this optional file to **tag** the Docker daemon with metadata like:

- Environment name
- Region or cluster ID
- Alert thresholds

Purpose:

To inject observable metadata about the Docker host for logging or metrics aggregation.

When to Use:

- With Prometheus exporters
- In environments using custom health dashboards or Grafana annotations

Benefits:

- Makes environments self-describing
- Allows deeper correlation between container health and infrastructure telemetry

Not natively used by Docker — but commonly used by monitoring systems and third-party exporters.

7.7 `/var/lib/docker/swarm/` — Docker Swarm Internal State

When you initialize Docker Swarm mode, this directory stores:

- Swarm CA certificates
- Node join tokens
- Raft consensus state
- Encrypted secrets

Purpose:

To manage Swarm clustering metadata.

When to Use:

- In Swarm clusters with multiple nodes
- When using `docker secret`, `docker service`, or `docker stack`

Benefits:

- Secure and self-contained cluster config
- Maintains consensus logs and CA chain

Avoid modifying this directory manually. Use Swarm CLI tools instead.

7.8 `/etc/docker/pidfile` — Daemon Process ID File (Ephemeral)

This file stores the **PID (Process ID)** of the running `dockerd` instance. It is auto-generated and deleted on daemon restart.

Purpose:

To track the active Docker daemon process.

When to Use:

- In custom restart scripts
- For debugging stuck or orphaned processes

Benefits:

- Enables monitoring agents to track daemon uptime
- Assists in graceful termination via scripting

Summary: Rare, Legacy, and Experimental Files

File or Path	Purpose	Use Case
`/etc/docker/daemon-cert.pem` & `daemon-key.pem`	Legacy TLS setup	Backward compatibility
`/etc/docker/daemon-proxy.conf`	Proxy config sourced externally	GitOps, templated infra
`/etc/docker-init.sh`	Custom pre-start scripts	Cloud-init, Packer, CI
`/etc/docker/builder.toml`	BuildKit (proposed) config	Experimental builds
`/etc/docker-compose/override.yml`	Compose service overrides	Dev vs prod deployments
`/etc/docker/daemon-health.json`	Custom monitoring injection	Prometheus, Grafana
`/var/lib/docker/swarm/`	Swarm CA, consensus data	Multi-node Swarm clusters
`/etc/docker/pidfile`	Daemon PID tracking	Health checks and scripts

You will rarely encounter all of these files in a single deployment — but knowing they exist helps you **troubleshoot uncommon bugs, integrate monitoring systems**, or **maintain legacy Docker stacks**. They form the hidden architecture that surfaces when you move beyond default Docker setups and into **real-world hybrid systems**.

Appendix A: Docker, Docker CLI & Compose Reference Cheat Sheet

A.1 Docker CLI Reference

Image Management

Command	Description
docker build -t myapp .	Build Docker image with the tag myapp from current directory
docker images	List all local Docker images
docker rmi myapp	Remove image named myapp
docker pull ubuntu:22.04	Pull Ubuntu 22.04 image from Docker Hub
docker tag myapp myrepo/myapp:v1	Tag an image for pushing to a registry
docker login	Authenticate with a Docker registry (e.g., DockerHub, private registry)
docker push myrepo/myapp:v1	Push a tagged image to a remote registry
docker save -o myapp.tar myapp	Save image myapp as a .tar archive for offline transport
docker load -i myapp.tar	Load image from a .tar archive back into Docker

Container Lifecycle

Command	Description
docker run -it ubuntu bash	Run interactive Ubuntu container
docker run -d -p 8080:80 --name web nginx	Run container with port mapping
docker ps -a	List all containers
docker stop <id>	Stop container
docker rm <id>	Remove container

Logs & Inspect

Command	Description
docker logs <container>	View container logs
docker logs -f <container>	Follow logs in real-time
docker inspect <container>	Show container metadata (JSON)

Exec & Shell Access

Command	Description
docker exec -it <container> bash	Open bash shell
docker exec -it <container> sh	Open sh shell

Cleanup

Command	Description
docker system prune -af	Remove all unused data
docker volume prune	Prune unused volumes
docker image prune -a	Prune unused images

A.2 Dockerfile Instruction Reference

Essentials

Instruction	Description
FROM	Base image
WORKDIR	Working directory
COPY	Copy files
RUN	Execute command
CMD	Default startup command
EXPOSE	Declare port usage
USER	Drop root
HEALTHCHECK	Add health monitoring

Best Practices

```
FROM node:18-alpine
WORKDIR /app
COPY package*.json ./
RUN npm install
COPY . .
EXPOSE 3000
CMD ["node", "index.js"]
```

Security Hardening

```
RUN adduser -D appuser
USER appuser
```

Cleanup Optimization

```
RUN apt clean && rm -rf /var/lib/apt/lists/*
```

A.3 Docker Volume Reference

Command	Purpose
`docker volume create myvol`	Create volume
`docker volume inspect myvol`	View volume metadata
`docker volume rm myvol`	Remove volume
`tar czvf vol.tar.gz`	Backup volume
`tar xzvf vol.tar.gz`	Restore volume

1. **Default Location**: `/var/lib/docker/volumes/`
2. **Types**: Named, bind mount, tmpfs, plugins (e.g., NFS, EBS)

A.4 Docker Network Reference

Command	Purpose
`docker network create mynet`	Create network
`docker network ls`	List networks
`docker network inspect mynet`	Inspect details
`docker network rm mynet`	Remove network
`docker exec -it <c> ping <c2>`	Test container connectivity

Network Types:

1. `bridge:` Default, isolated per container
2. `host:` Shares host network (Linux only)
3. `overlay:` Multi-host (Swarm mode)
4. `macvlan:` Gets its own IP on LAN

A.5 Compose YAML Reference

Basic Compose Sample

```
services:
  web:
    build: .
    ports:
      - "8080:80"
    volumes:
      - ./src:/app
    environment:
      - NODE_ENV=production
    depends_on:
      - db
    restart: unless-stopped
    healthcheck:
      test: curl --fail http://localhost || exit 1
      interval: 30s
      timeout: 10s
      retries: 3

  db:
    image: postgres
    volumes:
      - pgdata:/var/lib/postgresql/data

volumes:
  pgdata:
```

[✓] Tip: *This Compose file starts two services:* web *and* db. *The* web *service depends on the database, uses health checks, and automatically restarts unless manually stopped.*

Optional: Compose Profiles (Advanced)

What are Profiles?

Profiles let you conditionally run services only when explicitly enabled — useful for debugging, monitoring, or staging environments.

```
services:
```

```
  debug:
    image: busybox
    command: sleep 3600
    profiles:
      - debug
```

How to use:

```
$ docker compose --profile debug up
```

🔒 **Pro Tip:** *Services under a profile won't run unless the profile is explicitly enabled. This avoids cluttering your main runtime environment with optional or development-only services.*

A.6 Docker Compose CLI Reference

Command	Purpose
`docker compose up -d`	Start services
`docker compose down`	Stop + cleanup
`docker compose build --no-cache`	Rebuild images
`docker compose logs -f`	Live logs
`docker compose exec web bash`	Shell access
`docker compose config`	Validate config
`docker compose ps`	Show running services

A.7 Docker Security Configuration Summary

Security Goal	Context/Tool	Example Command or Configuration
Drop privileges	Dockerfile	`RUN adduser -D appuserUSER appuser`
Drop Linux capabilities	Bash (CLI flags)	`--cap-drop=ALL --cap-add=NET_BIND_SERVICE`
Scan images	Bash	`trivy image myappdocker scan myapp`
Secrets usage	Bash (Swarm)	`docker secret create db_pass ./db.txt`
User Namespaces	daemon.json (JSON)	`{ "userns-remap": "default" }`
Enable Content Trust	Bash (Env Variable)	`export DOCKER_CONTENT_TRUST=1`

A.8 System File Locations (Linux)

File	Purpose
`/etc/docker/daemon.json`	Daemon config
`/var/lib/docker/volumes/`	Volume data
`/var/lib/docker/`	Images and containers
`/var/run/docker.sock`	Docker socket
`journalctl -u docker`	System logs

A.9 Docker Environment Variables

Variable	Purpose
`DOCKER_BUILDKIT=1`	Enable BuildKit
`DOCKER_HOST=tcp://...`	Remote Docker
`DOCKER_CONTENT_TRUST=1`	Image verification
`COMPOSE_PROFILES=dev`	Enable specific profiles
`COMPOSE_PROJECT_NAME=app`	Custom project name

A.10 Build Optimization Patterns

Layer caching	Dockerfile	`COPY requirements.txt .` `RUN pip install -r requirements.txt`

Multi-stage builds	Dockerfile	`FROM node:18 AS build`
		`RUN npm run build`
		
		`FROM nginx`
		`COPY --from=build /app/dist`
		`/usr/share/nginx/html`

A.11 CI/CD Snippet (GitHub Actions)

```
- name: Build and Test
  run: |
    docker compose up -d
    docker compose exec -T app pytest
    docker compose down
```

Appendix B: Real World Project & Hands-On Lab

Lab: Docker Monitoring + Logging with Prometheus, Grafana, Loki

Difficulty Level: Advanced

Now we will create a **complete real-world hands-on lab**, covering:

- **Metrics stack**: Prometheus + Grafana + cAdvisor + Node Exporter
- **Logging stack**: Loki + Grafana or optional ELK Stack
- **Centralized Volume Logging**
- **Docker Compose project layout**
- **Run instructions**
- **Validation steps**

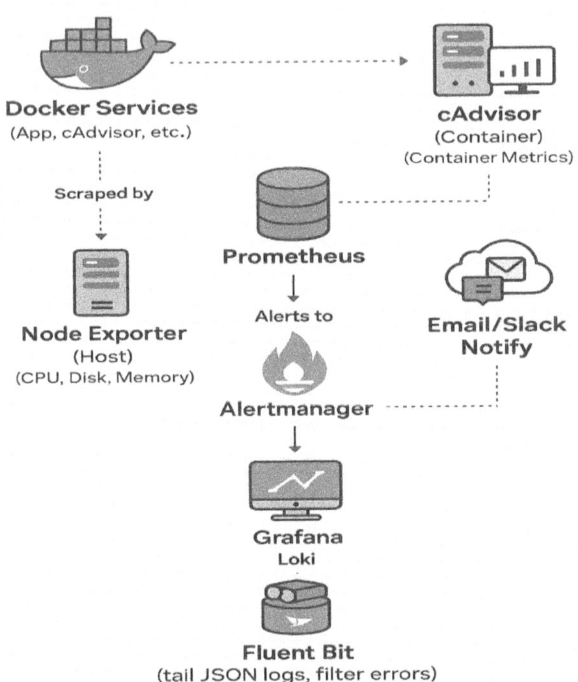

Prerequisites for Docker Monitoring + Logging Lab

1. Host Machine Requirements

The host machine must meet the following minimum and recommended specifications:

Resource	Minimum	Recommended
Operating System	Ubuntu 20.04 / 22.04, Debian 11/12, CentOS 8+, Rocky Linux	Ubuntu 22.04 LTS
CPU	2 cores	4 cores or higher
RAM	4 GB	8 GB or more
Disk Space	20 GB free	40 GB free or higher
Network Access	Internet connection	Internet + LAN access

Tip: *For better results when handling large logs or dashboards, aim for 8GB RAM and SSD storage.*

2. Installed Software

Ensure the following core software is installed and operational:

Software	Minimum Version	Installation Command
Docker Engine	20.10+	`` `curl -fsSL https://get.docker.com ``
Docker Compose Plugin	v2.5+ (plugin)	`sudo apt install docker-compose-plugin`
Bash Shell	Standard (latest)	Pre-installed on Linux
Git (optional)	2.30+	`sudo apt install git`

3. Email & Slack Setup (Optional for Alerting)

Service	Details
SMTP Server	Required for sending email alerts (Gmail, Office365, SES, etc.)
Slack Webhook	Required for Slack-based alert notifications

Slack incoming webhook URL format:

```
https://hooks.slack.com/services/Txxxx/Bxxxx/xxxxxx
```

4. User Permissions and Access

- Ensure the current user has been added to the Docker group:

```
$ sudo usermod -aG docker $USER
$ newgrp docker
```

- Sudo access is required to:
    - Install packages
    - Manage system services (systemd setup for Watchdog)

5. Essential System Packages

Install the following essential packages:

```
$ sudo apt update
$ sudo apt install wget curl msmtp jq
```

Tool	Purpose
`wget`	For healthchecks within containers
`msmtp`	For sending email notifications
`jq`	(optional) for parsing JSON outputs

6. Firewall and Port Access

Ensure the following ports are open on your host firewall:

Service	Port	Purpose
Grafana	3000	Grafana Web Dashboard
Prometheus	9090	Prometheus Web UI
Alertmanager	9093	Alertmanager Web UI
Node Exporter	9100	Node Metrics Export
cAdvisor	8081	Container Metrics Export
Loki	3100	Logs ingestion endpoint
Fluent Bit	2020	Fluent Bit Metrics (Optional)
Sample App	8080	Node.js Healthcheck App

UFW commands to allow the ports:

```
$ sudo ufw allow 3000/tcp
$ sudo ufw allow 9090/tcp
$ sudo ufw allow 9093/tcp
```

```
$ sudo ufw allow 9100/tcp
$ sudo ufw allow 8081/tcp
$ sudo ufw allow 3100/tcp
$ sudo ufw allow 8080/tcp
```

Also ensure inbound/outbound connectivity for pulling Docker images.

7. Docker Compose and Stack Services Summary

The following services will be deployed:

Service	Version	Purpose
sample-app	18.20.8	Node.js test app with health endpoint
prometheus	3.3.0	Scrape metrics from exporters
node-exporter	1.9.1	Host metrics (CPU, RAM, Disk)
cadvisor	0.47.0	Docker container metrics
grafana	11.6.1	Visualization and dashboards
loki	3.5.0	Log aggregation for containers
fluent-bit	4.0.1	Log shipper from Docker containers
alertmanager	0.28.1	Manage and route Prometheus alerts

All services are defined within `docker-compose.yml` properly.

8. Checklist Before Running Lab

Checklist Item	Status
Docker installed and running	☑
Docker Compose installed	☑
Project folders and files organized	☑
Ports opened (or firewall disabled)	☑
SMTP and Slack webhook configured (optional)	☑
Fluent Bit and Loki configured	☑
Systemd service created for Watchdog	☑
Internet access verified for pulling images	☑

Folder Structure

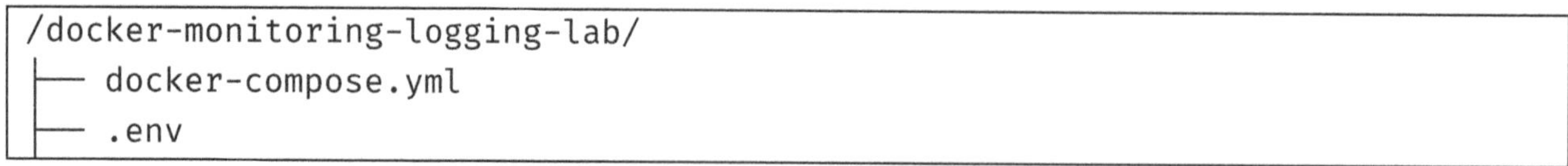

```
/docker-monitoring-logging-lab/
├── docker-compose.yml
├── .env
```

```
├── prometheus/
│   ├── prometheus.yml
│   ├── alerts.yml
├── grafana/
│   ├── datasources/
│   │   ├── prometheus.yaml
│   │   └── loki.yaml
│   ├── dashboards/
│   │   ├── docker-host-overview.json
│   │   ├── container-metrics.json
│   │   └── loki-logs.json
├── loki/
│   ├── loki-config.yml
├── fluent-bit/ (optional)
│   ├── fluent-bit.conf
│   ├── parsers.conf
├── sample-app/
│   ├── Dockerfile
│   ├── app.js
│   └── package.json
├── scripts/
│   ├── docker_health_watchdog.sh
├── alertmanager/
│   ├── alertmanager.yml
```

`docker-compose.yml` (Master File)

```
services:
  app:
    build: ./sample-app
    ports:
      - "8080:8080"
    logging:
      driver: "json-file"
    restart: always
    healthcheck:
      test: ["CMD", "wget", "--no-verbose", "--tries=1", "--spider",
"http://localhost:8080/health"]
      interval: 30s
      timeout: 10s
      retries: 3
```

```
    networks:
      - monitor-net

  prometheus:
    image: prom/prometheus:latest
    ports:
      - "9090:9090"
    volumes:
      - prometheus_data:/prometheus
      - ./prometheus/prometheus.yml:/etc/prometheus/prometheus.yml
      - ./prometheus/alerts.yml:/etc/prometheus/alerts.yml
    restart: always
    healthcheck:
      test: ["CMD", "wget", "--no-verbose", "--tries=1", "--spider",
"http://localhost:9090/-/healthy"]
      interval: 30s
      timeout: 10s
      retries: 3
    networks:
      - monitor-net

  node-exporter:
    image: prom/node-exporter
    ports:
      - "9100:9100"
    restart: always
    healthcheck:
      test: ["CMD", "wget", "--no-verbose", "--tries=1", "--spider",
"http://localhost:9100/metrics"]
      interval: 30s
      timeout: 10s
      retries: 3
    networks:
      - monitor-net

  cadvisor:
    image: gcr.io/cadvisor/cadvisor:v0.47.0
    ports:
      - "8081:8080"
    volumes:
```

```
      - /:/rootfs:ro
      - /var/run:/var/run:ro
      - /sys:/sys:ro
      - /var/lib/docker/:/var/lib/docker:ro
    restart: always
    healthcheck:
      test: ["CMD", "wget", "--no-verbose", "--tries=1", "--spider",
"http://localhost:8080/healthz"]
      interval: 30s
      timeout: 10s
      retries: 3
    networks:
      - monitor-net

  loki:
    image: grafana/loki:latest
    ports:
      - "3100:3100"
    volumes:
      - loki_data:/loki
      - ./loki/loki-config.yml:/etc/loki/local-config.yaml
    command: -config.file=/etc/loki/local-config.yaml
    restart: always
    healthcheck:
      test: ["CMD", "wget", "--no-verbose", "--tries=1", "--spider",
"http://localhost:3100/ready"]
      interval: 30s
      timeout: 10s
      retries: 3
    networks:
      - monitor-net

  grafana:
    image: grafana/grafana:latest
    ports:
      - "3000:3000"
    volumes:
      - grafana_data:/var/lib/grafana
      - ./grafana/datasources:/etc/grafana/provisioning/datasources
      - ./grafana/dashboards:/etc/grafana/provisioning/dashboards
```

```
    environment:
      - GF_SECURITY_ADMIN_USER=${GRAFANA_USER}
      - GF_SECURITY_ADMIN_PASSWORD=${GRAFANA_PASSWORD}
    depends_on:
      - prometheus
      - loki
    restart: always
    healthcheck:
      test: ["CMD", "wget", "--no-verbose", "--tries=1", "--spider",
"http://localhost:3000/login"]
      interval: 30s
      timeout: 10s
      retries: 3
    networks:
      - monitor-net

  alertmanager:
    image: prom/alertmanager
    ports:
      - "9093:9093"
    volumes:
      - ./alertmanager/alertmanager.yml:/etc/alertmanager/alertmanager.yml
    command:
      - '--config.file=/etc/alertmanager/alertmanager.yml'
    restart: always
    networks:
      - monitor-net

  fluent-bit:
    image: fluent/fluent-bit:latest
    ports:
      - "2020:2020"
    volumes:
      - /var/lib/docker/containers:/var/lib/docker/containers:ro
      - ./fluent-bit/fluent-bit.conf:/fluent-bit/etc/fluent-bit.conf
      - ./fluent-bit/parsers.conf:/fluent-bit/etc/parsers.conf
      - fluentbit_taildb:/fluent-bit/tail-db
    networks:
      - monitor-net
    depends_on:
```

```
      - loki
    restart: always
    healthcheck:
      test: ["CMD", "wget", "--no-verbose", "--tries=1", "--spider",
"http://localhost:2020/api/v1/health"]
      interval: 30s
      timeout: 10s
      retries: 3

volumes:
  prometheus_data:
  grafana_data:
  loki_data:
  fluentbit_taildb:

networks:
  monitor-net:
    driver: bridge
```

`.env` File (for cleaner security)

```
GRAFANA_USER=admin
GRAFANA_PASSWORD=admin
```

`prometheus/prometheus.yml` (Metrics Scraping Config)

```
global:
  scrape_interval: 15s
  scrape_timeout: 10s
  evaluation_interval: 15s
  external_labels:
    environment: 'production'

rule_files:
  - "alerts.yml"

scrape_configs:
  - job_name: 'prometheus'
    static_configs:
      - targets: ['localhost:9090']
```

```
  - job_name: 'cadvisor'
    static_configs:
      - targets: ['cadvisor:8080']

  - job_name: 'node-exporter'
    static_configs:
      - targets: ['node-exporter:9100']

alerting:
  alertmanagers:
  - static_configs:
    - targets:
      - 'alertmanager:9093'
```

/prometheus/alerts.yml

```
groups:

- name: node-health
  rules:
    - alert: HostDown
      expr: up{job="node-exporter"} == 0
      for: 2m
      labels:
        severity: critical
      annotations:
        summary: "Node Exporter Down (instance {{ $labels.instance }})"
        description: "The node {{ $labels.instance }} is down or unreachable
for more than 2 minutes."

- name: container-health
  rules:
    - alert: DockerContainerDown
      expr: up{job="cadvisor"} == 0
      for: 2m
      labels:
        severity: critical
      annotations:
        summary: "cAdvisor Down (instance {{ $labels.instance }})"
        description: "cAdvisor at {{ $labels.instance }} is down for more
than 2 minutes."
```

```
- name: resource-usage
  rules:
    - alert: HighCPUUsage
      expr: rate(container_cpu_usage_seconds_total{image!=""}[5m]) > 0.8
      for: 3m
      labels:
        severity: warning
      annotations:
        summary: "High CPU Usage (container {{
$labels.container_label_com_docker_swarm_service_name }})"
        description: "Container {{
$labels.container_label_com_docker_swarm_service_name }} CPU usage > 80% for
3 minutes."

    - alert: HighMemoryUsage
      expr: (container_memory_usage_bytes{image!=""} /
container_spec_memory_limit_bytes{image!=""}) > 0.8
      for: 3m
      labels:
        severity: warning
      annotations:
        summary: "High Memory Usage (container {{
$labels.container_label_com_docker_swarm_service_name }})"
        description: "Container {{
$labels.container_label_com_docker_swarm_service_name }} memory usage > 80%
for 3 minutes."

- name: disk-space
  rules:
    - alert: LowDiskSpace
      expr: (node_filesystem_avail_bytes{mountpoint="/"} /
node_filesystem_size_bytes{mountpoint="/"}) < 0.15
      for: 5m
      labels:
        severity: critical
      annotations:
        summary: "Low Disk Space on Host ({{ $labels.instance }})"
        description: "Disk space is less than 15% available on {{
$labels.instance }} root partition."
```

```
- name: application-heartbeat
  rules:
    - alert: AppHeartbeatMissing
      expr: absent(up{job="app"})
      for: 2m
      labels:
        severity: critical
      annotations:
        summary: "App Heartbeat Missing (Job 'app')"
        description: "No heartbeat detected for 'app' service. It may be
down."

- name: log-spike
  rules:
    - alert: ApplicationErrorSpike
      expr: sum(rate({severity="detected"}[1m])) > 10
      for: 2m
      labels:
        severity: critical
      annotations:
        summary: "Application Error Log Spike Detected"
        description: "More than 10 ERROR or WARN logs per minute detected
across containers."
```

grafana/datasources/prometheus.yaml

```
apiVersion: 1

datasources:
  - name: Prometheus
    type: prometheus
    access: proxy
    url: http://prometheus:9090
    isDefault: true
```

grafana/datasources/loki.yaml

```
apiVersion: 1

datasources:
  - name: Loki
```

```
    type: loki
    access: proxy
    url: http://loki:3100
```

Prebuilt Dashboards

Docker Host Overview Dashboard (Node Exporter + Host Metrics)

Monitors:

- CPU Usage %
- RAM Usage
- Disk Usage
- Network In/Out
- System Uptime
- Load Average

Dashboard

grafana/dashboards/docker-host-overview.json

```
{
  "annotations": {
    "list": [
      {
        "builtIn": 1,
        "datasource": "-- Grafana --",
        "enable": true,
        "hide": true,
        "iconColor": "rgba(0, 211, 255, 1)",
        "name": "Annotations & Alerts",
        "type": "dashboard"
      }
    ]
  },
  "title": "Docker Host Overview",
  "panels": [
    {
      "type": "graph",
      "title": "CPU Usage %",
      "datasource": "Prometheus",
```

```
      "targets": [
        {
          "expr": "100 - (avg
by(instance)(irate(node_cpu_seconds_total{mode=\"idle\"}[5m])) * 100)",
          "legendFormat": "{{instance}}",
          "refId": "A"
        }
      ]
    },
    {
      "type": "graph",
      "title": "Memory Usage",
      "datasource": "Prometheus",
      "targets": [
        {
          "expr": "(node_memory_MemTotal_bytes -
node_memory_MemAvailable_bytes) / node_memory_MemTotal_bytes * 100",
          "legendFormat": "{{instance}}",
          "refId": "A"
        }
      ]
    }
  ],
  "schemaVersion": 30,
  "version": 1,
  "editable": true
}
```

Show containing graphs for CPU, Memory, Disk, Network

Container Metrics Dashboard (cAdvisor Focused)

Monitors:

- Per-Container CPU %
- Per-Container Memory %
- Container Restarts
- Uptime
- Network Bytes In/Out
- Disk I/O per container

Dashboard

grafana/dashboards/container-metrics.json

```
{
  "title": "Container Metrics Overview",
  "panels": [
    {
      "type": "graph",
      "title": "Container CPU Usage %",
      "targets": [
        {
          "expr":
"rate(container_cpu_usage_seconds_total{name!=\"\",container!=\"POD\"}[5m])
* 100",
          "legendFormat":
"{{container_label_com_docker_swarm_service_name}}",
          "refId": "A"
        }
      ]
    },
    {
      "type": "graph",
      "title": "Container Memory Usage %",
      "targets": [
        {
          "expr":
"container_memory_usage_bytes{name!=\"\",container!=\"POD\"} /
container_spec_memory_limit_bytes{name!=\"\",container!=\"POD\"} * 100",
          "legendFormat":
"{{container_label_com_docker_swarm_service_name}}",
          "refId": "A"
        }
      ]
    }
  ],
  "schemaVersion": 30,
  "version": 1,
  "editable": true
}
```

Shows metrics **per container**, automatically.

Loki Logs Explorer Dashboard

Logs Search:

- Live view of logs from all containers
- Search by container name
- Highlight error keywords (error, warn)
- Timeline log graph

Dashboard

`grafana/dashboards/loki-logs.json`

```
{
  "title": "Loki Logs Explorer",
  "panels": [
    {
      "type": "logs",
      "title": "Container Logs",
      "targets": [
        {
          "expr": "{job=\"varlogs\"}",
          "refId": "A"
        }
      ],
      "datasource": "Loki"
    }
  ],
  "schemaVersion": 30,
  "version": 1,
  "editable": true
}
```

Grafana "Explore" mode for real-time logs is built-in too.

Dashboard Templates Summary

File Name	Dashboard
`docker-host-overview.json`	Host metrics
`container-metrics.json`	Docker container stats
`loki-logs.json`	Real-time container logs

How to Import the Dashboards in Grafana

Option 1: Manual Import

- Login to Grafana
- Left Sidebar → "+" → **Import**
- Upload each JSON file
- Set Data Sources:
  - Prometheus for metrics dashboards
  - Loki for logs dashboard

Option 2: Provision Automatically

In `docker-compose.yml` for Grafana:

```
volumes:
  - ./grafana/dashboards:/etc/grafana/provisioning/dashboards
```

Dashboard provision config inside

`/grafana/provisioning/dashboards/dashboard.yaml`

```
apiVersion: 1
providers:
  - name: 'docker-monitoring'
    orgId: 1
    folder: 'Docker Monitoring'
    type: file
    disableDeletion: false
    updateIntervalSeconds: 10
    options:
      path: /etc/grafana/provisioning/dashboards
```

Grafana will automatically load all dashboards on startup!

`loki/loki-config.yml`

```
auth_enabled: false

server:
  http_listen_port: 3100
  grpc_listen_port: 9095

common:
  path_prefix: /loki
```

```
ingester:
  lifecycler:
    ring:
      kvstore:
        store: inmemory
      replication_factor: 1
  chunk_idle_period: 5m
  chunk_block_size: 262144
  chunk_retain_period: 30s

schema_config:
  configs:
    - from: 2020-10-15
      store: boltdb-shipper
      object_store: filesystem
      schema: v12
      index:
        prefix: index_
        period: 168h
    - from: 2025-05-01
      store: tsdb
      object_store: filesystem
      schema: v13
      index:
        prefix: index_
        period: 24h

storage_config:
  tsdb_shipper:
    active_index_directory: /loki/tsdb-index
    cache_location: /loki/tsdb-cache
  filesystem:
    directory: /loki/chunks
  boltdb_shipper:
    active_index_directory: /loki/index

limits_config:
  reject_old_samples: true
  reject_old_samples_max_age: 168h
  allow_structured_metadata: false
```

```
compactor:
  working_directory: /loki/compactor
  compaction_interval: 10m
  retention_enabled: true
  retention_delete_delay: 2h
  delete_request_store: filesystem
```

Fluent Bit Sidecar (Advanced Optional)

Collect logs from all containers **as a sidecar** instead of JSON driver.

`fluent-bit/fluent-bit.conf`

```
[SERVICE]
    Flush        1
    Daemon       Off
    Log_Level    info
    Parsers_File parsers.conf
    HTTP_Server  On
    HTTP_Listen  0.0.0.0
    HTTP_Port    2020

[INPUT]
    Name          tail
    Path          /var/lib/docker/containers/*/*.log
    Parser        docker
    Tag           containers.*
    DB            /fluent-bit/tail-db/tail-containers.db
    Mem_Buf_Limit 5MB
    Skip_Long_Lines On
    Refresh_Interval 5

# Filter: capture only ERROR and WARN logs
[FILTER]
    Name          grep
    Match         containers.*
    Regex         log    (?i)(error|warn)

# Filter: add severity field
[FILTER]
```

```
    Name          modify
    Match         containers.*
    Add           severity detected

[OUTPUT]
    Name          loki
    Match         containers.*
    Uri           http://loki:3100/loki/api/v1/push
    Labels        job=fluent-bit, container_name=$container_name,
severity=$severity
    Remove_keys   stream,time
    Line_Format   json
```

What this config does:

- Reads every container's `/var/lib/docker/containers/<container-id>/<container-id>-json.log`
- Parses logs cleanly
- Sends logs into **Loki** automatically
- Each log line will have labels: `job, container_name`
- Database state tracking to avoid duplicate reading (`tail-db`)
- Proper GREP filter inserted (only keep ERROR/WARN logs)
- Set Prometheus alert **if too many errors happen** in a short time.

`fluent-bit/parsers.conf` (**Parses Docker's native JSON logs** correctly)

```
[PARSER]
    Name         docker
    Format       json
    Time_Key     time
    Time_Format  %Y-%m-%dT%H:%M:%S.%L
    Time_Keep    On
    Decode_Field_As escaped_utf8 log
```

Fluent Bit container can be added to `docker-compose.yml` to push all logs cleanly into Loki.

Add Fluent Bit to `docker-compose.yml`

Inside `services:`:

```
  fluent-bit:
    image: fluent/fluent-bit:latest
    ports:
      - "2020:2020"   # Optional: to view Fluent Bit metrics
```

```
    volumes:
      - /var/lib/docker/containers:/var/lib/docker/containers:ro
      - ./fluent-bit/fluent-bit.conf:/fluent-bit/etc/fluent-bit.conf
      - ./fluent-bit/parsers.conf:/fluent-bit/etc/parsers.conf
    networks:
      - monitor-net
    depends_on:
      - loki
    restart: unless-stopped
```

Fluent Bit will now join `monitor-net`, pull logs from Docker, and send directly into Loki!

Loki Will ingest the logs and Grafana will show in Dashboard

In Grafana ➔ **Explore** tab:

- Choose **Datasource: Loki**
- Query:

```
{job="fluent-bit"}
{severity="detected"}
{job="fluent-bit"}
```

`sample-app/Dockerfile`

```
FROM node:18-alpine

WORKDIR /usr/src/app

COPY package*.json ./
RUN npm install

COPY . .

EXPOSE 8080

HEALTHCHECK --interval=30s --timeout=10s --start-period=10s --retries=3 \
  CMD wget --no-verbose --tries=1 --spider http://localhost:8080/health ||
exit 1

CMD ["node", "app.js"]
```

sample-app/app.js

```
const express = require('express');
const app = express();
const port = 8080;

app.get('/', (req, res) => {
  res.send('Hello World! Docker Monitoring and Logging Lab');
});

app.get('/health', (req, res) => {
  res.send('OK');
});

app.listen(port, () => {
  console.log(`App listening at http://localhost:${port}`);
});
```

sample-app/package.json

```
{
  "name": "sample-app",
  "version": "1.0.0",
  "description": "A sample Node.js app for Docker Monitoring Lab",
  "main": "app.js",
  "scripts": {
    "start": "node app.js"
  },
  "author": "Sudipta Biswas",
  "license": "ISC",
  "dependencies": {
    "express": "^4.18.2"
  }
}
```

/scripts/docker_health_watchdog.sh

```
#!/bin/bash

# Docker Health Watchdog
# Monitors container health and restarts + notifies

while true
```

```
do
  for container in $(docker ps --format '{{.ID}}')
  do
    health=$(docker inspect --format='{{.State.Health.Status}}' $container 2>/dev/null)
    name=$(docker inspect --format='{{.Name}}' $container | sed 's/\///')

    if [[ "$health" == "unhealthy" ]]; then
      echo "$(date) : Container $name ($container) is unhealthy. Restarting..." >> /var/log/docker_watchdog.log

      docker restart $container

      # Email alert (adjust your msmtp or sendmail config)
      echo -e "Subject: [ALERT] Docker Container $name Restarted\nContainer $name was unhealthy and has been restarted." | msmtp youremail@example.com

    fi
  done
  sleep 60
done
```

Make it executable

```
$ chmod +x scripts/docker_health_watchdog.sh
```

Run manually

```
$ cd scripts
$ ./docker_health_watchdog.sh &
```

Systemd Service for Watchdog Script

Create a systemd service that auto-runs the watchdog at boot.

/etc/systemd/system/docker-watchdog.service

```
[Unit]
Description=Docker Health Watchdog Service
After=docker.service
Requires=docker.service

[Service]
Type=simple
```

```
WorkingDirectory=/path/to/your/docker-monitoring-logging-lab/scripts/
ExecStart=/bin/bash docker_health_watchdog.sh
Restart=always
RestartSec=10

[Install]
WantedBy=multi-user.target
```

Replace `/path/to/your/docker-monitoring-logging-lab/scripts/` with your real folder path.

Commands to Enable Watchdog at Boot

```
$ sudo systemctl daemon-reload
$ sudo systemctl enable docker-watchdog.service
$ sudo systemctl start docker-watchdog.service
$ sudo systemctl status docker-watchdog.service
```

Now **even after server reboot, the watchdog automatically starts.**

Alertmanager Integration (Email + Slack Alerts)

`/alertmanager/alertmanager.yml`

```
global:
  resolve_timeout: 5m
  smtp_smarthost: 'smtp.yourmailserver.com:587'
  smtp_from: 'alertmanager@yourdomain.com'
  smtp_auth_username: 'alertmanager@yourdomain.com'
  smtp_auth_password: 'yourpassword'

route:
  receiver: 'email-notifications'
  group_wait: 30s
  group_interval: 2m
  repeat_interval: 12h

receivers:
  - name: 'email-notifications'
    email_configs:
      - to: 'yourteam@yourdomain.com'
        send_resolved: true
  - name: 'slack-notifications'
    slack_configs:
      - api_url: 'https://hooks.slack.com/services/your/slack/webhook'
```

```
        channel: '#alerts'
        send_resolved: true
        title: '{{ .CommonLabels.alertname }} - {{ .CommonLabels.severity
}}'
        text: >-
          {{ range .Alerts }}
            *Alert:* {{ .Annotations.summary }}
            *Description:* {{ .Annotations.description }}
          {{ end }}
```

Replace:

- `smtp.yourmailserver.com`
- `yourteam@yourdomain.com`
- `your Slack webhook URL`

How to Run the Full Lab

Step 1: Navigate to lab folder

```
$ cd docker-monitoring-logging-lab
```

Step 2: Start services

```
$ docker compose up -d --build
```

Step 3: Access services

Service	**URL**
Grafana Dashboard	`http://localhost:3000` (admin/admin)
Prometheus	`http://localhost:9090`
Node Exporter Metrics	`http://localhost:9100/metrics`
cAdvisor Metrics	`http://localhost:8081/metrics`
Loki API	`http://localhost:3100`
Sample App	`http://localhost:8080`

Step 4: In Grafana

- Login
- Explore
- Add Prometheus Dashboards (Node Exporter Full, Docker Metrics dashboards)
- Explore Loki Logs (container logs)

Real-World Full Project — Production-Ready App with Docker & Docker Compose

Difficulty Level: Advanced

Project Goal

Deploy a **production-grade full-stack application** using Docker and Docker Compose, with:

- ☑ A React frontend
- ☑ A Flask (Python) backend API
- ☑ PostgreSQL database
- ☑ Redis (cache/queue)
- ☑ Celery for background tasks
- ☑ NGINX reverse proxy with HTTPS
- ☑ SSL (Let's Encrypt + Certbot)
- ☑ Prometheus + Grafana for monitoring
- ☑ Loki + Promtail for logs
- ☑ CI/CD integration (GitHub Actions or GitLab)
- ☑ Volume backups and restore hooks
- ☑ Secrets and configuration isolation

Project Structure

```
fullstack-app/
├── docker-compose.yml
├── .env
├── frontend/            # React App (Vite or CRA)
├── backend/             # Flask REST API
├── nginx/
│   └── nginx.conf
├── prometheus/
│   └── prometheus.yml
├── grafana/
├── certs/               # TLS certs (symlink or mounted)
├── logs/                # Centralized logs
└── backup/              # Volume backup script
```

`docker-compose.yml` (Simplified View)

```
services:
  frontend:
    build: ./frontend
    ports:
      - "3000:3000"
    depends_on:
      - backend
    networks:
      - appnet

  backend:
    build: ./backend
    env_file: .env
    depends_on:
      - db
      - redis
    networks:
      - appnet
      - dbnet

  db:
    image: postgres:15
    env_file: .env
    volumes:
```

```
      - pgdata:/var/lib/postgresql/data
    networks:
      - dbnet

  redis:
    image: redis:alpine
    networks:
      - appnet

  celery:
    build: ./backend
    command: celery -A app.celery worker --loglevel=info
    depends_on:
      - backend
      - redis
    networks:
      - appnet

  nginx:
    image: nginx:alpine
    volumes:
      - ./nginx/nginx.conf:/etc/nginx/nginx.conf:ro
      - ./certs:/etc/ssl
    ports:
      - "80:80"
      - "443:443"
    depends_on:
      - frontend
      - backend
    networks:
      - appnet

  prometheus:
    image: prom/prometheus
    volumes:
      - ./prometheus/prometheus.yml:/etc/prometheus/prometheus.yml
    ports:
      - "9090:9090"
    networks:
      - monitor
```

```
  grafana:
    image: grafana/grafana
    ports:
      - "3001:3000"
    networks:
      - monitor

  loki:
    image: grafana/loki
    ports:
      - "3100:3100"
    networks:
      - monitor

  promtail:
    image: grafana/promtail
    volumes:
      - ./logs:/var/log
    networks:
      - monitor

volumes:
  pgdata:

networks:
  appnet:
  dbnet:
  monitor:
```

Build and Run

```
$ docker compose build
$ docker compose up -d
```

Visit:

- React App: http://localhost:3000
- Grafana: http://localhost:3001
- Prometheus: http://localhost:9090

Secrets & Env (.env example)

```
POSTGRES_DB=appdb
POSTGRES_USER=appuser
POSTGRES_PASSWORD=supersecret
REDIS_URL=redis://redis:6379/0
SECRET_KEY=myjwtkey
```

Store this file securely. Never commit it to Git.

SSL with Let's Encrypt

Use Certbot inside or outside the Docker container to auto-generate certs.

```
$ sudo certbot certonly --standalone -d yourdomain.co
```

Mount `/etc/letsencrypt/live/` to `./certs` or use a volume.

Backup & Restore Script (Postgres Example)

```
#!/bin/bash
DATE=$(date +%F_%H-%M)
BACKUP=backup/pgdata_$DATE.tar.gz

docker run --rm \
  -v fullstack-app_pgdata:/data \
  -v $PWD/backup:/backup \
  busybox \
  tar czvf /backup/$(basename $BACKUP) /data
```

Healthchecks

In Compose:

```
healthcheck:
  test: ["CMD", "curl", "-f", "http://localhost:5000/health"]
  interval: 30s
  retries: 5
```

Add to `backend` and `frontend` services.

Monitoring with Prometheus + Grafana

- Add targets in `prometheus.yml`
- Mount `prometheus.yml` in `prometheus` service
- Configure Grafana dashboard to pull from Prometheus
- Add Loki as a data source for logs

GitHub Actions CI/CD (Basic Pipeline)

```
.github/workflows/deploy.yml

name: CI/CD

on:
  push:
    branches: [ main ]

jobs:
  build-and-deploy:
    runs-on: ubuntu-latest
    steps:
      - name: Checkout
        uses: actions/checkout@v3

      - name: Build and Deploy Stack
        run: |
          docker compose down
          docker compose build --pull
          docker compose up -d
```

Rollbacks & Recovery

- Keep `.env` and `docker-compose.yml` versioned in Git
- Maintain volume snapshots
- Use GitHub Actions or GitLab CI for auto rollbacks on failed deploys
- Use health checks to auto-detect bad deployments

Final Checklist for Production

- ☑ Use `.env` and do not commit secrets
- ☑ Use non-root Docker users in your Dockerfiles
- ☑ Add healthchecks to every service
- ☑ Monitor with Prometheus and Grafana
- ☑ Log with Loki/Promtail or ELK
- ☑ Use HTTPS with Certbot or Cloudflare
- ☑ Backup volumes daily
- ☑ Use CI/CD for safe rollouts
- ☑ Split networks: `frontend, backend, db, monitor`
- ☑ Scan images before deploy (`trivy, grype`)
- ☑ Harden Dockerfiles (drop root, slim builds)

Appendix C: Docker Deployment Resource Estimation

This appendix is your practical guide to sizing Docker-based deployments — whether you're running a development stack on a single VM or planning a multi-node production cluster. We'll break it down by:

1. Resource types (CPU, RAM, Disk, Network)
2. Key deployment drivers (App type, Sessions, Users)
3. Estimation formulas
4. Real-world case study examples

C.1 Resource Categories

Resource	Description
CPU	Affects concurrent request handling, latency
RAM	Holds in-memory processes, buffers, app state
Storage	Persists images, volumes, DBs, logs
Network	Determines throughput, egress, ingress, latency

C.2 Key Estimation Drivers

- Number of **concurrent users**
- Number of **active sessions**
- Application **type** (stateless, DB-heavy, caching, compute-intensive)
- Expected **I/O** and network load
- **Container architecture** (monolith vs microservices)

C.3 Estimation Formulas and Assumptions

Resource estimation is critical for designing containerized deployments that are resilient, performant, and cost-efficient. This section provides formulas, variable definitions, and a practical worked example.

Key Parameters and Definitions

Symbol	Description
`U`	Concurrent users expected
`S`	Average active sessions per user
`Rps`	Requests per second
`T`	Average CPU time per request (seconds)
`M`	Memory required per container (in MB)
`N`	Number of containers
`C`	vCPUs required per container
`D`	Disk requirement per container (GB)
`BW`	Bandwidth per request (in MB)
`RF`	Redundancy Factor (e.g., 2 for active-active)
`B`	Burst Buffer (10–30%)
`LR`	Log Retention Period (in days)
`IS`	Image Size (compressed, in GB)
`RPSz`	Avg. Request Payload Size (for ingress, in MB)
`SecO`	Security Overhead as percentage (e.g., 0.05 = 5%)
`GPU`	GPU units required per container (if applicable)
`UtilFactor`	CPU Utilization Factor (default = 0.7)

Estimation Formulas

CPU Estimation

```
CPU Cores Needed = ((U × S × Rps × T) / UtilFactor) × RF × (1 + B)Assume
Core Utilization Factor ≈ 0.7 (to leave headroom)
```

- Use `UtilFactor = 0.7` to leave 30% headroom.
- Add `RF` for high availability.
- Add `B` for burstable traffic.

RAM Estimation

```
RAM Required (in MB) = (N × M × (1 + B + SecO)) + System Overhead
```

- System Overhead (MB) ≈ 1024–2048 MB (OS + Docker + services).
- Add `SecO` for policy-hardened systems (AppArmor, Seccomp, SELinux).

Storage Estimation

```
Storage (in GB) = (N × D) + IS + (Log_GB_per_day × LR × RF) + 30%_BufferUse SSDs for IO-heavy apps. Add 20–30% buffer.
```

- `Log_GB_per_day depends on app verbosity.`
- Add redundancy and retention.
- Add 20–30% buffer for growth and resiliency.
- Use SSDs for databases or real-time write-intensive apps.

Network Estimation

```
Network Throughput (in MBps) = Rps × RPSz × RF x BW
```

- `RPSz` is request payload size in MB.
- Use this to determine required ingress/egress.
- Adjust for shared host environments or Kubernetes limits.

For example, 100 RPS × 0.5 MB/request = 50 Mbps

GPU Estimation

```
Total GPUs = N × GPU
```

- Only needed for workloads using NVIDIA or AMD GPU passthroughs (ML, video, inference).

Worked-Out Example – Internal Web App

Assume you're deploying a containerized dashboard app for internal users:

Parameter	Symbol	Value
Concurrent Users	U	300
Sessions per User	S	1.1
Requests per Second	Rps	6

Parameter	Symbol	Value
Avg. CPU Time per Request	T	0.015 sec
Avg. Memory per Container	M	256 MB
Number of Containers	N	5
vCPUs per Container	C	1
Disk per Container	D	3 GB
Bandwidth per Request	RPSz = BW	0.5 MB
Redundancy Factor	RF	2
Burst Buffer	B	0.2 (20%)
Log Retention Days	LR	7
Logs per Day	–	1 GB
Image Size	IS	1 GB
Security Overhead	SecO	0.05 (5%)
GPU per container	GPU	0 (not used)
System Overhead	–	2 GB
Utilization Factor	UtilFactor	0.7

Calculate Resource Estimates

CPU

Formula:

```
CPU_Total = ((U × S × Rps × T) / UtilFactor) × RF × (1 + B)
```

Calculations:

```
= ((300 × 1.1 × 6 × 0.015) / 0.7) × 2 × 1.2
= (297 × 0.015 = 4.455) / 0.7 = 6.364
6.364 × 2 × 1.2 = 15.2736
Recommended CPU: ~15.3 vCPUs → round to 16 vCPUs
```

RAM

Formula:

```
RAM_Total_MB = (N × M × (1 + B + SecO)) + System_Overhead
```

Calculations:

```
= (5 × 256 × 1.25) + 2048
= 1600 + 2048 = 3648 MB
Recommended RAM: ~3.6–4 GB
```

Storage

Formula:

```
Storage = (N × D) + IS + (Logs/day × LR × RF) + 30% buffer
```

Calculations:

```
= (5 × 3) + 1 + (1 × 7 × 2)
= 15 + 1 + 14 = 30 GB
30 GB × 1.3 = 39 GB
Recommended Storage: ~39–40 GB SSD
```

Network

Formula:

```
Network_MBps = Rps × BW × RF
```

```
= 6 × 0.5 × 2 = 6 MB/sec = 48 Mbps
Recommended Bandwidth: ~50 Mbps
```

Resource Summary Table

Resource	Corrected Estimate
vCPUs	16 cores
RAM	~4 GB
Storage	~40 GB SSD
Network	~50 Mbps
GPU	Not Required

C.4 Case Study 1: Internal Web App

- Users: 200 concurrent
- Sessions/user: 2
- Requests/sec: 5
- Response time: 0.2s
- Memory/container: 512 MB
- Disk/container: 1 GB
- Bandwidth/request: 0.3 MB

Resource Estimation:

```
CPU: (200 * 2 * 5 * 0.2) / 0.7 = ~571.4 CPU units → ~2 vCPUs
RAM: 3 containers × 512MB + 2GB = ~3.5 GB
Disk: 3 × 1GB + 2GB overhead = ~5 GB
Network: 5 RPS × 0.3 MB = 1.5 MB/s = ~12 Mbps
```

Note: 1 vCPU = 1000 millicores = 1000 CPU units

Resource	Estimate
vCPUs	~0.6 vCPU → recommend 2 vCPUs
RAM	~3.5 GB
Disk	~5 GB
Network	~12 Mbps
Suggested VM	2–4 vCPU, 8 GB RAM, 50 GB SSD

C.4 Case Study 2: E-commerce + Analytics Backend

- Users: 1000
- Sessions: 2
- 20 RPS
- CPU per req: 0.3s
- Memory: 1 GB/container
- Disk: 5 GB/container
- Network: 0.5 MB/request
- Services: API, DB, cache, frontend

Services split:

- API: 4 containers
- Frontend: 2 containers
- Redis: 1
- PostgreSQL: 1

Resource Estimation:

```
CPU: (1000 * 2 * 20 * 0.3) / 0.7 = ~17K CPU units = ~18 vCPUs
RAM: (4×1 + 2×0.5 + 1×0.5 + 1×2) + 2GB overhead = ~9 GB
Disk: ~20 GB (app + db + logs + volume)
Network: 20 RPS × 0.5 MB = ~10 MB/s = ~80 Mbps
```

Recommended infra:

- 2 × 8 vCPU, 16 GB RAM nodes (Swarm or K8s)
- SSD-backed storage
- NGINX + Prometheus + backup scripts

Practical Tips

- Always **monitor real usage** (Prometheus, cAdvisor, Grafana)
- Overprovision storage; Docker logs can grow
- Use **ulimits**, **healthchecks**, and `--memory`/`--cpus` flags
- Cache aggressively using Redis/Nginx
- For multi-tenancy: isolate workloads with namespaces or rootless Docker

Let's expand with more **real-world Docker deployment use cases** across diverse scenarios, such as ML workloads, video streaming, high-traffic APIs, internal dashboards, and IoT edge deployments.

C.4 Case Study 3: Machine Learning Inference Service (GPU-enabled)

Scenario:

• Service: PyTorch-based model served via FastAPI • Users: 50 concurrent model inference calls • Requests/sec: 10 • Model load time: 200ms • Each inference time: 1.5s (GPU) • RAM usage per model: 2 GB • Disk size: 10 GB (model weights + logs)	**Framework**: PyTorch + FastAPI **Inference Time (GPU)**: 1.5s **Concurrent Users**: 50 **RPS**: 10 **Model Load Time**: 200ms **RAM**: 2 GB per model container **Disk**: 10 GB per container **Payload per Request**: 0.2 MB **Replicas**: 2 **Inference is GPU-bound**, not CPU-heavy

Resource Estimation:

CPU: Minimal (offloaded to GPU)
GPU Memory: ~2 GB per model instance × 2 replicas = 4 GB
RAM: 2 containers × 2 GB + 2 GB base = 6 GB
Disk: 2 × 10 GB = 20 GB + logging (Recommend 30 GB SSD)
Network: 10 RPS × 0.2 MB payload = 2 MB/s = 16 Mbps

Tips:

- Use NVIDIA Docker Runtime
- Bind GPU memory per container (`--gpus device=0`)
- Mount model weights as a shared volume for multiple replicas

C.4 Case Study 4: High-Traffic Public API with Rate Limits

Scenario:

- Users: 10,000 concurrent
- Requests/sec: 300
- Response time: 100ms
- Stateless Node.js API
- Memory: 512 MB/container
- Redis rate limiter backend

Resource Estimation:

CPU: (10,000 * 1 * 300 * 0.1) / 0.7 = ~428K CPU units = ~430 vCPU (with autoscaling)
RAM: 20 containers × 512 MB + Redis (1 GB) + system = ~12 GB
Disk: Minimal, stateless containers = ~5 GB + Redis persistence
Network: 300 RPS × 0.25 MB = 75 MB/s = 600 Mbps

Infra:

- Kubernetes HPA for scaling
- Redis hosted on separate volume
- NGINX ingress with rate limiting per IP/token

C.4 Case Study 5: Internal BI Dashboard

Scenario:

- Stack: Superset + PostgreSQL
- Users: 25 analysts, 10 concurrent queries
- Each query: ~200 MB memory, ~0.5s compute
- DB size: 20 GB

Resource Estimation:

CPU: (10 queries × 0.5s) / 0.7 = ~7 vCPUs
RAM: Superset = 2 GB, DB = 4 GB buffer, + OS = 8 GB
Disk: PostgreSQL = 20 GB + 10 GB backup + 10 GB logs = ~40 GB
Network: 10 × 0.1 MB dashboard = 1 MB/s = ~8 Mbps

Considerations:

- Enable Superset caching
- Backup DB volume regularly
- Monitor long-running queries

C.4 Case Study 6: Video Streaming Platform

Scenario:

- 200 simultaneous viewers
- Video chunks served via NGINX container
- Avg bitrate: 2 Mbps
- Load-balanced backend: 3 nodes
- Disk: 1 TB of encoded video

Resource Estimation:

CPU: 3 NGINX nodes (1 vCPU each)
RAM: NGINX = 512 MB × 3 = 1.5 GB
Disk: 1 TB (SSD or fast NAS mount)
Network: 200 users × 2 Mbps = 400 Mbps sustained

Notes:

- Use `X-Accel-Redirect` for chunk offloading
- Mount video directory as a volume (bind mount or EBS/NFS)
- Deploy on nodes with 1 Gbps NIC or higher

C.4 Case Study 7: Edge IoT Data Aggregator

Scenario:

- Deployed on Raspberry Pi at 10 locations
- Stack: Python MQTT consumer + SQLite
- 1 data packet/sec/device × 50 devices
- Small payloads, low RAM

Resource Estimation (per device):

```
CPU: 1 vCPU
RAM: 256 MB
Disk: 1 GB local SQLite + logs
Network: 50 RPS × 0.01 MB = 0.5 MB/s
```

Key Strategies:

- Use Alpine images
- Log rotation (`log-opt`)
- Use `docker restart=always`

Assumptions Summary Table

App Type	RAM/Container	CPU Load	Disk (GB)	Bandwidth/Req
Web API (Node/Python)	512 MB	0.1–0.2s/req	<1 GB	0.1–0.3 MB
ML Inference	2–4 GB	GPU-bound	10 GB	0.2–1 MB
DB (Postgres/MySQL)	2–8 GB	CPU & IO bound	20–100 GB	Varies
Superset/Grafana	1–2 GB	Light	5–10 GB	0.1 MB
NGINX Reverse Proxy	128–256 MB	Low	<1 GB	High throughput

General Sizing Tips

- Always run **load tests** (Locust, Artillery, JMeter)
- Profile RAM usage with `docker stats`, `psrecord`, or `cAdvisor`
- Use **autoscaling policies** (K8s HPA or custom Swarm scaling)
- Prefer **multi-stage builds** to reduce container size
- Use `--memory`, `--cpus`, and healthchecks in production
- Enable **logging limits** (`max-size`, `max-file`) in Compose or daemon config
- Monitor network load per service (`vnstat`, `iftop`, `netstat`, or Grafana)

Perfect! Let's now work on high-impact **Case Studies based on Netflix, Amazon, and Flipkart**, showing how Docker-style containerization could apply to large-scale, real-world deployment architectures — extrapolated for educational and simulation purposes.

These will help you to understand **enterprise-scale container resource planning** in scenarios involving millions of users, globally distributed architectures, and high throughput demands.

Enterprise-Scale Case Studies – Netflix, Amazon, Flipkart

Note: These case studies are **educational simulations** based on publicly known architectural patterns and realistic assumptions. They illustrate how Docker containers and orchestration would scale at large enterprise levels.

C.4 Case Study 8: Netflix – Global Video Streaming Platform

Deployment Scenario:

- 200M+ users globally
- ~10M concurrent streams
- Distributed CDN, microservices
- Edge containers handling video chunks
- Backend containers: catalog, personalization, recommendation ML models, billing, analytics

Key Containerized Components:

- NGINX-based edge stream servers (GPU acceleration for encoding)
- ML inference containers (personalized recommendations)
- PostgreSQL/Redis-based metadata services
- Kafka + Flink for real-time analytics
- Grafana + Prometheus for monitoring

Estimated Container Resources (per region):

Component	Count	vCPU	RAM	Disk	Bandwidth
Edge streaming	200	4	1 GB	20 GB	200 Mbps/node
ML inference	100	GPU	4 GB	5 GB	10 Mbps
Metadata services	50	2	2 GB	100 GB	5 Mbps
Billing + Auth	50	2	1 GB	10 GB	2 Mbps

Notes:

- Container-level resource constraints (`--cpus, --memory`) strictly enforced
- Use of **multi-node Swarm/K8s** with autoscaling and failover
- Real-time logs streamed to Loki + ELK

Resource Summary – Netflix (Per Region)

Component	Containers	Total vCPUs	Total RAM	Total Disk	Total Bandwidth
Edge Streaming	200	800 (200×4)	200 GB	4 TB	40 Gbps (200×200 Mbps)
ML Inference	100	100 GPUs	400 GB	500 GB	1 Gbps (100×10 Mbps)
Metadata Services	50	100 (50×2)	100 GB	5 TB	250 Mbps (50×5 Mbps)
Billing + Auth	50	100 (50×2)	50 GB	500 GB	100 Mbps (50×2 Mbps)

Aggregated Totals (Per Region)

Resource	Value
vCPUs	1000 cores (excluding GPUs)
GPUs	100
RAM	~750 GB
Disk	~10 TB
Bandwidth	~41.35 Gbps

C.4 Case Study 9: Amazon – High-Scale E-commerce + Microservices

Deployment Scenario:

- 250M+ active users
- 50M daily sessions
- Highly decoupled architecture: 1000s of services
- Dockerized workloads for: cart, search, payments, fraud detection, order history, etc.

Docker Deployment Architecture:

- **Frontend gateways** (React/Next.js on NGINX containers)
- **Microservice APIs** for each domain (Node.js/Java/Python)
- **AI/ML fraud detection** services with PyTorch/TensorFlow
- **Containerized RDS proxies**, Redis, Kafka, MongoDB sidecars
- **Lambda-like event processing via Docker**

Containerized Service Group Sample:

Service	Containers	vCPU (avg)	RAM	Disk	Throughput
Search API	500	2	1 GB	10 GB	1000 RPS
Cart Service	300	2	1.5 GB	5 GB	800 RPS
ML Fraud Engine	100	GPU	8 GB	20 GB	200 RPS
Recommendation	150	4	2 GB	10 GB	500 RPS
Payment Gateway	200	2	1 GB	5 GB	300 RPS

Scaling Strategy:

- Use of **Node Affinity**, **Pod Autoscaling** (K8s)
- **Separate container registry per region**
- Internal APIs versioned, deployed via **Canary** releases in containers
- Distributed tracing with **Jaeger in Docker**

Resource Estimation (Per Region Peak)

Resource	Value
vCPUs	(500×2) + (300×2) + (150×4) + (200×2) = **~2600 vCPUs**
RAM	~500 GB (search) + 450 GB (cart) + 800 GB (ML) + 300 GB (rec) + 200 GB (payment) = **~2.2 TB**

Resource	Value
Disk	~11 TB total for combined services
GPU	100 GPU containers for ML inference
Network	~2800 RPS total per region sustained

C.4 Case Study 10: Flipkart – Regional E-commerce Platform with High Flash Sale Load

Deployment Scenario:

- 30M+ active users in India
- Peak concurrency during festive flash sales
- Requires fast autoscaling and API rate throttling
- Dockerized services for: catalog, checkout, delivery, coupons, inventory

Container Breakdown:

Microservice	Peak Instances	RAM (GB)	vCPU	Disk/Logs	Notes
Catalog API	100	1	1	5 GB	CDN caching on edge
Checkout Service	120	2	2	10 GB	Payment retries + lock system
Delivery Engine	60	2	2	10 GB	Real-time delivery maps
Coupons & Deals	40	1	1	2 GB	DB and Redis combo
Inventory Tracker	80	1.5	1	10 GB	Kafka triggers + alerts

Infra Characteristics:

- Burstable CPU via `docker run --cpus=".5"`
- Rate-limiting at container ingress layer (NGINX + Lua scripts)
- Backup via Docker volume plugins (EBS/S3 mount)
- Session persistence using Redis containers (Clustered)

Aggregated Resource Summary (Peak)

Resource	Estimate (Total Peak Load)
vCPUs	(100×1) + (120×2) + (60×2) + (40×1) + (80×1) = **540 vCPUs**
RAM	100 + 240 + 120 + 40 + 120 = **~620 GB**
Disk	500 + 1200 + 600 + 80 + 800 = **~3.2 TB**

Learnings from Enterprise Use Cases

Practice	Netflix	Amazon	Flipkart
High Availability	Global Swarm	K8s with HA	Regional Auto-scaling
Monitoring Stack	Grafana + Loki	Prometheus + CloudWatch	ELK + Grafana
Container Hardening	Seccomp/AppArmor	Docker Bench + Signatures	Private registries
Log Management	Loki / Fluentd	EFS + CloudLogs	Promtail + Rotation
CI/CD Pipeline	GitHub + Spinnaker	CodePipeline + GitOps	Jenkins + K8s Rollouts

Now move to next level of in-depth **Case Study** focused on a **robust, auto-scaling architecture**, tailored around a modern technology stack using **Docker**, **Docker Compose (or Kubernetes)**, **microservices**, and **event-driven design**.

C.4 Case Study 11: Auto-Scaling Architecture for a Cloud-Native E-Commerce Platform

Overview

Let's explore a case study of a **modern e-commerce platform** built with a **containerized microservices architecture**, deployed using **Docker** and orchestrated via **Kubernetes or Docker Swarm**. The architecture is designed to **horizontally auto-scale** based on traffic, system load, and business events (e.g., flash sales, holidays).

Technology Stack

Layer	Stack / Tools
Frontend	React (served via NGINX in Docker)
Backend APIs	Python (FastAPI), Node.js (Express), Go
Authentication	Keycloak (OAuth2/OpenID)
Database	PostgreSQL + Redis + MongoDB (as services)
Queue/Eventing	Kafka + Celery (for async processing)
Containerization	Docker + Docker Compose (local)
Orchestration	Kubernetes (EKS/GKE) or Docker Swarm
CI/CD	GitHub Actions + Docker Hub + ArgoCD
Monitoring	Prometheus, Grafana, Loki, Alertmanager
Storage	S3 (object), EBS (block), NFS (shared)
Load Balancing	NGINX Ingress + Cloud Load Balancer
Auto Scaling	Horizontal Pod Autoscaler (K8s) / Swarm Auto Scale Scripts
Secrets & Configs	HashiCorp Vault / Docker Secrets / K8s Secrets

Deployment Highlights

- **Each microservice** runs in its own Docker container with defined resource limits (`--memory`, `--cpus`).
- Stateless services are **scaled horizontally** using HPA (Horizontal Pod Autoscaler) based on:
    - CPU and memory thresholds
    - Queue length from Kafka (custom metrics)
    - Number of active sessions or API requests per second

- **Stateful services** like PostgreSQL run with persistent volumes and high availability enabled.
- Redis and Kafka are deployed as clustered containers using Docker Compose (dev) or Helm Charts (prod).
- CI/CD pipelines trigger auto-builds and image pushes with environment-based deployment promotion (dev → staging → prod).

Auto-Scaling Flow Diagram (Descriptive)

- **User traffic increases**
- **Prometheus metrics** detect high CPU/RAM usage or long queue
- **HPA triggers scaling**
- New Docker containers are spawned in seconds
- Load balancer (NGINX Ingress) routes traffic to new pods/containers
- Logs and metrics instantly picked up by Grafana & Loki
- Once traffic drops, containers are gracefully terminated based on cooldown rules

Resource Summary

Service Group	Base Replicas	Max Replicas	CPU/Container	RAM/Container	CPU (Base)	CPU (Max)	RAM (Base)	RAM (Max)
React Frontend	2	10	0.25 vCPU	512 MB	0.5 vCPU	2.5 vCPU	1 GB	5 GB
FastAPI Backend	3	30	0.5 vCPU	1 GB	1.5 vCPU	15 vCPU	3 GB	30 GB
Keycloak (Auth)	2	5	1 vCPU	2 GB	2 vCPU	5 vCPU	4 GB	10 GB
Redis Cache	1	3	0.25 vCPU	256 MB	0.25 vCPU	0.75 vCPU	256 MB	768 MB
Kafka Broker	3	6	2 vCPU	4 GB	6 vCPU	12 vCPU	12 GB	24 GB
Celery Workers	3	20	0.75 vCPU	1 GB	2.25 vCPU	15 vCPU	3 GB	20 GB

Security + Fault Tolerance Features

1. JWT token-based auth via OAuth2/OIDC
2. TLS/SSL enforced through NGINX + cert-manager
3. Resource quotas and namespace limits per environment
4. Circuit breakers using Istio (optional) or Retry/Timeout config in services
5. Liveness + readiness probes for all containers
6. Database replicas with streaming backup to S3
7. Canary rollouts with Argo Rollouts or Jenkins-X

Real-World Events Simulated

Event Type	System Response
Traffic Spike	10x scale in frontend/API replicas within 2 mins
Queue Overload	Celery workers doubled via HPA (based on lag)
DB Failover	Primary Postgres auto-switch with zero downtime
Node Crash	Kubernetes reschedules pods to healthy nodes
Log Surge	Loki buffer increases; Alertmanager notifies

Takeaways

- **Stateless services = easy to scale horizontally**
- **Resource estimation + metrics-driven autoscaling** = optimized cost and performance
- **Event-driven architecture** enables decoupling and fault tolerance
- **Container isolation** improves deployment velocity, rollback safety, and system observability

Next, we will move to **Case Study on DevSecOps in Dockerized Environments**, which show how **Docker and DevSecOps** practices are integrated to build secure, automated CI/CD pipelines from development to deployment.

C.4 Case Study 12: Implementing DevSecOps in a Dockerized CI/CD Pipeline

Scenario: A FinTech Startup Enabling Secure Payments APIs

A FinTech company is building a set of microservices for secure payments, identity verification, and fraud detection. These services are deployed via Docker and orchestrated using Kubernetes in a hybrid cloud environment. Given the industry (finance), **security, compliance, auditability, and continuous assurance** are critical at every stage.

Technology Stack

Category	Tools/Tech Used
Source Control	GitHub
CI/CD	GitHub Actions, ArgoCD
Containerization	Docker, Docker Compose
Orchestration	Kubernetes (self-hosted or EKS)
Infrastructure as Code	Terraform, Helm
Secrets Management	HashiCorp Vault, K8s Secrets
Image Scanning	Trivy, Grype, Docker Scan
Policy Enforcement	OPA (Open Policy Agent), Kyverno, Conftest
Runtime Security	Falco, AppArmor, SELinux
Logging & Monitoring	Prometheus, Grafana, Loki, ELK
Vulnerability Feeds	NVD, Snyk, Anchore

DevSecOps Flow

1. Code Commit (GitHub)

- Developer pushes code to GitHub
- Pre-commit hooks check for secrets, code quality, and security linting (e.g., Bandit, ESLint)

2. Build (CI Pipeline)

- GitHub Actions build a Docker image
- Trivy and Docker Scan, scan for OS + dependency CVEs
- SBOM (Software Bill of Materials) is auto generated for auditing

3. Test

- Unit tests, integration tests, and SAST (Static App Sec Test) run
- Secrets detection via `gitleaks`
- IaC scanning with `Checkov` or `tfsec`

4. Policy Gate

- OPA/Kyverno validates Kubernetes manifests for:
  - No `:latest` image
  - Mandatory resource limits
  - Disallowed root user
  - Required network policies

5. Push & Promotion

- Images pushed to a private Docker registry (Harbor or AWS ECR)
- Only images that pass scanning + policy gates are allowed

6. Deployment

- ArgoCD watches for changes in GitOps repo
- Promotes image to staging/production after approvals
- Helm templates used for reproducibility

7. Runtime Security

- Falco monitors containers for anomalies (e.g., shell spawn, network access)
- AppArmor profiles enforced in containers
- Live logs streamed to ELK or Loki for audit and alerting

8. Incident Response + Feedback

- Incidents trigger automated Jira ticketing and Slack alert
- Developers receive feedback on vulnerabilities and policy failures

Key DevSecOps Metrics Monitored

Metric	Description
Time to detect (TTD) vulnerabilities	How fast scans detect CVEs after commit
Policy violation rate	% of pipeline failures due to misconfigurations
CVE severity breakdown	Ratio of critical/high/medium vulnerabilities
Image freshness	Age of base image and dependency versions

Metric	Description
Secrets detection	How many secrets (API keys, tokens) caught
MTTR	Mean time to remediate a vulnerability

Security Controls Applied in CI/CD

Layer	Security Control
Docker Image	Trivy/Grype scans, SBOM, minimal base image
Dockerfile	Multi-stage builds, no root user, pinned tags
Compose/K8s Manifest	Policy validation, resource limits enforced
Runtime	Falco rules, AppArmor, seccomp profiles
Networking	NetworkPolicies, ingress/egress control
Secrets	Vault, Docker secrets (not ENV vars)

Outcome

- **80% CVEs** identified pre-deployment via Trivy + policy checks
- Reduced attack surface by shifting to Alpine-based images and removing unused packages
- Full **audit trail** of deployments with GitOps + CI pipeline logs
- 99.9% uptime maintained while continuously patching vulnerable containers

Resource Summary

Component	Replicas	vCPU (Each)	RAM (Each)	Disk (Each)	Notes
CI Agents (GitHub Runners)	2–3	2 vCPU	4 GB	10 GB	For builds, tests, image creation, SBOM generation
Trivy/Grype Scanners	1–2	1 vCPU	2 GB	5 GB	Container image CVE scanning
OPA/Kyverno Gatekeeper	2	1 vCPU	1 GB	<1 GB	Policy enforcement for K8s manifests
Vault Server	2 (HA)	2 vCPU	4 GB	10 GB	Secrets management with auto-unseal + audit logging
ArgoCD Controller	2	1 vCPU	1 GB	2 GB	GitOps sync and approval workflow

Component	Replicas	vCPU (Each)	RAM (Each)	Disk (Each)	Notes
ELK Stack (or Loki)	3–4	4 vCPU	8 GB	100–200 GB	Central logging, audit trail, real-time visualization
Prometheus + Grafana	2	2 vCPU	4 GB	10 GB	Monitoring, alerts, pipeline metrics
Falco Runtime Monitor	DaemonSet	1 vCPU/node	512 MB	<1 GB	Suspicious behavior alerts (runtime detection)
Docker Registry (Harbor)	1–2	2 vCPU	4 GB	50–100 GB	Secure artifact storage

Aggregate Resource Estimate (Production Tier)

Resource Type	Approximate Total
vCPUs	~28–32 cores
RAM	~48–64 GB
Storage	~300–400 GB SSD
GPU	[X] Not Required
Bandwidth	Moderate (limited to CI/CD + logs + image push/pull)

Summary: Key Takeaways for DevSecOps with Docker

- ☑ Scan containers early and often — shift left
- ☑ Automate CVE feeds and SBOM generation
- ☑ Enforce deployment policies (don't rely on human review)
- ☑ Use rootless containers and strict capabilities
- ☑ Monitor runtime behavior (Falco + audit logs)
- ☑ Integrate security feedback into CI/CD for continuous hardening

Next **Case Study** on **DevSecOps for Security Operations & Malware Analysis**, tailored to highlight how **Docker containers** and **DevSecOps pipelines** are used to automate, isolate, and accelerate security response and malware investigation - a crucial use case for modern DevSecOps practices.

C.4 Case Study 13: DevSecOps for Security Operations & Malware Analysis Lab

Scenario:

A cybersecurity team at a managed security service provider (MSSP) needs to continuously analyze suspicious files, URLs, and system logs for signs of compromise, malware, and zero-day exploits.

They want to:

- Build a **secure, containerized malware sandbox**
- Integrate this into a **DevSecOps pipeline** that automates detection, analysis, and reporting
- Ensure the entire environment is **isolated**, monitored, and auditable

Technology Stack

Layer	**Tools/Technologies**
Container Runtime	Docker (rootless, user namespaces)
Orchestration	Docker Compose / Kubernetes (air-gapped optional)
Malware Tools	Cuckoo Sandbox, YARA, ClamAV, Volatility, Suricata
SIEM Integration	Elastic Stack (ELK), Wazuh, OpenSearch
Automation	Python, Bash, Celery (for async scans)
Static Analysis	YARA, CAPA, Binwalk, Strings
Dynamic Analysis	Docker-in-Docker containers, Firejail isolation
CI/CD	GitHub Actions / GitLab CI for automating updates
Monitoring & Alerts	Grafana + Loki + Alertmanager
Secrets Management	Docker Secrets / Vault

DevSecOps + Security Workflow

1. File or URL Ingestion

- Analysts drop a suspicious file into a mounted volume or POST it via API
- File is tagged, hashed, and stored for traceability

2. Static Analysis Pipeline (Containerized)

- Containers run:
    - YARA rule scan
    - `strings` and `binwalk` extractors
    - Dependency/PE header checks
    - AV scanners (ClamAV container)

3. Dynamic Sandbox Execution

- Docker runs malware sample inside a **Firejail or DinD (Docker-in-Docker)** container with:
    - Limited networking
    - CPU/memory limits
    - Mount namespace isolation

4. Behavioral Logging

- All network calls, file system changes, and process spawns are logged
- Suricata captures all outbound traffic
- Logs forwarded to Loki/ELK for live threat hunting

5. CI/CD for Threat Intelligence

- GitHub pipeline updates YARA rules daily from open-source feeds (e.g., `rules.yara` repo)
- Updated rules trigger redeployments of analysis containers

6. Alerting and Reporting

- If malware indicators (IoCs) are found:
    - Analyst notified via Slack/email
    - Report auto-generated and stored as PDF
    - Alert raised in Wazuh/OpenSearch dashboard

Sample Container Layout

Container	Purpose	Runtime Flags
`yara_scanner`	YARA rules execution	`--read-only --memory=256m`
`clamav_scanner`	AV engine	`--pids-limit=50`
`static_extractor`	Binwalk + PE parse	`--cap-drop ALL`
`dynamic_sandbox`	Isolated malware execution	`--security-opt apparmor=unconfined`

Container	Purpose	Runtime Flags
`network_logger`	Packet capture (Suricata)	`--net=host` with BPF filters
`log_forwarder`	Sends to ELK	`--log-driver=json-file`

KPIs and Metrics Tracked

Metric	Target / Outcome
Time to first detection	< 1 minute from file drop
Alert generation rate	90%+ accuracy (verified false positives)
Pipeline completion time	< 3 minutes per file (average)
YARA rule update freq	Daily or on push to threat feed
Network IOC detection	Real-time with Suricata logs

Security and Isolation Practices

- ✅ **No privileged containers**
- ✅ Uses **AppArmor + seccomp** on sandbox containers
- ✅ All artifacts analyzed in **read-only or tmpfs volumes**
- ✅ **TLS-encrypted** container-to-SIEM data pipelines
- ✅ Separate **air-gapped analysis cluster** (optional)

Bonus: Sample DevSecOps CI Pipeline

```
name: YARA Rules Pipeline

on:
  push:
    paths:
      - 'rules/yara/**'

jobs:
  scan:
    runs-on: ubuntu-latest
    steps:
    - name: Clone Repo
      uses: actions/checkout@v2

    - name: Run YARA Scan
      run: docker run --rm -v ${{ github.workspace }}/samples:/samples \
```

```
           yara_scanner:latest -r /samples
```

Use Case Benefits

- ☑ **Secure-by-default** container sandboxing
- ☑ Easy to **version**, **reproduce**, and **rollback** analysis runs
- ☑ Quick integration into SIEM + alerting pipelines
- ☑ Scalable to run 100s of files/day
- ☑ Compliant with audit, forensics, and traceability requirements

Component Breakdown (Per Node / Analysis Cluster Estimate)

Container	Purpose	vCPU	RAM	Disk	Key Runtime Flags
`yara_scanner`	YARA rule execution	0.5	256 MB	1 GB	`--read-only, --memory=256m`
`clamav_scanner`	ClamAV-based antivirus scan	1	512 MB	1 GB	`--pids-limit=50`
`static_extractor`	Binwalk, strings, PE header parse	1	512 MB	2 GB	`--cap-drop=ALL`
`dynamic_sandbox`	Malware execution in isolation	2	1.5 GB	5 GB	`--security-opt apparmor=unconfined, no root`
`network_logger`	Suricata traffic monitor	1	1 GB	10 GB	`--net=host, BPF filters`
`log_forwarder`	Log shipping to ELK/Loki	0.5	512 MB	1 GB	`--log-driver=json-file`

Resource Summary (Per Malware File Analysis)

Metric	**Value (Approx)**
Total vCPUs	6–7 vCPU
Total RAM	~4 GB
Disk Usage	~20 GB per file
Analysis Time	≤ 3 minutes
Throughput Target	100–200 files/day/node

Additional Components (CI, Monitoring, Updates)

Component	**vCPU**	**RAM**	**Purpose**
GitHub/GitLab CI Agent	2	4 GB	YARA rule auto-update + test + redeploy

Component	vCPU	RAM	Purpose
Prometheus + Loki	2	4 GB	Monitoring and alert correlation
Vault	1	2 GB	Secure credential storage and audit logs
Wazuh/OpenSearch	2	6 GB	Alert visualization and dashboarding

Resource Summary

Total Node Resources	Estimate (Analysis Node)
vCPUs	~10–12 cores
RAM	~8–10 GB
Disk (SSD Preferred)	~100–200 GB
Network (Ingress/Egress)	Moderate (logging, updates)

Final Takeaways for Security Teams

- **Docker empowers modular and isolated malware labs**
- **DevSecOps pipelines enhance speed, reproducibility, and automation**
- Real-time monitoring and scanning help shift malware analysis **from manual to automated**
- Easily deployable in cloud, hybrid, or air-gapped on-prem environments

Next Cast Study on **Docker for Infrastructure Operations**, focusing on how Docker is used by IT/InfraOps teams for automation, repeatability, disaster recovery, diagnostics, and environment standardization. This is ideal for enterprise-level operations use cases.

C.4 Case Study 14: Docker in Infrastructure Operations (InfraOps)

Scenario:

A large IT services company manages hundreds of internal infrastructure services, legacy applications, and tools across multiple environments (on-prem, cloud, hybrid). The Infrastructure Operations team is tasked with:

- Standardizing development and deployment environments
- Automating backup, diagnostics, and recovery processes
- Minimizing "snowflake server" issues
- Supporting a wide range of tools (PostgreSQL, LDAP, ELK, Jenkins, DNS, legacy apps)

Docker provides the abstraction and repeatability they need.

Use Cases and Tech Stack in InfraOps

Function	Tool or Image Used	Docker Role
Backup Automation	Restic, Duplicity, Borg in containers	Run on cron with bind-mounts
Monitoring & Logging	Prometheus, Grafana, ELK Stack	Deployed as Docker Compose stack
Local DNS Server	CoreDNS, Bind9	Deployed via Docker
Jenkins CI	Official Jenkins container	Shared reusable config volume
LDAP & Auth Services	OpenLDAP container	Mounted with persistent volumes
Log Collection	Filebeat, Fluentd, Logstash	Sidecar or daemonset containers
Network Tools	Nmap, Netcat, tcpdump (as disposable containers)	Fire-and-forget diagnostics
Legacy App Hosting	Wine + X11 containers	Run old GUI apps inside container
Disaster Recovery	Docker Swarm backup services + mounted volumes	Auto-export and restore

Lifecycle Example: PostgreSQL Backup & Restore with Docker

- A backup container using **BorgBackup** is scheduled nightly via cron
- It mounts the host PostgreSQL data volume read-only
- The backup is encrypted, tagged, and stored to S3-compatible storage
- In DR scenarios, an identical PostgreSQL Docker container is spun up
- Data is restored automatically from S3 using a containerized recovery script

Benefits Realized

Goal	Docker-Enabled Outcome
Environment parity	Same container runs on staging/dev/production
Disaster recovery speed	From hours to minutes with scripted containers
Legacy app compatibility	Run old apps inside isolated Linux containers
Security and rollback	All ops containers are immutable and versioned
No package conflicts	No host pollution—everything isolated in images

Docker Images Built by InfraOps

1. `infra/postgres-backup:v1` → backs up any mounted PG data dir to cloud
2. `infra/dns-server:v2` → containerized BIND with reloadable configs
3. `infra/diagnostic-tools:v3` → Nmap, ping, curl, dig for fast on-demand diagnostics
4. `infra/log-forwarder:v1` → Filebeat+Loki forwarder with central config
5. `infra/jenkins-worker:v2` → Pre-baked Jenkins agents with Git, Python, Terraform

Real-World Scenarios Handled

Incident	Docker-Based Solution
VM crash, DB recovery	New container spun up with restored PG volume
Legacy service failed after update	Older image version rolled back instantly
Internal DNS misconfiguration	Isolated container-based CoreDNS verified before release
Manual diagnostic needed	`docker run --rm -it infra/diagnostic-tools` used safely
Log agent misbehaving	Container restarted or re-pulled in seconds

Security & Governance

- **Containers run as non-root with limited permissions**
- **Immutable images** signed and stored in private registry

- **Compliance reports** generated via Docker inspect + container logs
- **Volume encryption** for backups and sensitive mounts
- **Audit logging** via SIEM integration on every image pull/run

Resource Planning (Per Host)

Container Group	Average RAM	vCPU	Disk Use	Scaling Notes
Monitoring Stack	2–4 GB	2	10 GB	One stack per datacenter (Prometheus + Grafana + ELK)
Backup Automation	~1 GB	1	Variable	Cron-based; containers spin up and exit automatically
Diagnostics Tools	256 MB	0.5	100 MB	Run-on-demand; disposable container model
Auth Services (LDAP)	1 GB	1	1–2 GB	Long-running container with persistent volumes
Legacy App Hosting	2–4 GB	2	5–10 GB	Uses Wine + X11 containerized GUI apps
Jenkins CI Agents	2–3 GB	2	5 GB	Prebuilt containers with CI tooling (Git, Terraform)

Resource Summary Snapshot

Resource Type	Estimation Per Host
vCPUs	~4–6 cores depending on toolset enabled
RAM	~8–12 GB
Disk	~20–40 GB (excluding volume backups)
Network Load	Low (except during backup or logging bursts)

Summary: Why InfraOps Teams Love Docker

- **Standardizes tools across environments**
- **Easier DR/rollbacks** with images & version tags
- **Speeds up response** during incidents
- **Automates common infra tasks** in containers
- **Improves security** with isolation, non-root execution, and reproducibility

Next Case Study explores **Blockchain Infrastructure using Docker**, focusing on how **global supply chain consortia** deploy **scalable**, **permissioned Hyperledger Fabric** networks. Docker ensures **rapid peer onboarding**, **smart contract isolation**, **secure key handling**, **fault tolerance**, and **reproducibility**. **Kubernetes and Compose** streamline **development**, **orchestration**, and **disaster recovery**, reducing **DevOps overhead** across partners.

C.14 Case Study 15: Real-World Blockchain Infrastructure Using Docker Containers

Scenario:

A global consortium of supply chain vendors is building a **permissioned blockchain network** to ensure transparency, traceability, and integrity of goods across logistics partners.

The blockchain nodes must:

- Be deployed in a **multi-party, decentralized infrastructure**
- Support secure **smart contracts (chaincode)**
- Be easily replicated and **containerized for onboarding new peers**
- Handle **fault tolerance**, version upgrades, **consensus**, and **data persistence**

Docker is used across the board for building, distributing, running, and orchestrating the blockchain nodes and support services.

Use Case: Blockchain for Global Supply Chain Consortium

Objectives:

- Each supply chain partner runs its own **Dockerized blockchain node**
- Use of **Hyperledger Fabric** for a permissioned ledger
- Docker Compose for development and test networks
- Kubernetes for production-grade blockchain orchestration
- Integration of secure **chaincode logic**, **certificate authorities**, and **orderers**

Infrastructure Stack

Component	Technology Used
Blockchain Network	Hyperledger Fabric (v2.x)
Container Runtime	Docker (Compose for dev, K8s for prod)
Smart Contracts	Chaincode in Go, Node.js, Docker-packaged
Database Layer	CouchDB (Dockerized) per peer
Cert Authority	Hyperledger CA (Docker container)
Monitoring	Prometheus + Grafana for metrics, health
Backup/Recovery	Volume snapshots + Docker-based recovery scripts

Component	Technology Used
Logging	Fluentd + ELK stack

Docker-Based Architecture

Service	Image / Role
`Peer`	Runs blockchain peer node + CouchDB
`Orderer`	Maintains ordering service for consensus
`Ca`	Issues crypto material (certificates)
`Cli`	Admin client for channel/chaincode ops
`chaincode`	Deployed as Docker image per contract
`Explorer`	Web UI for blockchain state
`metrics-exporter`	Prometheus metrics exposure for peer

Core Container Components (Per Organization)

Service	Image Role	vCPU	RAM	Disk (Persistent)	Notes
`peer`	Blockchain node (ledger + gRPC)	2	2–4 GB	10–20 GB	Runs smart contract container per chaincode
`couchdb`	State database for peer	1	1 GB	5–10 GB	Key-value store backing the peer ledger
`orderer`	Ordering service (Raft/Kafka)	1–2	2 GB	5 GB	One per network, or per org in Raft mode
`ca`	Certificate Authority node	1	512 MB	1–2 GB	Manages TLS, mTLS, cert rotation
`cli`	Admin tool container	0.5	512 MB	1 GB	Used for joining channels, deploying chaincode
`chaincode`	Smart contract (containerized)	0.5–1	512 MB	Ephemeral	Separate container per contract per peer

Service	Image Role	vCPU	RAM	Disk (Persistent)	Notes
`explorer`	Blockchain Web UI	1	1–2 GB	1 GB	Optional for visibility into blocks, txns
`metrics-exporter`	Prometheus-compatible metrics	0.5	256 MB	–	Node and ledger performance metrics

Input Parameters (per org)

Parameter	Symbol	Value
Number of Peers	`P`	2
Chaincode Containers per Peer	`CC`	2
CouchDB per Peer	`CDB`	1
Orderer Containers	`O`	1
CA Containers	`CA`	1
CLI Admin	`CLI`	1
Explorer	`EX`	1
Metrics Exporter	`M`	1

CPU Estimation

Formula:

```
Total_vCPUs = (P × 2) + (P × CC × 1) + (P × CDB × 1) + (O × 2) + (CA × 1) +
(CLI × 0.5) + (EX × 1) + (M × 0.5)
```

Calculation:

```
= (2 × 2) + (2 × 2 × 1) + (2 × 1 × 1) + (1 × 2) + (1 × 1) + (1 × 0.5) + (1 ×
1) + (1 × 0.5)
= 4 + 4 + 2 + 2 + 1 + 0.5 + 1 + 0.5
= **15 vCPUs**
```

RAM Estimation

RAM per Component:

Component	RAM (GB)
Peer	2

Component	RAM (GB)
Chaincode	0.5
CouchDB	1
Orderer	2
CA	0.5
CLI	0.5
Explorer	1
Metrics Exporter	0.25

Formula:

```
Total_RAM = (P × 2) + (P × CC × 0.5) + (P × CDB × 1) + (O × 2) + (CA × 0.5)
+ (CLI × 0.5) + (EX × 1) + (M × 0.25)
```

Calculation:

```
= (2 × 2) + (2 × 2 × 0.5) + (2 × 1) + (1 × 2) + (1 × 0.5) + (1 × 0.5) + (1 ×
1) + (1 × 0.25)
= 4 + 2 + 2 + 2 + 0.5 + 0.5 + 1 + 0.25
= **12.25 GB RAM**
```

Storage Estimation

Assumptions:

- Ledger (per peer): ~10 GB for 1M txns
- CouchDB (per peer): ~5 GB
- Logs & snapshots: ~5–10 GB
- Explorer & metrics: ~1–2 GB
- Chaincode containers: ephemeral (no storage)

Formula:

```
Total_Storage = (P × 10) + (P × 5) + (Logs_Backups) + (Explorer + Metrics)
```

Calculation:

```
= (2 × 10) + (2 × 5) + 10 + 2
= 20 + 10 + 10 + 2 = **42 GB (rounded to 50 GB with buffer)**
```

Network Estimation

Assumption:

- gRPC sync, chaincode execution, monitoring metrics
- ~20 Mbps per peer at moderate load

Formula:

```
Total_Network = P × 20 Mbps + M × 2 Mbps + Explorer × 1 Mbps
```

Calculation:

```
= 2 × 20 + 1 × 2 + 1 × 1 = **43 Mbps**
(Rounded to **50 Mbps** for buffer)
```

Resource Summary

Resource	Estimate
vCPUs	~15 cores
RAM	~12–13 GB
Disk	~50 GB
Network	~50 Mbps ingress/egress
Startup Time	<5 sec per container
Chaincode Isolation	2 per peer (containerized)

Lifecycle: Adding a New Consortium Member

- New member pulls Docker Compose template from Git
- Uses Fabric CA to generate org-specific certs and keys
- Spins up `peer`, `couchdb`, and `cli` containers using Docker Compose
- Admin container uses `peer channel join` to connect to shared blockchain
- Smart contracts (chaincode) deployed using Dockerized CLI
- Logs sent to ELK for compliance

Performance Benchmark

Metric	Value (Sample)
TPS (Transactions/sec)	250–1000 (depends on consensus type)
Chaincode latency	~200ms avg
Ledger disk usage	~10–20 GB per org for 1M txns
Docker startup time	<5 sec/peer node
Horizontal scale-out	Add new peer via Docker image spin-up

Security & Resilience

1. All peers use **TLS + Docker secrets** for private key storage
2. Chaincode runs in its **own Docker container**, isolated per peer
3. Crash recovery via Docker volume restore or cloud snapshots
4. Uses **mutual TLS (mTLS)** for peer-to-peer and peer-orderer comms

5. Cert revocation built into Dockerized CA containers

Business Outcome

- Consortium onboarded 10 partners within 2 weeks using Docker images
- Full reproducibility ensured with containerized network setup
- 60% faster disaster recovery (peer restore) via volume mapping
- Docker Compose used for integration tests of chaincode before production
- Enabled secure multi-org governance without full DevOps team per node

Summary: Why Docker Works for Blockchain Infra

Advantage	Description
Reproducibility	Any org can spin up the exact same peer node
Chaincode Testing Isolation	Each smart contract tested in its own container
Onboarding Simplicity	Docker Compose templates + CLI = fast peer launch
Enhanced Security	Key isolation + TLS + container immutability
Automation Ready	Fit for CI/CD of chaincode and orchestration
Modular Deployment	Peer, Orderer, CA, Explorer = pluggable units

C.5 Runtime Flags for Resource Enforcement

Runtime Resource Enforcement with Docker Flags

After estimating your container requirements (CPU, RAM, logs, etc.), enforce those limits using the following production-grade Docker flags:

Flag	Purpose	Example
`--memory`	Set a hard memory limit per container	`--memory=512m`
`--cpus`	Limit container to a specific number of CPU cores	`--cpus=1.5`
`--ulimit`	Restrict max open files, processes, or memory locks	`--ulimit nofile=1024:2048`
`--log-opt`	Limit log file size or rotation count	`--log-opt max-size=10m --log-opt max-file=3`

Pro Tip: *Apply these flags in production to avoid noisy neighbors, container memory overruns, or unbounded log growth — all of which impact node stability and performance.*

C.6 Further Reading & Sizing Resources

For advanced resource estimation, observability, and cloud-native deployment planning, refer to the following trusted tools and documentation sources:

Explore these trusted tools and documentation to enhance your Docker deployment estimation and monitoring practices:

- **cAdvisor** – Real-time container resource metrics.

  🔗 `https://github.com/google/cadvisor`
- **Prometheus & Grafana** – Metrics collection, dashboarding, and alerting.

  🔗 `https://prometheus.io/docs/introduction/overview/`
- **Grafana Docker Dashboard** – Prebuilt Docker monitoring visualizations.

  🔗 `https://grafana.com/grafana/dashboards/893`
- **AWS EC2 Instance Sizing Guide** – Instance selection for container clusters.

  🔗 `https://aws.amazon.com/ec2/instance-types/`
- **Google Cloud Machine Types** – GCP VM sizing for Docker and GKE.

  🔗 `https://cloud.google.com/compute/docs/machine-types`
- **Kubernetes Resource Limits** – Configure memory/CPU boundaries.

  🔗 `https://kubernetes.io/docs/concepts/configuration/manage-resources-containers/`

Appendix D: Preparing for the Docker Certified Associate (DCA) Exam

The **Docker Certified Associate (DCA)** exam is one of the most recognized certifications in containerization and cloud-native technologies. It validates your core understanding of Docker's ecosystem, architecture, security, networking, storage, orchestration, and real-world troubleshooting.

Docker Certified Associate (DCA) – Official Domain Breakdown for Exam readiness and exam preparation

Domain: Orchestration (25%)

Core Responsibilities:

- Manage **multi-container services** across nodes.
- Run and **scale containers** using **Swarm Mode**.
- Convert standalone containers into **services and stacks**.
- Troubleshoot failed services and deployment issues.

Key Skills:

- Set up Swarm: `docker swarm init, docker swarm join`
- Create services: `docker service create, docker stack deploy`
- Define replicas, publish ports, mount volumes.
- Understand **replicated vs. global services**.
- Use **node labels** for task placement:
    - `docker node update --label-add role=db worker1`
    - `docker service create --constraint 'node.labels.role == db' ...`
- Interpret `docker inspect` output for services, tasks, containers.
- Convert apps into Compose files (`docker-compose.yml`) and deploy:
    - `docker stack deploy -c docker-compose.yml mystack`

Kubernetes (Introduced):

- Understand basics of `pod, deployment, configMap,` and `secret`.

Exam Tip:

Swarm Mode is still **heavily tested**, even if Kubernetes is mentioned. Be prepared to:

1. Troubleshoot services (`docker service ps`, `docker service logs`)
2. Deploy with `stack`
3. Use node constraints, templates, and secrets

Domain: Image Creation, Management & Registry (20%)

Core Responsibilities:

- Build efficient, secure, and tagged images.
- Store and share images across registries (DockerHub, GHCR, private).
- Sign images and manage versioning.

Key Skills:

- Write optimized **Dockerfiles**:
  - Use multi-stage builds
  - Minimize layers
- Common Dockerfile instructions:
  - `ADD, COPY, EXPOSE, CMD, ENTRYPOINT, VOLUME`
- Inspect layers with `docker history` and `docker inspect`
- Tag and push images:
  - `docker tag myapp:latest myrepo/myapp:v1.0.0`
  - `docker push myrepo/myapp:v1.0.0`
- Prune unused images: `docker image prune -a`
- Run private registries or use DockerHub, GHCR, AWS ECR.
- Sign images using Docker Content Trust (Notary):
  - `export DOCKER_CONTENT_TRUST=1`

Exam Tip:

You'll face questions on:

1. Building and tagging with CLI
2. Registry functions (push/pull/login)
3. Docker Content Trust
4. Image layer analysis and optimization

Domain: Installation and Configuration (15%)

Core Responsibilities:

- Install Docker across platforms (Linux/Windows).
- Choose the correct **storage** and **logging drivers**.
- Configure Docker for secure and reliable performance.

Key Skills:

- Install Docker Engine and set up `daemon.json`
- Choose correct **storage drivers** (`overlay2, aufs, btrfs`)
- Logging drivers: `json-file, syslog, journald, fluentd`
- Set Docker to start on boot: `systemctl enable docker`
- Use certificates for TLS authentication between client and server
- UCP/DTR installation on **AWS or on-premises** clusters
- Use cgroups, namespaces for resource control
- Configure HA for UCP (manager, DTR replica, worker)
- Manage users and teams in UCP

Exam Tip:

Know how to:

- Configure `daemon.json`
- Enable cert-based access
- Understand sizing and requirements for installing UCP/DTR
- Troubleshoot with Docker logs and error outputs

Domain: Networking (15%)

Core Responsibilities:

- Connect containers securely.
- Configure and inspect Docker networks.
- Understand **Container Network Model (CNM)**.

Key Skills:

- Docker network types:
  - `bridge:` default single-host
  - `host:` no isolation (Linux only)
  - `overlay:` multi-host (Swarm)
  - `macvlan:` containers on LAN with IP/MAC
  - `none:` isolated, no connectivity
- Create and inspect networks:
  - `docker network create mynet`
  - `docker network inspect mynet`
- Publish ports: `docker run -p 8080:80`
- External DNS configuration via `/etc/resolv.conf` or `--dns`

- Load balancing via **Swarm routing mesh** or **L7 (Traefik, HAProxy)**
- Understand **Ingress vs Host mode**
- Traffic flow between Docker Engine, registry, UCP
- Kubernetes networking: `ClusterIP, NodePort`

Exam Tip:

Expect scenario-based networking questions, e.g.:

- Why can't a container ping another?
- How to make services discoverable across nodes?

Domain: Security (15%)

Core Responsibilities:

- Minimize container attack surface.
- Use proper identity, role, and access control.
- Ensure integrity of images and secrets.

Key Skills:

- Drop unnecessary Linux capabilities:
  - `docker run --cap-drop=ALL --cap-add=NET_BIND_SERVICE ...`
- Use `--user` to run containers as non-root
- Apply **Seccomp**, **AppArmor**, **SELinux**
- Understand Swarm's default use of **MTLS** (secure node-to-node)
- Configure Docker Content Trust (DCT)
- Scan images for vulnerabilities
- Set up **RBAC** in UCP (users/teams/roles)
- Integrate UCP with LDAP/AD
- Create **UCP client bundles** for CLI login

Exam Tip:

Know which flags harden containers (`--read-only, --cap-drop, --user`) and how security roles and MTLS work in Swarm/UCP.

Domain: Storage and Volumes (10%)

Core Responsibilities:

- Persist data using volumes and bind mounts.
- Backup and restore container data.

- Use persistent storage with Kubernetes.

Key Skills:

- Volume types:
  - **Named volumes** (`docker volume create`)
  - **Bind mounts** (`-v /host:/container`)
  - **tmpfs** (in-memory)
- Graph drivers: `overlay2, devicemapper`, etc.
- Volume inspection, cleanup:
  - `docker volume inspect myvol`
  - `docker volume prune`
- `Backups with tar`:
  - `docker run -v data:/data alpine tar czf /backup.tar.gz /data`
- Kubernetes Persistent Volumes:
  - `persistentVolumeClaim`
  - `storageClass`
  - `volumeMounts`

Exam Tip:

Understand how Docker volumes work, how to clean up unused images, and how to provision Kubernetes storage.

DCA Exam Format:

- **Total Questions**: 55
- **Type**:
    - 13 Multiple Choice (MCQ)
    - 42 Discrete Option Multiple Choice (DOMC)
- **Time**: ~90 minutes
- **Pass Mark**: Not disclosed, but estimate ~70%+

What You Should Do Now

Task	Tool
Study each domain deeply	Use this guide, Docker docs
Practice every command	Docker CLI, Play-with-Docker
Use real-world Compose/Swarm stacks	DockerHub + GitHub Actions
Use image scanning tools	Trivy, Docker Content Trust
Simulate exam conditions	90-minute mock tests

How This Book Helps You Ace the DCA Exam

This book – *Mastering Docker from Scratch to Scale* – has been meticulously crafted to align with the official DCA exam domains and real-world expectations of DevOps, SRE, and container engineers.

What's Covered That Maps to DCA Objectives:

DCA Domain	Verified Chapters in Book
Orchestration	Ch. 7 (Compose Essentials), Ch. 8 (Advanced Compose), Ch. 10 (Swarm), Ch. 16 (CI/CD with GitHub Actions), Ch. 19 (Kubernetes Crash-Course)
Image Creation, Management	Ch. 2 (Install), Ch. 4 (Building Images), Ch. 17 (DockerHub), plus Appendix A.2 (Dockerfile), A.10 (Build Optimization)
Container Lifecycle Management	Ch. 3 (Architecture & CLI), Ch. 5 (Execution & Lifecycle), Ch. 11 (Security), Ch. 15 (Troubleshooting)
Networking	Ch. 5 (Networking Between Containers), Ch. 12 (Docker Networking), Appendix A.4 (Docker Network Reference), A.5 (Compose YAML Reference)
Volumes and Storage	Ch. 6 (Data Management), Ch. 14 (Backup & Recovery), Appendix A.3 (Volume CLI Reference)
Security	Ch. 11 (Docker Security), Ch. 13 (Hardening), Ch. 14 (DR & Secure Backups), Appendix A.7 (Security Config Summary)
Docker CLI / Compose Mastery	Throughout Chapters 2–17, especially Ch. 3, Ch. 6, Ch. 7, Ch. 10
Troubleshooting	Ch. 15 (Troubleshooting), Ch. 16 (CI/CD Lab Debugging), Appendix B/C Labs
CI/CD and Automation	Ch. 16 (GitHub CI/CD), Ch. 17 (DockerHub), Appendix A.11 (CI/CD Snippet), Appendix B/C (Real-World CI/CD Labs)

Why This Book Is Different:

- ☑ **Hands-on Projects & Labs** – Real-world case studies like *Malware Analysis Lab*, CI/CD pipelines, and security operations are included.
- ☑ **Knowledge Checks** – Every chapter ends with DCA-style MCQs and DOMC (Discrete Option Multiple Choice) questions.
- ☑ **Cheat Sheets & Appendices** – For quick revision before your exam day.
- ☑ **Production-Level Examples** – Beyond the exam, this helps you succeed in enterprise Docker deployments.
- ☑ **Covers Edge Cases** – Such as rootless containers, BuildKit, advanced Compose features, and monitoring.

Exam Readiness Checklist:

- Practice Docker CLI and Compose daily using the examples in this book.
- Revisit **Chapter 11 (Security)** and **Chapter 15 (Troubleshooting)** multiple times.
- Use **Appendix A** to drill CLI flags and YAML configurations.
- Try the **Case Study Labs** like malware sandboxing and GitHub Actions to build deep confidence.
- Complete all **Knowledge Check Questions** exercises per chapter.

Here's a detailed mapping of Book Chapters to the Docker Certified Associate (DCA) Exam domains, aligned with the official DCA curriculum and weights. This will help you to prepare for the exam by understanding which chapters contribute most toward each domain.

Docker Certified Associate (DCA) Exam – Chapter Mapping Guide

DCA Exam Domain	Weight (%)	Relevant Book Chapters / Sections	Chapter Titles
1. Orchestration	25%	Chapter 7	Docker Compose Essentials
		Chapter 8	Advanced Docker Compose
		Chapter 10	Advanced Docker
		Chapter 16	CI/CD Pipeline with GitHub Actions
		Chapter 19	Kubernetes Crash-Course
2. Image Creation, Management & Registry	20%	Chapter 2	Installing Docker and Docker Compose
		Chapter 4	Building Docker Images
		Chapter 17	Mastering DockerHub
3. Installation & Configuration	15%	Chapter 1	Introduction to Docker
		Chapter 3	Docker Architecture and Basic Commands
		Chapter 20	Docker Configuration Files and System Directories
		Appendix A.8	System File Locations (Linux)
4. Networking	15%	Chapter 5	Docker Containers in Action
		Chapter 12	Docker Networking

DCA Exam Domain	Weight (%)	Relevant Book Chapters / Sections	Chapter Titles
		Appendix A.5	Compose YAML Reference
5. Security	15%	Chapter 11	Docker Security
		Chapter 13	Best Practices and Container Hardening
		Chapter 14	Backup and Recovery
		Chapter 16	CI/CD Pipeline with GitHub Actions
6. Storage & Volumes	10%	Chapter 6	Data Management in Docker
		Chapter 14	Backup and Recovery
		Appendix A.3	Docker Volume Reference

Final Tip - Before Exams

Day 1 – Installation & Configuration (15%)

- ▢ 🕮 Review Chapter 1: Introduction
- ▢ 🕮 Review Chapter 2: Docker + Compose Installation
- ▢ 🕮 Review Chapter 3: CLI Basics
- ▢ 🕮 Review Chapter 20 + Appendix A.8: System File Locations
- ▢ Reinstall Docker & Compose locally or in Play With Docker
- ▢ Practice daemon.json tuning, systemd reloads, Compose V2 flags
- ▢ Review CLI flags in Appendix A.1

Day 2 – Image Creation, Management & Registry (20%)

- ▢ 🕮 Review Chapter 4: Dockerfiles
- ▢ 🕮 Review Chapter 17: DockerHub
- ▢ 🕮 Review Chapter 16: CI/CD Pipeline
- ▢ 🕮 Review Appendix A.2, A.10: Dockerfile & build optimization
- ▢ Create and optimize a multi-stage Dockerfile
- ▢ Push images to DockerHub
- ▢ Enable image signing (Content Trust)

Day 3 – Storage & Volumes (10%)

- ▢ 🕮 Review Chapter 6: Volumes & Networks
- ▢ 🕮 Review Chapter 14: Backup & Restore
- ▢ 🕮 Review Appendix A.3: Volume CLI Reference
- ▢ Create named volumes and mount them
- ▢ Run PostgreSQL/MySQL with persistent data
- ▢ Backup and restore a volume manually and via script

Day 4 – Networking (15%)

- ▢ 🕮 Review Chapter 5: Docker Containers in Action
- ▢ 🕮 Review Chapter 12: Docker Networking
- ▢ 🕮 Review Appendix A.4, A.5: Networking and Compose YAML
- ▢ Create custom bridge, overlay, and host-mode networks
- ▢ Connect multiple containers across networks
- ▢ Use --internal, --link, --network-alias

Day 5 – Security (15%)

- ▢ 🕮 Review Chapter 11: Docker Security
- ▢ 🕮 Review Chapter 13: Hardening
- ▢ 🕮 Review Chapter 14: Backup/DR
- ▢ 🕮 Review Appendix A.7: Security Config Summary
- ▢ Harden a container (rootless, AppArmor/Seccomp)
- ▢ Perform Trivy scan on a local image
- ▢ Simulate secrets management and user dropping

Day 6 – Orchestration (25%)

- ▢ 🕮 Review Chapter 7 & 8: Compose
- ▢ 🕮 Review Chapter 10: Swarm
- ▢ 🕮 Review Chapter 16: GitHub CI/CD
- ▢ 🕮 Review Chapter 19: Kubernetes Transition
- ▢ Deploy a Compose app with profiles
- ▢ Set up Swarm with scaling & update strategy
- ▢ Review .github/workflows/ YAMLs

Day 7 – Final Review & Mock Test

- ▢ 🕮 Review Knowledge Check questions (all chapters)
- ▢ 🕮 Review Appendix A cheat sheets
- ▢ Simulate exam: Attempt 55 practice questions
- ▢ Grade yourself and revisit weak areas

Use this book not just to pass the DCA, but to become a confident, production-ready Docker engineer. The exam is the start. Your container journey begins here.

"Containers aren't just about packaging apps – they're about thinking modular, secure, and scalable. DCA certification proves it. This book gets you there." – Sudipta Biswas

Glossary of Terms

Note: This glossary provides definitions for common terms, tools, and technologies covered throughout this book.

A

- **AppArmor**: A Linux kernel security module that restricts programs' capabilities through profiles attached to each application. Often used in container runtime hardening.
- **API Server**: Core Kubernetes component that handles REST operations and exposes the Kubernetes API.
- **Autoscaling**: The process of automatically adjusting the number of running containers or pods based on resource usage or performance metrics.

B

- **Base Image**: The foundational image in a Dockerfile from which other images are built. Typically defined with the FROM instruction.
- **Bind Mount**: A type of Docker volume that directly links a host directory to a container path.
- **Build Context**: The directory sent to the Docker daemon when building an image, including the Dockerfile and other necessary files.
- **BuildKit**: A modern, faster Docker image build engine supporting advanced features like cache imports.

C

- **Capability Dropping:** The practice of removing unneeded Linux capabilities from containers to reduce attack surface.
- **cAdvisor:** A container monitoring tool that provides real-time metrics on resource usage and performance.
- **Chaincode**: Smart contracts in Hyperledger Fabric, typically run in Docker containers to maintain network isolation.
- **CI/CD (Continuous Integration and Continuous Delivery/Deployment)**: A methodology for automating the build, testing, and deployment of applications.
- **Clair**: A static vulnerability analyzer for Docker images.

- **Cluster**: A group of machines (Nodes) running Kubernetes-managed applications.
- **Compose File**: A YAML file (docker-compose.yml) used to define and configure multiple Docker services.
- **ConfigMap**: A Kubernetes object used to inject non-sensitive configuration data into containers.
- **Container**: A lightweight, isolated runtime environment for executing applications with all their dependencies.
- **Containerd**: A high-performance container runtime that handles lifecycle and storage for containers.
- **Container Runtime Interface (CRI)**: A Kubernetes plugin interface for container runtimes like containerd or CRI-O.
- **CouchDB**: A NoSQL database used as the state database in Hyperledger Fabric peers.
- **CronJob**: A Kubernetes resource that schedules jobs to run at fixed times, dates, or intervals.
- **CVE (Common Vulnerabilities and Exposures)**: A list of publicly disclosed cybersecurity vulnerabilities maintained by the MITRE Corporation.

D

- **Daemon (dockerd)**: The background service running on a host that manages Docker containers.
- **Deployment**: A Kubernetes resource that defines desired number of Pods and manages scaling, rolling updates, and rollbacks.
- **Docker Compose**: A tool for defining and running multi-container Docker applications.
- **Docker Context**: A CLI feature that allows users to switch between Docker environments (e.g., local, remote).
- **Dockerfile**: A text file with instructions for building a Docker image.
- **Docker Hub**: A cloud-based repository service where Docker users can share container images.
- **Docker Image**: A snapshot or blueprint of a containerized application that includes the app code, dependencies, and OS libraries.

- **Docker Swarm**: Docker's native clustering and orchestration tool for managing containerized applications.
- **Docker Registry**: A server-side application for storing and distributing Docker images.

E

- **Entrypoint**: The main command that gets executed when a container starts, defined in Dockerfile.
- **Environment Variables**: Configurable parameters passed to containers for use at runtime.
- **etcd**: A distributed key-value store used by Kubernetes to store cluster state and configuration data.

F

- **Falco**: An open-source runtime security tool that monitors containers and alerts on suspicious behavior.
- **Firewall**: A network security device or rule set that filters incoming and outgoing traffic.
- **Fluent Bit**: Lightweight log processor and forwarder often used for container log aggregation.

G

- **GitHub Actions**: CI/CD platform allowing automation of workflows including Docker builds and Kubernetes deployments.
- **Grafana**: A tool for visualizing time-series data from sources like Prometheus, often used for monitoring Docker and Kubernetes environments.
- **GitOps**: A methodology that uses Git repositories as the single source of truth for declarative infrastructure and application deployments.

H

- **Helm**: A package manager for Kubernetes that helps define, install, and upgrade applications.
- **Horizontal Scaling**: The process of increasing capacity by adding more container instances rather than upgrading hardware.

I

- **Image Tag**: A version label applied to a Docker image (e.g., nginx:1.21).
- **Immutable Container**: A container that does not change state after initialization.
- **Infrastructure as Code (IaC)**: Managing infrastructure through configuration files instead of manual processes.
- **Ingress**: A Kubernetes API object that manages external access to services, typically HTTP.

J

- **Jenkins**: A popular open-source automation server used for building CI/CD pipelines.
- **JSON File Logging**: Docker's default logging mechanism that writes container logs in JSON format.
- **Job**: A Kubernetes resource that runs a task to completion.

K

- **Keycloak**: An open-source identity and access management tool that supports single sign-on, OAuth2, and more.
- **Kubelet**: Agent that runs on each Node and ensures containers are running in a Pod.
- **kubectl**: Command-line tool for interacting with Kubernetes clusters.
- **Kubernetes (K8s)**: A powerful open-source platform for container orchestration across clusters of machines.
- **kube-apiserver**: Kubernetes component that validates and configures data for the API objects.

L

- **Label**: Key-value pairs attached to Kubernetes objects used for identification and selection.
- **Liveness Probe**: A health check in Kubernetes that determines if a container is still running properly.
- **Loki**: A log aggregation system from Grafana Labs designed for storing and querying logs, optimized for containers.

M

- **Macvlan:** A Docker network driver that assigns a MAC address to containers, enabling LAN-level access.
- **Minikube:** Tool for running local single-node Kubernetes clusters.
- **Minikube**: A tool to run a single-node Kubernetes cluster locally for development and testing.
- **Mount**: Attaching a host directory or volume to a container path.
- **Multi-Arch Image:** Docker image supporting multiple CPU architectures.
- **Multi-Stage Build:** A Dockerfile technique that improves image optimization and security.
- **Mutual TLS (mTLS)**: A security protocol where both client and server authenticate each other using certificates.

N

- **Namespace**: In Kubernetes, a logical partition to divide cluster resources between multiple users.
- **Nginx**: A high-performance HTTP and reverse proxy server often used in containerized architectures.
- **Node**: A worker machine in Kubernetes, either a VM or a physical server.

O

- **Open Policy Agent (OPA)**: A general-purpose policy engine used to enforce security and compliance rules in Docker and Kubernetes.
- **Overlay Network**: A virtual network that spans across multiple Docker hosts or Kubernetes nodes, allowing containers to communicate securely.

P

- **PersistentVolume (PV)**: A piece of storage in Kubernetes provisioned by administrators.
- **PersistentVolumeClaim (PVC)**: A user's request for storage in Kubernetes.
- **Pod**: The basic deployable unit in Kubernetes, which may contain one or more containers.
- **Port Mapping**: The process of exposing container ports to the host or external networks.

- **Prometheus**: A time-series database used for monitoring and alerting in containerized systems.

Q

- **QoS Class (Quality of Service)**: Kubernetes classification of Pods based on their resource requests and limits (Guaranteed, Burstable, BestEffort).
- **Quota**: A limit on the amount of resources (CPU, memory, etc.) that a container or group of containers can consume.

R

- **Registry**: A repository for storing and distributing Docker images (e.g., Docker Hub, Harbor).
- **ReplicaSet**: A Kubernetes object that ensures a specified number of Pods are always running.
- **Resource Limits**: Constraints set on containers to limit CPU and memory usage.
- **Rollback**: Reverting a Kubernetes Deployment to a previous version.
- **Rootless Containers**: Containers that run as a non-root user on the host for added security.
- **runc**: CLI tool and runtime for spawning and running containers per OCI specification.

S

- **SBOM:** Software Bill of Materials—a list of all components in a container image.
- **Scaling**: Increasing or decreasing the number of container instances (Pods) to match load.
- **Secrets Management**: Handling sensitive information such as API keys, tokens, and passwords in a secure way (e.g., Vault, Docker Secrets).
- **Seccomp**: Linux security feature used to restrict system calls.
- **Service**: A Kubernetes abstraction that defines a logical set of Pods and a policy by which to access them.
- **Service Discovery**: A mechanism for containers or Pods to find and communicate with each other automatically.

- **Sidecar**: A helper container running alongside the main container inside the same Pod.
- **Sigstore**: A set of tools for signing and verifying container images.
- **StatefulSet**: A Kubernetes object managing stateful applications, ensuring stable storage and unique network identities.
- **Swarm Mode**: Docker's native clustering and orchestration tool for running containers at scale.

T

- **Tag**: A label assigned to a Docker image version for tracking and deployment.
- **Taints and Tolerations**: Kubernetes mechanisms that control Pod scheduling onto Nodes.
- **Trivy**: A vulnerability scanner for Docker images and file systems.
- **Tini**: A tiny init process used as PID 1 to handle signals and zombies properly in containers.

U

- **Ulimits**: Kernel-level constraints that control resource limits for containers (e.g., number of open files).
- **Update Strategy**: Deployment setting in Kubernetes to control how Pods are updated (e.g., rolling updates).

V

- **Vault**: A secrets management tool from HashiCorp that securely stores and controls access to sensitive information.
- **Vertical Pod Autoscaler (VPA)**: Kubernetes tool that adjusts CPU/memory requests automatically based on usage.
- **Volume**: A persistent storage mechanism used by Docker containers to store data across restarts.

W

- **Wazuh**: An open-source SIEM and host intrusion detection platform often used in container security monitoring.
- **Webhook**: HTTP callbacks triggered by CI/CD or orchestration events.

- **Worker Node**: Node in Kubernetes that runs Pods and is managed by the Kubernetes Control Plane.

X

- **X.509 Certificates**: Standard format of public key certificates used for authentication within Kubernetes.

Y

- **YAML (YAML Ain't Markup Language)**: A human-readable data format used in Compose files and Kubernetes manifests.
- **YARA Rules**: Pattern-matching rules for detecting malware and threats in static analysis pipelines.

Z

- **Zero Trust Architecture**: A security model where no device or user is trusted by default, even within a network perimeter.

Alphabetical Index

L

M

N

O

P

Q

R

S

T

U

V

W

X

Y

Z

www.ingramcontent.com/pod-product-compliance
Ingram Content Group UK Ltd.
Pitfield, Milton Keynes, MK11 3LW, UK
UKHW061547190726
13845UKWH00030B/1069